HEARTLAND

Midwestern History and Culture

GENERAL EDITORS

James H. Madison and Thomas J. Schlereth

Comparative Histories of
the Midwestern States

HEART
LAND

EDITED BY

James H. Madison

Indiana University Press

BLOOMINGTON AND INDIANAPOLIS

First Midland Book Edition 1990

© 1988 by Indiana University Press
All rights reserved

Manufactured in the United States of America

LIBRARY OF CONGRESS CATALOGING-IN-PUBLICATION DATA
Heartland.
(Midwestern history and culture)
Bibliography: p.
Includes index.
1. Middle West—History. 2. Regionalism—Middle
West—History. I. Madison, James H. II. Series
F351.C692 1988   977   87-45835
ISBN 0-253-31423-2
ISBN 0-253-20576-X (pbk.)
2 3 4 5 6 94 93 92 91 90

CONTENTS

Contents

Acknowledgments

This book is the work of many hands. The twelve authors who contributed essays undertook the task with an enthusiasm and co-operation that made an editor's job considerably easier. At Indiana University Press, John Gallman and Joan Catapano helped shape the idea for the book and supported the project to its conclusion. Thomas J. Schlereth, my coeditor for the Midwestern History and Culture Series in which this volume appears, also offered good advice. I am indebted as well to Martin Ridge, who long ago helped me understand the value of studying states and regions. Ken Goodall provided expert copyediting for a manuscript with many styles, and Bobbi Diehl kept us all on schedule and, once again, remained a friend. Suzanne Hull prepared the maps. I am grateful to all.

James H. Madison

HEARTLAND

James H. Madison

The States of the Midwest

An Introduction

THE ANNOUNCEMENT IN LATE 1986 that a midwestern town of 980 residents would be the site of a new Japanese auto-truck factory brought anxiety as well as celebration. One resident, who had lived in the community since 1916, voiced a suspicion others shared: "Oh dear," she said, "what are we going to do? It'll bring so much foreign element, people who know nothing about us."[1]

Of course, the Japanese executives knew something about this small midwestern town. They had good data on its access to interstate highways, its state and local tax structure, sewage treatment facilities, and labor pool. It is doubtful, however, if they really knew much else about the town, the state, or the region in which they were investing. In this regard the Japanese are little different from many Americans. Not only in Tokyo but also in Boston, Atlanta, and San Francisco there are many who know nothing about us in the Midwest; and even in Chicago, Omaha, and Trempealeau County, Wisconsin, there are midwesterners whose knowledge about their state and region is vague and incomplete. Midwesterners do have some sense that they live in a special region and a distinctive state, but they are often unsure about the origins and nature of these differences.

This collection of essays is intended to help all know more about the people who live in the American heartland, to know its residents

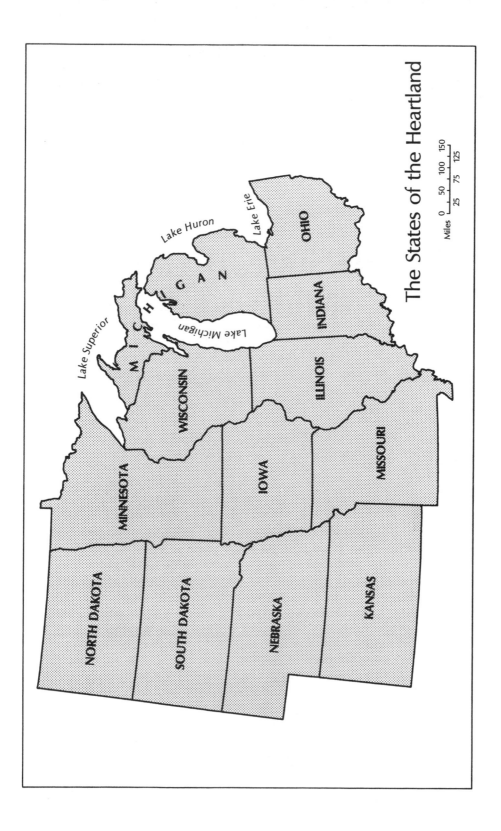

The States of the Heartland

Lake Superior

Lake Huron

Lake Erie

Lake Michigan

M I C H I G A N

OHIO

INDIANA

ILLINOIS

WISCONSIN

MISSOURI

IOWA

MINNESOTA

NORTH DAKOTA

SOUTH DAKOTA

NEBRASKA

KANSAS

Miles 0   50   100 150
        25   75   125

as citizens of a singular state and a singular region. To this end, the twelve essays in the volume have three major characteristics: they are historical; they are analytical; and they are comparative.

Planning for this collection began with the assumption that the best way to know the present is to know the past. The Midwest's past is relatively short—none of the states has yet celebrated a bicentennial of statehood—yet in this brief history are to be found the origins of the region's present and likely its future. There has been change in the Midwest, but it has been evolutionary rather than revolutionary. All midwestern states remain closely tied to their nineteenth-century origins, even though some have evolved more rapidly than others. With good reason, then, the twelve contributors to this collection are all historians. Their interests and methods are different from those of journalists, sociologists, economists, and others who deal in the present. In writing about their states, however, these historians interpret a past that is not dead, a past that directly informs the present.

The essays are analytical as well as historical; they are also highly interpretive. Each writer has selected subjects he or she thinks most informative and has shaped these chosen subjects around larger themes and broader questions. Each author is exceedingly well informed about his or her particular state, and each has ventured boldly to present its character through its history. None of the essays serve as complete reference works. The reference function is provided instead by the bibliographies that accompany the essays. The purpose of this collection is to provide a sophisticated and challenging introduction to the states and the region. The essays present history that engages the intellect, requires thinking about past and present, and, at times, sparks disagreement.

Finally, the essays are comparative. Each author analyzes one state's history and compares it with other states of the Midwest and with the nation as a whole. This comparative perspective, with its nested, three-layered approach of state, region, and nation, mitigates the provincialism of much state history and gives these twelve essays greater integration. Each historian thought in comparative contexts while writing the essay, and each circulated early drafts of the essay among all participants. All of us learned more about the Midwest and the nation as a consequence. We came also to understand better our own particular state. Our hope in presenting this collection is that readers will share the deepening and breadth of understanding that comes from comparative thought.

Heartland argues for understanding the diversity of the American nation, of the Midwest, and of the twelve states of the Midwest. Assumptions of homogeneity are omnipresent in twentieth-century America, particularly in the popular culture of music, dress, and food and in the national sweep of television news and entertainment. The common assumption of foreigners that Americans are all alike is not surprising. Many Americans themselves only dimly perceive their nation as a collection of states and regions. Academics are particularly likely to think in national and international contexts and to avoid strong attachments to place as they strive for career and geographic mobility. Journalists similarly seek the big story with a mass audience. A brief nod toward the regionally picturesque in food or manners or politics often serves to satisfy the occasional suspicion that all places in America are not alike.

When the Midwest is seen as distinctive, it is usually presented as the most representative part of the American nation. From the beginning of settlement to the present, midwestern boosters have conveyed such notions, implying thereby that other regions have fallen away from the Midwest's standard of the ideal American way. According to Meredith Nicholson, a midwesterner writing in the early twentieth century, "We are friendlier, less snobbish, more sanguine in our outlook upon public matters, and have a greater confidence in democracy than in the East."[2] Visitors and residents alike have often emphasized the bucolic and pastoral stability of the region, its traditional moral values, and its down-to-earth veneration of family and hard work. A colorful brochure, advertising the appearance in 1987 of a new magazine called *Midwest Living*, asserted that "something incredibly *strong*" holds the region together and that this something is a combination of "our appreciation of the land we live on. Clean air. Wide open spaces. Genuine friendships. Our family-oriented values."[3] In contexts such as these the Midwest is portrayed as the center of the nation, the most American part of America. New soap powders must play in Peoria, new presidential candidates in Iowa.

Such positive claims for the region can be matched with negative assertions. The Midwest is provincial and unsophisticated, pragmatic and materialistic, bland and boring—as stolid and reliable as the squares on the landscape that mark the region's rectilinear survey. There are many generalizations to be made about midwestern lag, retardation, or decline. All of its states endured at the outset of their history a kind of colonial status as territorial governments and as economic and cultural dependencies. Throughout the region there are remnants of a colonial mentality that looks eastward for approval and acceptance. In the late twentieth century the midwestern industrial and agricultural economies struggle to overcome the rusted factories and bankrupt farms that challenge notions of hard work and material progress. The lag here was due less to competition from the Northeast than from the growing Sun Belt.

As the essays that follow demonstrate, there is some validity to these images of the Midwest, positive and negative. Traditional values remain: newspapers in rural Iowa really do carry notices of bridal showers, inviting anyone who wishes to attend. And change has brought challenge and even despair: many young midwesterners have left the region for jobs and homes in the Sun Belt. But the Midwest is not as one-dimensional or as simple as these easy generalizations suggest.

The essays in this collection are powerful antidotes to assumptions of homogeneity in America and in the Midwest. Bound by the canons of midwestern modesty, the authors do not assert the superiority of the region, but they do assert its diversity and its complexity. The heartland is a heterogeneous place. Not only does its landscape take different forms, so too does its political, economic, and social life.

The diversity presented in this volume is organized around state boundaries. Artificial lines on a map, drawn for political convenience, state boundaries do in fact contain distinctive cultures. Each essay presents the essence and personality of a state, suggesting an identity that is economic and social as well as political. The Midwest is often described as the nation's breadbasket, the origin of its corn, wheat, pork, and beef. In Nebraska, Iowa, North Dakota, and South Dakota farming is indeed dominant. But in Ohio, Michigan, and Wisconsin factories and offices are more important than grain elevators and farmhouses. Social and political differences are even more complex. Iowa and Michigan created outstanding systems of public education, while Missouri and Indiana lagged behind other states in the region and in the nation. Kansas and North Dakota strongly supported prohibition in the late nineteenth century while Nebraska remained lukewarm. Populism caught fire in Minnesota and North Dakota but not in Indiana or Ohio.

Some of these differences derive from the physical geography of the twelve states. Natural resource endowment affected the mix of agriculture and industry and the patterns of population settlement, town location, and transportation routes. Nebraska and Kansas are different in part because their rivers are different. Michigan's lakes have influenced its choices from the beginning to the present. Differences in soil, topography, and climate make farming in South Dakota unlike that in Indiana. Important also has been the timing of white settlement. States in the eastern part of the region were settled earliest and have always been the most populous, the most urban, and the most industrial. Later settlement, less rainfall, and harsher climates have left the western edge of the region more sparsely populated.

The diverse physical environment accounts for variation through the region, but nature is not the primary source of diversity. More important in weaving the patterns of the midwestern fabric is the mix of peoples and cultures, interacting with the physical environment. Each state has a distinctive blend of people. Some, such as Wisconsin and North Dakota, are ethnic mosaics. Others, such as Iowa and Indiana, tend toward greater homogeneity. But all are great salad bowls or stews, if not melting pots, of peoples.

An essential ingredient in the past and present of each of the states is its particular pattern of migration and settlement. A large generalization can be ventured: the states of the Upper Midwest— particularly Michigan, Wisconsin, Minnesota, North Dakota, and Iowa—attracted a larger share of New England and upstate New York migration in the nineteenth century, while the states of the Lower Midwest, particularly Ohio, Indiana, Illinois, and Missouri, received a larger share of migration from the Upland South. The consequences were many. Patterns of speech, building construction, and religion reflected settler origins. The Civil War presented a much more div- isive force in the Lower Midwest, where real and imagined Copper- heads brought tension and conflict. Even more broadly, states with stronger Yankee influences developed a political culture in which a commonwealth tradition became more dominant. Citizens expected their government to be honest and efficient and to work in the best interests of the public good. Government was their ally rather than their adversary. In states with a stronger southern migration there was more tolerance and demand for political patronage and the spoils of office. As political scientist Daniel J. Elazar has argued, these Lower Midwest states tended to be more job-oriented and individualistic while their neighbors to the north were more issue-oriented and more moralistic. Thus, for example, the progressive reform movement flourished in Wisconsin but foundered in Indiana.

While these large patterns of migration and resulting cultures are helpful in understanding the Midwest and its states, they are not alone sufficient. As the authors of the essays indicate, there are many var- iations and glosses on this basic pattern. To the migrations of Yankees and southerners must be added the immigrants from Europe and, more recently, Asia, who created different culture mixes in each state. Another variation came from the movement of rural blacks from the Deep South to some but not all of the midwestern states in the twen- tieth century. In a few states a significant Indian population remained: Sioux Indians provide much of South Dakota's distinctiveness. And there are many features of a state's culture that are not fully explained in terms of migration patterns.

Even within state boundaries there is variation. Iowa may appear homogeneous, but its history includes the influence of Italian coal miners and Amana pietists. North Dakota's Red River Valley is more prosperous and politically conservative than the rest of the state. St. Louis and Kansas City and Cleveland and Cincinnati have different traditions though located in the same states. Most farmers in southern

Indiana would lack the know-how to succeed on a farm in central Indiana and vice-versa. Chicago has always played a special role in adding a singularly Byzantine complexity to Illinois politics. The hodgepodge of political and cultural variation within Wisconsin is such that only an expert can explain it—one reason, perhaps, why Wisconsin has provided so many of the nation's historians.

Despite intrastate diversity each of the twelve midwestern states is indeed an entity, a unit that is a political and cultural whole. Missouri has a less precise sense of state identity than Wisconsin or Indiana, but all states have meanings that are more than boundary lines on maps. The differences can be exaggerated, but these states do have personalities. Most important is the fact that midwesterners think of themselves as citizens of a particular state. They tell jokes about adjacent states that outsiders cannot understand. They cheer for the state university's basketball and football teams even though they may not be graduates of the institution. They travel to Florida or Arizona in the winter and seek out fellow North Dakotans or Ohioans. They support the nation's strongest state historical societies.

The essays that follow present a distinctive personality for each of the twelve midwestern states. Yet they demonstrate also that each state belongs to a region and that there are commonalities of culture that bind midwesterners together. The authors demonstrate too that this region truly is the heartland of the nation, not only geographically but politically, socially, and culturally. *Heartland* thus presents themes and suggests paradoxes that speak to the complexity and heterogeneity of the American people, to the differences that persist within the common bonds of state, region, and nation.

NOTES

1. *Indianapolis Star*, December 3, 1986.
2. Meredith Nicholson, *The Valley of Democracy* (New York, 1918), 375.
3. *Midwest Living* subscription brochure, mailed to author, January 1987.

BIBLIOGRAPHY

Among the books that have made the largest contributions to the study of regions are *The United States 1830–1850: The Nation and Its Sections* (New York, 1935), by historian Frederick Jackson Turner; *American Regionalism: A Cultural-Historical Approach to National Integration* (New York, 1938), by sociologists Howard W. Odum and Henry E. Moore; *American Federalism: A View from the States*, 3d ed. (New York, 1984), by political scientist Daniel J. Elazar; and *Regionalism in America* (Madison, Wis., 1952), a collection of broad-ranging essays edited by Merrill Jensen. Recent ways of thinking about regions are elaborated in Carl Abbott, "Frontiers and Sections: Cities and

Regions in American Growth," *American Quarterly* 37, no. 3 (1985), 395–410; David Goldfield, "The New Regionalism," *Journal of Urban History* 10 (February 1984), 171–86; and Frederick C. Luebke, "Regionalism and the Great Plains: Problems of Concept and Method," *Western Historical Quarterly* 15 (January 1984), 19–38.

Geographers have made important contributions to understanding regionalism and the Midwest. Good examples of their work are Raymond D. Gastil, *Cultural Regions of the United States* (Seattle, 1975); Wilbur Zelinsky, *The Cultural Geography of the United States* (Englewood Cliffs, N. J., 1973); and John Fraser Hart, ed., *Regions of the United States* (New York, 1972). Specific focus on the Midwest as place comes in the special issue of the *Journal of Geography* 85 (September–October 1986) and in James R. Shortridge, "The Vernacular Middle West," *Annals of the Association of American Geographers* 75 (1985), 48–57.

Early twentieth-century impressions of the Midwest include Meredith Nicholson, *The Valley of Democracy* (New York, 1918); Booth Tarkington, "The Middle West," *Harper's Monthly* 106 (December 1902), 75–83; and Graham Hutton, *Midwest at Noon* (Chicago, 1946). Assessments of the region at one of its more optimistic moments are provided in Thomas T. McAvoy, ed., *The Midwest: Myth or Reality?* (Notre Dame, Ind., 1961). A good study of its politics is John H. Fenton, *Midwest Politics* (New York, 1966). Recent popular accounts include Neal R. Peirce and John Keefe, *The Great Lakes States of America: People, Politics, and Power in the Five Great Lakes States* (New York, 1980); Neal R. Peirce, *The Great Plains States of America: People, Politics, and Power in the Nine Great Plains States* (New York, 1973); and Joel Garreau, *The Nine Nations of North America* (Boston, 1981).

Among the many books that deal with important parts of the region's history are Lewis Atherton, *Main Street on the Middle Border* (Bloomington, Ind., 1954); Richard Lyle Power, *Planting Corn Belt Culture: The Impress of the Upland Southerner and Yankee in the Old Northwest* (Indianapolis, 1953); R. Carlyle Buley, *The Old Northwest: Pioneer Period, 1815–1840*, 2 vols. (Indianapolis, 1951); Malcolm J. Rohrbough, *The Trans-Appalachian Frontier: People, Societies, and Institutions, 1775–1850* (New York, 1978); and James C. Malin, *The Grassland of North America: Prolegomena to Its History* (Lawrence, Kans., 1947). An interesting example of the diversity of regional traditions comes in Marlene Park and Gerald E. Markowitz, *Democratic Vistas: Post Office and Public Art in the New Deal* (Philadelphia, 1985). A good general introduction to state history is provided in John Alexander Williams, "A New Look at an Old Field," *Western Historical Quarterly* 9 (July 1978), 281–96.

Annette Atkins

MINNESOTA

Left of Center and Out of Place

MINNESOTANS TELL IOWA JOKES. Otherwise regular folks mock hog farming, endless stretches of corn, and Iowans' alleged provincialism. Minnesotans also tell North Dakota jokes, claiming there's nothing to see, nothing to do, and no good reason to go there. People in Duluth, Minnesota, say that the only good thing about Superior, Wisconsin, is that it has a great view of Duluth.

To a Bostonian, Californian, or other "outsider" such fine distinctions must seem puzzling, even laughable. Isn't the Midwest all the same? Saul Steinberg's map of the United States from a New Yorker's point of view blurs everything beyond the Hudson River. Journalists sometimes call the Midwest "flyover land"—the place between the coasts where nothing happens, where nothing needs to be noticed. National news comes from New York and Washington (with only a few, and usually human interest, exceptions—Charles Kuralt "On the Road," Peter Jennings anchoring the news from central Iowa); important art, music, theater, dance, and literature happen only on the East or West coasts. *Time* several years ago covered a major Picasso exhibit when it arrived in New York City but not when it opened—earlier—in Minneapolis at the Walker Art Center. The interesting, fashionable, and chic people of the country either come from the coasts or flee there from the barren Midwest, so the mythology goes.

MANITOBA

ONTARIO

KITTSON ROSEAU LAKE OF THE WOODS

Rainy River

MARSHALL KOOCHICHING

PENNINGTON *Red Lake R.* BELTRAMI

Red Lake RED LAKE

Red River of the North POLK CLEARWATER

Big Fork R. *Little Fork R.* COOK

NORMAN MAHNOMEN ITASCA SAINT LOUIS LAKE

CLAY BECKER HUBBARD CASS *Whiteface R.*

N. DAKOTA *Mississippi R.* *Louis R.* Duluth LAKE SUPERIOR

WILKIN OTTER WADENA CROW WING AITKIN CARLTON

Crow Wing R.

TRAVERSE TODD MORRISON MILLE LACS PINE

GRANT DOUGLAS BENTON KANABEC *St. Croix R.*

BIG STONE STEVENS *Chippewa R.* POPE STEARNS SHERBURNE ISANTI CHISAGO

SWIFT KANDIYOHI MEEKER WRIGHT ANOKA

WISCONSIN

LAC QUI PARLE CHIPPEWA HENNEPIN RAMSEY

Minneapolis St. Paul WASHINGTON

YELLOW MEDICINE RENVILLE McLEOD CARVER

LINCOLN LYON REDWOOD NICOLLET SIBLEY SCOTT DAKOTA *Mississippi River*

Minnesota River LA SUEUR RICE GOODHUE *Cannon R.*

PIPESTONE MURRAY COTTONWOOD WATONWAN BROWN BLUE EARTH WASECA STEELE DODGE OLMSTED WINONA WABASHA

ROCK NOBLES JACKSON MARTIN FARIBAULT FREEBORN MOWER FILLMORE HOUSTON

SOUTH DAKOTA

I O W A

MINNESOTA

Miles 0 10 20 30 40

✪ State Capital

Those same journalists, though, also talk about Midwestern virtues, if not with admiration at least with some grudging respect. The very absence of sophistication, of temptations, of occasions for sin that supposedly make the Midwest bland have also made it safe and somehow the repository of natural goodness. Salvation has long beckoned from the west in answer to a variety of eastern corruptions. Charles Loring Brace and the New York Children's Aid Society, for example, in the late nineteenth century combated juvenile delinquency in New York City by sending wayward boys and girls westward, usually to the Midwest. He too blurred the territory beyond the Hudson River and saw there the home of virtue. Removed from bad environments, bad associations, and the multiple temptations of urban life, Brace argued, a delinquent could be saved by farm life. From the mid 1850s to the mid-1880s, Brace's society relocated nearly fifty thousand children. So confident was he of the natural healthiness and virtues of the west that Brace placed children in foster homes with next to no investigation of the foster family's circumstances.

Many midwesterners share this grandiose notion about the Midwest. In *Midwest Politics*, John Fenton writes, "Unlike the citizens of Texas, Mississippi, or Vermont, who identify strongly with the Lone Star State or the South or New England, most Midwesterners think of themselves as Americans. . . . they live in America, for the Midwest is America."[1] Minnesotans like other midwesterners speak the *national* language—the dialect of so-called "standard" American English. Dan Rather took speech lessons to disguise his Texas roots, while South Dakotan Tom Brokaw speaks in his native midwestern tongue. Actors and actresses, too, usually talk like they grew up in Cold Spring or White Bear Lake, even when they're playing characters from other places.

Minnesota is part of that Midwest. Except for changes in the pavement, road signs, and the speed of cars, there are few clues to tell drivers that they've entered or left Minnesota. The rolling, open prairie land of southwestern Minnesota cannot be distinguished from the rolling, open prairie land of southeastern South Dakota or northern Iowa. The Red River of the north joins North Dakota and Minnesota more than it divides them. The Minnesota side of the valley has more ties—agricultural, economic, social, political, and ethnic—with North Dakota than with the Iron Range or the Twin Cities. The people involved in mining and recreation in northern Minnesota have more in common with the people of northern Wisconsin and Upper Michigan than, say, with the health-care professionals who dominate Rochester's economy and society.

But when Minnesota acquired territorial status in 1849 and statehood in 1858, it began to develop an identity, to make a history, and to create a sense of itself, so Minnesota is also not its neighbors. Its boundaries enclose more than eighty-four thousand square miles, almost twelve thousand lakes, eighty-seven counties, five cities with a population over fifty thousand, and more than four million people. To single out any one characteristic of the state and call it uniquely Minnesotan would be foolish. But in combination, particular factors do add up to a state's identity. In Minnesota the most important factors are a distinct political climate, three regions quite different from each other, and a divided consciousness.

Minnesota politicians have long found ideological allies in other midwestern states. When Ignatius Donnelly, John Johnson, Floyd B. Olson, Harold Stassen, Hubert Humphrey, Eugenie Anderson, Eugene McCarthy, Walter Mondale, and Arvonne Fraser leaned left (admittedly at different angles), they leaned with the La Follettes in Wisconsin, William Langer in North Dakota, George McGovern in South Dakota, and Albert Cummins and Harold Hughes in Iowa. Minnesota's third parties have found inspiration and support in other states, and its people have joined political organizations that bridged state boundaries—from Donnelly's Anti-Monopolist party in the 1870s to the Populists in the 1890s to A. C. Townley's Non-Partisan League in the 1910s.

Minnesota's string of liberal leaders has not, however, been unbroken. Governor J. A. A. Burnquist, yielding to war hysteria in 1917, appointed a Commission of Public Safety to protect the state against all threats (especially from the large and largely loyal German-American population in the state). As historian W. W. Folwell noted: "If a large and hostile army had already been landed at Duluth and was about to march on the capital of the state, a more liberal dictatorship could hardly have been conceded to the commission."[2]

Disloyalty, in the commission's view, required swift, decisive, and vigilant attention. The commissioners issued a "white list" of acceptable German textbooks; they required English as the language of instruction; they limited the rights of noncitizens to teach; they ousted a University of Minnesota faculty member and several officials in Brown County; they prohibited strikes; they cleared Industrial Workers of the World organizers from the streets by passing a strict vagrancy ordinance; they closed dance halls and beer parlors.

The commissioners saw the greatest need for their work in politics. Disloyalty threatened on all sides, they thought: Minneapolis voters elected a socialist mayor; five Minnesota congressmen opposed American entry into the world war; pacifist organizations attracted Minnesota members; political candidates—including Charles Lindbergh, Sr.—denied the legitimacy of the war. The committee rejected claims of First Amendment protection. Arrests, harassment, indictments, injunctions were common. A few men, including Townley, spent time in jail for sedition. But the Public Safety Commission was an exceptional, if not a singular, example of repression in Minnesota political history, and generally Minnesotans have felt they had little to fear from their state government.

Thomas Jefferson saw government as a necessary but dangerous force. Because so many eighteenth-century European governments served the interests of the few and oppressed the many, Jefferson and other American colonial thinkers feared the power of the state and saw the people pitted against government in a battle for their liberty. This suspicion of government and belief that government had to be restrained in order for people to be free underlay the formation of the American Republic.

Minnesota, however, was born into a different world. The reform spirit of America's early nineteenth century encouraged confidence in the beneficence of the government, the belief that people and their lives could be made better through the agency of the government. The romantic and mostly Yankee reformers of antebellum America believed that people were basically good and simply needed sufficient education, guidance, and help to allow their true interests to emerge. Government, as an arm of the people, could do this good work and the world could be improved.

President Abraham Lincoln's words about government of the people, by the people, for the people, have been repeated so often and so mechanically by so many fourth graders that in the late twentieth century it can be difficult to hear the words at all, let alone to hear in them Lincoln's profound disagreement with Jefferson. Lincoln envisioned government and people not as adversaries but as allies in a common struggle. That is the atmosphere in which Minnesota came to statehood, and it has shaped the state's dominant political mood.

If Minnesotans didn't fear the accumulation of power by government, they did fear its concentration in the hands of big business. And if Minnesotans identified threats that needed to be restrained, they were corporate not governmental. From a nineteenth-century Minnesota point of view, it was big businesses that endangered people's freedom, diminished their opportunities, held too much power, and made mock of American equality. Corporations knew no public interest. Even the state's more conservative critics called for reform and government regulation.

Minnesotans found an ally against corporate power in the political system. Only the state government, they believed, was powerful enough to defend the people's rights, opportunities, and interests against the interests and power of big business.

This adversarial relationship—between the people and the corporations—and this alliance—between the government and the people—characterizes Minnesota's political life. Like all generalizations, this one has its flaws. It ignores people's feuds with government; it

overlooks state and corporate alliances; it excludes examples of corporate and community cooperation; it hinges on a particular nineteenth-century definition of *the people* that included the so-called producing classes and excluded bankers and industrialists. Even so, it
does highlight a significant feature of Minnesota's identity, one that
many contemporary politicians are trying hard to erase. Four examples will suggest how this alliance has functioned in the last one
hundred years in Minnesota and how its form has varied.

Nineteenth-century farmers in Minnesota wanted railroads—in
their backyards if possible. Trains transported goods and people and
connected isolated places to the rest of the world. The railroads were
nearly magical and the railroad companies were powerful. Only the
weather exerted more economic influence on the fate of farmers.
Discriminatory rates and injustices hurt the individual farmer, and
the farmers constituted a kind of captive audience. They could not
choose another carrier if the local one did not please them. A single
farmer had neither the money nor the clout to fight the big railroad
companies, but the government could and, in nineteenth-century
Minnesota, did.

A series of governors took up the farmers' defense. In 1870, only
three years after rails first connected St. Paul and Chicago, Governor
Horace Austin declared that "wise legislative supervision of our railroad corporations is a public necessity," and in 1871 the state legislature passed its first railroad regulations. When Cushman Davis
assumed the governorship in 1874 he announced that complaints
from the "producing classes" were "universal" and "the grave questions which exist *between* the State and the railroad corporations are
not yet settled." The "evil" of corporate monopoly, he asserted, "is
a public one, affecting every citizen," and the state should act.[3]

Governor Lucius Hubbard in the 1880s stated that "The increasing
aggressiveness and the bolder defiance of corporate power, especially
represented by great railroad corporations, must ultimately be met
and restrained by the power and authority of the State." In 1889,
Governor William Merriam reminded the legislature that

> powerful corporations are thoroughly equipped . . . to protect them-
> selves, as they have the advantages that always come to the concentration
> of capital; hence, while your board of [railroad] commissioners should
> be a just and impartial umpire . . . it becomes its province to supply, in
> itself, to the people of the state an organization worthy to combat that
> with which it comes in contact; and in such sense, and to that extent,
> the board of commissioners may be said to represent the state and to
> act in its interest.[4]

When in 1901 Governor Samuel Van Sant tried to break up the
Northern Securities Company—a merger that established virtual mo-

nopoly over the state's railroads—he acted in accord with nearly thirty years of state action. When President Theodore Roosevelt fought the same company the following year, he emerged as a "trustbuster" and signaled a new direction in federal government action and initiatives, the Progressive Era. Minnesota had not changed much, but the federal government had.

Minnesota's suspicion of big business also partially accounts for the state's tradition of isolationism. From 1906 to 1946 "isolationism was a dominant strain in Minnesota foreign policy thought," argues historian Barbara Stuhler.[5] Among the motives for isolationism, the most powerful in Minnesota were economic. Charles Lindbergh, Sr., opposed World War I because he believed that it benefited only eastern bankers and munitions makers. Once again, he said, the people would be made to pay for the gain of the profiteers. He found many listeners who agreed with his charges. It was his duty, he believed, to protect people from the corporate warmongers.

In another example of this alliance between the producing classes and the state, Governor Floyd B. Olson intervened in the 1934 Minneapolis truckers' strike and the 1935 Strutwear Knitting Company strike and helped break the power of antiunion forces in the city. This story really begins in 1903, when a group of bankers and businessmen organized the Citizens' Alliance (CA) to "discourage strikes, walkouts, and unfair practices by either employer or employee," to "secure for the employer and employee freedom of contract," and to "uphold the principles of the Open Shop." The CA operated a free employment bureau and supported a number of trade schools. It also surreptitiously circulated regular reports on "radical activities in the city and state" that belied its public rhetoric of equal commitment to owners and workers. And the CA's main purpose was to fight unions. In 1934 the organization bragged that it had "defeated every major strike in the city since the end of World War I."[6]

But labor fought back, using political weapons. In 1916 in Minneapolis Thomas Van Lear—machinist, union man, and socialist—won election as mayor. He had sought political office, he said, because he "believed that municipal political action could curb the power of the capitalists and set the stage for labor's eventual victory." In one campaign speech he gave this advice to his listeners:

> when fat, slick, well-fed, well-dressed men, who never missed a meal in their lives, come down here and tell you workingmen that you should be patient and satisfied with things as they are, I think you ought to tell them to go to hell.[7]

In 1934 Minneapolis truckers walked off their jobs in the spring and summer ostensibly over wages, but the larger issues were union recognition and employees' right to organize. During the strike two deputies and two strikers were killed and sixty strikers were wounded. Some accounts labeled the fight "civil war" or "class warfare." In 1934 Governor Olson called out the National Guard to keep the trucks from moving. In 1935 during the Strutwear Company strike he called out the troops to keep the factory closed. In both cases his actions effectively supported the strikers. These strikes did not kill the Citizens' Alliance but did mark the beginning of its decline. And Minneapolis unions did increase and strengthen. The growth of unions on the national level was assisted by the Wagner Act and on the local level by Olson's intervention. From the point of view of the "producing classes," the power of the government had been brought to bear to help workers confront business.

In the final example, the popular definition of *the people* may have broadened, but the state government still intervened in the public interest against big business. At the end of World War II, reaching the bottom of the richest of the iron ore deposits, Iron Range companies developed a processing system that made the mining of low-grade iron ore profitable. The Reserve Mining Company located its processing plant on the scenic Lake Superior shore to draw water from the lake and dispose of wastes easily. According to its plans, the heavy wastes would settle harmlessly at the bottom of the deepest of the Great Lakes. Agreeing that the dumping caused no serious risks, the state and federal governments approved this plan in 1947. Reserve, heralded as the "economic savior of the Iron Range," employed twenty-five hundred people and kept the industrial North Shore alive. It also dumped into Lake Superior about sixty-seven thousand tons of taconite tailings daily.

Beginning in 1969 legal suits challenged Reserve's use of the lake. The discovery of asbestos-like fibers in the wastes and fears about their carcinogenic effect added health worries to complaints that Reserve was destroying the natural beauty of the lake and the shore. The suits united concerned citizens, private environmental groups, the state Pollution Control Agency, the federal Environmental Protection Agency (after 1970), the U.S. Justice Department, and the State of Minnesota against Reserve Mining. The key trial lasted nine months and concluded when Judge Miles Lord of the federal district court ordered Reserve to halt dumping immediately. An appeals court temporarily stayed the order and removed Judge Lord from the case, but it too ended Reserve's dumping and enforced on-land waste disposal.

In this case the state government defended the people's health and the environment against the interests of big business. Any state must defend its citizens, of course, but as one author argues, "Reserve Mining Company was not forced out of Lake Superior by science or environmental laws but by a succession of value-laden political decisions."[8] These values and politics follow a long pattern in Minnesota's political life—and they distinguish the state from its neighbors.

These examples of the state government's willingness to fight or control business interests and the pattern they suggest are a distinctive aspect of Minnesota's political climate and help account for Minnesota's traditionally big and powerful government. A high but generally progressive income tax was originally accepted and persists because an activist government has been popularly accepted. Not seen as a threat, government has been allowed to be big in order to do what a society needs done. In the 1984 presidential election Walter Mondale spoke out of this Minnesota tradition and Ronald Reagan out of a different tradition when they each used the term *special interests*. To Reagan it meant organized labor, women, minorities. But to Mondale it meant corporations, capitalists, big businesses. He was speaking in a Minnesota voice, using Minnesota language.

But Minnesota has been changing in the past twenty years. The agricultural part of the state's liberal coalition has diminished in size, power, and authority. The abortion issue has been divisive in both major parties. Labor unions have been weakened by hard financial times. Citizens increasingly complain about a disproportionately high income tax; they worry about insufficient attention to the needs of businesses, about too generous welfare benefits. The new Right has found real strength among Minnesota's social conservatives. The state government has more and more tried to identify itself with businesses. The legislature, for example, recently strengthened the Institute of Technology at the University of Minnesota and established a Super Computer Institute to increase state support of local high-tech industries. Both the governor and the state legislature are committed to removing Minnesota from among the top ten states in tax rates. It's an important symbolic statement, they say.

Organizations such as the Minnesota Association of Commerce and Industry have lobbied hard for tax breaks and incentives for businesses, and few politicians today can resist this pressure. But the state is slow to reduce its workmen's compensation and state services or to offer too many incentives to lure outside businesses. It hasn't, for example, raised its legal limits on interest rates—as South Dakota did—to attract credit card companies. Traditions build strong habits and Minnesota is still standing further left than its neighbors. When Minnesota Republicans today call themselves the IR (Independent Republicans) and Democrats call themselves DFLers (Democratic-Farmer-Laborites) they are announcing that Minnesota's internal political life differs from that of the rest of the nation, a claim only partially false.

Minnesota's identity derives not only from its politics but also from its geography and landscape. Using a north woods chain saw rather than a Mayo Clinic scalpel, Minnesota can be cut into three predominant regions: rural Minnesota, the Cities, and Up North.

Europeans "discovered" and explored Minnesota north to south. Frenchmen searching for a northwest passage found furs, Indians, and the makings of a thriving trade instead. Accompanied and followed by Catholic priests, these Frenchmen altered the native culture with European goods, and were altered themselves. Their livelihood depended on cooperation with the native peoples. And, as historian Gary Clayton Anderson argues, whites and Indians often formed reciprocal social, economic, and political bonds.

The construction of Fort Snelling in the mid-1820s at the junction of the Mississippi and Minnesota rivers symbolized the transition to a new, more impersonal and antagonistic relationship between Indians and whites. American soldiers and settlers did not form bonds as the French and earlier traders had. They felt no reliance on Indian people nor any affection for native ways. The immigration of land-hungry agricultural settlers resulted in land cessions, reservations, unmet treaty obligations, and finally armed conflict. Following the Dakota War in 1862, the Dakota were dispersed and their influence on and in the state was severely limited. The Ojibway fared little better.

After the 1850s farming was crucial to the identity of Minnesota; it continues to be despite the fact that in the 1980s only a minority of the state's people farm for a living and a majority of the state's wealth is invested outside of agriculture. Nonetheless, rural Minnesota occupies most of the state's physical space—excluding only the Twin Cities metropolitan area and the northeast arrowhead—and makes up a large part of the state's identity.

The quality of the state's farmland ranges from excellent to awful; the farms vary in size from only a few dozen acres to mid-sized family operations to corporate holdings upward of a thousand acres. Since farmers first turned the soil, the natural environment and the economic climate have been alternately generous and stingy; the only certainty has been uncertainty. Bad weather, bad prices, high interest rates, early frosts, droughts, and insect plagues have alternated unpredictably with good weather, good prices, low interest rates, and bountiful harvests.

In the late nineteenth and early twentieth centuries, farm troubles sent people from the land but also evoked angry political responses that led farm people to found and join political organizations attuned to their needs. Led by such men as Ignatius Donnelly, farmers organized to protect their interests in the 1870s and 1880s. In succession they founded, joined, or supported the Anti-Monopolist party, the Greenback and Greenback-Labor parties, the Farmers' Alliance, and the People's party, the Non-Partisan League, and the Farmer-Labor party.

Since the 1930s more and more farm people have coped with trouble by leaving the land—sometimes by choice but more often because they couldn't afford to stay. A land boom in the 1970s made some farmers wealthy and encouraged expansion, but the bust of the 1980s killed land values, impoverished some farm families, brought ruin to those who had overexpanded, and accelerated the forced exodus from the countryside.

Rural townspeople share the fortunes of the farmers, but the two groups often clash. Their mutual dependence means that they can help or hurt each other. Asking for credit in the local store, denying credit to a family already overdrawn, needing a loan extension, having already made too many extensions, farm people and town people powerfully affect each others' fates. Farmers find sympathy with other farmers; business people and bankers turn to other business people and bankers. The small-town banker and the farmer, whatever their personal relationship, must look differently on a foreclosure moratorium. These differences have generated competing political positions and commitments. The Republicans have long had a strong foothold in the towns, the Democrats on the farms.

The tension is social as well as political and economic. To town kids the word *farmer* is an insult; to farm kids city kids don't know anything. Willa Cather describes a version of this tension in her novel *My Ántonia*, set in rural Nebraska. Jim Burden and the other town boys are attracted by the vitality and sensuousness of the immigrant country girls, but "their respect for respectability" is too great and they all marry the prim, reserved, and properly respectable town girls.[9]

If the same tensions have long strained rural life, the same topics have occupied rural conversations for over a hundred years: prices, interest rates, how to get ahead, the role of government, machinery, the neighbors, and the weather. Though it might sound like urban small talk, discussion of weather is serious rural business. It's the farmers' shop talk, their equivalent of office gossip about stock market prices and Dow Jones averages.

In the mid- to late nineteenth century Hans Mattson, the state's immigration director, Father John Ireland, Catholic bishop and archbishop of the St. Paul diocese, and the railroad companies all eagerly sought settlers. Apart from a rural colonization project sponsored by Father Ireland, most Irish immigrants forsook farming for city life. So it was mostly Germans, Scandinavians, and Yankees who settled these farms and small towns in the nineteenth century. These proverbially restrained people—this "sternly undemonstrative race," as one novelist labels them—have set the emotional tone of the region and much of the state.[10] Talk about the neighbors comes easy, but revealing discussions of personal issues, when possible at all, often stumble and falter. Disagreements are muffled by "that's different"— a phrase that signals polite disagreement *and* the end of a conversation. The local commandment "Don't make a fuss" quiets and conceals anger, sadness, joy, love, hate, any strong emotion. The joke about the Norwegian who loved his wife so much he almost told her isn't a joke in many Minnesota places.

In the 1870s Governor John S. Pillsbury distinguished between farmers "worthy" and "unworthy" of state help by whether or not they talked. The worthy had too much self-respect, Pillsbury believed, to tell their troubles. In the 1980s the farm crises have cracked some of the restraint. Rural newspapers and small-town radio stations carry advertisements about coping with stress, getting help, the necessity of talking about emotions. Hot lines have been set up. Mental health clinics are meeting more and more clients. But these new and strange messages bring little response in places where people have long equated silence with strength, self-respect, and virtue. The tradition is strong. The *Minneapolis Star and Tribune* once labeled Minnesota the land of 10,000 hints.

Rural Minnesota differs only slightly from rural areas in the Dakotas, Iowa, and Wisconsin: more rainfall (on average) than in North and South Dakota, fewer hogs and less corn than in Iowa, and more turkeys and fewer dairy cattle than in Wisconsin. Generally, though, the midwestern rural similarities are greater than the state differences.

The second region, the seven-county metropolitan area around the Twin Cities of Minneapolis and St. Paul, dominates the state's public life but occupies the smallest space of the three parts. The concentration of state legislative and government offices, the main campus of the state university, six liberal arts colleges, major corporate and banking firms, nearly half the population, the only international airport, huge shopping malls, and the state's major daily newspapers creates a sense of power, life, and vitality that can eclipse the rest of the state. This division has spawned a value-laden vocabulary of *instate* and *outstate* that rural Minnesotans object to but can't erase.

If Minnesota has yuppies (in a Midwestern version), they generally live in the Twin Cities and indulge in a kind of conspicuous consumption—a term coined by Thorstein Veblen, a graduate of Carleton College in Northfield, Minnesota—that seems slightly out of place against Minnesota's rural background, where wealth like emotion is traditionally concealed or saved or invested in land, and where show and bragging are discouraged. The suburb most closely associated with wealth in the public's imagination is Edina, but many of the Cities' wealthiest people live in more restrained and secluded suburbs. Television and national advertising have diminished the power of this modesty, but it persists.

Banks and office buildings dominate the skyline of the Twin Cities; clean companies and so-called brain industries—electronics, insurance, medical technology, computers, corporate headquarters, education—dominate their economy; they've replaced grain elevators, flour mills, stockyards, and railroad yards. A small amount of heavy manufacturing has been carried on in the Twin Cities, including the production of ammunition and car and tractor parts. But it has long been overshadowed by such companies as Control Data, 3M, Pillsbury, IDS, Dayton-Hudson, Northwest Airlines, Lutheran Brotherhood, Honeywell, Univac Division Sperry Rand, St. Paul Companies, Medtronic, Cargill, General Mills, International Multifoods, West Publishing, and the Farmers' Union Grain Terminal Association.

Many of these businesses have been good citizens, and the state has been a "leader in corporate donations" (perhaps because of the antibusiness politics). The Minnesota Project on Corporate Responsibility and the 5 Percent Club actively encourage local charitable giving. In a 1978 *New York Times* study, thirty-three of the thirty-seven corporations in the nation that donated 5 percent of their pretax profits to charity were headquartered in Minnesota.[11] The Bush, Jerome, McKnight, and Northwest Area foundations are only four of the major Twin Cities–based foundations that support the arts, education, and community development. The St. Paul Junior Chamber of Commerce lobbied vigorously in the 1950s to gain an open-occupancy ordinance to fight local discrimination (especially anti-Semitism). The same chapter in the 1970s and 1980s defied Jaycees tradition and bylaws by admitting women and then fighting the national organization all the way to the Supreme Court (and winning) over the issue of female membership.

At the same time, for over twenty years some Minnesotans have vocally opposed Honeywell's involvement in the production of weapons for the U.S. Defense Department. They have regularly demonstrated, obstructed traffic, and faced arrest (the wife of the Minneapolis chief of police among them) in order to compel Honeywell, from their point of view, to put peace over profits.

Urban Minnesota offers more ethnic diversity than the rural part of the state, although it is still very homogeneous. People only half joke when they say Minnesotans all look alike. Minneapolis is traditionally Scandinavian and Protestant; today it also has one of the largest urban Indian populations in the country (though still under 5 percent). St. Paul is more German, Irish, and Catholic, and even today good traditional Irish and British Isles music can be heard in St. Paul.

The black population of the state in 1980 was under 2 percent overall and located almost entirely in the Twin Cities. Some Mexicans, Asians, and other non-Europeans have made urban Minnesota home, and since the Vietnam War large groups of Vietnamese and Hmong have located in the Twin Cities.

The most noticeable diversity is European—southern and eastern, Christian and Jewish. These ethnic minorities have a presence beyond their numbers because many have settled or stayed in neighborhoods that retain ethnic culture and consciousness. Church services are conducted in Ukrainian, Russian, Greek, Spanish, French. The enthusiastic eater can find food other than midwestern meat and potatoes, but otherwise these minority groups command little notice from the dominant population, except for the anti-Semitism that has existed for so long in the Twin Cities.

Artists, writers, hippies, vegetarians, punk rockers, ne'er-do-wells, and other people living across the grain, live everywhere in the state but more often find comrades, support, freedom, and privacy in the Cities. Racism and a narrow range of acceptable diversity, though, make even the Twin Cities inhospitable to many people.

In other midwestern states, the capital, the university, and the business centers are split up, so no one city dominates or exerts quite so much influence over the rest of the state. This urban dominance plays a key role in Minnesota's development and identity. Milwaukee, Chicago, Detroit, and other midwestern cities all host much greater ethnic and racial diversity. This lack of diversity in the Twin Cities also plays a key role in the state's identity.

Minnesota's third region most distinguishes the state from its midwestern sisters. Up North includes the mines of the Iron Range; the woods, even a few virgin pine; hundreds of lakes and rivers; a few farms; Lake Superior; dozens of small towns; and the City of Duluth. This region is also quite different from the rest of the state in politics, economy, ethnicity, and social patterns.

Duluth, at the base of Lake Superior, anchors the area. Built long and narrow on the side of a ridge of hills, the city looks like an impoverished version of San Francisco. It once provided the setting for a film that needed a Soviet port city background. It is the state's third largest city and, though it is able to accommodate half-a-million people, its population has never risen much above 100,000. The heavy industry missing in the Twin Cities exists in Duluth and in the smaller range cities. On nights when the wind is wrong, the odors of the wood-processing plant hang over the city. The comings and goings of the lakers and salties under the aerial lift bridge remind Duluthians of their industrial roots and of distant places—hinted at by Cyrillic characters and exotic place names lettered on the ships' bows.

Duluth has its share of Germans and Scandinavians but, like the Iron Range, also attracted Finns, Greeks, Italians, Poles, Croats, and other southern and eastern Europeans as the agricultural frontier closed in the late nineteenth century and wage-labor jobs opened. This ethnic variety makes for a different emotional climate Up North. Expressiveness is stronger than restraint. The proximity to Duluth of the Fond du Lac and Grand Portage Indian reservations and the local presence of Indian people make Duluth more aware of the Ojibway past, if not always more sensitive. During the post–World War I Red Scare, when Ku Klux Klan chapters sprouted up throughout the Midwest, including Minnesota, John Fedo reports that racial tension ran especially high in Duluth as employers imported job-hungry southern blacks to quiet union activity. In the summer of 1920 a white mob lynched three black circus hands on a main Duluth street. Postcards of the dead men surrounded by respectable-looking mob members circulated through the city within a few days.

Fishing, shipping, repairs, transportation, loading, and carting, as well as supplying miners and loggers, provided work to sustain Duluth for nearly a hundred years. But in the past twenty years the city has suffered. Dozens of empty storefronts, high unemployment, and hard times have presented staggering problems. Tourism might be able to revive the town and its economy, but the transition from an industrial to a service economy will be painful.

Traditionally a union town, Duluth remembers corporate power. It is more class-conscious and class-divided than any other Minnesota city. At the turn of the century it boasted of more millionaires per capita than any other city of its size. The workers traditionally lived in the west end, in West Duluth. People with money lived in the east end, along the shore, or overlooking the lake.

The French voyageurs of the sixteenth and seventeenth centuries who married native wives, wore skin clothing, and raced along in native canoes provided later Minnesotans with a romantic heritage of paddling misty lakes, learning magic Indian ways, living unencumbered by European restraints and laws. This mythology lives on and contributes to the tension that most defines the north country: development versus preservation. On the side that sees the range's brightest glory in development stand some of the biggest businessmen in Minnesota and American history: Andrew Carnegie, J. Pierpont Morgan, and John D. Rockefeller in iron ore and steel; Frederick Weyerhaeuser in lumbering; and James J. Hill and Jay Cooke in railroads. Mining, lumbering, and transportation virtually monopolized economic activity in the region for seventy-five years. Most of the owners lived elsewhere (some never set foot in the state) and their huge fortunes made in the region usually flowed out of the state. When the good times passed, even the managers moved on, leaving behind some of the most glorious and elegant homes in all of Minnesota, fabulous township and county buildings—and depleted natural resources, a floundering work force, and a tradition of union activity.

Unlike Minnesota farmers, angry range laborers did not found and join political parties. Most of them spoke little or no English and even the men could not vote. They could not express their grievances or receive redress through electoral politics. Over three dozen ethnic groups made up the unskilled labor force and even the Western Federation of Miners had organizing troubles—not ideological, but verbal. According to labor historian Neil Betten, "The American organizers and the appointed American leaders of the locals could speak neither for the workers nor to them." In the 1907 Mesabi strike against the Oliver Iron Mining Company, the strikers—nearly three-quarters of them Finnish—were led out by a Finn, an Italian, and a Scotch-Irish immigrant.[12]

Range strikes were often bitter and violent. The presence of United Mine Worker organizer Mother Jones and Industrial Workers of the World activists frightened and angered management. The use of Pinkerton-like company police and of infiltrators and the firing and blackballing of union activists seriously alienated workers. Violence and bloodshed during a 1916 range strike and a 1917 timber strike left both sides hostile, angry, and unforgiving.

Despite these and other strikes when northern laborers and employers were pitted against each other, owners, management, and workers have found themselves in agreement in their opposition to conservation. Conservation threatened them all by challenging the hegemony of development.

On the side of preservation have stood those who want a chance to get away from it all and to shed a few of the restraints and laws of society, and those who are aware of the finite nature of natural resources and wilderness. The state has spawned committed conservationists, from C. C. Andrews—the state's first fire warden and passionate proponent of the Superior National Forest—to Sigurd Olson, an active political worker and nature writer. What makes the north country valuable to conservationists is the seclusion, beauty, isolation, quiet, clear water, and absence of development. The preservationists have tried to limit or prohibit roads, hydroelectric generators, sawmills and lumbering, resorts, powerboats, airplanes, and snowmobiles. This isolation and quiet also attracts tourists—many of them the kind who don't spend much money.

The tensions between development and preservation, restraint and growth, beauty and jobs run deep and strong. They divide people within the area and across the state. The tensions are acutely felt and bitterly fought because they pit two value systems against each other. Unencumbered individualism, the frontier, freedom, progress, growth, development, technology, return to nature, self-determination, and getting ahead are words that tap into the emotional reservoir of strong American values. Questions and issues cast in value terms and using such loaded language have been difficult to resolve in northern Minnesota. A tree can't both be cut down and remain standing, though that's the nature of this conflict.

In the 1920s and 1930s, conservationist Ernest Oberholzer and entrepreneur Edward Backus embodied this conflict in their fight over the future of Rainy Lake. Historian Newell Searle tells the story: "Backus found in the Quetico-Superior country a last outpost where he could fashion in unfettered isolation a powerful industrial empire of food and water. Oberholzer saw in the region a vast wilderness, traditional Indian ways, and silence whose conservation would protect and perpetuate for others the idyllic life he had fashioned for himself."[13] Two world views clashed when these men faced each other. The triumph of one meant the demise of the other.

In the mid-1970s Congressman Donald Fraser of Minneapolis supported strict federal regulations of the Boundary Waters Canoe Area that restrained development, limited the access of motorized vehicles, and resulted in the closing of numerous resorts (where tourists did spend money). In 1978 angry iron rangers helped defeat Fraser's senatorial bid; he had voted against their interests. The conflict endures.

Of course, the sides within the conflict are more numerous and complicated than these two. Some northern laborers stand among the most avid and loyal of wilderness devotees. Many campers want electric hookups, motorboats, and fast food along the trail. Conservationists argue among themselves about what protection means. Some Minnesotans don't pay much attention at all; others don't want tax dollars spent to save either the Arctic Cat Company or Hungry Jack Lake. Who is the public, then, and what is its interest? That is an especially painful range question.

A third characteristic of Minnesota is that it is confused about its identity. The state doesn't have an easy label. Its people don't know exactly what they are because they're several things (though not enough things to claim "diversity" as their identifying tag). It is a liberal state with strong forces of conservatism. It is an agricultural state where the majority of the population is concentrated in a single (and relatively small) metropolitan region, but even with this majority the state can't really be called urban. It is the state of 10,000 lakes, as the license plates have long read, and it has a wilderness dotted with iron mines. And, like other Americans, Minnesotans consider themselves part of what's best in America and part of what's negligible.

Minnesotans relish being a part of the Midwest that is admirable and noble. Two national network television programs have been set in Minnesota: "Little House on the Prairie" and "The Mary Tyler Moore Show." Both portray Americans, Minnesotans, at their most wholesome. The main characters honor the traditional American values of home, family, hard work, and success. The people are nice, clean, white, richly innocent, and fairly naive. They seem to represent the so-called best in both pioneer and mid-twentieth-century America. And it seems somehow right to place them in Minnesota rather than New Jersey or Colorado or Texas. While the exaggerated ruthlessness of the characters in "Dallas" matches Texas's legendary extravagance, not only the program's title but also its people's behavior would have to change if it were relocated in Minnesota. It's not that "Dallas"-like behavior doesn't happen in Minnesota, it's only that it conflicts with the state's image. Within the state, there is no pleasure taken in extravagance of any kind, let alone in extravagant evil. Outside the state, the thought of Minnesota intrigue and extramarital dalliance must seem comical.

In the same self-congratulatory vein, Minnesotans like to think of themselves as the truest of the true Americans, the most superior of the morally superior. Garrison Keillor and his tales of Lake Wobegon have come recently to represent Minnesota in the popular imagination. In his fictional Minnesota town "all the women are strong, all the men are good looking, and all the children are above average." It's this last phrase that suggests so pervasive a truth about Minnesotans, about a part of the state's personality. Midwesterners might be normal, but Minnesotans want to claim that their advanced, modern, and up-to-date features put them ahead of their regional neighbors and even, sometimes, in the forefront of the nation.

The Mayo Clinic in Rochester and the University of Minnesota Hospitals stand among the foremost medical centers in the United States and make Minnesotans proud. The "Minnesota method" is a way of treating the chemically dependent that is followed and practiced in progressive clinics throughout the world. The "Minnesota miracle" is the label affixed to the state's way of funding schools. White Minnesotans attribute the general racial harmony of the state to extraordinary tolerance (rather than to the relatively small sizes of racial minorities—and some members of the minority populations might disagree). The state has lower crime rates and higher voter turnout rates than most of the rest of the country. It boasts of early laws on child labor, workmen's compensation, and direct primaries. It prides itself on its clean state government and its clean air and water. Minnesotans watch with satisfaction while other states copy the state's Clean Indoor Air Act.

The presence of the Twin Cities in the state supports this sense of superiority. In contemporary America, urban is modern, progressive, and considerably more hip than rural; Iowa and the Dakotas have nothing to offer in competition. The skyscrapers, upscale shopping centers, big-name stores, progressive businesses, and wealth make Minnesotans the equal of any urbanites in the country, they think.

Sometimes Minnesotans' pride collapses into smugness, into the self-satisfied assertion that this is simply the best place to live—rural values, urban sophistication, clean industry, quiet places, and weather that makes people more noble. Perhaps it's this attitude that has prompted so much satire from Minnesota writers. Satire often makes the strongest retort to alleged superiority. The smugness of fictional Gopher Prairie in *Main Street* infuriated Sinclair Lewis. He rails against the locals who elevated their town, glorified their own activities, and deified their beliefs and then expected Carol Kennicott, if not the world, to follow their lead. They knew they were "the best people," and they didn't need to look beyond themselves.

Novelist Jon Hassler uses a gentler satire in *Staggerford*, but the narrator's affection for Miss McGee doesn't keep him from taking swipes at her primness, her certainty about truth and error, her conviction of her own rightness. Miss McGee's greater powers of introspection save her from sisterhood with the self-righteous of Gopher Prairie, but she's not more distant than a cousin. J. F. Powers's Father Urban is driven to distraction by the stumbling, bungling complacency of his confreres in rural Minnesota, and the book is entitled *Morte d'Urban*.

Keillor's satire is the kindest, but it is still satire. His fictional Toast 'n Jelly Days, for example, differs only slightly from the Korn and Klover Karnival held every summer in Hinckley or from any one of dozens of annual community festivals.

If Minnesota could just be a progressive state, one that stood in the forefront of the nation, and was not in the Midwest, it might have a less divided consciousness. But Minnesotans have in addition to their superiority complex an accompanying inferiority complex. They fear that the state is not really the best place on earth. And there's lots of evidence to confirm their suspicion. They know that most of the really interesting and exciting things, the temptations, are elsewhere. They can easily imagine European or Asian tourists coming to America and skipping Minnesota (unless they have relatives there).

And not just tourists. American historians seem often to skip Minnesota. For example, a standard generalization in American history is that the United States became an urbanized nation in 1920. A majority of Minnesota's population did not live in urban places until 1950, and in several essential ways the state (or big parts of the state) is still not really urbanized.

Similarly, coming to statehood about seventy-five years after the ratification of the Constitution and two hundred years after the original settlement of the first colonies, Minnesota has grown up in the shadow of the East. As colonists looked to England and Europe for their culture, history, education, norms, and rules, Minnesotans have long looked to the East Coast. Many of Minnesota's early leaders— Henry H. Sibley, Alexander Ramsey, Jane Grey Swisshelm, Charles Pillsbury, Edmund Ely, Harriet Bishop, Samuel and Gideon Pond, Maria Sanford—were transplanted Yankees. Settlers walked westward, but they kept looking over their shoulders and carried eastern baggage. It's a modified version of Frederick Jackson Turner's frontier thesis: civilization starts in the northeast and moves westward.

In other historical generalizations, too, Minnesota is ignored. In the best accounts of American poor-relief practices, historians recount that by the time of the American Revolution local and relatively informal modes of caring for the poor were waning. Such practices as families taking care of their own, auctioning off the poor to the lowest bidder, and warning out strangers were falling into disuse. By the early nineteenth century, more and more communities adopted the poorhouse as the mode of relief. Before the Civil War, David Rothman writes, "Institutionalization became the standard public response to the problem of poverty."[14] After the war, scientific charity and state bureaucracies emerged and then everything changed in the twentieth century. This story has almost nothing to do with Minnesota's experience.

Minnesota's relief practices at least through the 1870s were still like those of colonial Massachusetts. More than half of Minnesota's counties finished the century without ever establishing poor farms (there were almost no poorhouses). Outdoor aid was common well into the twentieth century, and more than one county was still auctioning off its poor. Yet the story of "American" practices prevails.

And then there's American literature, which can be divided into four major categories: southern, western, midwestern, and American. The last might more accurately be called eastern, but it's rarely identified regionally. Almost no one calls John Updike or John Cheever a regional writer (and it seems almost sacrilegious to do so), but place and provincial issues infuse the work of these men. Cheever's "The Swimmer" is not running through the backyards of Avon or St. Cloud, Minnesota. Similarly, in art, critics call Grant Wood a regional artist because of his Iowa settings but call Winslow Homer American because of the New England and Atlantic locale of much of his work.

Many Minnesotans share this notion that the really important things are happening elsewhere. Minnesota author Carol Bly writes, "A natural problem of living in the country is that one is always behind the times,"[15] and Minnesota is rural enough to believe it and to care.

Fashions, trends, fads, styles start elsewhere. By the time they get to Minnesota and the Midwest, they're already out of style on the East Coast. Recalling his youth in Minneapolis, *New York Times* editor Harrison Salisbury wrote, "I knew that New Yorkers were very sophisticated people. In fact, I was ashamed of coming from a place way out west where, as I understood the New York view, no one really lived and certainly no one from New York ever ventured. I felt very gawky, very provincial." After a month in New York, "I went back to Minneapolis and felt very superior. I knew how to do things in the New York way."[16]

Minnesotans have often tried to do things in the New York or East Coast way. The status symbols of the Midwest acquire their status partly out of being eastern—Cape Cod or colonial houses, sailing, the *New Yorker*, the *New York Times*. One of the largest mansions on Lake Superior ignored its view of the lake for thirty years and looked out instead onto a small, formal garden, appropriate for a cramped backyard in Boston.

Minnesotans' smugness takes other occasional lashings. When Mary Tyler Moore's program ended and Ed Asner continued in the "Lou Grant" spinoff series, the program's tone, format, and locale changed. Moore's program had been a half-hour comedy set in a fairly chaotic and inconsequential television newsroom in Minneapolis, populated by the egotistical and foolish anchor man and the dippy star of the cooking program. Asner's program was changed to one hour; the comedy became serious drama that took up significant political and social issues; a few people in the newsroom may have been cranky or difficult to get along with, but they turned out serious and high-quality work nonetheless; and most importantly for Minnesota's image, the program's locale was moved to California.[17]

This sense of being both superior and negligible leaves Minnesotans confused. The state is urban enough, diverse enough, corporate and artistic enough to make a claim to sophistication. It is rural, safe, homogeneous, and isolated enough to be decidedly unsophisticated and proudly American. The state is in the center of everything, but central to almost nothing. It's ahead of the times and behind the times. Minnesotans make fun of themselves, but then they know they have a lot to make fun of. They have strong politicians but can't get one elected president. The state has professional sports teams but doesn't win national titles. It's a state of vice-presidents and contenders. It's urbane and plagued by what Minnesota poet Barton Sutter calls our "insane Bergmania."[18] It's in the Midwest, though the sisterhood is sometimes uncomfortable. This conflict, this divided consciousness, this sense that the state is many things gives the state energy and an enlivening vitality.

It also, however, leads Minnesotans to tell Iowa jokes. As historian Bruce White points out, Minnesotans tell jokes about the more rural Iowa because they fear the "fragility of their metropolitan sophistication. . . . In telling Iowa jokes they are saying: We are not rural anymore."[19] And they're right and they're wrong.

N O T E S

1. John H. Fenton, *Midwest Politics* (New York, 1966), 19.
2. William Watts Folwell, *A History of Minnesota*, 4 vols. (St. Paul, 1921–30), III, 556.
3. Horace Austin, Inaugural Address, in Minnesota, *Executive Documents of the State of Minnesota*, 1870, 5. Cushman K. Davis, Inaugural Address, ibid., 1874, 6, 11 (italics added).
4. Lucius B. Hubbard, Governor's Message, ibid., 1883, 28. William Merriam, Inaugural Address, ibid., 1889, 17.
5. Barbara Stuhler, *Ten Men of Minnesota and American Foreign Policy, 1898–1968* (St. Paul, 1973), 6.
6. Theodore C. Blegen, *Minnesota: A History of the State* (Minneapolis, 1963; reprinted 1975), 295. Quoted in collection notes for Citizens Alliance of Minneapolis Papers, 1903–1958, Division of Archives and Manuscripts, Minnesota Historical Society, St. Paul. Thomas E. Blantz, C. S. C., "Father Haas and the Minneapolis Truckers Strike," *Minnesota History* 42 (Spring 1970), 6.
7. David Paul Nord, "Minneapolis and the Pragmatic Socialism of Thomas Van Lear," *Minnesota History* 45 (Spring 1978), 7; Van Lear quoted on 4.
8. Robert V. Bartlett, *The Reserve Mining Controversy: Science, Technology, and Environmental Quality* (Bloomington, Ind., 1980), 161.
9. Willa Cather, *My Ántonia* (Boston, 1918), 202.
10. Cornelia James Cannon, *Red Rust* (Boston, 1938), 58.
11. Don Larson, *Land of the Giants* (Minneapolis, 1979), 3.
12. Neil Betten, "Strike on the Mesabi—1907," *Minnesota History* 40 (Fall 1967), 341.
13. R. Newell Searle, *Saving Quetico-Superior: A Land Set Apart* (St. Paul, 1977), 59.
14. David Rothman, *The Discovery of the Asylum: Social Order and Disorder in the New Republic* (Boston, 1971), 202.
15. Carol Bly, *Letters from the Country* (New York, 1981), 126.
16. Harrison E. Salisbury, "A Victorian City in the Midwest," in Chester G. Anderson, ed., *Growing Up in Minnesota: Ten Writers Remember Their Childhoods* (Minneapolis, 1976), 71.
17. I am indebted to Susan Meyer, "Mary Tyler Moore: An American Institution," unpublished manuscript, December 1986, for the insights in this paragraph.
18. Barton Sutter, *Pine Creek Parish Hall and Other Poems* (Ord, Nebr., 1985), 59.
19. Bruce M. White, "Did You Hear the One About . . . ," *Twin Cities Reader*, December 8, 1982.

BIBLIOGRAPHY

William Lass, *Minnesota: A History* (New York, 1977), gives a quick over-view of the state and provides a basic bibliography up to 1977. The standard works on the state are W. W. Folwell's *A History of Minnesota* (St. Paul, 1921–30) and Theodore Blegen's *Minnesota: A History of the State*, 2d ed. (Minneapolis, 1975). Especially helpful as well is *Minnesota History*, the journal published by the Minnesota Historical Society that covers an array of fascinating, arcane, and substantial issues in the state's past. The volumes themselves provide a record both of the changing definition of state history and of historians' different interests over time. See also Barbara Stuhler and Gretchen Kreuter, *Women of Minnesota: Selected Bibliographical Essays* (St. Paul, 1977), and Annette Atkins, *Harvest of Grief* (St. Paul, 1984).

The Minnesota Historical Society Press is preparing a collection of essays on twentieth century Minnesota, edited by Deborah L. Miller, to be published in 1988. Rhoda R. Gilman and Stephen Sandell are writing *Northern Lights*, also to be published by the society; it is a textbook for children, but adults will delight in it, too.

The state's politics have inspired substantial writing. Since 1977 Carl Solberg's biography of *Hubert Humphrey* (New York, 1984) and John Haynes's *Dubious Alliance: The Making of Minnesota's DFL* (Minneapolis, 1984) have been valuable and controversial additions to the scholarship. For a different angle there is Meridel Le Sueur, *Crusaders: The Radical Legacy of Marian and Arthur Le Sueur* (St. Paul, reprinted 1984). Gary Clayton Anderson, *Little Crow: Spokesman for the Sioux* (St. Paul, 1986), focuses on Little Crow, especially in his role as politician.

The best recent writing on Minnesota's ethnic groups is available in *They Chose Minnesota: A Survey of the State's Ethnic Groups* (St. Paul, 1980). The humble title only hints at the richness of the material, which includes sections on dozens of groups, including native Americans and Afro Americans. Patricia Hampl's *Romantic Education* (Boston, 1981), Ignatia Broker's *Night Flying Woman* (St. Paul, 1983), Era Bell Thompson's *American Daughter* (St. Paul, reprinted 1986), Gordon Parks's *A Choice of Weapons* (St. Paul, reprinted 1986), Justine Kerfoot's *A Woman of the Boundary Waters* (Grand Marais, Minn., 1986), and Chester Anderson, ed., *Growing Up in Minnesota* (Minneapolis, 1976), present quite different accounts of life in Minnesota. For a full account of the Duluth lynching, see Michael W. Fedo, *"They Was Just Niggers"* (Ontario, Calif., 1979).

Minnesota is rich in writers and literature. Jean Irvin, *The Minnesota Experience* (Minnesota, 1979), offers a substantial bibliography of Minnesota prose. For examples of poetry, see *25 Minnesota Poets* (Minneapolis, 1972) and *25 Minnesota Poets #2* (Minneapolis, 1977). A third volume is in prep-aration. For fiction see Seymour Yesner et al., eds., *25 Minnesota Writers* (Minneapolis, 1980). Another fiction collection is also in preparation. The most notable of Minnesota's fiction writers are Sinclair Lewis, F. Scott Fitzgerald, J. F. Powers, Jon Hassler, and Frederick Manfred; and of its poets, John Berryman, Robert Bly, Tom McGrath, and Meridel Le Sueur.

Martha Mitchell Bigelow

MICHIGAN

A State in the Vanguard

M ICHIGAN IS A STATE of fascinating, and at times extreme, dichotomies. It is agrarian and midwestern, yet urban, industrial,
and dominated by water. Its heritage is Yankee and international. It
was one of the first and last midwestern states to be settled. It has
led both in exploitation and in conservation of natural resources.
Often conservative in politics, it has been a leader in quality-of-life
reforms. Beneath this rich diversity, however, there are constant historical themes—water, an air of internationalism, industrial and urban
expansion, and a sense of always being in the vanguard.

Michigan is first of all midwestern. A midwesterner's allegiance
is more to state than to region; yet there is a definite midwestern
character. Midwesterners are conscious of their importance to the
nation. They know they feed the United States and much of the world.
They know that their cities dominate the industrial landscape. They
take conscious pride in being middle American, and in their minds
that means moderation in all things—politics, social institutions, cultural activities. They are able to be moderate, and therefore modest,
because they know their power. They are the heart of the continent
and they know it. Midwesterners believe that the south is backward,
that the West is a place of extremes, and that the East, although
culturally advanced, is effete in character; therefore, all are to be

MICHIGAN

Miles 0 10 20 30 40 50

⭐ State Capital

ISLE ROYALE
(TO KEWEENAW CO.)

LAKE SUPERIOR

ISLE ROYALE

Same Scale
as Main Map

WESTERN PART OF MICHIGAN

Same Scale as Main Map

LAKE SUPERIOR

ONTONAGON

BARAGA

HOUGHTON

KEWEENAW

MARQUETTE

Montreal R.

GOGEBIC

IRON

Brule River

DICKINSON

KEWEE-NAW

LAKE SUPERIOR

MARQUETTE

ALGER

LUCE

SCHOOLCRAFT

CHIPPEWA

Escanaba

DICKINSON

DELTA

MENOMINEE

Menominee R.

MACKINAC

Mary's R.

WISCONSIN

ONTARIO

WISCONSIN

LAKE MICHIGAN

EMMET

CHEBOYGAN

PRESQUE ISLE

CHARLEVOIX

OTSEGO

MONT-MORENCY

ALPENA

ANTRIM

LAKE HURON

LEELANAU

GRAND TRAVERSE

KALKASKA

CRAWFORD

OSCODA

ALCONA

BENZIE

Au Sable R.

MANISTEE

Manistee R.

MISSAUKEE

Muskegon R.

ROSCOMMON

OGEMAW

IOSCO

WEXFORD

MASON

LAKE

OSCEOLA

CLARE

GLADWIN

ARENAC

OCEANA

NEWAYGO

MECOSTA

ISABELLA

MIDLAND

BAY

HURON

Muskegon R.

MONTCALM

GRATIOT

SAGINAW

TUSCOLA

SANILAC

MUSKEGON

KENT

Grand River

IONIA

CLINTON

SHIAWASSEE

GENESEE

Flint

LAPEER

ST. CLAIR

OTTAWA

Grand Rapids

Kalamazoo R.

BARRY

EATON

INGHAM

Lansing

LIVINGSTON

OAKLAND

Pontiac

St. Clair R.

MACOMB

Detroit

ALLEGAN

Kalamazoo

JACKSON

WASHTENAW

Dearborn

WAYNE

VAN BUREN

KALAMAZOO

CALHOUN

Raisin R.

MONROE

BERRIEN

CASS

ST. JOSEPH

BRANCH

HILLSDALE

LENAWEE

LAKE ERIE

ONTARIO

ILLINOIS

INDIANA

OHIO

pitied—only midwesterners are true Americans. As true Americans they are people of action with a strong optimistic belief in their ability to create economic, political, and social change that results in progress. Coupled with this strong belief in progress, however, is a staid, conservative streak that says, "We are fine just like we are. Don't try to change us, leave us alone! We are bedrock Americans in our love of land, country, family, and God, and we don't want to change."

Michiganians have all these traits—in extremes. They are different and changeable like their weather. They even debate whether they are Michiganians or Michiganders. They see themselves as different from the rest of the Midwest even while they reflect its values.

In assessing this difference, or what makes Michigan distinctly Michigan, we must look at the major elements that shaped its history: water, internationalism, industrialism, a varied ethnic composition, a high regard for education, and humanitarianism. First and foremost is water. Water has shaped the Michigan character in every way. Michigan has but two relatively short land borders; the rest is water. It is the only state surrounded by four of the five Great Lakes, and its 3,121-mile coastline is surpassed only by the coastlines of Hawaii and Alaska. I once flew sixteen hours in a small plane, viewing the length and breadth of Michigan. We were seldom out of sight of water. Fly over most of the Midwest and you see miles and miles of unbroken farmland. Fly over Michigan and you see miles and miles of unbroken water. In Michigan water shaped the lives of the Indians; the lines of settlement of the pioneers; the growth of the lumber, mining, and chemical industries; the development of the automobile; and the recreation and tourist industries. Today the potential of the fresh water of the Great Lakes is shaping the future industrial and recreational expansion of the state even as that same water is being looked at longingly by other states. Water, the first element of life, shapes us all; in Michigan it is so ever-present that Michiganians forget its significance.

Water gives Michigan its unique shape—two separate peninsulas. You could not even reach the Upper Peninsula from lower Michigan except by water until 1957. If you stand at the Straits of Mackinac, a vast inland sea stretches around you. You know the oceans are greater, but the ocean view is cut off by the horizon. Here you seem to see water everywhere.

Separation by water has created two psychologies in the state. Southern Michiganians like to call their state the mitten state. That infuriates people from the Upper Peninsula, called UPers, because it leaves them out. UPers generally feel abused and ignored by downstaters, as they call people from lower Michigan. UPers, however, are caught in one of Michigan's many dichotomies. They want money and development from the south because they are poor, but they do not want downstaters destroying their forests, polluting their crystal-clear streams, and crowding their wild, wonderful, isolated north woods. They demand progress and economic development at the same time that they cry "Leave us alone." As the tourists pour across the bridge, you hear such phrases as "Building that bridge was the biggest mistake we ever made!"

The second element, internationalism, seems strange at first glance. But Michigan began as a vital part of the struggle for empire between France and Great Britain. It shares international waters with Canada, and throughout its history it has had an important trade with foreign nations. Today the state maintains offices in Japan and Belgium. In addition to its commercial contacts, the ethnic diversity of its immigrants has turned Michigan outward. Michigan is conscious of playing a world role. Hence, it is not surprising that during World War II Michigan's Senator Arthur Vandenberg turned from typical midwestern isolationism to internationalism and became instrumental in creating the United Nations.

A third factor common to all the Midwest but more significant in Michigan is the effect of industrialism. Michigan is different from the rest of the Midwest in the depth, breadth, and age of its industrial-commercial-urban revolution. Agriculture was and is important in Michigan, but even at its height it never dominated the economic life of the state. Michigan began not as an agricultural state but as part of the fur industry. From the earliest settlement its good agricultural land was centered in the lower half of the lower peninsula. The great preponderance of the state was settled with the development of timber, mining, chemical, and related industries. Michigan entered the Union in 1837 with an economy based on fur trading and fishing. Agriculture had only begun to take over in the land rush of the late 1820s and 1830s, and its period of dominance was over by the Civil War. As the state entered the Union, big business and big fortunes were already a part of its psyche. John Jacob Astor, with the headquarters of his American Fur Trading Company located at Mackinac Island, had already made one of the first major American fortunes and was moving on to new conquests. The industrial-commercial-urban revolution so important in Michigan also had another effect: the labor movement shaped Michigan's history more than that of any other state of the Midwest. And Michigan's labor history in turn shaped the rest of the nation.

The last factor that makes Michigan different is the character of her people. They partake in midwestern optimism to the extreme of boundless enthusiasm. They see themselves in the vanguard of all movements and activities that enhance and protect the quality of life and the rights of human beings. They can be found in the vanguard of such educational, humanitarian, and civil rights reforms as abolishing capital punishment, forming the Republican party on an anti-slavery platform, and creating the first comprehensive public school system west of the Alleghenies. Michigan was the first state in the Union to constitutionally mandate a civil rights commission, and one of its representatives in Congress, Martha Griffiths, was responsible for including "sex" in the protection clauses of the 1965 Civil Rights Act. In the twentieth century, Michiganians have also evinced a deep concern for protection of the environment.

In its diversity Michigan has also exemplified the converse of the above traits. There has been a strong nativist, isolationist strain in the state. The agricultural tradition has remained strong; agriculture today vies with tourism for second place in economic returns to the state. There have been strong reactions against efforts to reform. The state's civil rights record is marred by race riots in Detroit in 1863, 1943, and 1967. The Ku Klux Klan was strong in the state in the 1920s and the 1960s, and conservative politicians won elections to state office more often than liberal ones. Conservation of natural resources did not become important until Michiganians had massively exploited their mines, timber, and streams—and, in many instances, their neighbors. These trends, however, seem to be only countercurrents in shaping the state's history.

Michigan is a beautiful state. Its varied topography was created in the ice age by pushing, gouging glaciers. Four glaciations covered Michigan, pushing the soil off the hard crystalline rocks of the Laurentian Shield, which reaches south into the Upper Peninsula, and combining it with soil created by the erosion of soft shale and limestone to create the fertile farmlands of southern Michigan. The land north of a line drawn across the state and intersecting the town of Clare was left relatively infertile, though it supported vast forests of great white pine and hardwoods. The melting glacial waters created the Great Lakes and thousands of inland lakes and vitally important river systems. The Great Lakes were linked by strategically important waterways: the St. Mary's River between Lakes Superior and Huron, whose rapids were bridged in 1855 by the "Soo" Locks; the Straits of Mackinac connecting Lakes Michigan and Huron—bridged in 1957 by "Mighty Mac," which, between its anchorages, is the longest and most beautiful suspension bridge in the world; and the St. Clair River, Lake St. Clair, and the Detroit River connecting Lakes Huron and Erie. The French, the British, and the Americans all recognized the importance of these links, and the struggle for empire centered on these strategic points. Today through the locks at the Sault Ste. Marie flows a higher tonnage of commerce than that traversing the Suez and Panama canals combined. The Detroit River is one of the busiest lanes of commerce in the world, and Michigan considers its ports on the Great Lakes to be seaports, linking it through the St. Lawrence Seaway to the rest of the world and emphasizing its international character.

The first humans appeared in this area after the retreat of the ice approximately twelve thousand years ago. They must have marveled at the mountains of the Keewenaw, the bare rocks of the eastern Upper Peninsula, the lush forests covering the state, and the grass prairie lands and oak openings of the south. The Paleo-Indians had a simple hunting-gathering culture that eventually took them south of Michigan's modern borders. There is no archaeological evidence that humans occupied Michigan between 8000 B.C. and 4000 B.C., when the Indians moved back into the state from the south, bringing with them a rich ceremonial life centered on a burial cult. The Paleo-Indian culture reached its height as influences from the Hopewell culture of Ohio and Illinois reached into the state around 100 B.C. By A.D. 1000 Indian economic patterns had stabilized and were essentially the same as they would be in the contact period. In summer the Chippewa (Ojibway) in the north gathered large family groups around rich fishing locations such as Sault Ste. Marie. Smaller groups went out on their own in the winter. In the south, agricultural groups, including the Miami and the Potawatomi, lived in settled villages and farmed. Large groups made hunting trips during winter. In the middle were the Ottawa, who did some farming but were primarily traders.

Water played a key role in the life of the Indians. They placed their dwellings on high, defensible points close to water for food and transportation. They traded throughout the river systems far to the south and west. For instance, copper from the old copper culture of the Keewenaw has been found as far south as the Gulf of Mexico and as far west as Missouri. The Indians developed birchbark canoes strong enough to travel the rivers and the Great Lakes if they clung to the shore but light enough to be carried easily over portages. The routes plied by the Indians through the rivers and the lakes later enabled the French to penetrate the continent and develop the fur trade.

The French did not intend to destroy the way of life of the Indians, but they did. As the Indians became dependent on European guns, knives, axes, cooking utensils, and textiles, trade and trapping came to dominate their economic life.

The French, who arrived in the upper lakes through the waterways of the St. Lawrence River valley, were the first to give Michigan its international character. Etienne Brule and a companion named Grenoble probably reached Michigan's Upper Peninsula in 1622, Jean Nicolet in 1634, and Jesuit missionaries Father Isaac Joques and Father Charles Raymbault in 1642. The first mission in Michigan was founded at Sault Ste. Marie in 1668 by Father Jacques Marquette, and it was from Michigan that Marquette and Joliet set out in 1673 to explore the Mississippi River.

The explorers set the geographic framework of French influence, but policy was created in France. Thus, the tradition of being a part of an international community was set. As English settlement grew on the East Coast, French policy was to control the hinterland through military posts, Jesuit missions, and licensed traders. It was less destructive of the Indian way of life than occupation by settlers, and it forced the French to cultivate the western tribes as allies.

French military posts were located in territory that was to become part of the midwestern states of Wisconsin, Minnesota, Illinois, Indiana, and Missouri, but their major settlements were in Michigan at Michilimackinac and Detroit. Antoine de la Mathe Cadillac understood the strategic importance of the straits at Detroit and convinced the French government to allow him to establish a post there in 1701. That and subsequent French moves into the Ohio Valley enhanced the struggle for empire between the British and the French, precipitating the French and Indian War. The French withdrew after the Treaty of Paris of 1763, and the English took over. The way of life in Detroit and Michilimackinac changed little in the British period, 1763–96; however, Michigan's continuing role as a center of Indian and British activities both in the American Revolution and the War of 1812 gave it a historical perspective different from that of other states of the Midwest. This sense of being a part of the world of international intrigue has remained in the consciousness of the state.

Michigan's late settlement also gave it a different perspective from that of the other states of the Old Northwest. Organized under the Northwest Ordinance of 1787 and becoming a territory in 1805, Michigan stagnated during the first two decades of the nineteenth century. While the Indians and the proximity of the British in Canada may have been partly responsible for that, it was more likely the tales of the Black Swamp and poor land that prevented migration. Thus in the first decades of the nineteenth century, when settlers were pouring into Ohio, Indiana, and Illinois, Michigan's population was standing still. The migration of southern settlers northward and westward into Ohio, Indiana, Illinois, and Missouri gave these states a political and social history different from that of Michigan, whose early settlement was dominated by Yankees from New England and New York.

Michigan's first wave of settlement from the eastern states began with the opening of the Erie Canal in 1825 and the dissipation of the myth of poor land. The territory's population jumped from 9,000 in 1820 to 86,000 in 1835 and 212,000 in 1840. These settlers experienced the humanitarian and educational leadership that the state would maintain into the twentieth century, the boom-and-bust economy that has been extreme in Michigan, the development of political and governmental systems that were comparatively clean and honest, a magnificent obsession with transportation that eventually catapulted Michigan into the automobile industry and changed the face of the nation, and the development of a diversified economy that from its inception was more industrial, commercial, and urban than that of many of the states of the Midwest.

Michigan's tendency toward extremes is exemplified by its stormy entry into the Union. This entry also demonstrates an extreme example of midwestern independence of character that Michiganians associate with their state. Midwestern states other than Missouri were admitted to the Union smoothly and easily. Michigan's fight for statehood, like Missouri's, involved state's rights, but it differed in not involving slavery.

Lewis Cass, who had been territorial governor since 1813, resigned his office in 1831 to serve in President Andrew Jackson's cabinet. His friend John T. Mason of Virginia was secretary of the territory. When Mason moved to Texas, Cass persuaded Jackson to appoint Mason's son, nineteen-year-old Stevens T. Mason, as secretary. Governor George B. Porter was often absent from the territory, leaving Mason as acting governor. In 1834 Porter died, and Mason, called the "Boy Governor," took up his duties on a more permanent basis. Mason took the lead in establishing Michigan's statehood, but the legal steps to accomplish that in the United States Congress were held up by a border controversy between Michigan and Ohio. A ten-mile strip along Michigan's southern border was in dispute. The Toledo Strip, as it was known, contained the mouth of the Maumee River, and in an era of canal building it was thought that a canal connecting the Maumee with the Wabash and thus the Ohio would make Toledo the commercial metropolis of the Midwest.

Mason argued that a territory with a population of sixty thousand or more had under the Ordinance of 1787 the right to become a state. In September 1834 he asked the Legislative Council to provide for a census of the territory. When the census showed that the territory contained 85,856 people, Mason requested that the council call an election for delegates to a constitutional convention, although Congress had not authorized such action. The council complied, and delegates met in May 1835 in Detroit. In thirty-one days they produced a forward-looking constitution that included a bill of rights, suffrage for adult white males, and the then unique office of state superintendent of public instruction. The constitution fit perfectly with the democratic impulses of the Jacksonian period.

Then occurred the comic-opera "Toledo War." Ohio and Michigan called out their militia, and armed forays were made by both sides. Legal right appeared to be on Michigan's side, but political might lay with Ohio, whose electoral votes Jacksonians needed in the election of 1836. Congress offered a compromise—the western half of the Upper Peninsula for the Toledo Strip.

A special convention of elected delegates assembled in Ann Arbor in September 1836 and voted to reject the compromise. (No wonder that even today the Upper Peninsula feels unwanted.) But some Michiganians had second thoughts. Only states, not territories, would share in the distribution from the federal treasury of the surplus collected from the sale of public lands, and Michigan stood to lose about $650,000. Moreover, only states had true federal representation. So Mason let it be known that he would accept a citizen-called convention. The convention, dubbed by its opponents the "frost-bitten convention," met in Ann Arbor in December 1836 and ratified the compromise. The western Upper Peninsula became a part of Michigan, and Michigan became the twenty-sixth state on January 26, 1837.

Michigan drew up its constitution during an optimistic time in United States history. After the opening of the Erie Canal, the entire Old Northwest experienced such a decade of growth that the opportunities must have seemed unlimited. Jacksonian democracy had brought the government closer to the people, change and progress were in the air, and men felt free to question their institutions. Humanitarian reforms of all kinds flourished, education for the masses assumed an importance never before experienced, and business grew. It was the time of the flowering New England culture, and many of New England's tenets spilled through New York to Michigan.

By 1850, the first year for which figures are available, Michigan immigrants from the Northeast outnumbered those from the South forty-five to one. (In Indiana and Illinois, southerners outnumbered northerners seven to five.) The immigrants retained their traditional New England values. They were interested in local government. In New England, towns (rather than counties, as in the South) played the important role in local government, and Michigan, influenced by "Yorkers," developed the county-township form of government that spread across the rest of the Midwest.

The Yankees were Protestant in religion and interested in education. Michigan's concern for its citizens' quality of life is most evident in education. Denominational colleges were founded in the 1830s and 1840s in Kalamazoo, Olivet, Albion, Hillsdale, and Adrian. These colleges, however, were never as prominent and strong as those in other midwestern states such as Ohio, partly because of the strength of the state university system and partly because Michigan passed the first law west of the Alleghenies setting up minimum standards that an educational institution would have to meet before it could incorporate. Michigan played her vanguard role as the university was part of an innovative, farsighted educational system that was adopted by other states of the Midwest and influenced the rest of the country.

The founding of this public school system is credited to two young men from Marshall, John D. Pierce and Isaac Crary. Crary was chairman of the committee that drew up the article on public education for the 1835 constitution. He and Pierce based their plan on Victor Cousin's report on education in Prussia. Michigan thus was the first state in the Union to create an office of superintendent of public instruction, and its constitution envisioned a state system of schools rather than a series of local systems of schools. Pierce became the first superintendent.

Michigan's constitution was unusual in other particulars. It was the first state constitution to include a specific prohibition against the appropriation of state funds for the use of sectarian or religious institutions. It provided for the forfeiture of state financial aid in case of failure to maintain a school for the required three months, and it made financial provisions for establishing libraries in the townships. The crowning achievement of this system was a state university free from sectarian control. The university was a heritage of Michigan's territorial days when the Catholepistemiad or University of Michigan was founded in 1817 under the leadership of a Catholic priest and a Protestant minister. Michigan's comprehensive system of education, reaching from the elementary through the secondary schools into the university, drew such outstanding educators as Henry Simmon Frieze, Andrew Dixon White, Henry Philip Tappan, and James B. Angell from the East to this fledgling university, and they in turn brought many educational innovations.

The University of Michigan both demonstrated and helped increase Michigan's commitment to internationalism. From its inception it welcomed foreign students, and by the latter half of the nineteenth century the university had become a mecca for students from the Far East, partly a result of President James B. Angell's 1880 trip to China as a special envoy from the president of the United States to the Chinese Empire. This special interest in the Far East has continued. One of the largest foreign student groups on campus is Asian, and the university ranks among the first four American educational institutions in the enrollment of foreign students.

Michigan also pioneered in agricultural education. The 1850 Michigan constitution stated: "The Legislature shall encourage the promotion of intellectual, scientific and agricultural improvement; and shall, as soon as practicable, provide for the establishment of an agricultural school." On February 12, 1855, the legislature created the agricultural school that became Michigan State University, the first such agricultural college in the nation. When Justin Morrill spoke in support of federal legislation to create land grant colleges, his example of what he wanted to create was the college in Michigan "liberally supported by the state, in the full tide of successful experiment."

Michigan's place in the vanguard of educational change extended to all levels. The state established the first normal (teacher training) school west of the Alleghenies and the first university chair in the nation for the science and art of teaching. The Michigan Supreme Court, in a precedent-setting legal case used across the Midwest to support public financing for high schools, in 1872 enunciated the principle of public support for secondary education.

Michigan's concern for the quality of life was evident in its participation in the reform movements of its statehood era. The 1830s and 1840s saw revivalism sweep the frontier; utopian communities were created; there were crusades for penal reform, temperance, and women's rights. Cudgels were also taken up in defense of the poor, the sick, and the insane. Michigan participated in all these reforms. Various temperance laws were passed. In 1839 the legislature abolished imprisonment for debt. In 1848 it abolished capital punishment, and in 1850 married women were given the right to use or dispose of their own property without their husband's consent. Although co-education began in Ohio, where before the Civil War both Oberlin and Antioch opened their doors to women, the University of Michigan in 1870 was the first large state university to take this step.

The reform that eventually swallowed up all others was the movement against slavery. Michigan was in the vanguard here, too. With its northern border touching Canada, it early became a route for the underground railway. Escaping slaves were aided particularly by the congregational churches and the Quaker settlements in the southern tier of counties. James G. Birney, leader of the Liberty party, moved to Bay City, Michigan, in 1841. He ran for governor in 1843 and for president in 1844. In both cases Michigan gave him a large number of votes. By 1848 the Free-Soil party, successor to the Liberty party, was polling 10 percent of Michigan votes. Michiganians felt particularly strong outrage against Kentucky slave hunters who came into their state. In 1848, for example, a group of people in Marshall, Michigan, took a black family away from a raiding party and spirited them to Canada. The ensuing legal cases and publicity enhanced bitter feelings, and the reform movement slipped over into politics.

Prior to this time, the political development of Michigan had centered on the Democratic and Whig parties, and the primary issues had been economic. The two parties were fairly evenly balanced, so compromise was the order of the day (a situation still current in Michigan politics). But out of the antislavery struggle came drastic change in the Democratic party, the destruction of the Whig party, and the creation of the Republican party—born in Michigan. Although antislavery groups had already met in Ripon, Wisconsin, and called themselves Republicans, the first statewide Republican party meeting that fielded a full slate of nominees for statewide offices took place in 1854 at Jackson, Michigan, at the "convention under the oaks." The convention's nominee, Kingsley Bingham, was elected governor.

As a result of the Civil War, Republicans became so powerful in Michigan that from 1854 to 1932 Democrats held the office of governor for only eight years. Yet despite being a one-party state, Michigan during this period was remarkably free, as it has been in recent times, of political corruption. Again some measure of credit must go to the moral attitude and tradition of good government brought into the state by New Englanders.

Michigan's poststatehood waves of immigration reinforced this commitment to good government and the state's early sense of internationalism. German settlements began in the early 1830s around Ann Arbor and spread across much of southern Michigan. Led by Frederick Schmidt, who spent fifty years as a missionary, Germans settled Frankenmuth—which still celebrates its German traditions. In the late 1840s Albertus Van Raalte led the Dutch to Allegan County, where they established cities called Zeeland and Holland that commemorate their heritage today with a week-long tulip festival. The English and Scotch fanned out along the Chicago Road, and Detroit retained much of its French tradition as French-speaking Canadians added to its ethnic diversity. Following the potato famine in Ireland in the 1840s, floods of Irish came to the United States. Their Michigan settlements were largely in Detroit, Grand Rapids, Marquette, and Houghton. Churches were the predominant cultural influences in the lives of all the immigrants. The Germans, however, were known particularly for such higher cultural interests as musical events, social clubs, and German language newspapers.

German immigration was considered so desirable by state officials that Michigan maintained immigration offices abroad, as did railway and steamship companies. One historian argues that Michigan attracted a more stable and prosperous immigrant in this period because of the advertising of these offices. He also argues that part of Michigan's emphasis on clean government and human rights came from these prosperous middle-class citizens.

Black migration to Detroit also increased rapidly in the 1850s and 1860s, but it was always small. In Detroit in 1870 there were only 2,235 blacks in a population of 80,000—3 percent of the total. A larger number of blacks settled along the route of the underground railway, particularly in Cass County.

The major attraction for all these immigrants was the state's expanding economic opportunities. Land was the first attraction, but quickly Michigan's commercial and industrial character began to take over. Michigan had been a state only four years when in 1841 Douglas

Houghton, state geologist, called attention to the massive copper deposits of the Keweenaw Peninsula. Almost immediately the first major mining boom in United States history was foreshadowing the 1849 gold rush. The Ontonagon boulder, a three-ton chunk of copper "spirited" away from Michigan by the federal government and now on display at the Smithsonian Institution, still excites the imagination of Michigan schoolchildren. By 1864 the day of the individual miner had ended, and Boston and Pittsburgh mining companies had taken over. Some of these mines, such as the Cliff had paid fabulous dividends; others had swallowed the fortunes of their creators.

On the heels of the copper rush came the discovery in 1844 of large deposits of iron ore near present-day Negaunee. Following this discovery, there occurred the usual business ventures and failures. The first efforts to refine iron ore at the site occurred at the Carp River Forge in Negaunee. The opening of the Sault Canal in 1855, however, created a cheap means of moving the ore south, and Michigan ore began to play a vital role in such developing steel centers on the lakes as Toledo, Cleveland, Gary, and Chicago. Michigan's major iron company was Cleveland Cliffs—today the only company still producing iron in the Upper Peninsula. By 1860, only two decades into statehood, an industrial and transportation revolution had already come to Michigan. In addition to mining, the state was in the midst of a lumber boom.

In the Midwest, with the exception of the prairie states, the production of lumber for local construction was always important. Water played a key role as towns and villages sprang up where water could power a gristmill and a lumber sawmill, the first steps toward industrial enterprises. In Michigan, however, by the 1840s and 1850s commercial logging and lumbering were also well under way. The drawing card was Michigan's magnificent white pine trees growing close to river systems that could transport the lumber to the lakes. Commercial lumbering began in the Saginaw Valley, and in 1860 seventy-two sawmills there produced 131 million board feet of lumber. The same story was repeated in other river valleys. Two industries that developed as adjuncts of the lumber industry were the salt industry—forerunner of the chemical industry—and the furniture industry of Grand Rapids.

All this industrial activity was predicated on the development of transportation. The first railroad west of the Appalachian Mountains was the Erie and Kalamazoo from Toledo to Adrian, Michigan, built in 1836. Michigan's entrepreneurial spirit is demonstrated by the fact that this railroad was begun in the wilderness only eleven years after the first railroad in England. The new state began other lines, but the panic of 1837 destroyed state credit, and by the late 1840s private enterprise had taken over. Plank roads served as feeders to the railroads and rivers, and hundreds were chartered in this period. River traffic was at its height. Steamships and sailing vessels were built in Detroit for lake traffic, and keel boats and shallow-draft boats were built in the ports of Saginaw and St. Joseph, among others.

Agriculture also boomed in this period. Through this network of transportation more than 380,000 new inhabitants came to Michigan between 1840 and 1860. Rural population almost doubled each decade. By the 1880s the state ranked fourth in the nation in the production of wool and ninth in the production of wheat. There was much interest in scientific agriculture. The state perceived itself as agricultural; however, to the perceptive observer, it must have already been obvious that the wave of the future was industrial development.

The Civil War spurred economic development. Rural acreage and population increased by 45 percent due to a demand for products and the Homestead Act. Wool and wheat remained the principal cash export crops, and mechanization on the farm increased dramatically. However, the big drama lay with the extractive industries. Copper and iron were sorely needed for war material—copper for cannons, canteens, and brass buttons and iron for arms and railroads. By 1870 Michigan was providing three-fourths of the nation's copper and one-fifth of its iron. Iron-ore production had grown eightfold in the preceding decade.

Immediately following the war, between 1865 and 1870, Michigan was the number one producer of lumber in the nation. Michigan timber helped rebuild Chicago after the disastrous 1871 fire and provided much of the lumber for homes on the Great Plains. Manufacturing also grew. Detroit produced locomotives, steam engines, stoves, and freight cars. It became a center for drugs (Parke-Davis), varnish, paint, shoes, and seeds (D. M. Ferry Co.) Grand Rapids was already an important furniture center, as well as a center for the wagon and carriage trade. Kalamazoo, Jackson, Pontiac, Lansing, Flint, and other cities developed comparable industries, while mining spurred the growth of Marquette, Houghton, and Hancock.

The year 1870 was a turning point. After that year more of Michigan's work force was involved in commerce and industry than in agriculture. Michigan's industrial development had run in tandem with its agricultural development, then passed and superseded it more quickly than in other states of the Midwest. Thus, although Michigan's tension between rural and urban industrial values has been great, it has not been as dominant a theme as it has been in states where the period of agricultural dominance was much longer.

Following 1870, industry and the people involved in it dominated the economic and the political life of Michigan. It was the heyday of the lumberman, and as lumber flowed across the Midwest making Michigan the leading lumber producer for thirty years, the folklore and the way of life of the lumberman entered the state's consciousness forever. So did the tales of the copper miners. Michigan ranked first in the nation in copper production until 1887, and the migration of British settlers from Cornwall to mine the copper brought "Cousin Jack" jokes and a distinctive food, the pasty, into the lives of all Michiganians, especially UPers. The Scandinavians too left permanent marks across the UP with their distinctive outdoor saunas.

In the last half of the nineteenth century the states farther west took over Michigan's role in wool and wheat production, and Michigan farmers turned to specialized crops, including peppermint, celery, and fruit. But agricultural change was secondary to the industrial juggernaut. By 1880 capitalization in Michigan industry had superseded that in Michigan's agriculture. Michigan industry in 1870 had 64,000 employees and a capitalization of $72 million; by 1900 it had 160,000 employees and a capital investment of $280 million. W. K. Kellogg and Charles W. Post had already made Battle Creek "the Cereal City." Using Michigan salt brines, Herbert H. Dow had by 1888 made Michigan the largest producer of bromine in the nation. By the turn of the century Dow Chemical Company had made Midland "the Chemical City" and W. E. Upjohn had created a drug industry in Kalamazoo. Flint with its Durant-Dort Carriage Works was already calling itself "the Vehicle City." The manufacturing economy of Detroit became more diversified, adding products like tobacco, clothes, and other personal items. Because of its cigar production, Detroit was known as "the Tampa of the North." Detroit was also the center of the car industry, but it was railway cars. Shipbuilding flourished, ironworking grew, and engine making (primarily marine engines) took hold.

It was this diversified industry with its ability to produce paint and varnish, wheels, axles, engines, and car bodies that was a major factor in attracting the automobile industry to Michigan. Ironically, this industry destroyed diversification and gave Michigan the reputation of being a one-industry state in the twentieth century. In addition to the diversity, Michigan's transportation system, the pool of capital available from the lumbering and mining industries, and, most important of all, outstanding entrepreneurs made the auto industry possible. The automobile quickly dominated the psyche of Michiganians. It was an easy shift because the rapid industrial growth from 1840 to 1900 had already prepared the mind-set of Michiganians for the progress and change usually associated with an industrial-urban economy. It is this age, depth, and breadth of Michigan industrialization that makes the state different from the rest of the Midwest.

Industrial-urban dominance is also reflected in the dominance of the Republican or Grand Old Party with its support from lumber barons and manufacturers. Democrats, Greenbackers, and Progressives operating out of a depressed farm economy raised issues of reform, but they never gained control in Michigan as they did in other states of the Midwest. The first successful reform movement came out of the Republican party and, more important for the urban-industrial thesis, Detroit. In 1889 Hazen Pingree, a shoe manufacturer, won election as mayor of Detroit on a platform of regulating the street railways. For the next seven years he waged a lonely battle on a city and state level. During the panic of 1893 he pressed for direct relief for the unemployed and created urban gardens, known as "Pingree's potato patches," the forerunner of victory gardens in the two world wars. Pingree was opposed by the old-line Republicans, but they accepted his nomination for governor in 1896 because they thought his popularity would offset the Fusion-Democratic ticket. Pingree was frustrated in Lansing, but succeeding governors, including one Democrat, Woodbridge Ferris, were all reformers. Most of the reforms of the Progressive Era—including railroad regulation, initiative, referendum and recall, the rewriting of the state's constitution, and various social changes—were enacted in Michigan, but largely by leaders associated with the industrial cities. This period of reform also saw major steps taken toward conservation of natural resources. That was largely the work of Governor Chase Osborn, Michigan's only Upper Peninsula governor.

When the historian looks at Michigan in the twentieth century, the amazing thing is that despite the accelerating pace of change the major themes of the state's history have remained constant. Industry dominates. Every schoolchild knows the story of Henry Ford and how his use of the assembly line at his Highland Park plant created the mass production of the twentieth century and brought the price of cars so low that the average American could afford a Tin Lizzie. The automobile industry has always been highly competitive, and literally hundreds of makes and manufacturers have come into being, flourished briefly, then died. By the end of the twenties, the Big Three—General Motors, Ford, and Chrysler—had emerged. Like the Civil War, World War I spurred more industrial expansion. The face of Michigan and of the nation was changed by the growth of roads, filling stations, and motels. As was fitting, Michigan was a leader in the development of good roads. Horatio ("Good-Roads") Earle, a leader in the fight for better roads in the state, was appointed the first highway commissioner in 1913. The first mile of concrete road in the United States was laid in Michigan along Woodward Avenue in 1909. U.S. Senator Charles Townsend of Michigan introduced and fought for the Federal Highway Act of 1921, which envisioned an interstate network of roads, and Michigan introduced the motor bus that would destroy the interurbans and eventually the railroads. Michigan pioneered in building bypasses and divided highways and developed the first roadside parks and picnic tables. By 1930 Michigan was preeminently "the Motor State."

This rapid growth did what previous growth had done. It brought immigrants into the state—again reinforcing Michigan's international character. This migration, however, was almost entirely to Detroit. Detroit's population increased sixfold between 1900 and 1930 as the new immigration, as it was called, came largely from eastern and southern Europe. The most numerous of the new immigrants were the Poles, and Hamtramck became the suburb most closely associated with their culture. Large numbers of Russians, Hungarians, Slovakians, Rumanians, and Greeks added to the ethnic complexion of the city. As the mining industry began to decline in the Upper Peninsula, many Finns, Norwegians, and Italians migrated south to join those coming from Europe to Detroit. Migration from the Near East also swelled. By the 1970s Detroit had the largest Arabic-speaking population in North America. Blacks from the South also migrated to Detroit and increased tenfold in thirty years.

Detroit's polyglot population jumped from 250,000 in 1900 to 1.5 million in 1930. They found jobs and opportunity in the 1920s, but in the thirties the Great Depression hit Michigan like a sledgehammer. By 1932–33, 50 percent of the workers in the southern cities of the state were unemployed. Unemployment in the mining counties of the Upper Peninsula was even higher. Starvation, misery, and crime exploded in the cities. Michiganians and Michigan ideas played significant roles in the Democratic party and the New Deal, but the major change in Michigan was on the industrial front, where labor organizations emerged as one of the most influential forces in the state.

Labor organizations in Michigan had their origins in the nineteenth century and basically reflected the trends of the Midwest and the nation: that is, they were ineffective. The first mechanics' organizations in Detroit in the early nineteenth century were largely fraternal. More formal organizations came with the Knights of Labor in the 1860s. The Knights participated, for example, in the unsuccessful strikes in the lumbering industry of the Saginaw Valley in 1872 and 1876. After the 1887 Haymarket riot in Chicago, the American Federation of Labor (AF of L) took the Knights' place. Organized by Samuel Gompers as a conservative craft union, the federation at first seemed to be a growing success. However, Michigan's company towns were difficult to organize. Battle Creek, for example, was dominated by the cereal companies. The Seventh-Day Adventists had come to Battle Creek in the 1840s, and their emphasis on health had led to John Harvey Kellogg's establishment of a health sanitarium and W. K. Kellogg's creation of the breakfast food industry. C. W. Post had come to the sanitarium and stayed to become Kellogg's principal competitor. Post, despite strikes, fought the unions to a standstill in "his" town. A similar paternalism dominated Calumet, Michigan. In 1913 the Calumet and Hecla copper miners struck for an eight-hour day and a minimum wage of three dollars a day. The strike dragged on for nine months with strikebreakers, interference by state and federal troops, cries of Red socialism and atheism, and death when a false alarm caused the trampling of women and children attending a miners' Christmas program in the Italian Hall. The strikers finally returned to work in April 1914. The defeat of the industrial miners' union left the craft unions of the AF of L in control of labor organization in the state. The craft unions played an important role in successfully advocating legislation favorable to labor, but labor was not yet a political and economic force.

In 1914 Michigan's automobile industry provided 36.7 percent of the state's manufacturing output. By 1930 Michigan's Big Three produced 75 percent of the cars in America. Until the depression, however, unions had played a negligible role in the industry. For one thing, the craft unions of the AF of L simply were not suited to the massive unskilled work force of the automobile industry. Seeing this, John L. Lewis of the United Mine Workers organized the Committee for Industrial Organization under the AF of L. In Michigan various industrial unions joined together in 1935 to form the United Automobile Workers and affiliated with the CIO. In 1936 they followed its leadership out of the AF of L.

In 1936 the UAW decided that if it were to make headway it must organize the workers in the Big Three. General Motors was chosen as the most logical target, and organizing began in earnest in June 1936. Union leaders, however, did not plan the strike that began that December. The workers seized the initiative and sat down in the Fisher Body plants in Cleveland and Flint. Within one week thirteen GM plants had closed, practically shutting down production of cars by GM. GM said it would not negotiate until the workers left the plants and then only at the plant level, a stance that would effectively destroy the united bargaining power of the UAW. The story of this tense time has passed into labor history. Governor Frank Murphy's role in bringing the two sides together was probably crucial. The end came on February 11, 1937. General Motors agreed to sign a national contract with the United Automobile Workers. Other sit-down strikes followed all over the country, and Michigan's name became anathema to some. A *New York Times* editorial entitled "Oh Michigan!" asked:

> Isn't that uneasy peninsula between the lakes the place where all the trouble that afflicts this nation starts? Didn't the banking panic of 1933 rear its ugly head in Michigan and slither madly across the rest of the country? And haven't we now a plague of sit-down strikes made and patented in Michigan and ready to export?

Nevertheless, the union movement had received its great impetus. The UAW picked off companies one by one until only Ford was left, and it finally capitulated in 1941.

Throughout the 1930s, union contracts in Michigan set the pattern for the nation, reinforcing Michigan's sense of leadership and being in the vanguard. By the 1940s a new leader of the UAW, Walter Reuther, had appeared. He led the union into a stronger political stance with an emphasis on another Michigan theme—socially progressive programs.

The growing influence of labor in politics in Michigan influenced labor's political gains elsewhere. In 1947 there were only five Democrats in Michigan's 100-member house of representatives and four in its 32-member senate. In 1948 four Michiganians—Neil Stabler, wealthy oil businessman; G. Mennen ("Soapy") Williams, heir of the Mennen soap fortune; and Hicks and Martha Griffiths—sat down in the Griffiths' basement and decided to try to take over the leadership of the Democratic party. The result was that Williams ran for governor and Stabler became the Democratic state chairman. A split in the Republican party, the support of labor—particularly Walter Reuther and Gus Scholle—and the organizing skills of Hicks Griffiths helped Williams win. With his green polka-dot tie and his friendly smile, he became one of the most popular governors the state has had. The gubernatorial term was for two years, and he was reelected six times. Labor, led by Reuther, was interested in political action that would enhance rights and increase jobs for labor. As political observer Neal Peirce noted:

> In area after area—civil rights, compulsory health insurance, training programs for the unemployed, public recreation, education—Williams and Reuther sought to make Michigan a laboratory for social democracy. They took advanced stands, already ahead of their time, and permanently altered the political complexion of the state.[1]

Unfortunately, there was a bitter fight over taxes to finance the resulting record budgets. Democrats supported corporate taxes; Republicans, who still controlled the legislature, wanted a sales tax. Williams pushed for a graduated income tax. The stalemate that resulted caused state employees to go a couple of paydays without money and Michigan bonds to plummet.

The legislature finally rammed through a sales tax, but Michigan's "payless paydays" had destroyed the Williams luster. He became assistant secretary of state in Washington and was succeeded in Michigan by Democrat John B. Swainson, whose term saw the culmination of the fight of citizen groups and labor to remodel Michigan's outdated 1908 constitution. Then occurred one of those interesting reversals in Michigan politics. George Romney, a reformer, emerged from the

1961–62 constitutional convention as a leader—seen as basically non-partisan. As a Republican governor, he was able to enact an income tax that at least temporarily solved the financial problems of state government. Reelected overwhelmingly in 1966, he carried into office a Republican legislature.

Ironically, after his second election Romney had to deal with a Democratic legislature because of the Supreme Court decision (*Baker v. Carr*) requiring one-man one-vote. The role that Michigan labor played in this national decision is often overlooked. Gus Scholle had been fighting for an end to unequal legislative districts since the 1940s. In 1959 he filed a suit, *Scholle v. (Secretary of State) Hare*, arguing the one-man one-vote principle. The Michigan Supreme Court, relying on earlier precedent, decided against Scholle in 1960. In the meantime the U.S. Supreme Court was hearing the Tennessee case, *Baker v. Carr* (1962). Theodore Sacks of Detroit, chief counsel for the AFL-CIO, who did the basic research on Scholle's case, passed his work on to the plaintiff in *Baker v. Carr*. It was the Sacks-Scholle argument that the Supreme Court accepted. The Michigan case arrived at the Supreme Court just after *Baker v. Carr* and was remanded to the state court, which reversed its earlier decision. The Michigan court's July 1962 decision made it the first state court in the country to hand down a one-man one-vote decision.

The one-man one-vote rule meant that in the 1970s Michigan Republican governors would have Democratic legislatures. William G. Milliken, the popular moderate Republican who followed Romney, remained in office for thirteen years and brought bipartisanship to a new level of accomplishment. Reflecting Michigan's tradition of good, honest government, Michigan politics in the 1970s focused on issues rather than personalities, and these issues again centered on the dominant themes of Michigan history: industrial-urban dominance reflected in the growing plight of the cities, quality-of-life reforms in education and in minority and civil rights, and recreational and environmental issues involving the water and the land. Milliken, working with a Democratic legislature, made impressive gains in all these areas, thus helping to implement Reuther's vision of a state (and nation) dedicated to racial equality and nondiscrimination, aid for the poor, better medical care and housing, and a cleaner environment. Before Proposition 13 in California, he introduced the "circuit breaker," which gave tax relief when a person's property taxes exceeded a certain percentage of his income.

Milliken also recognized that Michigan cities, particularly Detroit, had to have help to deal with their problems. He engineered a change in the formula for revenue sharing that benefited the cities. State assistance to the cultural institutions of Detroit was also provided. As Milliken worked to aid the cities, he formed a tacit alliance with the

Democratic mayor of Detroit, Coleman Young—another example of bipartisanship, or, as Neil Peirce designated it, issue-oriented politics. At this point, it is too early to tell if the tradition will continue through the 1980s, but it is interesting that the first major act of Michigan's next governor, Democrat James Blanchard, was to push through an unpopular tax increase to save Michigan bonds and credit. He was able to accomplish this feat with a one-vote margin provided by a Republican senator.

All Michigan administrations in the twentieth century have continued the state's support of education and particularly of the three large universities—Michigan, Michigan State, and Wayne State, which together enroll over 120,000 students. Michigan's system of education, as envisioned by its founders, still reaches from kindergarten to the universities and in quality is generally considered to be second only to California's. The issue of how to pay for excellence, however, will not go away. School aid formulas, support for parochial schools, college tuition grants, and loans continue to be social and political issues. Michigan's continuing concern for this element of the quality of life is shown by a vanguard proposal by Governor Blanchard: an innovative plan for parents to pay into a state administered fund that would guarantee their children's college tuitions.

The problem and the opportunity most stark and demanding for all elected officials in the twentieth century, but particularly for Mayor Young and Governors Milliken and Blanchard, are found on the changing industrial-urban scene. Detroit is the epitome of the change. The problem lies in overcoming an image as a one-industry city, which in today's world breeds high chronic unemployment. The opportunity is to create a diversified economy open to all citizens. The second urban-state problem is the growth of the inner-city black population and the flight of whites to the suburbs. The opportunity here is to create a true interracial, democratic society in one of the nation's major cities. In 1972 the chairman of the Greater Detroit Chamber of Commerce, Lawrence M. Carino, observed:

> Detroit is the city of problems. If they exist, we've probably got them. We may not have them exclusively, that's for sure. But we probably had them first. The city has become a living laboratory for the most comprehensive study possible of the American urban condition.[2]

Detroit has always been an ethnically diverse city. In 1880 over forty nationalities were listed in its census, and the largest group was German. In 1920 the largest group was the Poles, and over half of the skilled and semiskilled workers had been born out of the country. In 1930 Detroit still had the third largest number of foreign-born citizens in the nation. During World War II, massive numbers of whites and blacks from the South migrated to work in Michigan's war factories. They stayed to work there in the fifties. The ethnic base was shifting, but as late as 1970 some 22 percent of the people in Detroit were foreign born or had foreign-born parents. The big shift, however, was between 1966 and 1970, when the black population jumped from 20 percent to 43 percent. In 1967 came destructive riots in Los Angeles and Newark, but Detroit had the most disastrous riot of all. Forty-three people were killed, hundreds were wounded, thousands were arrested, and property damaged totaled in the millions of dollars. All this took place in a city where a popular young mayor, Jerome Cavanaugh, had opened lines of communication and supposedly had a good rapport with black leaders.

Leadership, however, could not stop what happened. The riot was a result of anger and despair over the long delay in fulfilling the American promise of equality and opportunity. The newly gutted blocks joined with the empty lots left from the mass urban renewal of the fifties, when over eleven thousand Detroit housing units were torn down but not replaced, giving some areas of Detroit the appearance of a wasteland. Nay-sayers wrung their hands in despair, and Detroit was back in the news as it had been during the depression, the sit-down strikes, and other difficult times—as a terrible place to be.

Under these circumstances the mayoral election in 1969 pitted the first black candidate in the city's history, Richard Austin, against Roman Gribbs, the police commissioner. Austin, a thoroughly competent candidate and a gentle man given to compromise and accommodation, lost by only seven thousand votes. (Austin won statewide office the next year as secretary of state and became one of the state's most popular elected officials, winning the highest number of votes of any official in 1982 and 1986.) Gribbs became a caretaker for transition, appointing blacks to boards, commissions, and police and fire-fighting forces.

Sometime between 1969 and 1973 the racial balance in Detroit shifted and the majority in the city became black. Coleman Young, a black state senator, became mayor in 1974. Young was a former labor leader, the first black national Democratic committeeman in the state and the nation, and a respected member of Michigan's constitutional convention of 1962–63. The business and union leadership of Detroit—represented by New Detroit, the Detroit Economic Council, and the Detroit Renaissance group—immediately initiated an ongoing dialogue with the mayor. Young, an astute politician and a lover of his city, began the delicate tightrope walk that he made into an art. For the city to survive, he had to have white business support; for his political future, he had to keep the support of his black constituency. Young moved with dispatch in some areas, immediately dismantling a hated police organization called Stress. In the area of jobs he moved more slowly but continued the shift of control to blacks. White flight to the suburbs slowed as it became obvious that the rights of all would be protected.

The recent story of Detroit is one of the movement of affluent young professionals into deteriorating historic neighborhoods, the expansion of convention and hotel space that allowed Detroit to host the 1980 Republican convention, and continuing urban problems through the ups and downs of the oil crisis of the seventies and the Japanese import crisis of the eighties. Political power, jobs, and appointed positions have shifted to the black community. In many ways Young has operated like the political bosses of the nineteenth century whose power rested on the foreign-born in their cities. The shift of power, however, has been supported by Michigan's and Detroit's white leadership. When the history of the twentieth century is written, one of the bright highlights may well be this interracial cooperation, which oversaw the successful transition of a major American city to black control.

Urban Michigan still has massive problems, including high unemployment among blacks in inner cities and an unemployment rate for black teenagers that is over 50 percent. The needs of the urban-industrial society continue to dominate the politics and consciousness of the state, but there is also a growing sense of optimism and assurance.

The administration of James Blanchard developed innovative programs for diversification based on the state's strengths. In addition to instituting a job training program and a youth corps, eliminating red tape, and starting a capital venture fund, Blanchard turned to Michigan's traditional belief in education and created two institutes that hold promise for its future. The Industrial Technology Institute in Ann Arbor is designed to work on industrial automation; the Molecular Biology Institute in East Lansing spearheads research. Their location allows them to take advantage of the resources of the state universities. Both institutes have received support from private industries and Michigan foundations (particularly Kellogg and Dow). A center for the development of small businesses has been started in Detroit as an adjunct of Wayne State University, and other centers of excellence are planned around the state. Only time will tell if such programs can cushion drastic swings of the economy, but the entire leadership of the state is clearly working toward this end.

The need for diversification is reflected in the state government's efforts to push two other major prongs of the state's economy—agriculture and tourism. These two endeavors alternate with each other for second and third place in value added to the state's economy. Agriculture provides only 1.9 percent of Michigan jobs, but Michigan is second only to California in the variety of its agricultural products.

Michigan is the nation's leading producer of navy beans, sweet and tart cherries, soft winter wheat, and spearmint. The present administration has targeted food processing as an industry to develop since much of Michigan's agricultural produce is shipped out of state for processing. Despite the small number of people working in agriculture, most of the vast geographical area of Michigan is composed of small towns and countrysides where traditional rural values predominate. With the exception of a string of counties in the western Upper Peninsula where the union tradition is still strong, the rural area is predominantly Republican. Its citizens take very seriously their position as God-fearing, straitlaced, basic midwesterners who form the backbone of the state and the nation.

This rural area is also important because it encompasses most of the great scenic beauty and recreational opportunities of the state. There lie the clear limpid streams, the unmarked forests, the tallest, largest ski hills, and the water wonderland that the Michigan Travel Bureau touts as it beckons those interested in hunting, fishing, camping, and water and winter sports.

Michigan's history as a tourist attraction began early. By 1838 people from Chicago were "watering" at Mackinac Island, and in the late nineteenth and early twentieth centuries the entire western shore of the state became studded with the summer homes of wealthy midwestern industrialists. This trend continues but it is far more democratic today. In 1980 Michigan had 215,958 temporary homes—more than any other state except Florida.

Water is the primary element in the recreational appeal of the state. No Michiganian, even one who lives in the interior of the state, is further than four hours from one of the Great Lakes. A small lake or river is less than an hour away. Michiganians seem to have an almost mystical feeling about the water and the north woods—that dark, mysterious, wonderful land that lies north of Clare. There the forests are green, dark, and impenetrable; the wildflowers are profuse; and the colors are brilliant. The lakes and streams are cold, crystal clear, and unpolluted; people can get back to nature. This feeling seems to be strongest in urban areas. It is the urban worker who grabs a camper and heads for the north woods on vacation and who provides much of the support for environmental and recreational programs.

Michigan ranks fifth in the nation in the number of recreational parks and first in the number of modern campsites. Its park system attracts over twenty million visitors yearly. The two major tourist attractions in the state are historic: Mackinac Island, a state park with three historic elements, and Greenfield Village and Henry Ford Museum, which contains the most outstanding collection of Americana in the nation. Together they attract over two million visitors a year. An effort is under way to showcase the many other historic attractions owned by the state, such as Fort Wilkins, Fayette, Cambridge Junction, Hartwick Pines, and Father Marquette Memorial.

Michigan has the largest number of registered boats and registered snowmobiles of any state. It ranks fifth in the nation in hunter days and angler days. These uses have had an impact on Michigan's environmental movement. The quality-of-life issue is reflected in the effort to clean up rivers and lakes wherever industrial pollution has created problems and to handle air and chemical pollution. Cleaning up water in joint efforts with Canada has resulted in some successes; people are able to eat fish from the Detroit River for the first time in decades. In chemical pollution, however, Michigan follows only New York and New Jersey in the number of major toxic sites that need to be cleaned up. The Blanchard administration has pushed a $300-million toxic-waste cleanup fund.

One of the most interesting environmental issues arises each fall when a resounding outcry greets the army of hunters (over 750,000— larger than the U.S. Army) hits the woods on November 15 for the opening of the deer season. Opposition to deer hunting has never been successful, but it brings to the forefront Michigan's centuries-old tension between exploitation and conservation. In the eighteenth and nineteenth centuries, Michiganians thought resources were infinite as they destroyed the furbearing animals and gutted the forests and mines. In the twentieth century the finiteness of these resources has become painfully apparent. The environmental movement, so vocal in the nation in the 1960s, has been especially strong in Michigan, partly because the state's industry has been such a drastic polluter. In 1968, when Michigan passed a $100-million bond issue for state parks, it passed a $330-million bond issue to clean up pollution.

The Milliken administration responded to conservation concerns with the creation of a new environmental quality commission. Michigan became the first state to ban the sale and use of "hard" pesticides and one of the first to require deposits for beer and soft-drink containers. Unfortunately, Milliken's record was stained by the poor handling in 1973 of the situation that occurred when a fire-retardant chemical, PBB, was accidentally mixed in cattle feed. The resultant death of cattle, poisoning of the soil, and fear for health and public safety provided a lesson to the state in the dangers of pollution. The Blanchard administration has continued a strong positive stand on environmental issues, reflecting what appears to be a nonpartisan stand in the state.

Environmental issues touch all the themes that have spun through Michigan's recorded history: Michigan's water and other natural resources are as essential to modern tourism as they were to the Indians, the fur traders, the lumbermen, and the miners. Their preservation depends on the international vision begun as part of the French Empire and continued through the waves of immigration. Yet these resources must still balance against the industrial-commercial-urban growth that has dominated the state since 1870. At the heart of conservation is Michigan's concern for the quality of life of its citizens. This quality has been especially evident in Michigan's educational system, its support of abolition and civil rights, and its union movement. Michigan's confidence today that all such problems can be resolved is an echo of its self-confident drive for statehood and its self-perception as a people in the vanguard of education, of the automotive industry, of unionization, and of political and social change.

To Michiganians the bridge that spans the Straits of Mackinac, "Mighty Mac," is a symbol of their state, with its two beautiful peninsulas. It is also a symbol of the unity of all human beings and of the beneficent use of technology, which can build a bridge that soars like a startled white bird high above a vast expanse of water, water, water. And it is a symbol of the triumph of a vision and a determination to create a better world—a vision that is, of course, both American and midwestern. But to Michiganians, the bridge is above all a symbol of a particular vision, that of Michigan; "Mighty Mac" means "Mighty Michigan."

NOTES

1. Neal R. Peirce and John Keefe, *The Great Lakes States of America* (New York, 1980), 185.
2. Quoted in Dan Georgakas and Marvin Surkin, *Detroit: I Do Mind Dying: A Study In Urban Revolution* (New York, 1975), 4.

BIBLIOGRAPHY

There is no modern-day bibliography on Michigan materials and resources. The 1917 bibliography by Floyd Streeter, *Michigan Bibliography* (Lansing, Mich., 1921) is still useful. The bibliographic essay in the appendix of Willis Dunbar and George May, *Michigan: A History of the Wolverine State* (Grand Rapids, Mich., 1980) is excellent for secondary works on twentieth-century Michigan. Essential to the study of Michigan history are the primary and secondary resources found in the *Michigan Pioneer and Historical Collection* and *Michigan History Magazine*. Since 1917 *Michigan History* has been published continuously by the Bureau of History, Michigan Department of State. Also helpful is the Library of Michigan's quarterly publication *Michigan in Books*.

The two major one-volume works on state history are F. Clever Bald, *Michigan in Four Centuries* (New York, 1961), and Dunbar and May. The first is out of date but still contains useful information; the second is a detailed textbook useful for college classes. Bruce Catton's *Michigan: A Bicentennial*

History (New York, 1976) is primarily a nostalgic lament by a native for a "lost" Michigan and deals almost entirely with the nineteenth century. Still useful as a tour guide to the state and sprinkled with insightful comments is the Works Progress Administration's *Michigan: A Guide to the Wolverine State* (New York, 1941). Two interesting and useful compilations, particularly for college classes, of current topics are Alan Brown et al., *Michigan Perspectives: People, Events and Issues* (Dubuque, Iowa, 1974), and the two-volume *Michigan Reader*. The first volume was edited by George May and Herbert Brinks, the second by Robert Warner and C. Warren Vander Hill. For those interested in a variety of information displayed through innovative mapping computer technology there is Lawrence M. Sommer, *Atlas of Michigan* (East Lansing, Mich., 1977). For a variety of information on state government, see the *Michigan Manual* published biennially by the Department of Management and Budget. The publications of this department and the Departments of Commerce, Agriculture, and Natural Resources provide a wealth of information about Michigan's economy, commerce, recreation, and resources. Typical of these publications are *Michigan Agricultural Statistics* (Michigan Department of Agriculture, 1985) and *Reaching for Recovery: New Economic Initiative in Michigan*, sponsored by the Department of Commerce (Washington, D.C., 1985). All state government publications are located in the document room of the Library of Michigan.

There are county histories and city histories too numerous to mention, and Detroit particularly has been the subject of numerous sociological and historical studies. I found particularly helpful David M. Katzman, *Before the Ghetto: Black Detroit in the Nineteenth Century* (Urbana, Ill., 1973); Dan Georgakas and Marvin Surkin, *Detroit: I Do Mind Dying: A Study in Urban Revolution* (New York, 1975); August Meier and Elliot Rudwick, *Black Detroit and the Rise of the UAW* (New York, 1979); Neal R. Peirce and John Keefe, *The Great Lakes States of America* (New York, 1980); Davis B. McLaughlin, *Michigan Labor: A Brief History from 1818 to the Present* (Ann Arbor, Mich., 1970); and the three-volume biography of Frank Murphy by Sidney Fine. Helpful for the study of Michigan's ethnic diversity are all the publications of Michigan's Ethnic Heritage Center of Wayne State University, Detroit. There is such a wealth of material available for the study of Michigan's history that one's ambition is limited only by time and energy.

John D. Buenker

WISCONSIN

as Maverick, Model, and Microcosm

WISCONSIN IS A STATE of impressive topographical, climatic, economic, demographic, ethnocultural, political, and regional diversity. Its topography is perhaps the most varied in the entire Midwest, with five distinct physiographic areas connected and divided by an intricate network of rivers, lakes, bogs, marshes, and swamps from whence it derived its Indian name meaning "a gathering of the waters" or "the stream of a thousand isles." Its climate includes every element except moderation and predictability, with winters that rival North Dakota's and Minnesota's, an appreciable number of hot, humid summer days that would do justice to St. Louis, and short transitional seasons that frequently fail to materialize. Although justly touting itself as America's Dairyland, Wisconsin boasts a variegated economy that relies substantially on mining, fishing, canning, brewing, insurance, dairy farming, light and heavy industry, and tourism. Much of the state is sparsely populated. There are, however, seven distinct areas of population concentration, and nearly 70 percent of Wisconsin's people live within a hundred miles of the Lake Michigan shoreline. With an indigenous Indian population, a history of being both the "most German" and the most foreign stock state in the Union, and growing black, Hispanic, and Asian populations, Wisconsin is something of a "living ethnological museum," to quote Richard Cur-

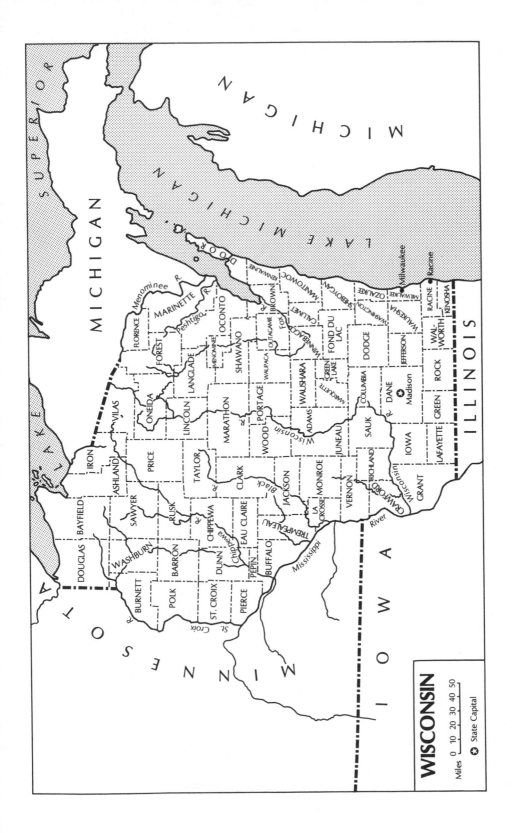

WISCONSIN

Miles 0 10 20 30 40 50

✪ State Capital

rent.[1] Despite a highly prized and usually deserved reputation for tolerance and pride in ethnic diversity, the state has had more than its share of ethnocultural conflict. At least since the 1890s Wisconsin has experienced frequently bitter, issue-oriented political conflict that has usually pitted regular Republicans against two generations of La Follette Progressives, Social Democrats, or rejuvenated urban-labor-liberal Democrats. Finally, various sections of Wisconsin are frequently conscious of belonging to geoeconomic subregions, such as the Great Lakes industrial belt, the hay and dairying region, the "cutover," the corn belt, and the north woods, that link them to other states.

Yet, for all this variety, the Badger State is also marked by a well-defined public culture—the set of institutions, values, beliefs, attitudes, mores, and myths that give order and meaning to the social and political processes, provide the underlying assumptions and rules that govern social and political behavior, and constitute the standards by which ethnocultural, socioeconomic, and regional segments of the population are defined and granted legitimacy and participation. Its main elements were initially the product of settlers from New England and New York, but they were modified by the contributions of later arrivals and by the inexorable march of modernization, urbanization, and industrialization. This dynamic consensus functions as a universal model to which no individual or group conforms entirely and which is refracted by each through the prism of its own particularistic world view.

It is the interaction, the creative tension, between Wisconsin's tremendous diversity and its well-established public culture that constitutes the state's unique character and that defines much of its relationship to region and nation. As Current has noted, this relationship has generally cast the state in the role of maverick or model.[2] In many important ways, Wisconsinites perceive of themselves as being sui generis, with no real counterparts anywhere. It is this self-conscious sense of uniqueness that is most boldly expressed in the slogan "When you say WIS-CON-SIN, you've said it all." Wisconsin has also been, especially in the organization and operation of its university outreach programs and in the emulation of its legislation and administrative agencies, a model which other states have often copied, even if not as self-consciously, rigorously, or frequently as Badger State chauvinists allege. But Wisconsin has also been, in its value system, patterns of ethnic and economic succession, and relations with its Indian population, a microcosm of region and nation.

Any discussion of Wisconsin's diversity perforce begins with its topography, a product of the glacial age that ended about twelve thousand years ago. For thousands of years, glaciers covered most of Wisconsin, exempting only the southwestern quarter, which became

known as the Driftless Area, a region of gently rolling hills with the
same terrain as adjacent areas of Illinois, Iowa, and Minnesota. The
glaciers divided the state into five distinct physiographic regions: (1)
the Lake Superior Lowland; (2) the Northern Highland, which covers
most of the northern third of the state and is dotted with small lakes,
streams, and marshes; (3) the Central Plain, which constitutes the
middle of the state and is characterized by rock formation similar to
the buttes and mesas of Colorado; (4) the Western Upland, which
includes much of the Driftless Area, and (5) the Eastern Ridges and
Lowland, an 80- to 100-mile-wide strip abutting Lake Michigan from
Green Bay to the Illinois border.

Glacial action and the subsequent melting blessed Wisconsin with
over ten thousand lakes, thirty-three-thousand miles of river and
stream frontage, and a collage of marshes, bogs, and swamps to go
with five hundred miles of Michigan and Superior lakeshore. The Fox
River and Wisconsin River systems link Lake Michigan to the Mississippi River. Although Wisconsin has no appreciable deposits of
petroleum or iron ore and only small deposits of lead, zinc, sandstone,
and limestone, it has become an important industrial state largely
through determination, ingenuity, location, and waterpower. Glacial
action also helped divide the state into the pine, evergreen, and hard-
wood forests that once covered the northern two-thirds of the state
and the grassy prairie that constituted the remainder. Finally, glaciers
left Wisconsin with significant variations in soil quality, thus profoundly affecting the fortunes of agriculture. While very little of the
state's soil is equal to that of Iowa or Illinois, much of it in the Eastern
Ridge and Lowland and some in the lower Driftless Area does not fall
far short. But most of the soil in the Northern Highland and the
Central Plain rates only poor to fair.

This topographical dissimilitude is matched by the state's extreme
climate. Wisconsin has a continental forest climate that features
temperature extremes varying from 60 degrees below zero to 110
degress above zero Farenheit. The state has long, cold, snowy winters
and short, unpredictable transition seasons. The southern part tends
to have hot, humid summers, while northern areas usually have summers that are shorter and cooler but equally moist. This climate, so
hard on people, is favorable for the production of high yielding crops,
at least in the southern half. The latter enjoys a "corn-belt summer"
induced by hot, humid gulf air that sustains a growing season of about
175 days. In the Northern Highland, by contrast, the growing season
varies from 80 to 120 days. Precipitation ranges from 28 to 44 inches,
more than enough to sustain most types of vegetation and crops. Snow
cover averages 140 days near Lake Superior and around 85 days in
the southeast, protecting against soil erosion, killing pests, and providing adequate moisture. These significant climatological differ-

ences, added to those of soil quality, guarantee that the fortunes of agriculture vary appreciably by region.

Given its topographical and climatic variety, it is not surprising that Wisconsin has developed what is probably the most diversified economy in the Midwest. The state seal features a plow for agriculture, a crossed pick and shovel for mining, an anchor for navigation, and an arm and hammer for manufacturing. To update the seal, it would be appropriate to add a lumbering ax and saw, a piece of heavy machinery, an Illinois tourist, a beer bottle, and, of course, a cow. The early French and British trappers and traders conducted a flourishing fur trade with the Indians that nicely sustained the small European population but began the long, steady degradation of Native Americans. From just after the War of 1812 through the Civil War, a flourishing lead and zinc mining frontier existed in the southwest corner of the state centered on Galena, Illinois, and Dubuque, Iowa. When the 1833 Treaty of Chicago opened southern Wisconsin to white settlement, thousands of Yankees and immigrants quickly grabbed up the choicest land available. In less than half a century, they built a thriving economy based primarily on grain farming, agriculturally based light industry, lumbering, and lake and river shipping. Despite some serious production fluctuations, Wisconsin ranked second only to Illinois in spring wheat production by the onset of the Civil War. Until the 1880s Milwaukee rivaled Minneapolis as a grain milling and shipping center, causing the *Milwaukee Sentinel* to proclaim that "wheat is king and Wisconsin is the center of the empire."[3] The J. I. Case Company in Racine and Allis-Chalmers in Milwaukee soon challenged Illinois-based farm implement manufacturers; Milwaukee, Racine, and Kenosha became important producers of wagons and fanning mills; and Sheboygan became an important cog in the furniture industry. Tanning and quarrying also flourished in the southeast, while its production of a certain sudsy beverage produced by German *braumeisters* made Milwaukee famous. Meanwhile, other Wisconsinites were busily exploiting the incredible treasures of the northern pines forests, making the state the leading lumber producer in the country for most of the latter half of the nineteenth century. Between 1840 and 1898, lumber barons cut over eighty-six billion board feet of lumber, sixty-six billion of that between 1873 and 1898.

But as early as the 1870s a combination of national and international competition, internal problems, and new technologies forced Wisconsinites to undergo a transformation that produced an almost entirely new economic base by the 1920s. The wheat boom collapsed as the plains states and eastern Europe provided stiff competition and soil exhaustion, rust, and cinch bugs blighted crops. Ever adaptive, the state's farmers responded by venturing into the production of wool, flax, sorghum, sugar beets, tobacco, hops, cranberries, ginseng, maple syrup, corn, oats, and hay, and by raising horses, pigs, sheep, and cows. Eventually, though, most of them turned to dairy farming, introduced into Wisconsin by settlers from New York and by Swiss, German, Dutch, and Scandinavian immigrants. But the major impetus came from the efforts of William Dempster Hoard, a New York–born newspaper editor who became governor of the state and president of the University Board of Regents. Hoard founded the Wisconsin Dairy-men's Association (WDA) in the 1870s, published *Hoard's Dairyman*, lobbied for laws to regulate and promote the industry, and pressured the university and its extension division to engage in basic dairying research. He also popularized the industry with such slogans as "The cow is queen" and "Speak to a cow as you would to a lady." By 1899 more than 90 percent of the state's farms kept at least some milk cows and Wisconsin was producing more than 28 percent of the coun-try's cheese. By 1919 the state accounted for almost 67 percent of cheese and led the nation in the production of creamery butter, fluid milk, and condensed and evaporated milk.

A similar but less successful transformation resulted from the disastrous decline of the lumbering industry. Although Wisconsin still ranked first in the nation in output as late as 1904, it had fallen to tenth place by 1920. The lumber companies had "cut and run," head-ing for new frontiers in the Pacific Northwest, while forest fires had destroyed nearly twenty-six billion board feet. The state, the univer-sity, the railroads and the local communities in the cutover region responded with an ambitious program for the settlement and eco-nomic development of the north. They recruited actively in other states and in Europe, promoting the cutover as a twentieth-century frontier. But the poor soil and the short growing season were unfit for any but the barest subsistence agriculture. Most homesteaders eventually gave up on agriculture and survived by hunting and fishing or by working in the mines of the Gogebic Range or the industries in the Fox and Wisconsin valleys. After the initial influx of people, the population of the cutover declined steadily, except during the depression-ridden 1930s. The prosperity that did return to the north country resulted from the establishment of diversified industries, es-pecially those using wood and its by-products, the resurgence of the Lake Superior iron-ore traffic, and the interrelated movements of conservation and tourism. The Fox and Wisconsin valleys became the pulp and paper capital of the country, and the aluminum cookware and canning industries also flourished. The increasing affluence of the southern half of the state, combined with the proliferation of the automobile, guaranteed a steady stream of tourists, campers, boaters, fishermen, hunters, and skiers.

The third leg of the modern Wisconsin economy was provided by the transformation from light to heavy industry that characterized the eastern third of the state, especially the southeastern corner. This corner is essentially the northwest loop of the Chicago industrial district, which also extends along the southwestern shore of Lake Michigan well into Indiana. In its own right, Milwaukee is the tenth largest manufacturing city in the United States. The expertise and experience gained in the milling, brewing, millworking, wagon, and farm implement industries proved transferable when new technologies and the modernization of industry mandated significant change. Farm implement companies incorporated the internal combustion engine and continued to be among the nation's leaders in their field. Even though it was without iron and coal, southeastern Wisconsin became an important center for the fabrication of steel because of its lakefront location, skilled labor, and technological expertise. It also became one of the country's largest manufacturers of heavy and electrical machinery. The once-flourishing wagon industry was gradually displaced by the manufacture of automobiles and automobile parts.

One important consequence of this economic transformation was the emergence of well-organized, activist, and politically sophisticated movements of farmers and industrial workers. The Grange, American Society of Equity, National Farmers Union, National Rural Life Movement, and, of course, the Wisconsin Dairymen's Association, Farm Bureau, National Farmers' Organization, and American Milk Producers Institute gave farmers impressive clout in the marketplace and the legislature. They made the state a leader in the development of producer and marketing cooperatives. The WDA remained powerful enough to prohibit the sale of colored oleomargarine into the 1960s and to retain "America's Dairyland" on license plates to this day. By the turn of the century, the State Federation of Labor and the Milwaukee Federated Trades Council were politically militant and heavily tinged with socialism. Milwaukee's unions were the economic arm of the Social Democrats, who dominated the city's politics for nearly half a century. Organized labor exerted enough influence during the Progressive Era and the 1930s to make the state a model of labor and welfare legislation, and it became a major force in the rejunevated Democratic party in the 1950s. More recently the power of farmers and labor organizations has been counterbalanced not only by business associations but also by professional societies and political action committees of consumers, conservationists, women, and taxpayers. Unions of public employees and schoolteachers have also achieved prominent status.

Wisconsin's socioeconomic complexity is surpassed by its ethnocultural mix. In a population of 4.5 million, there are significant concentrations of at least twenty-five ethnic groups. Most Wisconsinites are readily able to rattle off the particulars of their own heritage, even if it runs to six or seven varieties. Ethnic festivals rival county fairs as the state's most representative cultural observances, and the State Historical Society has established a living historical museum called Old World Wisconsin to commemorate ethnic roots. The state's ethnic history begins with the Indians, whose ancestors have inhabited the state for over a thousand years. It is estimated that there were about twenty thousand Indians living in what is now Wisconsin at the onset of the seventeenth century, chiefly Menominee, Winnebago, Chippewa, and Sauk and Fox. They were joined in 1822 by the displaced New England–New York tribes of Stockbridge, Oneida, and Brotherton. By 1980 Wisconsin, with about thirty thousand Indians living largely in the northern counties and in Milwaukee, had the largest native population east of the Mississippi except for North Carolina and New York and the most diversified in the nation except for Oklahoma, Arizona, New Mexico, and California. The earliest permanent white settlers were the French fur traders and missionaries who settled around Green Bay and Prairie du Chien. They were followed by southern Americans and Cornish, Welsh, English, and Irish immigrants, who occupied the southwestern lead and zinc mining region around the War of 1812. In the early 1830s the southeastern region was quickly overrun by thousands of Yankees from New York and New England, who quickly assumed enduring leadership. Close on their heels came hundreds of thousands of immigrants from northern and western Europe, who soon earned Wisconsin the distinction of being the most foreign stock state in the union. As early as 1860 the foreign born and their children comprised half the state's population; by 1890 the proportion had nearly reached 75 percent. So anxious was the state to attract industrious immigrants that it created a bureau of immigration in the 1850s and its constitution granted the right to vote to any male resident who had lived in the state for one year and who had filed his declaration of intention to seek citizenship.

About half the immigrants were of German origin, 124,000 by 1860. By 1914 the majority of Wisconsinites were of German origin or background, most of them living in the eastern third of the state. Although sharply divided by religion, politics, and regional variations, Germans soon challenged the Yankees for hegemony. Whatever the reality, Wisconsin was widely perceived as the most German state in the union from the Civil War to World War I. With an unprecedented array of churches, parochial schools, newspapers, and fraternal, benevolent, athletic, musical, dramatic, military, and literary societies, Milwaukee was the "German Athens." Although German high culture largely disappeared with World War I, Gemütlichkeit—the popular culture of beer, bratwurst, and polkas—largely supplanted Yankee austerity.

Holding the balance between the Yankees and Germans were the smaller groups of northwestern European immigrants, most of whom came from the British Isles and Scandinavia. Most of the English, Welsh, and Scots settled in the southeastern part of the state and found the Yankee way of life generally compatible. The Catholic Irish, on the other hand, despite frequent clashes with the Germans over politics, control of the Catholic church, and education, usually maintained a sharp hostility toward anything British or Yankee. The sizable Scandinavian contingent, second only to the Germans, was headed by Norwegians, over sixty-five thousand of whom had arrived by 1890. Although predominantly farmers, the Norwegians also settled in river cities and in the lakeports, where their nautical heritage served them in good stead. Much less numerous were the Swedes, over twenty thousand of whom concentrated in the St. Croix River valley of northwestern Wisconsin, and the Danes, who settled mostly in and around the cities of Racine and Kenosha. These sizable populations were joined by less numerous but significant immigrant groups, chiefly Dutch, Belgians, English and French Canadians, Swiss, and Czechs. By 1890 Wisconsin was a state of persisting Yankee values, a British-German-Scandinavian population core, and hundreds of ethnic enclaves, both rural and urban, inhabited largely by people with northern and western European roots.

For the next three decades Wisconsin's ethnic composition was further enriched by an influx of immigrants chiefly from southern and eastern Europe, who settled mostly in the urbanizing, industrializing southeast and the cutover region. Far and away the largest of the newer immigrant groups were the Poles, who contributed over forty thousand foreign born to the state's population by 1930. In addition, there were sizable numbers of Italians, Czechs, Slovaks, Serbians, Croatians, Russians, Greeks, Lithuanians, Armenians, Hungarians, and eastern European Jews. Nearly all of them resided almost exclusively in the Milwaukee-Racine-Kenosha industrial complex, although most of the state's Finns and a sizable proportion of its Russians settled in the far north.

Thus Euro-Americans, in a bewildering variety of combinations and permutations, comprise nearly 95 percent of Wisconsin's population. Still, the Indians are not the state's only significant racial minority. By 1860 there were just over a thousand blacks in Wisconsin, most of them in Milwaukee and Racine and a few rural enclaves in the southwestern corner of the state. By 1910, there were still only about three thousand, a third of whom were in Milwaukee County. By 1930, however, the black population of the Cream City had risen to 7,500 and by 1980 to 150,000—over 15 percent of its population. Although blacks constitute only about 4 percent of the state's people, their concentration in the southeast lakefront cities significantly intensifies their impact. By 1980 the state also had over sixty thousand Spanish-speaking people, mostly Mexican-Americans from Texas and New Mexico, who like the blacks were concentrated in the southeastern counties. Japanese, Chinese, Filipinos, and Southeast Asians account for the remaining 1 percent of the population. The Indians, blacks, Hispanics, and Asians still live largely on the fringes of Wisconsin society. Clashes between Indians and whites have been ongoing, as whites have fluctuated between policies of segregation on reservations and forced assimilation, both marked by economic exploitation. In recent years there have been an increasing number of conflicts over fishing and timber rights and land ownership. Black-white conflicts over jobs, housing, and school segregation have been frequent occurrences in Milwaukee and Racine over the past forty years. Recent Southeast Asian arrivals have also been victims of overt hostility and discrimination.

Nor have relations among the members of the state's Euro-American majority always been without conflict. Prohibition and Sunday observance regularly pitted the state's Scandinavian, British, and Yankee Protestants against its Catholic, Lutheran, Jewish, and Eastern Orthodox populations. The Bennett Law controversy of 1889 arrayed groups seeking to retain their foreign languages against those insisting upon the exclusive use of English. The Know-Nothing movement of the 1850s, the American Protective Association of the 1890s, and the proposal to erect a statue of Father Marquette in the nation's capital all stirred up scurrilous anti-Catholic campaigns. The Ku Klux Klan enjoyed a brief popularity in the 1920s. The outbreak of World War I generated an anti-German hysteria that all but destroyed the state's bountiful Teutonic culture. In the main, though, Wisconsinites have been tolerant of the state's ethnic diversity, at least as it involves Euro-American heritage.

Given Wisconsin's significant heterogeneity, it is only natural that it divided into several sections, some of which orient their residents in an outward mode. This tendency is reinforced by the state's single most important demographic characteristic—its dramatically uneven population distribution. Nearly 70 percent of Wisconsin's people live east of a line from Green Bay–Oshkosh southwestward through Madison to Janesville-Beloit. Forty percent of them live in the southeast corner formed by metropolitan Milwaukee-Racine-Kenosha, 13 percent in Madison, and 16 percent in Green Bay–Lake Winnebago–Fox River Valley. Over 80 percent of Wisconsinites reside in seven population centers comprising less than 10 percent of the land. Milwaukee, easily the most densely populated county, has 4,447.5 people per square mile, while Sawyer County has but 7.7. Milwaukee has nearly a million people, Menominee County but 3,373.

Based on these conditions, Wisconsin is divided into at least four or five sections. The southeast lakeshore is part of the Chicago industrial district, while the Green Bay–Lake Winnebago–Fox and Wisconsin River Valley area is mainstream Wisconsin. So to a lesser degree is the south central and southwest section that centers primarily on Madison. But the far southwest counties are still, to a great degree, part of the old Tri-State lead and zinc mining complex centered on Dubuque, Iowa. Madison itself is an anomoly. As the state capital, the seat of the university system, and the center of the dairy region, Madison is the embodiment of Wisconsin. But the first two conditions also sharply separate it from the rest of the state and create an atmosphere of mutual suspicion, hostility, and condescension. Nor is there much love lost between Madison and Milwaukee as they vie for status as the state's premier city. The northwest section centered on La Crosse and Eau Claire is tugged and pulled between Madison and the Twin Cities of Minnesota. Finally, there is the north central section, which in many ways is a separate state, constantly at odds with Madison over conservation and taxation policies and exhibiting a love-hate attitude toward the "foreigners" downstate who sustain the section's economy and invade its privacy.

Not surprisingly, this complexity has been faithfully mirrored in Wisconsin politics. On the surface, politics has been dominated by two interrelated conditions: Republican hegemony and progressive orientation. The GOP has won fifty-three of the sixty-five gubernatorial elections since statehood and the La Follette legend and the Wisconsin Idea are articles of progressive-liberal faith nationwide. But a closer look reveals that the state has been much more competitive, in terms of both partisanship and ideology. Actually, the state's political history divides fairly neatly into three periods: (1) the era of ethnocultural partisan politics, 1848–96; (2) the era of intraparty Republican conflict, 1896–1959; and (3) the era of ideological two-party politics, 1959–present. Although the Democrats won only six gubernatorial elections out of twenty-three in the first period, they were much more competitive then. The Democratic party was led by businessmen from Milwaukee and the southwest counties, but its mass support came from Catholic immigrants of German, Irish, Czech, and other national origins who were attracted to the party primarily because of its hospitality to immigrants and its belief in "personal liberty." The Republicans were led largely by Yankees and supported by Scandinavian, British, and other Protestant immigrants who shared the Yankees' convictions favoring public regulation of personal conduct. In this delicate balance, German Lutherans frequently tipped the scale, voting Republican when economic or political issues were paramount but favoring the Democrats on personal liberty questions.

The critical election of 1896 was especially disastrous for Wisconsin Democrats, and they won only one gubernatorial election out of the next thirty-one. Partisan conflict was transformed into intraparty Republican battles between conservative "stalwarts" and progressive "half-breeds." The latter were dominated by two generations of La Follettes, who successfully downplayed ethnocultural issues, remodeled the political process, and appealed to "fair-minded" Democrats. The latter were further undermined by the rise of the Social Democratic party, which commanded the allegiance of tens of thousands of German and working-class voters. The elder La Follette owned the western two-thirds of the state, especially Scandinavian and British dairy farmers, and made common cause with lakeshore progressive Republicans led by Francis E. McGovern, who was governor of the state during the high point of Progressive Era productivity from 1911 to 1915. The progressive Republicans under McGovern cooperated with Milwaukee socialists in Madison, were sensitive to German sensibilities over prohibition and related issues, and wooed the industrial working class with a myriad of labor and welfare measures. But a power struggle between McGovern progressives and those of Governor and U.S. Senator Robert M. "Fighting Bob" La Follette and a conservative backlash against high taxes and big government allowed stalwarts to capture the governorship in 1915. For the next forty-four years, the governor's chair alternated between progressive and stalwart Republicans, except for a brief Democratic hiatus from 1933 to 1935. While the nation swung into the Democratic column in the 1930s, Wisconsin voters were more attracted by the second generation of La Follettes—Phil and young Bob—who endorsed the New Deal and formed the Progressive party in 1934. That and the continued strength of the Social Democrats under longtime Milwaukee mayor Daniel Hoan kept the Democrats dormant until the 1950s.

It was the election of William Proxmire as U.S. senator in 1957 and Gaylord Nelson as governor in 1958 that signaled the revival of the Democratic party and the emergence of a new era of ideologically based, partisan politics. The new Democratic party was essentially a coalition of union labor from the eastern lakeshore counties and liberals from Madison, the Milwaukee suburbs, and other university communities. It included both industrial workers and the newly organized and militant public employee and teacher unions. This coalition was symbolized by the conversion of Hoan and other Social Democrats, on one hand, and Bronson La Follette, grandson of "Fighting Bob," on the other. This uneasy coalition has been severely shaken by such issues as the Vietnam War, campus unrest, and civil rights and by the battle for hegemony between Madison and Milwaukee, but the new Democrats have controlled the governor's mansion for eighteen of the past twenty-eight years. With the Democrats usurping the progressive end of the political spectrum, the Republicans have cast themselves as the party of economic development, local autonomy, and morality.

Counterpoised against its impressive diversity is Wisconsin's distinctive public culture, that set of reasonably universal values, mores, and institutions that aggregate or transcend particularistic qualities and constitute the ground rules for social and political intercourse. Actually, the state's public culture includes two well-differentiated strains that have significantly different origins and orientations and vary greatly in the comprehensiveness of their application. The first, which a *Holiday* magazine writer of the 1940s dubbed "bucolic Gemütlichkeit,"[4] is concerned primarily with informal social behavior and relationships in the intimate areas of life. It constitutes a common bond among the state's three sizable blue-collar constituencies: the "jackpine savages" of the north country, the industrial workers of the lakeshore and riverfront cities, and the farmers of the southern and central sections. It is essentially the adaptation of continental European folk culture, with its emphasis on family, church, locale, hard work, food, drink, music, entertainment, and recreation, to the diverse environment of America's Dairyland. It originated with the Catholic and Lutheran Germans whose clannishness and drinking habits thoroughly shocked their Yankee and pietist neighbors but were adopted by most Catholic and Eastern Orthodox immigrants.

Basically a "private-regarding" vision of life, bucolic Gemütlichkeit's quintessential political premise is personal liberty, a catchall sentiment unalterably opposed to government regulation of personal moral conduct. Such an outlook was fundamentally compatible with the ethnocultural partisan politics that dominated Wisconsin and most other states during the nineteenth century. It is also a world view that flourishes in the "job-oriented" or "marketplace" politics that generally prevail in Illinois, Indiana, Ohio, and states farther east and south.[5] Such a system assumes that politics is a competitive arena in which socioeconomic, ethnocultural, and other interest groups vie for jobs, benefits, and recognition, and that government exists to enhance individual and group opportunities and to facilitate the pursuit of private, particularistic goals. The public interest is nothing more than the sum total of competing private interests, and politicians are essentially brokers who mediate disputes and distribute benefits on the basis of clout.

Marketplace politics in Wisconsin was largely a casualty of the Progressive Era. La Follette progressives and Social Democrats succeeded in equating it with exploitation and special privilege at a time when farmers, workers, and middle-class Wisconsinites had been highly sensitized to such concerns. Once in power they effectively destroyed the infrastructure of marketplace politics through such devices as the open primary, civil service, and nonpartisan local elections. Although significant numbers of Wisconsinites continued to vote according to the ethnocultural partisan affiliations of their progenitors, they were increasingly bereft of the cues that had informed such actions.

On the level of informal social behavior and relations, bucolic Gemütlichkeit provides whatever measure of satisfaction and fulfillment there is for the majority of Wisconsinites who earn their daily bread by physical labor. Its focus is intensely parochial, centering on families, friends, churches, ethnic and fraternal lodges, union and grange halls, villages and neighborhoods, bars, bowling alleys, softball teams, county fairs, and ethnic festivals. Social occasions are generously lubricated by alcoholic beverages; Wisconsin consistently leads the nation in per capita consumption of beer and brandy. Wisconsinites also play hard, favoring bowling, softball, and other forms of competitive athletics. Many bowl or play softball for their neighborhood bar, repairing to the latter to replay the contest or to watch the Packers, Brewers, Bucks, or Badgers on television. Wisconsinites are also outdoors people who love hunting, fishing, camping, and crosscountry skiing. Vacations usually involve going "up north" to engage in these activities, and it is common to remove male children from school for a week during deer-hunting season. Hunting and fishing trips are an important bonding process between male generations, and fishing contests are the high point of the summer social season in many communities. Wisconsinites also have a love affair with motorized forms of recreation; the state is proud of its reputation as the snowmobile capital of the country. Technological advances have expanded the definition of personal liberty to include opposition to vehicle inspection, motorcycle helmet laws, automobile seatbelt legislation, and raising the drinking age.

The major strain in Wisconsin's public culture was much more the conscious creation of intellectuals, politicians, clergymen, civic leaders, and the mass communications media. It is fundamentally the world view of the original Yankee settlers modified over time by technological change, economic development, and the influence of other ethnocultural groups. Because they arrived first and had a strong sense of community and mission, Yankees were able to transplant New England institutions, values, and mores, altered only by the conditions of frontier life. They established a public culture that emphasized the work ethic, the sanctity of private property, individual responsibility, faith in residential and social mobility, practicality, piety, public order and decorum, reverence for public education, activist, honest, and frugal government, town meeting democracy, and a belief that there was a public interest that transcends particularistic ambitions. Regarding themselves as the elect and just in a world rife with sin, error, and corruption, they felt a strong moral obligation to define and enforce standards of community and personal behavior. For the same reason, Yankees rarely entertained any serious doubts that the public interest and their own were identical.

This pietistic world view was substantially shared by British, Scandinavian, Swiss, English-Canadian and Dutch Reformed immigrants, as well as by German Protestants and many of the "Forty-Eighters." German Catholics and Lutherans, while frequently suspicious of and hostile toward one another, generally subscribed to the work ethic, a strong sense of community, and activist government but were less committed to economic individualism and privatism and ferociously opposed to government supervision of their personal habits. Southern and eastern European immigrants generally leaned more toward the Germanic view of things, while modernization, industrialization, and urbanization modified nearly everyone's sense of individual economic responsibility and put a premium on organization, political involvement, and education.

It was the fusing of these cultural elements with the innovative thought of the Progressive Era that solidified the state's formal public culture, which became widely known as "the Wisconsin Idea." Many progressive concepts regarding positive government, social planning, countervailing powers, democratization of the political process, the welfare state, and government-by-expert were developed and disseminated by such Wisconsin-based intellectuals as John R. Commons, Richard T. Ely, Edward A. Ross, Thorstein Veblen, Isaac Rubinow, and Charles McCarthy. Only the University of Chicago rivaled Madison as the intellectual seat of progressive thought. The ideas were made operational by progressive Republicans and Social Democrats, the former predominantly a Yankee-British-Scandinavian coalition and the latter heavily Teutonic. They were used as rationales by a variety of emerging interest groups making unprecedented demands on state government.

Especially crucial to the formation of the Wisconsin Idea were the dairymen, the Wisconsin State Federation of Labor, and the university. By its very nature, dairying requires a much heavier commitment of time and attention and a greater capital investment than do most other forms of agriculture. It also demands that farmers acquire and update a considerable body of scientific and technological knowledge in a systematic and sustained fashion and that reasonably uniform standards regarding production, storage, and sale of milk, butter, and cheese be established and enforced. Inevitably, dairymen looked to the university for the former and to state government for the latter. The university responded by establishing a demonstration dairy farm in its College of Agriculture, founding a department of rural sociology, teaching dairying courses, and sending extension agents into every nook and cranny of the state. Its researchers found solutions to such practical problems as how to determine the butterfat content of milk, how to detect and prevent bovine tuberculosis, and how to ascertain milk's suitability for making cheese. The government responded with the establishment of a dairy commission, the passage of a flurry of regulatory laws, the banning of colored oleomargarine, the setting of guidelines for the formation of producer cooperatives, and the addition of agricultural and domestic science to public school curricula.

A similar, though less comprehensive, response greeted the demands of labor unions for improved working conditions and greater economic security. Several distinguished university faculty members, led by Commons, produced well-documented reports, drafted legislation, and served on public, labor-oriented commissions. The university also established a department of labor economics and eventually a school for workers that provided on-the-job training for union officials. The legislature enacted one of the nation's first comprehensive workmen's compensation systems, an industrial commission to monitor the enforcement of scores of laws regulating the work place, and legislation controlling conditions of child and women's labor. In the 1930s it pioneered a statewide unemployment compensation system. Similar private sector–government–university cooperation characterized efforts to settle the cutover region and to create its economic base. In all three enterprises, the government and the university brought their considerable resources to bear in an endeavor that was perceived to be in the long-range common welfare of the state and its citizens even though the immediate and primary beneficiary was a particularistic, self-interested segment of the population.

The essence of the Wisconsin Idea, then, is the concept that there is a definable public interest that transcends particularistic concerns and is best achieved through the enlightened cooperation of the government, the university, and the private sector. The government's role is to generate the required social capital, build the necessary infrastructure, establish and monitor the operational guidelines, guarantee that the benefits are distributed equitably, provide for the welfare of the "worthy poor," and protect the public interest from exploitation. The university's function is to supply the theoretical knowledge and the technological expertise necessary to ensure the success of the enterprise. Together, the government and the university provide the social investment for a variety of endeavors whose immediate and obvious beneficiaries are private citizens and organizations but which will ultimately redound to the general prosperity, security, and quality of life. Cooperatively, the government, the university, and the private sector generate an environment conducive to the realization of individual potential and the pursuit of all goals that are deemed legitimate.

Central to the Wisconsin Idea is what Daniel Elazar has defined as a "commonwealth" concept in which both citizens and politicians conceive of politics as a public activity animated by a shared sense of the general good and properly devoted to the advancement of the public interest.[6] Good government is therefore measured by the extent to which it promotes that general good, rather than how well it responds to the requests of constituents, and by the honesty, selflessness, and commitment to the public welfare of those who govern. This is a perception, Elazar says, that Wisconsin shares with North Dakota and Minnesota; it is in direct contrast to Elazar's marketplace concept, which he says informs life in Illinois, Indiana, and Ohio. In Wisconsin the commonwealth concept flowed originally out of the sense of community that animated Yankee settlers on their "errand in the wilderness." The elder La Follette's followers appealed to this vision of community by promising to establish a government that would represent the common good of all Wisconsinites against the handful of special interests that sought to use the system for selfish gain. La Follette's crusading style and moralistic rhetoric always cast him as the champion of "the people," and he never entertained a serious doubt that the triumph of his movement and the general welfare were one and the same. This commonwealth orientation was also substantially compatible with the corporatist-organic conception of society held by most immigrants from continential Europe, who generally came from traditions that had long emphasized the responsibility of the strong and powerful for the weak and unfortunate and the prerogative of church and government to regulate economic life. Wisconsin's Scandinavian and German farmers were nationally instrumental in the agricultural cooperative movement, and the ideal of a cooperative commonwealth was also at the heart of the Social Democrats' program.

The importance of formal education in general and the university system in particular to the Wisconsin Idea cannot be overstated. During the Progressive Era, the Madison campus was widely celebrated as "a university that runs a state," as a "service university" dedicated to "the democratization of knowledge,"[7] and as one where "the boundaries of the campus are the boundaries of the state."[8] La Follette instituted a Saturday Lunch Club to bring faculty and legislators together, and by 1911 some forty-six faculty members were serving state government in some capacity. But, as Commons observed, most faculty members were totally absorbed in their own professional pursuits and even he "was never called in except by Progressives, and only when they wanted me."[9] Faculty members have generally been more impressed with the university's commitment to academic freedom: "Whatever may be the limitations which trammel inquiry elsewhere we believe that the great State University of Wisconsin should ever encourage that continued and fearless sifting and winnowing by which alone the truth can be found."[10] Although the university has frequently been flayed by conservatives for being too politically involved and by progressives for being too elitist and esoteric, it nevertheless persists as the state's most universally respected institution. Its level of financial support is significantly above the national average. With thirteen four-year campuses and thirteen two-year centers enrolling nearly 165,000 students at a comparatively low tuition cost, it makes higher education readily available. Its extension program is probably the most comprehensive in the nation; it offered 5,823 programs to 224,464 students in 1985. Significantly, its largest enrollments are in such practical areas as agriculture and agribusiness, small business and economic development, and family living. It is the university's accessibility as an avenue of social mobility and as a practical economic and political resource that accounts for its popularity and its centrality to Wisconsin's public culture.

This same devotion to practical knowledge and technical expertise caused Wisconsin to develop the nation's first Legislative Reference Bureau in 1907. Its head was Charles McCarthy, author of *The Wisconsin Idea*, who wanted to make Wisconsin the "one state in the country whose written law will be to some degree better than that of other states." Its supporters touted it as an instrument for "applying the scientific method to legislation"[11] The bureau provides lawmakers with the information needed to legislate and assists them in drafting legislation, carefully cultivating its image as an agency of apolitical technicians serving only the public interest.

Equally central to the Wisconsin Idea is an extraordinary level of public services financed by high taxes. The state spends 29.6 percent of its budget on welfare and 28.7 percent on education. A pioneer in workmen's and unemployment compensation, Wisconsin also ranks sixth in the nation in aid to dependent children and old-age assistance and twelfth in help for the blind. One-seventh of the state consists of public parks and forests, a measure of its devotion to conservation, recreation, and tourism. With nearly 10 percent of the budget going to environmental resources, Wisconsin is a national leader in reforestation and conservation, the prevention of soil erosion, and the reversal of water pollution. Its Department of Natural Resources enforces some of the toughest standards possible, despite the ongoing and frequently bitter opposition of the state's industries and its hunters, fishers, farmers, and campers. Wisconsinites are also proud of their free highway system, especially in contrast to the Illinois toll roads. As a result of this high service level, Wisconsin ranks fourth nationally, and second only to Minnesota in the Midwest, in combined state and local revenues as a percentage of personal income; its tax burden was 112 per cent of the U.S. average in 1977. Of the nation's industrial states, only California and Massachusetts rank higher in "effort," that is, in the proportion that per capita tax revenue represents of per capita income.

In keeping with their commonwealth conception that those who govern should be honest, selfless, and firmly committed to the public welfare, the architects of the Wisconsin Idea designed a state government and an electoral system that earned it a richly deserved reputation of being, in the words of political scientist John Fenton, "almost painfully honest."[12] Much of the administration of state government is vested in the hands of independent, nonpartisan, quasi-judicial agencies headed either by individual commissioners or full- or part-time boards of private citizens appointed by the governor. Since the terms of the governor and the board members rarely coincide, the governor's ability to pack these agencies is extremely limited. Because board members depend on other means of livelihood, they can afford to exercise independent judgment in the public interest. Nearly all state employees are classified civil servants and the state also has extremely stringent laws regulating lobbyists and campaign expenditures, a tough open meeting law, and a tradition that all legislative bills be given a public hearing. "Few states, if any," political observers Neal Peirce and John Keefe have concluded, "so jealously guard the public's right to know about and participate in policymaking as Wisconsin does."[13] Since most local government officials are either elected on a nonpartisan ballot or appointed under civil service, there is almost no material for building courthouse gangs or urban political machines. The state also has strict antinepotism rules and requires that all contracts be awarded through an impersonal bidding process. When scandals do occur, they are generally on the level of using an office telephone to make personal calls or driving a state car on private business. Wisconsinites, as Peirce and Keefe observe, "make major issues of incidents considered penny-ante elsewhere."[14]

While the Wisconsin Idea's emphasis on probity, expertise, and efficiency has considerably reduced the number of elective offices, it has also provided that those remaining are contested for in an issue-oriented, candidate-centered, programmatic politics that places enormous responsibility upon individual voters. Decades of civil service and nonpartisan local elections separated from state and national contests have all but destroyed the infrastructure of the Democratic and Republican parties. Wisconsin's unique open primary generates a substantial amount of crossover voting. As a result, candidates play down party affiliation and emphasize their personal qualities and positions on the issues. Governors have to build personal political organizations to be nominated and elected and bipartisan coalitions to govern. Organized interest groups and political action committees have largely appropriated the traditional functions of political parties. Compared with voters in Ohio, Illinois, and Indiana, those in Wisconsin are generally more liberal, more sophisticated, and better able to link individual candidates to issues and election outcomes to public policy. They generally have little patience with arguments that such an open-ended system benefits the educated, affluent, and well organized at the expense of the less advantaged or that the absence of party discipline in the legislature significantly inhibits the enactment of coherent public policy.

Given this open-ended system, Wisconsin's voters have shown an unusual proclivity to back charismatic mavericks and third parties that claim to represent "the people" against "special interests." The elder La Follette and his progressive followers established the prototype and his sons resurrected it in the 1930s. Social Democrat Dan Hoan was mayor of Milwaukee for twenty-four years; current incumbent Henry Maier has parlayed vociferous feuds with the city's establishment and with state government into an even longer tenure. At the other end of the spectrum, Senator Joseph R. McCarthy enjoyed notable success by flaying the liberal establishment in Madison and Washington. Senator William Proxmire, a veritable institution, regularly defies his fellow Democrats. Most recently, Wisconsin voters elected maverick Republican Senator Lee Dreyfus, who publicly challenged his party to get out of corporate board rooms and country clubs. In all these cases, it would seem that ideology was less significant than a colorful personality, exciting rhetoric, and a stance as a champion of "the people" against their enemies.

Wisconsin's public culture still contains a strong preference for local autonomy, despite the growth and importance of state government. Wisconsin is one of the few states outside New England to have town government, the primary unit of governance for the nearly one-third of its citizens who live in unincorporated areas. Town governments have responsibility for maintenance of roads and bridges, creation of sanitary districts, establishing zoning and building ordinances, and making public improvements. On the first Tuesday of April, each of the 1,280 towns holds its required annual meeting where all citizens are allowed to attend, speak, and vote. Cities and villages were also granted a considerable measure of home rule in 1924, although the state retained close scrutiny over bonded indebtedness. Over 35 percent of the state budget is in the form of aid to and shared revenues with school districts and local units of government, chiefly for education, health and welfare, transportation, and conservation, ranking the state tenth in the nation in this respect. The University of Wisconsin Center system is a cooperative venture between local government and the state, with the former providing the buildings and the latter the educational process.

Succinctly put, Wisconsinites in general have a self-image of their state as progressive; its motto is "Forward." Wisconsin reached the zenith of its reputation during the Progressive Era when it showed, according to Peirce and Keefe, "what an individual state, if it has the will, can do to enhance the quality of life of its people."[15] But each period of progressive success has produced a conservative backlash, and the state that produced the La Follettes also produced Joe McCarthy. Some have suggested that Wisconsin has been trading on its Progressive Era reputation for the past seventy years, except for the period of the later La Follettes. Even during the Progressive Era, backers of the Wisconsin Idea insisted that it was basically "new individualism," using the state to produce greater opportunity for the individual to become prosperous and secure. Its highest value was as much social stability as social justice and much was done to blunt the popularity of the socialists. Whatever the reality, the popular identification of Wisconsin with progressivism seems likely to endure.[16]

It is the dynamic interaction among the major and minor strains of its public culture and its considerable diversity that constitutes the essence of Wisconsin's unique character. Not surprisingly, this character consists primarily of a series of apparent anomalies or paradoxes. Having built a modernized, activist state government with one of the highest service levels in the nation, Wisconsin also permits more local autonomy than almost any other jurisdiction. After collecting taxes at one of the highest per capita rates in the Union, it returns more than a third to local government. With a competitive, ideologically based two-party system on the state level, it mandates nonpartisan elections for local government. Even though it has one of the highest per capita expenditure rates, it insists that most programs be funded on a pay-as-you-go basis. Extremely concerned about decorum and propriety in its public culture, it is also the home of bucolic Gemütlichkeit and personal liberty. Justly proud of its state university system for its international reputation and service to the state and its citizens, Wisconsinites also frequently regard it as a hotbed of radicalism and immorality. Demanding more of its public officials than most states in the way of intellectual clarity and probity, it also has a pronounced weakness for mavericks with colorful personalities.

This same creative tension between diversity and public culture defines Wisconsin's relationship to its sister states, making it at once maverick, model, and microcosm. Any such exercise in comparative taxonomy is, by its very nature, arbitrary. A great deal clearly depends on which qualities you choose to compare—and to what. What one person views as a difference in kind may be regarded by another as only a matter of degree or emphasis. There is also often a substantial difference between the image a state's citizens have of their own collective character, how they are perceived by the residents of other states, and the "objective reality" discerned by "impartial" observers. With these caveats in mind, it still seems fair to argue that Wisconsinites have a strong sense of identity as maverick and model, that people in other states frequently share this impression, and that an impressive amount of evidence can be marshaled to buttress such claims. But it is also true that Wisconsinites often exaggerate such claims, that people in other states are frequently irked by their hyperbole, and that much af the state's perceived uniqueness can just as readily be explained as variations on regional or national themes.

Wisconsin's identity as maverick dates from its earliest history. It established the nation's first state immigration bureau and its most liberal policy for the enfranchisement of newcomers. It abolished the death penalty permanently in 1854, only the third state to do so. Its cutover region remained one of the country's few twentieth-century frontiers for many years after its native son Frederick Jackson Turner proclaimed the end of this phenomenon. More rural but also more industrialized than the United States as a whole, Wisconsin is noteworthy for its unusual number of medium-sized industrial cities and for its "intricately meshed mosaics"[17] of rural ethnic enclaves. It is one of the few midwestern states with Indian reservations and it has one of the largest and most diversified Indian populations east of the Mississippi. Its status as America's Dairyland clearly sets it off from nearly all other states and both defines and reflects its character. Its diversity in both its economy and its ethnic population outstrips all but a handful of states. Its "squeaky clean" politics have few if any rivals. Milwaukee is the largest American city ever to be governed by a socialist mayor—and that for a record thirty-eight years. This circumstance and Wisconsin's fondness for La Follettes and progressive Republicans set Wisconsin apart when most of the rest of the country was embracing the New Deal and the Democratic party. The party's resurgence came eventually, but it came twenty-five years later in Wisconsin than it did elsewhere. Wisconsin successfully resisted the party's attempts to proscribe the state's unique open primary and loudly proclaimed the victory. Only a threat by the federal government to withdraw highway funds from Wisconsin caused the legislature to raise the drinking age to twenty-one when all the states around her had already done so. This obsession with "personal liberty" has also extended to refusal to enact automobile seatbelt or motorcycle helmets laws. And yet Wisconsin is one of the few states in the region not to have government-run lotteries or pari-mutuel betting. The list could be extended, but it would only serve to belabor the point that Wisconsinites are people who frequently think and do otherwise.

By the same token, Wisconsin has undoubtedly pioneered an unusual number of laws and programs that have served as models for other states. The tradition began in the 1850s when several states emulated its promotion of immigration. Its State Historical Society, founded during the territorial period, is widely regarded as an exemplar. By far the greatest degree of modeling, of course, occurred during the Progressive Era when the state's reputation as a "laboratory of democracy" and an "experiment station for political action" was at its zenith. No other state surpassed Wisconsin in the frequency with which reformist politicians, theorists, and publicists urged emulation of its ideas, laws, and institutions. Midwestern and western insurgents eagerly joined La Follette's crusade to do with the Republican party nationally what he and his followers had done to it in Wisconsin. In 1914 Governor McGovern boasted that Minnesota Republicans, Pennsylvania Progressives, and Ohio Democrats "all have recognized the leadership of Wisconsin among the commonwealths of the country and have sent delegations here to learn from us."[18] Rhetoric aside, it is clear that Wisconsin pioneered several laws and institutions during the Progressive Era and that many other states subsequently instituted similar innovations. Beyond that, the degree of causation and emulation varied significantly from case to case.

Twenty-seven states established legislative reference bureaus, in the first decade after Wisconsin did so; many came to Madison to study its bureau's operation or corresponded with the bureau's chief for guidance. George, Alabama, North Carolina, Ohio, Arkansas, California, Michigan, and New York all instituted county schools of agricultural and domestic economy by 1917, most of them consciously following Wisconsin's lead. Commons, chief architect of the 1911 workmen's compensation and industrial commission systems, regularly appeared before the legislatures of other states to explain his handiwork, while the American Association for Labor Legislation pronounced Wisconsin's legislation the model for that adopted in California, Massachusetts, New York, Ohio, and Pennsylvania. Several states, most notably Texas and North Carolina, deliberately followed Wisconsin in developing their university extension systems and in the service role that the campus provided for state government. North Carolina is proud of its reputation as "the Wisconsin of the South," while Austin, Texas, enjoys its status as another Madison. On the other hand, none of the other forty-three states that adopted the direct primary by 1940 completely duplicated the mechanics of Wisconsin's system, and recent scholars have substantially demolished La Follette's claim for the pathbreaking role of his railroad and tax commissions. Although Wisconsin has frequently been credited with proving the feasibiity of a state income tax in 1911, New York and Massachusetts, at least, deserve substantial credit. Although most of Wisconsin's reputation as a model rests on its pre-1914 accomplishments, it also introduced state unemployment compensation in the 1930s. Many authorities agree that the Social Security system owes much to Wisconsin expertise and example, while several states have copied its pioneering 1961 Outdoor Recreation Act. Although Wisconsinites have undoubtedly exaggerated their state's importance as a model, their basic claim is clearly on solid ground.

But while Wisconsin's self-concept as maverick and model is certainly valid, there are still many senses in which the state is also a microcosm of region and nation—quintessentially middle American. While comparing it to Illinois, Ohio, or Indiana yields a strong sense of Wisconsin's uniqueness, matching it up with Minnesota, or even Michigan, makes the differences seem much less striking. Living in the hay and dairy region, the Chicago industrial belt, the cutover, or the Lake Superior ore district often makes Wisconsinites more conscious of their similarities with neighboring states than of any distinctive identity. Breaking the state's public culture down into its core values reveals the latter to be adaptations of those widely assumed to be middle American—heroic habits of work and self-reliance; a preference for the "immediately useful and practical",[19] a devaluation of the purely intellectual and aesthetic; an egalitarian disdain for hierarchy, deference, formality, and special privilege; scrupulous frugality and honesty; an almost mystical belief in mobility and progress; a desire for public propriety; and the measurement of success by competence and responsibility. While Wisconsin may have institutionalized these values to an unusual degree, it has not introduced any new or conflicting set of norms. While it is reasonably unique for its retention of an indigenous Indian population, its experience with them has been essentially a slice of the national experience. "From treaty to termination," the most thorough student of the state's Indian policy has concluded, "the boundaries of the state of Wisconsin encompass an astonishingly representative illustration of the total development of federal Indian policy and Indian adaptation and resistance to it."[20] Similarly, the state's ethnic diversity, while remarkable, is the product of the general pattern of ethnic succession that has characterized much of the nation outside the South: an indigenous Indian population displaced by Yankee migrants followed by northern and western European immigrants in the nineteenth century, by southern and eastern Europeans in the early twentieth, and by southern blacks, Hispanics, and Asians in the post–World War II era. Finally, Wisconsin's economic history has been a veritable microcosm of the national experience outside the South—evanescent fur trading, mining, and lumbering frontiers; the evolution from subsistence farming to agribusiness; the transition from light to heavy industry; and efforts to respond to the challenges presented by postindustrialism and the Sun Belt phenomenon. All of these have placed Wisconsin squarely within the national and regional mainstream.

Thus the interaction between Wisconsin's impressive diversity and its distinctive public culture defines both its paradoxical personality and its anomalous role as maverick, model, and microcosm. It is hard to quarrel with the conclusion of Peirce and Keefe that Wisconsin is "an amalgam of strong political traditions and self-perpetuating political myths, of high government expectations and high taxes to prove it, of economic diversity in the extreme (cows to heavy machinery) and of a distinctive quality of life found in few of its sister states."[21]

N O T E S

1. Richard Nelson Current, *Wisconsin: A Bicentennial History* (New York, 1977), 56.
2. Current, *Wisconsin*, 214.
3. *Sentinel* (Milwaukee), November 8, 1861.
4. Mark Schorer, "Wisconsin," *Holiday* 6 (July 1949), 34–53.
5. The term *job-oriented* is used in John Fenton, *Midwest Politics* (New York, 1966), 1–7. The marketplace orientation is developed by Daniel Elazar, "Political Culture on the Plains," *Western Historical Quarterly* 11 (July 1980) 262–83.
6. Elazar, "Political Culture," 275–83.
7. Quoted in Robert Nesbit, *Wisconsin: A History* (Madison, Wis., 1973), 426.
8. Quoted in Nesbit, *Wisconsin*, 426. See especially the inaugural address of President Charles R. Van Hise, a college classmate of La Follette's, in *The Jubilee of the University of Wisconsin* (Madison, 1905), 98–128.
9. John R. Commons, *Myself: The Autobiography of John R. Commons* (Madison, 1964), 110.
10. These words, probably written by President Charles Kendall Adams of The University of Wisconsin, are inscribed on a plaque on Bascom Hall on the Madison campus.
11. Charles McCarthy, *The Wisconsin Idea* (New York, 1912), 214–32.
12. Fenton, *Midwest Politics*, 74.
13. Neal R. Peirce and John Keefe, *The Great Lakes States of America* (New York, 1980), 122.
14. Ibid., 109.
15. Ibid., 108.
16. McCarthy, *Wisconsin Idea*, 29–33, 294–303; Richard T. Ely, *Ground under Our Feet: An Autobiography* (New York, 1938), 279–82.
17. Wilbur Zelinsky, *The Cultural Geography of the United States* (Englewood Cliffs, N.J., 1973), 26.
18. Francis E. McGovern, *Francis E. McGovern on Campaign Issues, 1914* (Milwaukee, 1914), p. 5.
19. Lewis Atherton, *Main Street on the Middle Border* (Bloomington, Ind., 1954), 109–11.

20. Nancy Ostereich Lurie, "Wisconsin: A Natural Laboratory for North American Indian Studies," *Wisconsin Magazine of History* 53 (Autumn 1969), 3.

21. Peirce and Keefe, *The Great Lakes States of America*, 108.

BIBLIOGRAPHY

A wealth of published material is available on Wisconsin. Much of the best periodical literature is found in the *Proceedings of the State Historical Society of Wisconsin* from 1887 onward; the *Wisconsin Historical Collections* (1855–1915); the *Wisconsin Historical Publications* (1916–1931); and the *Wisconsin Magazine of History*, 1917 to the present. Theses and dissertations may be located by using Roger E. Wyman, [comp], *A Guide to Theses on Wisconsin Subjects* (Madison, Wis., 1964).

The best introduction to Wisconsin is through several fine general histories. Richard Nelson Current, *Wisconsin: A Bicentennial History* (New York, 1977), is a succinct, lively analysis that captures much of the state's essence. William F. Raney, *Wisconsin: A Story of Progress* (New York, 1940; reprinted 1963), is the classic statement of the state's self-perception. More up-to-date and skeptical is Robert C. Nesbit, *Wisconsin: A History* (Madison, 1973). For the past two decades, the State Historical Society and the Wisconsin Foundation have been sponsoring the research and writing of a projected six-volume history of the state. Three outstanding volumes have been published: Alice E. Smith, *From Exploration to Statehood* (1973); Richard N. Current, *Wisconsin in the Civil War Era, 1848–1873* (1973); and Robert C. Nesbit, *Wisconsin: Industrialization and Urbanization, 1873–1893* (1985).

Beyond that, space limitations dictate including only several "must" books, recognizing that everyone's list of such items will vary. Lawrence Martin, *The Physical Geography of Wisconsin* (Madison, 1965), is the classic treatment of the state's variegated topography and climate. Robert F. Fries, *Empire in Pine: The Story of Lumbering in Wisconsin, 1830–1900* (Madison, 1951), examines the rise and decline of an important industry. Joseph Schafer, *A History of Wisconsin Agriculture* (Madison, 1922), chronicles the transition from wheat farming to diversified agriculture. The evolution of America's Dairyland is brilliantly analyzed by Eric E. Lampard, *The Rise of the Dairy Industry in Wisconsin: A Study in Agricultural Change, 1820–1920* (Madison, 1963). Unfortunately, no comparable study is available for the state's industrial development. Much material on industrial development may be found, however, in Bayard Still, *Milwaukee: The History of a City* (Madison, 1965), which also contains interesting material on ethnocultural and political diversity. The rise of the labor movement in response to industrialization is discussed in Robert W. Ozanne, *The Labor Movement in Wisconsin: A History* (Madison, 1984). Vernon Carstensen, *Farms or Forests: Evolution of a State Land Policy for Northern Wisconsin, 1850–1972* (Madison, 1958), illustrates the cooperation of the government, the university, and the private sector.

The state's rich ethnocultural mix has not received the systematic scholarly analysis it deserves. Kathleen Neils Conzen, *Immigrant Milwaukee, 1836–1860: Accommodation and Community in a Frontier City* (Cambridge, Mass., 1976), is a classic study of Milwaukee's emergence as the German Athens. Fred L. Holmes, *Old World Wisconsin: Around Europe in the Badger State* (Eau Claire, Wis., 1944), is a popular account that captures the flavor of bucolic Gemütlichkeit. The state's political culture and history have attracted considerable scholarly attention. Roger E. Wyman, "Voting Behavior in the Progressive Era: Wisconsin as a Test Case" (Ph.D. dissertation, University of Wisconsin–Madison, 1970) stresses the persistence of ethnocultural voting under the pressures of programmatic politics. Leon D. Epstein, *Politics in Wisconsin* (Madison, 1958), is the most thorough study.

The emergence, meaning, and impact of the Wisconsin Idea is best understood by balancing early analyses with those of more recent scholars. Charles McCarthy, *The Wisconsin Idea* (New York, 1912), is the most complete statement by the man who coined the term. Equally indispensable is Robert M. La Follette, *La Follette's Autobiography: A Personal Narrative of Personal Experiences* (Madison, 1968). Especially enlightening and better balanced than McCarthy's and La Follette's books are Richard T. Ely, *Ground under Our Feet: An Autobiography* (New York, 1938), and John R. Commons, *Myself: The Autobiography of John R. Commons* (Madison, 1963). A thought-provoking critique by an articulate exponent of marketplace politics is Emmanuel L. Philipp, *Political Reform in Wisconsin: An Historical Review of the Subjects of Primary Election, Taxation, and Railroad Regulation* (Madison, 1973). Merle Curti and Vernon Carstensen, *The University of Wisconsin: A History, 1848–1925*, 2 vols. (Madison, 1949), lovingly details the development of the institution's various components and its critical role in the state's public culture. In contrast to accounts by the architects of the Wisconsin Idea, those of more recent scholars tend to underscore its complexity and ambiguity. David P. Thelen, in both *The New Citizenship: The Origins of Progressivism in Wisconsin, 1885–1900* (Columbia, Mo., 1971) and *Robert M. La Follette and the Insurgent Spirit* (Boston, 1976), stresses La Follette's co-option of a grass-roots reform movement for his own political advantage. Robert S. Maxwell, *La Follette and the Rise of Progressivism in Wisconsin, 1890–1920* (Madison, 1956), and Herbert F. Margulies, *The Decline of the Progressive Movement in Wisconsin, 1890–1920* (Madison, 1968), delineate the important conflicts and personal political rivalries that undermined the Wisconsin Idea. Stanley P. Caine, *The Myth of a Progressive Reform: Railroad Regulation in Wisconsin, 1903–1910* (Madison, 1970), is highly skeptical of the efficacy of La Follette's landmark reforms.

Lawrence O. Christensen

MISSOURI

The Heart of the Nation

ONE HISTORIAN RECENTLY described Missouri as "a bewildering blend of geography, humanity, and events." He added: "I am the first to confess that Missouri is difficult to understand."[1] And it is, for, like the Midwest region and the United States, Missouri is composed of diverse geographical features, has been occupied by a variety of people, and has experienced a long history. Just as historians and other scholars have searched for the "American character" without much success, so have historians sought to characterize Missouri. Writers who have offered central themes to explain the state's history have had difficulty making the events fit their theses. Therefore, a rejection of the notion that the state can be fit into a central thesis seems appropriate, except to state that Missouri is truly a microcosm of the nation and its history mirrors the complexity that characterizes the country's history. Indeed, just as Howard Odum and Harry Moore called the Middle States "the most American" region of the six into which they divided the country, it may be argued that Missouri is the most American state in the Midwest.[2]

The state's diversity begins with its land. North of the Missouri River to the Iowa border, glaciated plains provide soil for raising grain and livestock. The northwest corner of the state has some of its most productive land. South and southeast of the river are the Ozark High-

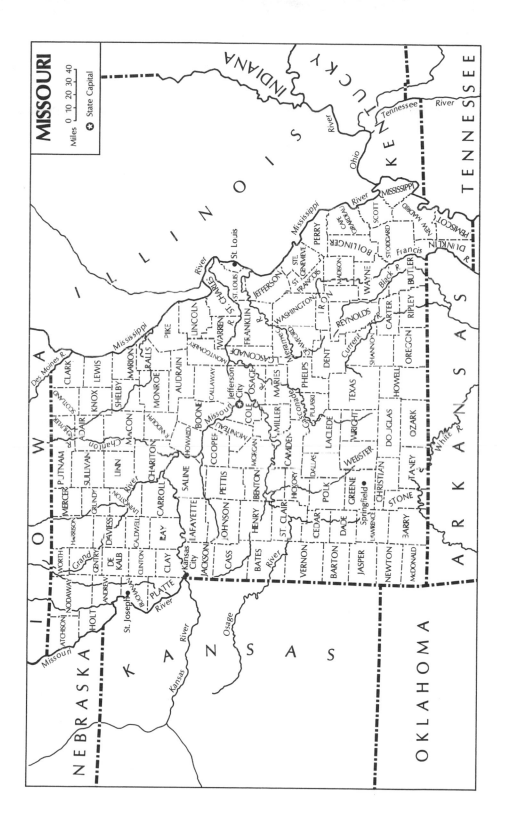

lands, or mountains, with their scenic vistas, fast-flowing clear streams, national forests, and rocky ridges. To the west and southwest lie the Osage Plains, with their fertile grasslands and low rolling hills. Extensive dairy and cattle herds dot the countryside today just as buffalo roamed the area before the Revolutionary War. In southeast Missouri are the lowlands, the Bootheel, with a more than two-hundred-day growing season producing cotton and soybeans. This great alluvial plain, a part of the Mississippi River valley, forms the eastern border of the state. The rich lands of the valley attracted early settlers as did the great Missouri River valley, which divides the state north and south and provides its western border from Kansas City to the Iowa line. In south central Missouri and in the state's southwestern corner, lead, zinc, and iron are mined. Coal underlays about one-third of the state, and limestone, silica, barite, lime, sand, gravel, copper, and silver round out the state's mineral resources. West central Missouri houses the fire clay industry, helping it rank among the top twenty mineral states. Rural Missouri offers great variety even though it fails to have any of the Great Lakes or a shoreline on an ocean.

Offering diverse land does not in itself make Missouri a microcosm of the nation. Its two major cities, St. Louis and Kansas City, provide the needed urban dimension, and they reveal characteristics that fit the assertion that Missouri mirrors the nation.

St. Louis has the characteristics of an eastern city. Founded in 1764 and dominated by its French founders during the first fifty years, St. Louis reached a populaton of more than ten thousand by 1820. By 1860 its population had more than doubled from its 1850 total, reaching 160,773 and placing it seventh among the nation's largest cities.

St. Louis's location near the confluence of the Missouri and Mississippi rivers made it, like other cities on the Mississippi and Ohio rivers, a trading center. The arrival of steamboats on the western waters quickened growth, expanding St. Louis's trade area into the northwest frontier and to the upper reaches of the Missouri River. St. Louis manufacturers began building the boats that added so much to the city's commerce. Workers also produced wagons, guns, saddles, furniture, barrels, and clothing as manufacturing became more important than trade to the city's economy. In addition, St. Louis became a financial center providing capital to develop the lead-mining industry in Missouri, Illinois, and Wisconsin. Manpower, supplies, and transportation equipment also went from Missouri's eastern city to the mines. By 1860 St. Louis produced two-thirds of Missouri's manufactured goods, representing an output of $42 million.

Because of its age, its diverse economic activities, and the variety of its people, St. Louis resembled eastern cities in both its appearance and ambience. A small but instructive example is the sport of soccer.

St. Louisans have enjoyed playing soccer for more than one hundred years, whereas the sport generally penetrated the Midwest only in the 1970s.

No one mistakes Missouri's other city as being eastern. Kansas City looks westward, and it has the feel of a western city. Officially organized in 1850, Kansas City remained a village of just over four thousand in 1860, while its neighbor to the north, St. Joseph, counted almost nine thousand. Aggressive entrepreneurs, such as Robert T. Van Horn, provided the impetus for the construction of a railroad bridge across the Missouri River linking the city with Chicago. Kansas City completed its bridge construction four years before St. Joseph and therefore quickly outdistanced its rival for the western trade.

Railroad construction westward benefited Kansas City as settlers occupied the plains, produced crops, and shipped them for processing to the Missouri city. In 1880 farmers shipped just under a million cattle, hogs, and sheep to the Kansas City market. Minneapolis businessmen who saw the potential of Kansas winter wheat invested their capital and milling know how in Kansas City, and it became a major producer of flour. In addition to being connected to the West economically, Kansas City took on the appearance of the broad plains that it serviced. Urban planner Henry Kessler, supported by newspaper publisher and city-beautiful promoter William Rockhill Nelson, created a city with wide boulevards, city parks, and broad expanses of green during the 1890s. And in the words of historian Paul C. Nagel, Kansas City, like the West, "remained preoccupied with the future."[3]

The people who settled Missouri's two cities and its land shaped the state's history. The first Missouri residents, the Indians, had little lasting impact on Missouri except to facilitate the earning of wealth by such prominent Missouri fur traders as Auguste and Pierre Chouteau and Manuel Lisa. By treaty the last Indians left Missouri in 1836. Similarly, the Spanish who controlled the territory for almost forty years during the eighteenth century left little legacy except clouded land titles. After the Louisiana Purchase of 1803, residents east of the Mississippi River joined the French who had established the first white settlement in Missouri at Ste. Genevieve in about 1750. The Lewis and Clark expedition helped publicize Missouri and other parts of the Midwest, and settlers poured across and up the Mississippi River, traveled up the Missouri River, and occupied the fertile rolling hills and bottomlands. By 1819, when the steamboat *Independence* arrived in the central Missouri town of Franklin, one thousand people lived there. By 1820, central Missouri, known as the Boonslick area, held twenty thousand of the territory's sixty-seven thousand people.

Settlers from Kentucky, Tennessee, and Virginia brought their slaves with them when they came to Boonslick and what came to be called Little Dixie. Although the Osage Indians had held slaves earlier, the French became the first Europeans to hold slaves in the territory when they used blacks from Santo Domingo to work the lead mines in 1720. Since the Northwest Ordinance of 1787 forbade slavery, southerners seeking new lands found Missouri attractive. In Boonslick and Little Dixie these southerners used their slaves to produce tobacco, hemp, corn, and livestock. Missouri became the only midwestern state with significant southern and slave populations. By 1820 Missouri's slaves composed almost one-sixth of its population. Like the nation, Missouri struggled with the institution of slavery.

Those central Missouri areas where southerners composed the majority of the population developed a culture captured in a poem by Albert Edmund Trombly entitled "Little Dixie":

> It's the heart of Missouri, blooded of three, Virginia,
>   Kentucky, and Tennessee.
> It's a tall spare man on a blue-grass hoss.
> It's sugar-cured ham without raisin sauce.
> It's son or brother named Robert E. Lee.
> It's tiger stalking a jay-hawk bird.
> It's fiddler fiddlin' you out of your seat,
> Fiddler fiddlin' you off your feet.
> It's a bluebird singing in a hawthorn thicket.
> It's vote to a man the Democratic ticket.
> It's crisp brown cracklin's and hot corn pone.
> It's catfish fried clean off the bone.
> It's hominy grits and none of your scrapple.
> It's mellow papaws and the Jonathan apple
> It's sorghum sweetenin' and belly-warming corn.
> It's old Jeff Davis a-blowin' on his horn.
> Unreconstructed it rares and bites
> At touch of a rein that would curb its rights.
> It's come in, stranger, draw-up a chair:
> There ain't no hurry and we'll all get there.[4]

As the poem implies, this area mirrored the culture of the American South and its Democratic politics.

Other southerners established another way of life in the Ozarks. Some Kentucky and Virginia settlers along the borders of the area brought slaves with them. But the majority of Ozark settlers came from Tennessee and occupied the central and western hill country. Poorer than the Kentuckians or Virginians, the Tennesseeans came from the eastern hill country of their former state and had probably migrated from the North down the Great Valley to Tennessee. They occupied an area of thirty-one thousand square miles in the Missouri Ozarks and brought their Republican politics with them.

Combining southern and Appalachian cultural characteristics, Ozarkers even in the 1980s retain aspects of their traditional culture. Brush arbors still house revivals in some locations, and during turkey and deer seasons it might be difficult to find someone to fix a leaky pipe or a malfunctioning furnace. Ozarkers know who their distant cousins are and can trace interfamily connections through marriages that occurred many years ago. An attachment to place and a strong sense of belonging to the countryside informs the Ozarkers' cosmic view. One might leave family and home to seek economic advance, but always with the desire to return to the rugged hills, deep valleys, and swift-flowing clear streams of the Ozark region.

A poem by Ralph Wyman Cox, "The Seasons of Their Years," depicts some characteristics of Ozark men:

The Missouri that I know
is a Missouri of boy-men
never really getting to be old men:
men who sit in small-town cafes
every morning, quietly talking
about snagging on the Osage
or gigging the Meramec;
talking about the big gobbler that
still makes scratchings under the Ozark oaks;
men who quietly smile into their coffee cups
at the loud talkers and smooth dressers
who hawk their cars and their insurance policies.
There are men who would rather make
a float trip than a dollar;
men who measure their worth in dogs, guns, and families—
Quiet, seemingly slow men who value their time
upon this earth.
Value the waters and the woods,
value the stillness of our Missouri.
These things, like a secret tonic, keeps them young
through all the seasons of their years.[5]

Besides southerners, individuals from other midwestern states chose to settle in Missouri. By 1870 more than 250,000 residents of Missouri claimed southern birth (102,861 from Kentucky, 70,212 from Tennessee, and 51,306 from Virginia), while almost 200,000 people born in Ohio (76,000), Illinois (72,000), and Indiana (51,000) had settled in Missouri. An additional 70,000 people born in New York, Pennsylvania, and New Jersey lived in the state, and almost 14,500 New Englanders contributed to the total population of 1,721,295. According to the 1870 census the number of native-born Missourians stood at 874,000, up from only 475,246 in 1860. Thus, the various parts of the nation contributed to Missouri's population, making the state's people a composite of the country's citizens.

Another element in the population came from Europe. After the early French influences, the most important foreign contribution to Missouri was from Germany. Many Germans came because of Gottfried Duden's *Report of a Journey to the Western States of North America*, which appeared in 1829. The first wave arrived during the 1830s. They often sought to establish a new Germany in a rural setting. Hermann, founded in 1837 by the German Society of Philadelphia, is a good example. Located about one hundred miles from St. Louis on the bluffs of the Missouri River, Hermann became a center for wine making. In 1848, Hermann wineries produced 10,000 gallons, and in 1856 they produced more than 100,000 gallons. Hermann's German architecture and people continue to reflect its origins, and the names of two of its pre–Civil War wineries still appear on the labels of Missouri wines.

A group of seven hundred Saxons followed Martin Stephan to Perry County and St. Louis during 1838. Expelled from the group as an adulterer in 1839, Stephan moved to Illinois and leadership passed to Carl Walther. Walther created the German Evangelical Lutheran Synod of Missouri, better known as the Lutheran Church–Missouri Synod.

In 1845 William Keil and five hundred of his followers settled in Shelby County. There they experimented in communal living much like the Amana settlement in Iowa. Bethel survived as a communal village until 1883, but Keil left the settlement soon after the Civil War, creating a new community in Oregon.

After the failure of the 1848 revolts in Germany and Europe, another wave of immigrants entered Missouri. Called Forty-Eighters, more liberal, better educated, and politically concerned, these Germans settled in St. Louis in large numbers, adding another dimension to life in that city. Between 1830 and 1850 St. Louis's population grew from 7,000 to 77,000, and fewer than half were born in the United States. Of the 40,000 foreign born, more than half claimed German birth. By 1860, St. Louis's population had grown to more than 160,000 and 50,000 had been born in Germany.

As they did throughout the Midwest, particularly in Ohio, Illinois, and Wisconsin, the Germans contributed scholars, clergymen, musicians, writers, and artisans to Missouri's culture. By the 1830s German gunsmiths in St. Louis had produced the finely crafted "Hawken" or "Missouri rifle" used extensively by western migrants. As noted above, Germans brought their wine-making and brewing skills to Missouri, but they also became steamboat builders and fine cabinet makers. They contributed tasty sausage and sauerkraut to Missourians' diets. Important in the development of St. Louis, which for a time in the

1870s became the center of Hegelian thought in America, they also pioneered in scientific agriculture in Missouri. They helped create a state board of agriculture in 1856, and two German immigrants served on the first board. Germans hated the institution of slavery, and they greatly influenced Missouri's course when the Civil War erupted in 1861. German Lutherans and Catholics joined American Protestants and French Catholics to give Missouri religious diversity.

Irish Catholics added further to the religious mix and contributed the second largest group of immigrants to Missouri, numbering some forty-three thousand in 1860. Potato famines during the 1840s drove the Irish out of their homeland. Irish poverty forced them to leave farming, and they became day laborers in American cities. In St. Louis, Irish laborers worked on the wharves and aboard the steamboats that plied the Mississippi. When the opportunity to work on the railroads came, the Irish provided the manual labor needed to build them. Before the Civil War only the Irish and Germans sent many of their sons and daughters to Missouri.

After the Civil War Missouri's population swelled to more than 1,700,000 in 1870, and while German- and Irish-born immigrants continued to contribute the largest number to the total, some 3,500 Bohemians, 2,300 Swedes, 14,314 English, 6,300 French, 3,200 Scots, 6,500 Swiss, 1,000 Austrians, and a smattering from practically every European country lived in Missouri that year. Whereas Missouri had ranked eighth among the states in population in 1860, it rose to fifth in 1870 and retained this position until 1910. Missouri's population grew at a rate at least equal to that of the rest of the country, and immigrants continued to make up a key element in this growth.

In relation to the rest of the population, the black percentage declined. Blacks composed more than 10 percent of Missouri's people in 1860 with 118,503. In 1890 blacks totaled only 150,184 of Missouri's 2,528,458 people.

While blacks have been a relatively small percentage of the population, they have played an important role in the state's history. Their presence as slaves brought Missouri to the forefront of national politics in 1819. Between 1804 and 1819 Missouri passed through the various stages of territorial government established by the Northwest Ordinance of 1787. When the issue of Missouri's statehood came before Congress, eleven free states and eleven slave states composed the Union. Since population determined representation in the House of Representatives, the eleven northern states held a majority in this body, and Missouri's addition as a slave state would not give the South sufficient representatives to change the North's advantage. However, since each state was entitled to two senators, Missouri's addition would have given the South a majority in the Senate.

The question of Missouri's entrance into the Union created the first national debate over the institution of slavery. In 1819 the northern-dominated House of Representatives passed legislation calling for the gradual elimination of slavery from Missouri. The Senate refused to accept the House action, and statehood for Missouri stalled. During the months that followed, most Missourians condemned the House effort to restrict slavery. They interpreted it as congressional meddling in their affairs. Across the North, antislavery proponents held meetings in support of restricting slavery, while meetings in the South denounced northern attempts to interfere with the peculiar institution.

When Congress reconsidered Missouri's statehood during its next session, the deadlock between the House and Senate over slavery in Missouri reoccurred, with an additional complication: Massachusetts had granted its district of Maine the right to seek statehood. Speaker of the House Henry Clay of Kentucky and Senator Jesse B. Thomas of Illinois saw opportunity in the Maine request. Their proposal paired Maine with Missouri, thus retaining the balance between the slave and free states. The compromise also prohibited slavery in the remainder of the Louisiana Purchase north of the southern boundary of Missouri.

Congress accepted the Clay-Thomas proposal, and Missourians prepared to write a constitution as the last step in entering the Union. In the process of electing delegates, individuals advocating restrictions on slavery from Cape Girardeau, Jefferson, St. Louis, Lincoln, and Washington counties filed for seats, but none secured election. Drawing upon the constitutions of Alabama, Kentucky, and Illinois, the proslavery delegates produced a document that followed standard lines, except that it prohibited the abolition of slavery without full compensation to each slaveholder. The constitution also required the first state legislature to pass a law forbidding the immigration of free blacks into Missouri.

When the constitution and newly elected representatives to Congress reached Washington in late 1820, antislavery forces argued that the provision about free black immigration violated the United States Constitution, and the House of Representatives rejected the Missouri charter by a vote of ninety-three to seventy-nine. Henry Clay again offered a compromise. It allowed Missouri to be admitted to the Union through presidential proclamation if the legislature agreed never to pass a law barring free black immigration. President Monroe proclaimed Missouri a member of the Union on August 21, 1821. Subsequently, a Missouri legislature violated the compromise and passed a law banning free black immigration, but by then Missouri had been in the Union for two decades.

While Missouri's constitution reflected the dominance of pro-southern attitudes, the fact that individuals favored the restriction of slavery as early as 1820 suggests that attitudes toward the institution of slavery in the state mirrored those in the nation. Similarly, the Elijah P. Lovejoy affair is proof of the tension that slavery produced in the state. An abolitionist editor in St. Louis, Lovejoy experienced mob violence and the destruction of his press during the 1830s. He fled to Alton, Illinois, where a mob threw his press into the Mississippi River and killed him. Lovejoy became the first martyr to the abolitionist cause. That antislavery sentiment in Missouri, as in the nation, had little widespread support before the Mexican War is indicated by the 1845 constitutional convention. When a delegate introduced an antislavery petition, it lost by a vote of sixty-four to zero, with even the introducer voting against it.

The Mexican War and the land acquired as a result of it brought a new dimension to the debate over slavery in Missouri. Thomas Hart Benton's career illustrates the change. From the mid-1820s until the late 1840s, Benton dominated Missouri politics. In 1848, when Benton's close friend Martin Van Buren split the Democratic party by running on the Free-Soil ticket and Benton did not try to persuade him to abandon Free-Soil, many of Benton's rural Missouri supporters, led by the ardent proslavery advocate Claiborne Jackson, accused him of allowing the Whigs to win the election.

Benton's ally Frank Blair edited a pro-Free-Soil paper during the 1848 election, giving more substance to the idea that Benton had failed his former supporters. Benton saw that contention over slavery could split the Union; he believed that slavery could not be sustained in the West; so he argued that debating the issue of extending slavery to the territories acquired from Mexico would only do damage and for no reason.

In an effort to bring Benton into line, Jackson offered and the legislature passed resolutions asserting that Congress had no power to limit slavery in the territories and denouncing antislavery agitation by northerners as threatening the peace established by the Missouri Compromise. The legislature also instructed Benton and his fellow senator David Rice Atchison to cast their votes in the Senate according to the principles stated in the resolutions.

Atchison supported the Jackson resolutions, and, during the summer and fall of 1849, Benton and his opponents crisscrossed the state attacking and defending the resolutions and each other. Division in the Democratic party led to the Whig party's dominating the legislature by 1850, and that resulted in the loss of Benton's Senate seat.

Although the Democrats came together in 1852 to elect Sterling Price governor, the question of slavery in the territories continued to agitate the state, as it did the nation. Benton won election to the House

of Representatives in 1852 and announced that he would challenge
Atchison for his Senate seat in 1855.

The passage of the Kansas-Nebraska bill in 1854, which repealed
the Missouri Compromise and allowed the people of the territories
to decide whether slavery should exist in them, diverted attention
from elections to what became a Civil War in miniature in the Kansas
territory. Senator Atchison organized proslavery Missourians into a
"self-defensive association." Antislavery people created the New England Emigrant Aid Company. In March 1855, during an election of
a territorial legislature, Missourians crossed the border, represented
themselves as Kansans, and voted in such numbers that a Kansas
population of fewer than three thousand voters cast sixty-three hundred
ballots and elected a proslavery body.

More immigrants from free states arrived in Kansas during the
next three years, and the free-staters won control of the territory in
1858, but not without violence erupting from time to time as the
emotionally charged issue of slavery and its extension proved intractable to compromise. Even after 1858 free-staters and proslavery people crossed each other's borders, killing, burning, and leaving a deep
legacy of hatred.

Thomas Hart Benton died in the same year that the free-staters
won in Kansas, but his political career had been in decline since he
lost his House seat in 1854. He tried to make a comeback in 1856,
accepting the Democratic nomination for governor, but he lost this
race, too. Benton's son-in-law, John Charles Frémont, won the nomination for president of the newly formed Republican party the same
year, but the old war-horse could not desert his party to support Frémont. Benton's political demise and his family's division showed the
potency of slavery as an issue in Missouri and the nation.

During the same time, Missouri also entered the national con-
science through the Dred Scott decision. A Missouri slave whose master took him to Illinois and Wisconsin Territory, Dred Scott brought
suit after his return to St. Louis, seeking freedom on the grounds that
he had been in a territory that was forbidden slavery by the Missouri
Compromise. When the case reached the Missouri Supreme Court,
it overturned eight previous decisions in which it had ruled in favor
of slaves who had similar experiences and decided in favor of Scott's
owner. Circumstances allowed the case to reach the U.S. Supreme
Court, which handed down its decision on March 7, 1857. The majority on the court decided against Scott on two counts: as a black he
could not be a citizen and hence had no right to use the federal courts,
and under the federal Constitution Congress had no right to legislate
regarding slavery in the territories. Thus, the Missouri Compromise
should never have had the force of law. With the Dred Scott decision,
the country came another step closer to Civil War.

When war came Missouri reflected the deep divisions that beset the nation. Like many in the nation, both North and South, Missourians expressed ambiguity over the issue of slavery, and like many in the North, righteous certainty concerning the question of secession. In 1860 Missourians elected the proslavery candidate, Claiborne Jackson, as governor and Thomas C. Reynolds, an even stronger slavery advocate, as lieutenant governor; proslavery men also won a majority of the legislative races. But in the presidential contest Missourians rejected both Abraham Lincoln and John C. Breckinridge, considered the extreme candidates, and gave a plurality to Stephen A. Douglas. After secession began, Jackson called for the election of a convention to decide whether Missouri should leave the Union. When the convention assembled in Feburary 1861, not a single proslavery delegate appeared, and the convention naturally decided against secession. Recent German immigrants, especially those who had settled in St. Louis, opposed slavery and secession and helped keep Missouri in the Union.

In his superb biography of Ulysses S. Grant, William S. McFeely summarized the significance of Missouri during these opening stages of the Civil War:

> Missouri, rising north of the line defined in the compromise to which the state gave its name, was a psychological and strategic threat to the Unionists. It represented the extension of slavery as well as the thrusting of the Confederacy into the North. If slaveholding Missouri had followed the wishes of its governor, Claiborne Jackson, and joined the Confederacy, there is no reason why its precedent could not have been followed elsewhere. People in southern Illinois sympathetic to the idea of keeping a black population controlled could have followed Missouri out of the Union, and if they had done so could not Indiana have followed?
>
> It was critical to the control of the Mississippi River. Had Missouri gone with the South, St. Louis, a riverport and railtraffic center, would have been the largest city in the Confederacy. . . .[6]

Governor Jackson tried his best to lead Missouri out of the Union, but to no avail. He and Thomas Reynolds, with some legislators, fled the state, and Missouri became the only state with a government in exile and representation in the Confederacy. A provisional government headed by Hamilton R. Gamble functioned in Jefferson City and maintained loyalty to the Union. While loyal, Gamble's government frequently clashed with Union Army officials because Missouri was also under martial law, and Jefferson City was an occupied city.

The reality of the Civil War hit Missourians flush in the face. Brothers literally fought each other, as did fathers and sons. Opposing forces conducted 1,162 battles or skirmishes in the state, 11 percent

of the total fought in the nation. Only Virginia and Tennessee surpassed Missouri's number of incidents. Missouri provided 40,000
troops to the Confederacy and 110,000 to the Union. Governor Gamble raised another army, a home-front militia of 50,000 to 75,000
men, to keep order within the state. At times the militia conflicted
with the Union Army's provost marshal forces, also charged with
keeping order. With the state so divided in outlook, the provisional
government established a test oath in an effort to separate the loyal
from the disloyal. Officials accepted as loyal those who swore allegiance to the Union by mid-December 1861. Those who refused to
take the oath were labeled "secesh" and were subject to fines and
confiscation of property. Suspected disloyalists in out-state Missouri
had to post bonds of from $1,000 to $10,000.

Nevertheless, guerrilla warfare plagued the state. Two groups
caused problems for the Union Army: the genuine southern sympathizers, who were sought by such Confederate recruiters as Joseph
Porter, and the bushwhackers, including William Quantrill and Bloody
Bill Anderson. Conditions on the state's western border became so
aggravated that Union general Thomas Ewing ordered all those suspected of proslavery sympathies removed from the area. Artist George
Caleb Bingham, although he was a loyal Union man, became so angry
at the order that he painted *Order No. 11* in repudiation of it. Missourians felt the ramifications of the Civil War with unusual acute-
ness.

Missourians dealt with slavery in their own way. After President
Lincoln revoked General John Charles Frémont's order of 1861, which
would have freed Missouri's slaves, Governor Gamble called the old
state convention into session. It wrote an emancipation plan that
would have abolished slavery gradually, with completion of the process scheduled for July 4, 1870. Meanwhile, Missouri blacks sought
their freedom by fleeing slavery and often serving in the Union Army.
Some eight thousand former Missouri slaves fought for the Union
cause. With Radical Unionists (Republicans) in control of the state
as a result of the election of 1864, the legislature ended slavery on
January 11, 1865, some months before ratification of the Thirteenth
Amendment to the federal Constitution.

The Radical Union party emerged in Missouri in 1863. Composed
of German immigrants, poor whites of the Ozarks, St. Louis merchants, other would-be capitalists, and a few ardent abolitionists, the
party dominated Missouri politics between 1864 and 1870. Besides
supporting rights for blacks, the Radical Unionists stood for development of public education, lenient laws toward banks, corporations,
and railroads, and revenge against political enemies. During the five
years of radical rule, Missouri's railroad mileage increased by about
twelve hundred miles, bringing it to over two thousand. The legis-

lature chartered two normal schools, provided the first state appropriations for the University of Missouri and Lincoln University, and established the College of Agriculture in Columbia and the School of Mines and Metallurgy in Rolla as parts of the University of Missouri. It also expanded the public school system for whites and created one for blacks. Perhaps because the Radicals pushed the state in new directions so quickly, but certainly because they feared their prosouthern political opponents and thirsted for revenge, they went down to defeat before they had accomplished all their objectives.

Of the midwestern states, only Missouri experienced Reconstruction. Indeed, Missouri proved to be a replica of the nation during this period of Civil War and Reconstruction: its people divided and fighting; its slave population seeking freedom and willing to fight to gain it; and, after the fighting, its people consumed by revenge and anger so that reconciliation became quite difficult, although economic growth and industrialization cried out for unity in addressing problems.

In 1870 the Radicals split over whether to liberalize the harsh test oath for political participation, and a coalition of Liberal Republicans and Democrats won control of the state. Two years later the Democrats won outright power and did not relinquish it for the next thirty-five years. Reunited, the Radicals changed their name to Republican and continued to exhibit strength in southwestern and northern border regions and German-dominated counties along the Missouri River. Blacks voted for the first time in 1870 as a result of the Fifteenth Amendment, and although they went to segregated schools and experienced segregation in public accommodations and discrimination in a variety of ways, they never lost the right to vote, nor, after 1867, did they experience segregation on public transportation. In politics, then, Missouri followed the South in empowering the Democratic party, but in race relations it rejected the extreme course of southern segregation and created a pattern that reflected elements of both North and South.

Despite the state's return to Democratic control and the election of former Confederates to important offices, including U.S. Senate seats, the legacy of violence and lawlessness that marked the Civil War in Missouri continued into the 1870s and 1880s. Because of Jesse and Frank James, the Younger boys, and others, Missouri became known as the "Outlaw State." The James boys did not end their careers until 1882, when Bob Ford murdered Jesse and Frank surrendered to the governor. Another form of lawlessness continued in the Ozark Highlands as "Baldknobbers," or vigilantes, sought to impose their notions of law and order on individuals and communities. Their violence soon fell of its own weight as Ozarkers rejected the arbitrariness of self-appointed monitors of their behavior.

Lawlessness and vigilantism seemed out of place in the bustling Missouri of the post–Civil War era. St. Louis's population reached 575,238 by 1900, and Kansas City added another 163,752 urban residents to the state's total. Railroads crisscrossed the state, connecting the two major cities with such increasingly important towns as Springfield, Sedalia, and Joplin. While Kansas City replaced St. Joseph as the state's second most important city, the latter town counted more than fifty-two thousand people in 1890. In 1910 more than 41 percent of Missouri's population lived in cities as compared to less than 13 percent of Arkansas's, 30 percent of Iowa's, and more than 61 percent of Illinois's.

Like many other cities, St. Louis and Kansas City came under the influence of political machines. St. Louis's Ed Butler attracted the attention of Lincoln Steffens when the *McClure's* editor wrote his famous exposé of urban corruption. A more effective and longer-lived machine dominated Kansas City for more than twenty years. Begun by Jim Pendergast and fully developed by his brother, Tom Pendergast, the Kansas City machine provided citizens with services in exchange for their votes, with huge sums of money ending up in the Pendergasts' pockets because of corruption. Among other results of machine rule, Kansas City in the 1920s became known for gambling, drinking, and prostitution. Its wide-open character and job opportunities attracted talented jazz musicians, who created the famous Kansas City sound. Similar conditions in St. Louis at the turn of the century had seen the flowering of ragtime under the leadership of Scott Joplin and Tom Turpin.

The forces of industrialization and urbanization that produced city growth and machine politics also spawned the farmer's protest movement, called Populism, and the labor movement. While Missouri's farmers attempted to organize politically, they never achieved the success of their counterparts in some other midwestern states, in part because the Democratic party proved adept at co-opting Populist issues. The farm protest movement in Missouri followed the national pattern in that it raised important issues but failed to achieve political power. Missouri's labor movement also followed the national pattern, although St. Louis's general strike in 1877 briefly drew national attention to the river city. Both St. Louis and Kansas City became major centers of organized labor during the twentieth century. The strength of labor was shown in 1978 when an antilabor "right to work" amendment to the state constitution failed by more than 300,000 votes. The two major metropolitan areas voted overwhelmingly against it, while rural areas tended to support it.

The other major response to industrialization and political corruption, the Progressive movement, found Joseph W. Folk destroying the effectiveness of boss Butler and riding this success to the governorship. Folk brought a number of changes to Missouri, including compulsory attendance laws in public education and a number of political reforms. Herbert W. Hadley, Folk's attorney general and his successor as governor, became the first Republican elected governor since 1870. He and his successor, Democrat Elliott W. Major, attacked special interests, including the Royal Baking Company, Standard Oil, and International Harvester. While Missouri progressivism made important contributions to the state, it failed to have the long-lasting and deep effect that the movement had on such midwestern states as Wisconsin.

During World War I Missouri reflected the experiences of much of the Midwest. Early in the war, opinion divided over the country's proper role, with those of Irish and German heritage supporting Germany. When Woodrow Wilson asked for war, Missouri Senator William J. Stone, chairman of the Foreign Relations Committee, and 25 percent of Missouri's congressmen voted no. Stone simply believed the United States had no business in the European war. Only five senators joined him in voting against American entrance. A variety of factors influenced the congressmen, including isolationist beliefs, opposition to the influence of U.S. bankers on policy, large German and Irish constituencies in their districts, and midwestern distrust of England. Only 8 percent of the nation's congressmen agreed with their Missouri colleagues. Unfortunately, Missourians of German heritage experienced discrimination during the war; the German language was dropped from school curriculums, and even street names were changed.

While voters in the nation elected Republican presidents during the 1920s, Missourians elected Republican governors. And, as in the rest of the nation, automobiles became important in Missouri during this decade. Missouri voters passed two bond issues totaling $135 million for road building. Improved roads stimulated car purchases. Registrations went from 151,027 in 1917 to 392,896 in 1922 to 764,375 in 1930. Highway construction and the automobile industry caused economic growth, fostered the tourist industry, and changed the face of the state as gas stations, roadhouses, and billboards rose along the roadways. In general, the automobile reduced provincialism, causing rural-urban experiences to become less dissimilar and life to become more standardized.

With improved roads and increased use of automobiles, some Missourians tried to improve rural educational opportunities by consolidating schools. Governor Sam A. Baker, formerly state superintendent of schools, attempted to establish a permanent school fund during the mid-1920s, but the legislature refused to go along. Instead, the state reduced its percentage of support for schools even more—and local districts were already supplying 85 to 93 percent of school money.

As a result, Missouri fell well below the national average in support of its schools. The state's lack of support affected all districts, including St. Louis, which, under William Torrey Harris as superintendent during the 1870s, had created a system that was copied by other cities and continued to be one of the better city systems well into the twentieth century. In 1931, during Republican Governor Henry Caulfield's administration, the legislature finally passed a school law that distributed state money so that every district could support a school program of at least minimum standard. Consolidation of school districts did not begin until 1947 and was not completed until after passage of the 1969 Consolidation Act. Funding for Missouri's schools continued to lag behind. In relation to its taxpayers' ability to pay, Missouri ranked forty-first among the fifty states in 1978–79 in spending for primary and secondary education and forty-third in 1976–77 in spending for higher education. Since 1980 the state's position has declined in both categories.

When the Great Depression replaced the prosperity of the 1920s, Missourians emulated the nation's turn to the Democratic party by electing Democratic governors and legislatures. Farmers had failed to share in the 1920s prosperity, and Missourians living in rural areas declined from 53.4 percent in 1920 to 48.8 percent in 1930. For the first time in the state's history, a majority of its citizens lived in towns and cities with populations of twenty-five hundred or more. Neither rural nor urban Missourians escaped the ravages of the depression. From 1929 to 1933 more than three hundred banks and savings institutions failed in Missouri. Industrial employment dropped from 370,787 in 1930 to 141,196 in 1933. New Deal programs helped relieve material suffering and quite importantly put people to work, but in Missouri, as in the nation, it took World War II to bring the depression to an end.

A strong New Deal supporter and a key figure in supervising the production of war material represented Missouri in the U.S. Senate during the depression and the war. Harry S Truman won his Senate seat after surviving a hotly contested primary election in 1934. Truman had been associated with the Tom Pendergast machine since 1922, when he won a Jackson County office. After losing an election in 1924, Truman became chief county administrator in 1926, compiling an exemplary record in this office and gaining a statewide reputation for his administrative ability. Although he was associated with the corrupt machine, he remained honest throughout his career. Boss Tom needed Harry's appeal in rural Jackson County and accepted his honesty in order to keep his support. Much later, in 1940, Senator Truman won another contested primary election by a close vote, surviving the destruction of the Pendergast machine when the boss was sent to prison for income tax evasion. Truman won the general election easily, although the electorate chose a Republican governor. During the war Truman chaired the important Committee to Investigate National Defense Programs. The Truman committee saved the government about a billion dollars and made its chairman a national political figure. Elected vice-president in 1944, Truman went on to the presidency after Roosevelt's death in April 1945 and distinguished himself as a leading figure in the last stages of World War II and the early years of the Cold War.

In 1948 Missourians joined a majority of the nation's voters in electing Truman to a full term as president. During the next almost thirty years, the state's voters served as a pretty fair political barometer of national voting trends. While they returned to electing Democratic governors and Democratic-controlled legislatures during most of the 1950s and 1960s, Missourians in presidential elections supported Dwight D. Eisenhower in 1952, rejected him by just under four thousand votes in 1956, gave only a ten-thousand vote majority to John F. Kennedy in 1960, provided Lyndon B. Johnson with a half-million majority in 1964, and went with Richard M. Nixon by ten-thousand votes in 1968 and by a landslide in 1972.

In the latter year Christopher Bond won the race for governor, becoming the first Republican elected to this office in Missouri since 1940. Bond's success had been anticipated. Two years earlier John Danforth had become the first Republican to win statewide office since 1946 when he won the race for attorney general. After serving as attorney general for two years, Danforth barely lost a race to unseat Missouri's longtime U.S. Senator Stuart Symington. In 1976 Danforth succeeded in winning Symington's old seat after the distinguished senator retired.

When the national electorate gave a majority to Jimmy Carter in 1976, Missourians followed suit and elected "Walking Joe" Teasdale in an upset over the Republican gubernatorial incumbent, Bond. And like Carter in 1980, Teasdale lost his attempt at reelection, as Missourians emulated the nation by giving Ronald Reagan a majority of their votes in the presidential contest and Bond a majority in the gubernatorial race. In 1984 Missourians again gave the balance of their votes to Republicans: Reagan in the presidential race and John Ashcroft in the governor's race. For almost twenty years Missouri's political preferences have exactly mirrored those of the nation.

By the end of the 1970s a touch of California had even come to Missouri in the form of limiting the state government's taxing power. Californians had adopted an antitax measure called Proposition 13, and in 1980 Missourians passed the Hancock Amendment through initiative and referendum. The amendment stipulates that taxes cannot be raised without a positive vote of the people and that if revenue exceeds a ratio connected to the level of personal income, the state must refund income taxes at a rate equal to the excess in taxes.

In the 1980s Missouri remains as diverse as ever. Agriculture, manufacturing, and tourism continue as important segments of its economy, but mining also engages its people. Missouri ranks second only to Michigan in automobile manufacturing, but an aircraft company, McDonnell-Douglas, is the state's largest private employer. St. Louis, like other great cities, suffered a population decline after peaking in 1950 with 856,796. The 1980 census counted only 453,088 people in the city. St. Louis County more than matched the city's decline with increases, going from 406,349 in 1950 to 973,896 in 1980 as Missourians, like their counterparts across the nation, abandoned central cities for suburbs. Jackson County, the home of Kansas City, grew from 541,035 in 1950 to 654,554 in 1970, but then declined to 629,266 in 1980. Much of the Kansas City area's growth in the past twenty years had occurred in Kansas. The populations of rural counties in Missouri decreased, except in the Ozarks, where retirement and recreation opportunities attracted thousands from all over the country. Greene County, the home of Springfield, for example, grew from 105,823 in 1950 to 185,302 in 1980. Camden County, one of the Lake of the Ozarks counties, went from 7,861 in 1950 to 20,017 in 1980. At the last census, Missouri's population stood at 4,908,288.

Even with all of the change experienced by the state, Samuel Clemens would still recognize it. Arguably the nation's greatest writer, Clemens set his most famous novel, *The Adventures of Huckleberry Finn*, in Missouri. Critics have called the book the all-American novel because its Missouri themes and characters capture the essence and diversity of the nation.

Indeed, diversity and variety define Missouri and the United States. Missourians from the Ozark region think of themselves as Ozarkers first and occupants of the state second. St. Louisans and Kansas Citians identify with their cities before they do with their state and certainly do not like to be confused with each other, rejecting common identification as urban Missourians, although both do use the term *outstate* to identify rural and small-town Missourians. Residents of the Bootheel refer to the rest of Missouri as "upstate." Folks who live in Kennett do more business with Memphis, Tennessee, than St. Louis. Even rural Missourians find a difference between those who live north of the Missouri River and those who live south of it. North Missouri tends to be devoted to raising crops, while grazing of animals dominates agriculture in the less fertile south central region. Such sources of unity as pride in a common history, veneration of important native sons and daughters, and pride in the natural beauty of the state cannot overcome localism, the attachment to region and place.

This diversity explains what one astute historian, David D. March, calls Missourians' elemental conservatism. It is this conservatism that is the basis of the nickname "Show Me State," which implies that Missourians demand proof and are slow to embrace change. March views Missourians' low-tax sentiments over the past fifty years as a manifestation of this conservatism. But both the conservatism and low-tax attitudes seem to stem from a lack of state unity, a failure to overcome local attachments and concerns in order to address state-wide needs. In 1985 Missouri ranked last in state government taxation per capita. Thinking of oneself as an Ozarker, St. Louisan, Kansas Citian, or resident of the Bootheel instead of as a Missourian produces fragmentation rather than unity.

Publicist Robert Townshend captured the essence of the state when he wrote, "But that's the way it is with Missouri. It's never definable, although it's a whole of many parts, each of which can be identified."[7] In this respect Missouri is just like the nation, and thus the most American of the midwestern states.

NOTES

1. Paul C. Nagel, *Missouri: A Bicentennial History* (New York, 1977), xiii.
2. Howard W. Odum and Harry Estill Moore, *American Regionalism: A Cultural-Historical Approach to National Integration* (Gloucester, Mass., 1966, reprint of 1938 edition), 462.
3. Nagel, *Missouri*, 81.
4. Albert Edmund Trombly, "Little Dixie," quoted in Milton D. Rafferty et al., *Atlas of Missouri* (Springfield, Mo., 1970), 8.
5. Ralph Wyman Cox, "The Seasons of Their Years," *Missouri Conservationist* 47, no. 5 (May 1986), 17.
6. William S. McFeely, *Grant: A Biography* (New York, 1981), 82.
7. Robert S. Townshend, "The 'See' in Scenery," *Missouri: Sequicentennial Edition: Vacation and Travel Guide* (Jefferson City, Mo., 1971), unpaginated.

BIBLIOGRAPHY

No history of the state surpasses David D. March, *The History of Missouri*, 4 vols. (Chicago, 1967). Floyd C. Shoemaker, *Missouri and Missourians: Land of Contrasts and People of Achievements*, 5 vols. (Chicago, 1943) remains a central and useful work. Two one-volume histories are Duane G. Meyer, *The Heritage of Missouri: A History*, rev. ed. (St. Louis, 1982), and William E. Parrish, Charles T. Jones, Jr., and Lawrence O. Christensen, *Missouri: The Heart of the Nation* (Arlington Heights, Ill., 1980). A delightful treatment of the state appeared in the Work Projects Administration's series of guides, *Missouri: A Guide to the "Show Me" State*, rev. ed. (New York, 1954). It combines personal views of the state, good history, and vignettes of various places. Paul C. Nagel's *Missouri: A Bicentennial History* (New York, 1977) provides an extended, individualistic interpretation of the state's history.

A project that has been under way for some time is *A History of Missorui* (Columbia, Mo., 1971–). Four volumes have appeared: William E. Foley, vol. 1, covering the period 1673–1820; Perry McCandless, vol. 2, 1820–60; William E. Parrish, vol. 3, 1860–75; and Richard S. Kirkendall, vol. 5, 1919–53. Vol. 4 is scheduled for completion in 1989. The volumes cover their periods in a comprehensive manner, have excellent bibliographies, and read well.

A number of books have appeared recently to enrich our understanding of Missouri's past. James Neal Primm, *Lion of the Valley: St. Louis, Missouri* (Boulder, Colo., 1981); A. Theodore Brown and Lyle W. Dorsett, *K.C.: A History of Kansas City, Missouri* (Boulder, Colo., 1978); and Lorenzo Greene, Gary R. Kremer, and Anthony F. Holland, *Missouri's Black Heritage* (Arlington Heights, Ill., 1980), treat the neglected areas indicated by their titles. William E. Foley and C. David Rice, *The First Chouteaus: River Barons of Early St. Louis* (Urbana, Ill, 1983), reveals the important role that family played in Missouri and the West. Howard Wight Marshall, *Folk Architecture in Little Dixie: A Regional Culture in Missouri* (Columbia, 1981), and Charles Van Ravenswaay, *The Arts and Architecture of German Settlements in Missouri: A Survey of a Vanishing Culture* (Columbia, 1977), provide a broad view of two different cultures. Robert K. Gilmore, *Ozark Baptizings, Hangings, and Other Diversions: Theatrical Folkways of Rural Missouri, 1885–1910* (Norman, Okla., 1984), recaptures the social life of the Ozark region. A broadly interpretive treatment of a period of the state's history is David Thelen's *Paths of Resistance: Tradition and Dignity in Industrializing Missouri* (New York, 1986). David W. Detjen, *The Germans in Missouri, 1900–1918: Prohibition, Neutrality, and Assimilation* (Columbia, 1985), and Steven Rowan and James Neal Primm, eds., *Germans for a Free Missouri: Translations from the St. Louis Radical Press, 1857–1862* (Columbia, 1983), add greatly to an understanding of the role of the Germans in Missouri's history.

A number of very good biographies and autobiographies are available along with excellent specialized studies. Reviews of many of these works are available in the state's premier journal, the *Missouri Historical Review*, which is the most important single source of writing about the state. The student of Missouri history should also consult the two publications of the Missouri Historical Society of St. Louis. The *Bulletin* of the society published a number of significant articles during its years of existence, and its successor, *Gateway Heritage*, continues to contribute important scholarship.

David B. Danbom

NORTH DAKOTA
The Most Midwestern State

UNLIKE MOST STATES of the Midwest, North Dakota never realized its future. In 1889 it came into the Union a sparsely populated commonwealth, with an economy based on wheat monoculture and dependent on outside capital, physically isolated from the rest of the country. Like Xanadu or Atlantis, it was already a place of myth and legend. But the legend of North Dakota was much less attractive than the legends attached to these other fabled places. North Dakota was the American Siberia, the nation's icebox, where locusts blotted out the sun, mosquitoes reached the size of sparrows, and winter blizzards flayed the naked landscape.

North Dakota aspired to be like the rest of the Midwest, and especially like Iowa and Wisconsin. It dreamed of a future with a dense and prosperous population based on a mixed economy of diversified farming and light industry. It dreamed of moving into the national mainstream and overcoming its negative image. When the cornerstone of the capitol was laid in Bismarck, a speaker predicted seriously that the prairie town on the Missouri River would someday be the center of Western civilization. If North Dakotans could dream of that, they could reasonably expect their state to become a Wisconsin or an Iowa. To settle for anything less was to commit state treason.

But North Nakota's anticipated future never came. As it approaches its centennial, it remains a sparsely populated state. Indeed,

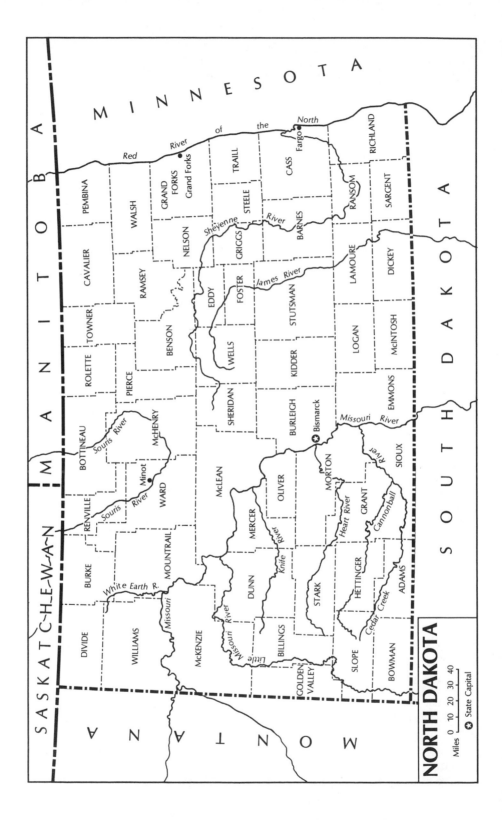

NORTH DAKOTA

it has a smaller population today than it had in 1930. Its agriculture is more diverse than it was a century ago, and lignite and oil have provided another economic dimension, but the economy remains colonial. North Dakota exports raw fossil fuels, unfinished farm products, and young people and imports finished products and capital. Modern transportation and communications and the development of national business have diminished the isolation of North Dakotans. Now they can be on either coast in a few hours; they dress as others do, read and hear and watch the same things others do, and eat at the same fast-food outlets. Still, North Dakotans have a sense of apartness and even inferiority; they are flattered when even second-rate performers or public figures visit the state, and outsiders invariably receive an appreciative standing ovation from the audience. On the other hand, North Dakota audiences remain seated after performances by local people, no matter how skilled they may be. Thus is North Dakota's inferiority complex subtly manifested: if you come from outside you are doing us a favor; if you are from here, you can't be very good. Small wonder North Dakotans have this attitude, given the fact that for the nation as a whole the state remains a synonym for nowhere; in 1986 Bill Cosby's television daughter got a huge laugh when she told him she was considering attending the University of North Dakota, and a second when she informed the family it was one of a handful of schools at which she knew no one.

There is a bright side to North Dakota's inability to realize its future. Better than most other midwestern states, it has been able to retain the values associated with a rural past of material scarcity. North Dakotans value community, church, and family. They prize independence and hard work, but they value neighborliness and mutual help as well. They sacrifice for their children, living for tomorrow rather than today. Relatively unthreatened by the problems of the modern society on the fringe of which they live, they are tolerant, friendly, open, generous, and respectful of others and their opinions. They are private and unobtrusive, people of decency and integrity, conservative but not reactionary, and remarkably friendly to practical innovation. On the edge of the Midwest, North Dakota reflects the values associated with it better than most of the other states in the region.

Much of the history of North Dakota is explained by its colonial status. All the midwestern states endured a colonial phase, in which they were dominated economically, socially, culturally, and politically by outsiders. But in North Dakota this phase never ended.

The state's colonial status comes in part from its location and climate. North Dakota is in the middle of the continent but on the edge of the United States, far from heavily populated areas. The closest major national urban center is Minneapolis–St. Paul, two hundred miles from the southeast corner of the state. Chicago, the hub of the region, is six hundred miles away.

North Dakota might overcome some of the disadvantages of isolation with an attractive climate, but it lacks that. Like the rest of the Midwest, North Dakota has a "continental" climate. But because North Dakota is farther than any other state from a moderating body of water, the continental effect is much more dramatic there. Winters are relatively severe, though natives claim the cold contributes to the long lives most inhabitants enjoy. Summers can be hot. In 1936 state extremes ran from 60 degrees below zero in the winter to 121 degrees above in the summer. Blizzards, "snirt" storms (snow and dirt mixed and windblown), violent thunderstorms, and tornadoes add variety to an already unpleasant climate. All but a tiny sliver of the state receives fewer than twenty inches of precipitation a year. Minimum moisture, short growing seasons, and long distances combine to effectively limit most farmers to small grains and beef cattle.

Geography has helped shape the state's development and even its social and political dimensions. The Red River Valley, a rich agricultural area developed from an ice-age lake bed, runs along the Minnesota border on the eastern edge of the state. Only 10 percent of the state's surface, it holds 40 percent of the population. Relatively prosperous and conservative politically, the Red River Valley has been resented historically by less-favored regions farther west. The other two major regions, about equal in size, are the Drift Prairie and the Missouri Slope. The former covers most of central and much of northwestern North Dakota. The bulk of the state's small grain production comes from this region's rich chernozem soils, and 40 percent of the people live there. West of the Drift Prairie lies the Missouri Slope. Relatively dry and less well endowed in soil resources, this region holds only 20 percent of the state's population. Cattle raising predominates, but deposits of lignite and petroleum add diversity to the slope's economy. While the valley and the prairie have a midwestern flavor, the slope's ambience is more western.

Historically, the land itself has been a major factor in the lives of most North Dakotans. It is more than a foundation on which to build and in which to plant; it is a palpable, living essence, sometimes beckoning and sometimes repelling, usually imperfectly understood and always compelling. It was the major factor that drew Europeans from narrow mountain valleys and crowded agricultural villages. What they found was a vast, unbroken, and monotonous landscape. It fairly breathed of openness, freedom, possibility, and abundance; it inspired awe, and sometimes fear. It promised a life that could not be duplicated in Europe. Unfortunately, early settlers tried to tame the land with the methods of Europe and the older Midwest. Eventually, the land forced them to adjust. They adopted new methods and crops, planted shelter belts of trees, and talked of irrigation. They learned to live with the land, but on its terms.

The land remains a capricious force in the lives of North Dakotans, now giving and now taking away. Observed in an early summer's sunrise or during an abundant harvest, it is benevolent and kind beyond belief. Baking in a drought or lying frozen and barren, it seems malevolent and cruel. But it is always there, never out of sight and, even for those who flee it, never out of mind.

Before the Europeans and Americans came, Native Americans struggled to adjust to the land. Along the Missouri River, Mandan, Hidatsa, and Arikara lived in settled agricultural villages. They were well adapted to the climate, but their habit of living in villages rendered them especially vulnerable to the smallpox carried by whites. The Red River Valley was dominated by the Chippewa and Métis (people of mixed Indian—usually Chippewa—and European—usually French—blood). Tied intimately to the world economy, these skillful hunters and trappers had denuded the valley of much of its furbearing game by 1865. Over most of the rest of the state ranged the Sioux, whose nomadic life-style and exploitaton of the buffalo represented as appropriate an adjustment to the demands of the plains as has ever been seen.

After the Civil War the government initiated the policy of confining North Dakota Native Americans to limited reservations. The Missouri tribes were placed at Fort Berthold, the Sioux were given Fort Totten and Standing Rock, and the Chippewa and Métis were concentrated in the Turtle Mountains. Many of their descendants continue to live on these reservations and to suffer disproportionately high rates of mortality, hunger, and unemployment. Relative to surrounding areas, reservations are seriously overcrowded, and residents lack capital, education, and marketable skills.

White North Dakotans, who tend to be so tolerant and sensitive to one another, show relatively little interest in the travails of Native Americans. Native Americans find themselves the victims of prejudice and contempt from whites, and their particular problems stimulate little concern in the larger community. A national study in 1986, which identified eleven "hunger" counties in the state, was widely dismissed by the remark that most of them were "just Indian counties." Ironically, these early North Dakotans remain residents of North Dakota, without being fully accepted as North Dakotans by their white neighbors.

The treatment of Native Americans by white North Dakotans is remarkable in part because it is similar to the treatment of North Dakota by the country as a whole. Like most other colonial areas, North Dakota has historically been dominated by outside interests.

In its early years North Dakota was controlled by its creators, the railroads. Without the Northern Pacific, the Great Northern, and the Soo Line, the state would have remained a vast territory inhabited mainly by Native Americans, hunters, and soldiers. With the railroads came the farmers and the farmers of the farmers—professionals, tradesmen, bankers, and merchants who settled in the dusty, treeless towns which they were sure were destined for greatness. Outside capital also came, in the form of banks, insurance companies, line elevators, commission houses, and so forth. The big money was invested in North Dakota, but control reposed elsewhere, mainly in Minneapolis and St. Paul.

Initially, the wealth that flowed out took the form of wheat. Hard red spring wheat, which could be produced more easily in North Dakota than anywhere else, was ground in the Twin Cities into the finest bread flour in the world. At the turn of the century 80 percent of North Dakotans were farmers, and 80 percent of farm income came from spring wheat. Public officials recognized from the beginning that dependency on wheat was dangerous. The state's prosperity was tied to a commodity that fluctuated erratically in price and was vulnerable to rust, insects, and weather. The answer was agricultural diversification. The railroads, bankers, merchants, state officials, and agricultural scientists favored more mixed farming and intensive cultivation. They attempted to introduce new crops, encouraged livestock and dairy production, and urged vegetable farming. They were successful to a limited extent, in part because the state's farmers have always been friendly to practical innovation. Barley, potatoes, flax, sugar beets, durum wheat (used for the manufacture of pasta), and sunflowers all became major crops, though spring wheat is still king. But farming did not become more intensive, nor did the new crops form the base for a denser population. And such endeavors as dairy farming and vegetable production limped along, exploiting small local markets, until transportation improvements after World War II allowed more efficient outside producers to undercut North Dakotans.

Others with an eye to the future saw commercial and industrial development as the key that would free the state from the prison of colonialism. Boosters promised all the things other states promised to prospective entrepreneurs—subsidies, low taxes, a cheap, dependable, nonunion work force, and so on. These factors gave North Dakota a "favorable business climate," which it still enjoys, but they were insufficiently strong to overcome the negative factors—limited local markets, isolation, expensive transportation, and shortages of skilled labor and local capital. The result has been that while some industry has developed—mostly related to agriculture—the main increases in employment have been in retailing, the professions, government, and service. These are the very areas that provided the bulk of nonfarm employment one hundred years ago.

Those who saw self-help in a capitalist context as the way out of North Dakota's colonial status did not go unchallenged. From the early years of statehood on, there were those who believed mutual, cooperative endeavor, with state sponsorship if necessary, was the preferable means to independence. Farmers and their organizations have been drawn especially to cooperation. The Farmers' Alliance and the American Society of Equity struggled in the state's early years to create a cooperative structure that would allow farmers to keep the profits that went to middlemen and were largely lost to the state. In the 1920s the Farm Bureau gained support for its ill-fated plan for cooperative grain marketing. In the 1930s the Farmers Union, then and now the major farm organization in North Dakota, took advantage of loans from the Farm Security Administration and other New Deal agencies to create and expand an impressive and enduring vertically integrated cooperative structure. Even today a large number of North Dakota farmers buy and sell through Farmers Union cooperatives, which strive to remain democratic, member-run economic institutions in an inhospitable age.

North Dakota farmers made a national reputation in their attempts to get state help in replacing private capital. The Alliance and the Equity both worked for state-owned terminal elevator facilities in the Twin Cities or Duluth-Superior. During the middle and late teens, the Nonpartisan League, an organization that was led by ex-socialists but functioned within the dominant Republican party, gained control of state government and attempted to enact a broad program of state ownership of facilities and provision of services on which farmers depended. Much of the program was defeated or undermined, but a state-owned bank and a state-owned flour mill and grain elevator complex were created.

The divisions engendered by the Nonpartisan League experience highlighted existing fissures in North Dakota society and embittered political life for many years. On one side were most farmers—who were also largely immigrants or their children—who saw the League as a means of escaping oppressive and grasping middlemen. On the other side were the town business and professional people—largely old stock Americans—who believed the League was frightening capital away from the state and harming their own interests. The conflicts opened by the appearance of the League continued for a generation, stimulated in part by such strong and charismatic personalities as William Lemke and William Langer. The latter, a sort of Huey Long of the Great Plains, revivified the League in the 1930s and made it his personal political vehicle. He added little to the list of state economic activities, but he reopened social and political wounds that had just started to heal through his imaginative and controversial attempts to fight the Great Depression. In the 1950s conservative Republicans finally succeeded in expelling the League from their party. Following the example of Farmer-Laborites in neighboring Minnesota, the League merged with the Democratic party, transforming it from a patronage party to a viable political entity.

With the Republican expulsion of the League and the death of the remaining major League figures, North Dakota politics entered a more quiescent and generally conservative phase. While resentments flair from time to time, the town-country divisions of earlier years have faded. Gone, too, are the vicious, slashing campaigns of the League era. Most contemporary political figures are most accurately described as colorless, and campaigns are commonly short on issues. North Dakotans distrust slick media campaigns and other signs of political sophistication. They like accessible politicians, and once they come to trust them they rarely turn them out. The governor's home phone number is listed in the Bismarck telephone directory, and the senior senator mows his own lawn in Fargo. That is the North Dakota style. Today, ideology counts for relatively little. For twenty years Quentin Burdick, a very liberal Democrat, and Milton Young, a very conservative Republican, served together in the Senate, and both regularly received around 70 percent of the popular vote. Obviously, many of the same people were voting for both.

The relative calm of North Dakota politics over the past generation has not altered other long-standing political tendencies in the state. The "commonwealth" tradition, so important in Wisconsin and Minnesota, is strong in North Dakota as well. The people expect elected officials to do the public's business fairly and impartially, and officeholders try to satisfy this expectation. The tradition of clean politics also remains vital. Most public servants are honest and serious about their responsibilities. Corruption is rare, and those caught in apparent peculations are virtually always convincing when they plead ignorance. North Dakota politicans are more often fools than knaves. North Dakotans exhibit a strong sense of civic responsibility. As is true in most other states of the Upper Midwest, electoral participation in North Dakota is high, standing at around 65 percent in presidential election years. North Dakotans also take full advantage of the initiative and referendum to legislate directly. These Progressive Era devices, which were instituted in Wisconsin and then spread to many other midwestern and western states, enjoy a vibrant existence in North Dakota due to permissive petition requirements and a politically active citizenry. In the past few years, the voters have revolutionized the state revenue system and legalized charitable gambling through the initiative process.

Perhaps the dramatic change in the state's political style is the result of North Dakotans' tiring of the bitter and vitriolic politics of earlier years. Certainly that style seems incongruent with the self-effacement, agreeability, and diffidence often associated with the German and Scandinavian characters. Equally important, perhaps, is the fact that both sides in the colonization debate have made concessions to the other. Those who emphasize self-help have accepted much of what their opponents have done. The state-owned bank is no longer an issue, and most North Dakotans appreciate its role of refinancing farm mortages, providing low-interest loans to beginning farmers and students, and returning a profit to the state. The state-owned mill and elevator continues to function, and state-produced "Dakota Maid" flour continues to be sold, in liberal and conservative administrations alike. Conservatives have also accepted the fact that North Dakotans, like other midwesterners, want a high level of state services in such areas as health, welfare, education, and transportation. On the other side, enthusiasts for state action have recognized that it is not possible to function effectively *in* a capitalist economy without being *of* it. North Dakota has always needed outside capital and cannot operate without it. Cooperation and state enterprises can mitigate some of the effects of colonial status, but they can never overcome these effects. As long as the state lives by producing basic commodities, in a country in which most capital remains in private hands, it cannot solve its economic problems internally.

The inability of North Dakota to industrialize in the way much of the rest of the Midwest has means that the state remains overwhelmingly dependent on agriculture for its economic survival. That places the state in a position of vulnerability to the operation of natural and economic forces over which it has no control. North Dakota can trace its history by booms and busts. The Great Dakota Boom of the 1870s and 1880s, fueled by high demand for the "Minnesota Patent" flour milled from hard spring wheat and stimulated by the dramatic example of the large-scale "bonanza" wheat farms of the Red River Valley, made North Dakota a state. Rust and low prices brought disaster in the nineties. Rising farm prices stimulated a second boom, between 1905 and 1915. In the 1930s the Great Depression and the Great Plains drought conjoined to bring the state close to destruction as a viable entity. By late 1936 fully half the people in the state were on relief, and many of the rest depended on payments from the U.S. Department of Agriculture. North Dakota had become a ward of the United States. Small wonder that some scholars have concluded the state suffered more than any other during the Great Depression.

Since that time federal programs, in which North Dakota farmers participate in large numbers, have buffered the state to a certain degree against precipitous price declines. Moreover, the development of more appropriate crops and methods, eagerly adopted by the state's generally progressive farmers, have even mitigated environmental problems to some extent. Still, fairly dramatic economic fluctuations continue. Agriculture languished following the boom stimulated by World War II, then boomed again during the late seventies. Since 1980, low farm prices have returned the state to its accustomed position of relative economic hardship. Ironically, the lignite and petroleum resources that have allowed some diversification of the state's economy have also contributed to its erratic character. Petroleum, for example, boomed in the fifties and again in the seventies but approached collapse in the mid-eighties as world oil prices declined.

Few North Dakotans forget the history from which their state has been unable to escape. They realize that every boom has a bust, that every silver lining has a cloud. They tend to be cautious and conservative, to avoid risk and husband resources against the inevitable rainy day. During the seventies, when Agriculture Secretary Earl Butz spread his gospel of "get bigger, get better, or get out" throughout the Midwest, most North Dakota farmers sat on their wallets. Those who followed Butz's advice now labor under a crushing burden of debt, while their neighbors nod in agreement about the dependability of the undependability of agriculture in North Dakota's history.

The state government reflects the prudence of the people. The state constitution requires a budget surplus, braking the spending impulses of governors and legislators. In good times the state builds reserves and is conservative about spending. It, too, has learned from the past. In the mid-1890s, state government was forced virtually to stop functioning for two years because of short revenue, and in the 1930s it had to curtail services sharply. Experience has been a stern teacher in North Dakota.

As is the case in the rest of the Midwest, North Dakota agriculture has been transformed in this century. It has become more technologically oriented, more dependent on such off-farm inputs as chemicals and machinery, and more capital intensive. The productivity of the average farmer has increased dramatically, as has the amount of land he or she can farm. In 1920 there were nearly 80,000 farms in the state, averaging about 450 acres in size. Today there are about 35,000 farms, and the average farm is about 1,200 acres.

This decline in farm numbers has not resulted from any weakness in the commitment to the family farm. Indeed, the state does and has done much to preserve that entity. During the thirties, for example, foreclosures were halted, it was made illegal for corporations to own farms, and those that did were forced to sell them. Even today, family corporations are the only type that can farm in North Dakota. During World War II, state government disposed of much of its land holdings to small farmers, and considerable sentiment existed for a graduated land tax that would penalize large farmers. Today a vigorous "Beginning Farmer" program attempts to place young producers on family farms. It is not the will of North Dakota, then, but the seemingly inescapable economic and technological realities of agriculture that have given the state fewer and bigger farms.

Those same realities have rendered much of the on-farm population superfluous and have altered rural demographics as well. Increasingly, farm families resemble town families in the state. Needing less labor and finding it difficult to provide for offspring, rural couples are having fewer children and are spacing births more closely together. In 1980 the average farm household had but 3.47 members, not dramatically greater than the average household size of 3.19 in North Dakota cities. The fact is that much of the population on the land is not needed. Beginning in 1915, outmigration from the countryside has consistently exceeded the natural increase in population and inmigration.

Some of those who have left—and are leaving—the land go to the larger towns. Fargo, Bismarck, Minot, Grand Forks, and the other major places in the state have grown as the countryside has languished. But North Dakota lacks the industrial base enjoyed by many other midwestern states, and the towns cannot begin to absorb the surplus population. Consequently, most of the rural surplus has gone to other states, such as Minnesota, Montana, Washington, Oregon, and California. So many have left that as early as 1960 as many native North Dakotans lived in other states as lived in North Dakota.

Steady outmigration has been a demoralizing experience, reflected in humorous comments ("Will the last person to leave North Dakota please turn out the lights?") as well as regretful remarks ("North Dakota's main export is its young people"). There are a number of famous North Dakotans (Lawrence Welk, Louis L'Amour, Eric Sevareid, Peggy Lee, Angie Dickinson), but there is no famous North Dakotan who lives in the state. Commemorated by the state's license plates are its three great heroes, Sakajawea, George Armstrong Custer, and Theodore Roosevelt. None was born here, and each lived here only a short time and under inauspicious circumstances. The first was a captive, the second was a soldier, and the third was suffering from depression. Even the state's unofficial poet laureate, the beloved James Foley, moved to California when he got the opportunity.

Outmigration and declining rural population have harmed more than morale. Those most likely to leave are young adults, who are educated in the state but are productive elsewhere. North Dakota has a relatively high birthrate and a high percentage of people over age sixty-five; it is adults between eighteen and sixty-five who are in short supply. Declining rural population, coupled with improved transporation, is slowly suffocating most of the state's small towns. And as the population dwindles it becomes more difficult to provide essential public services and maintain schools, churches, and other community institutions. Still, one wonders what the position of the state would be without the safety valve of outmigration. Given its economic base, it could not begin to provide public services or a decent standard of living to the hundreds of thousands who have gone. The alternative to outmigration would be overpopulation and impoverishment on a scale rivaling that in some Third World countries.

One positive consequence of outmigration has been a higher standard of living for those who remain on the land. Greater productivity, farm consolidation, and electrification have allowed North Dakota farm people to close what was once a massive gap between themselves and people in town. Per capita farm income is still below nonfarm income, indicating continuing relative deprivation and perhaps overpopulation, but the dramatic differences between rural and urban life of just a few decades ago no longer exist.

Providing improved living standards for themselves and meeting the capital requirements of modern agriculture have placed stress on North Dakota farm families. They have been forced to become progressively more commercial and less self-sufficient, with all the uncertainties this shift entails. They have been forced to become more scientific, more businesslike, and better educated. More recently, farmers and spouses have had to turn to town employment to supplement dwindling incomes. Historically, many people have been willing to sacrifice to remain on the land in North Dakota, and this tendency continues today.

In addition to its colonial status and agricultural character, and in part because of these factors, North Dakota has always had a sense of being apart from the rest of the country and isolated from it, of being a sort of outsider or country cousin in the family of states. Part of this feeling derives from the fact that North Dakota is and always has been relatively isolated physically from the rest of the country. Part of it derives, too, from the national attitude toward the state, compounded of ignorance, wonderment, and bemusement.

Another important contributor to the sense of apartness is the nature of the state's population. In the early years of the century, North Dakota led the region in the proportion of residents who were immigrants. In 1910, for example, over 70 percent of North Dakotans were immigrants or children of immigrants. These immigrants came from an impressive variety of places, but, as in the rest of the Upper Midwest, most had northern European backgrounds. Specifically, Norwegians, Germans from Russia, and Germans from Germany, in that order, composed the bulk of the immigrants. The first two of these groups were outsiders in Europe, so it is not surprising that they carried a sense of apartness to North Dakota.

Immigrants imparted to North Dakota much of what is characteristic of the state. The strong commitment to family, church, and place owe much to them and their tendency to form ethnic communities. The emphases on hard work, integrity, sobriety, and mutual aid also draw sustenance from their presence. So, too, do the sense of self-sufficiency, insularity, and, in the case of the Germans from Russia, suspicion of outsiders. The sort of fatalistic tendency to struggle with one's situation in silence, which Annette Atkins sees in Minnesota, can also be seen in the largely German and Norwegian population of North Dakota. Ethnicity has also been a source of political divisions, in North Dakota as elsewhere in the region. For example, natives and Norwegians favored prohibition, which Germans opposed, and Norwegians were early stalwarts of the Nonpartisan League while Germans from Russia joined more slowly.

The fact that North Dakota is populated by outsiders living far from the nation's mainstream strengthened the tendency of residents in the early years to see sinister external forces manipulating the state for their own benefit. Usually, Twin Cities banks, railroads, commission houses, and other business interests have been the villains in this piece, along with their local hirelings in the towns, especially Fargo. Early organizations such as the Farmers' Alliance, the American Society of Equity, and the Nonpartisan League took advantage of this sense of exploitation and furthered it, and even today one hears its echo in the state. One might be tempted to deride this attitude were it not so firmly based in reality. The state, especially in its early years, was dominated by Twin Cities interests, and its own leading businessmen were subservient to these interests. The interests hoped North Dakota would thrive, and they did much to benefit the state, but their major goal was always their own profit. That many North Dakotans recognized this fact and resisted these interests was exemplary more of political sagacity than of paranoia.

The sense of isolation has also been expressed politically by North Dakotans, as by other midwesterners, in isolationism in foreign policy. The insularity of the state and the ethnic composition of many of its citizens made North Dakota congressmen leaders in the struggle to keep the United States out of both world wars. Isolationism has faded over the past generation, in part because Germany is no longer our enemy and in part because it is more difficult to feel invulnerable to outside threats. The presence of major air and missile bases in Grand Forks and Minot has probably made North Dakota one of the more vulnerable states in the nuclear age.

North Dakota's sense of isolation and apartness affects its place
in national politics in another, more subtle way. North Dakotans tend
to liken their congressmen to ambassadors from a client state to a
friendly foreign power. Their job is to mediate between the citizens
of that state and the foreign power, and to get as many resources as
possible from the latter for the former. As long as congressmen do
this job in a satisfactory manner, they will hold the support of their
constituency. Hence, when Usher Burdick defended domestic Com-
munists on the floor of the House in the early fifties, or when William
Langer voted against Earl Warren's confirmation to the Supreme Court
because he thought it was time for a North Dakotan to be chief justice,
they could do so with impunity. Home folks cared mainly about con-
stituent service; their congressmen's postitions on national issues were
of secondary importance. By the same token, congressmen who become so wrapped up in national issues that they seem to neglect their
primary duties lose support at home, even when the positions they
take on these issues are popular in North Dakota. William Lemke's
activism in Father Charles Coughlin's Union party weakened him in
North Dakota by making him appear to be too interested in national
affairs. Likewise, Gerald Nye's prominence in the America First Committee during the early 1940s eroded his base of support, even though
most North Dakotans heartily approved his efforts to keep the country
out of war.

Generally, North Dakota congressmen have been successful ambassadors. The state's relative poverty and heavy federal agricultural
and defense expenditures have combined to regularly return several
tax dollars to the state for every one that leaves. Only a few other
midwestern states enjoy so favorable a relationship with the federal
government. It is not surprising that Senator Milton Young reveled
in the title "Mr. Wheat," even though it connoted parochialism. The
sobriquet showed that he knew what North Dakotans wanted him to
do, and he did it.

It is possible to make too much of North Dakota's isolation. Certainly it has been diminished in recent years. Modern air travel and
the vastly improved highway system have made North Dakota more
accessible to the outside world, and vice versa, than used to be the
case. More than ever before, the state is part of an hegemonic national
culture. North Dakotans spend more time outside the state than their
parents or grandparents did. Indeed, it has become the fashion among
many state residents to winter in the Southwest. By the same token,
isolation is diminished by the movement of outsiders into the state.
Employees of national businesses transferred there and professionals
relocating there have swelled the population of outlanders. So, too,
have the military bases and the universities. The latter have given

North Dakotans the opportunity to come in contact with people not only from all over the country but also from all over the world.

Still, North Dakota remains a relatively homogeneous and isolated state. Nearly 73 percent of the state's people were born there, ranking it eleventh among the states in percentage of natives. Moreover, the sense of apartness which the state so long held continues to be reflected in attitudes of mind and patterns of behavior, even if the fact of isolation is less dominant today than ever before.

Colonialism, isolation, the agricultural and rural emphasis of the state, and the ethnic background of the people make North Dakota what it is. At least some of these characteristics also apply to the other states of the region. Consequently, in many ways North Dakota is similar to the rest of the Midwest—especially the Upper Midwest. One might argue, though, that because North Dakota has changed less than most of the rest of the region, it remains *more* midwestern. While other states have escaped the colonialism and isolation of their early histories, and while they have become more ethnically and racially pluralistic and more diverse economically, North Dakota has remained relatively unchanged. Perhaps for this reason, characteristics identified as traditionally midwestern enjoy a vital existence in this state on the fringe of the region.

North Dakota is a land of strong, tightly knit families. The proportion of adult North Dakotans who marry is among the highest in the nation, and the divorce rate is the lowest. In 1980, 88.8 percent of all households included a married couple, and a parent was absent from only 5.3 percent of households with children under eighteen years of age. Divorce is not unheard of, but it continues to carry a stigma, especially in rural areas, that surprises outsiders. Strong family ties reach beyond conjugal units to include cousins, nephews, nieces, and others. The continuing rural nature of the state and its group settlement patterns encourages such familial closeness. This is not to say that North Dakota is a sort of idyllic land for families. Familial pathologies exist there as elsewhere, and families come under stress due to changing social and economic realities. But most people are in families, and find them to be comfortable and sustaining insitutions. Nor do they apparently believe the family to be under any generalized threat, if the weakness of nationally prominent "profamily" organizations in the state is any indication.

North Dakota is also a land of strong churches. In 1980, 73.9 percent of North Dakotans were church members, placing the state behind only Rhode Island and Utah. The Catholic and Lutheran churches held the allegiance of most of the immigrants in the young state, and they continue to dwarf all other denominations. Catholicism or Lutheranism in North Dakota is an integral part of most people's identity. Along with the family and the community, the church fixes one's position in the universe. Most North Dakotans are comfortable with the churches and their function, just as they are comfortable with the other institutions that define their lives. The sort of alienation traditionally associated with modern society is not a prominent feature of North Dakota life. In religion, this means that proselytizing churches can make very little headway. The Latter-Day Saints, for example, are growing rapidly in most other parts of the country, but in North Dakota they consist almost entirely of Mormons who have moved to the state from elsewhere. Like other groups, they have been frustrated by the tendency of North Dakotans to be comfortable with who and what they are.

North Dakota religiosity is not only important as a component of identity. It has traditionally had an impact on public policy. The state came into the Union dry in 1889 and was loath to surrender prohibition even in 1933. In 1986 the voters decided that North Dakota should remain the only state in the nation to keep retail stores closed on Sundays, and they made it the first state in the modern age to turn down a statewide lottery. North Dakota voters commonly march to a different beat, and the cadence is often religious.

On the other hand, North Dakota exhibits a high level of tolerance. During the twenties the Ku Klux Klan was a weak, marginal, and much-derogated group in North Dakota, though it was popular elsewhere in the region. Anti-Semitic incidents are so rare as to be virtually unheard of, and Fargo, overwhelmingly Lutheran and Catholic, has been presided over for most of the past generation by a Jewish and then a Presbyterian mayor. The latter won reelection overwhelmingly in 1986, despite having made Fargo the first city in the Dakotas to proclaim a gay and lesbian pride week. One might well argue that North Dakota's tolerance, in religion and other areas as well, derives mainly from the absence of a credible threat to its way of life. The population is, after all, relatively homogeneous, and the attitude toward Native Americans indicates that the potential for intolerance exists. Moreover, tolerance for others and their opinions does not imply enthusiasm or even curiosity. "He's different" or "she's different," the phrases North Dakotans commonly apply to persons out of the mainstream, imply tolerance and acceptance but not a desire to seriously consider alternative views or to alter one's own. North Dakotans are comfortable with much in their lives, and are not looking to change.

Just as they are firmly tied to family and church, North Dakotans are strongly committed to community. The hometown or rural neighborhood is a very important component of North Dakotans' identity, and place pulls strongly on the loyalty of most people. North Dakotans feel a strong sense of community pride. Most towns are clean, attractive, and well maintained. Centennial celebrations, county fairs, and even high school homecomings are well attended, drawing not only current residents but also many who have moved away. Local schools often become the foci of community pride, and it is not unheard of for so many residents to attend state basketball tournaments in which local boys or girls are playing as to necessitate prevailing on residents from nearby communities to safeguard their nearly abandoned towns. Of course, there is another side to community pride, manifested at times in a tendency to gloat over some feature on one town that makes it superior to its neighbors. On balance, though, the good that individuals and the state derive from pride of place outweighs the bad.

North Dakota's civic pride and sense of civic responsibility are reflected in a remarkable willingness to sacrifice to maintain a high level of public services. For many years a common North Dakota cliché was "Thank God for Mississippi and Alabama" because these states kept North Dakota from the bottom in per capita spending for a variety of social services. But North Dakota, like the two southern states that served as its safety net, always spent a large amount for public services as a percentage of per capita income. By this more telling measure, North Dakota is one of the biggest spenders among the states for highways, health, welfare, agricultural experimentation, and education. Means, rather than will, has always been North Dakota's problem when it comes to providing services. Even in 1979, at a time of agricultural prosperity and an energy boom, the state ranked only thirty-third in per capita income. The irony is that North Dakota, with a small and realtively unaffluent tax base, has always been forced to tax itself heavily for services that can be no better than mediocre. In this area, as in so many others, North Dakota deserves better than it has received.

Education is an area North Dakotans emphasize, as do most other midwesterners. Foundation aid for elementary and secondary schools is the largest single item in the state's budget, and it is apportioned in such a way as to benefit poor districts especially. The state supports eleven institutions of higher learning. It has historically been a leader in educational innovation, from consolidation of rural schools at the turn of the century to the open classroom in the 1960s. This emphasis on education has borne fruit. North Dakota's literacy rate is among the highest in the country. A higher percentage of adults holds high school diplomas in North Dakota than in any other state. North Dakota produces more National Merit scholars per capita than any other state. And more North Dakota high school graduates attend college (about 75 percent) than is the case anywhere else. Substantial sacrifices by taxpayers have created schools that are adequate but certainly not lavish. The state is consistently in the bottom half—or even the bottom fifth—in teacher salaries. Expenditures for higher education are spread among so many institutions that none can really be a place of quality by national standards.

The history of the people of North Dakota is a story of struggle in a difficult environment. People made lives for themselves and their families through hard work and determination. Some of the traits of the pioneers continue in their descendants. North Dakotans are hard working, dependable, and conscientious. They display the traits developed in lives of face-to-face relationships—they are people of integrity, truthfulness, and fair dealing. They also display some of the traits associated with their European forebears—diffidence, fatalism, self-effacement, agreeability, and tolerance. Having suffered themselves, they are usually sensitive to the sufferings of others and generous and open-handed to those in distress. The state's history is replete with instances of generosity to those less fortunate, even though at times there have been few who were less fortunate.

As they prepare to embark on their second century, North Dakotans continue to face the old problems. The economy remains a colonial one, tied to agriculture. The state remains isolated. As always, there is more to do than resources to do it with. North Dakotans remain painfully aware of being outside the national mainstream. They resent the real slights of outsiders and are overly sensitive to the imagined ones. They think the country pays too little attention to them, but they are often hurt when the attention paid is demeaning. A negative comment about cold weather or blizzads invariably elicits the rejoinder that Florida is too wet, Arizona is too dry, California has earthquakes, or Hawaii has volcanoes. For the North Dakota chauvinist, the grass is always browner on the other side of the fence.

In a way, the grass elsewhere is browner. Many aspects of life in North Dakota are good, and people there have reason to be content. Being on the periphery of American society, away from so many social trends, has not been all bad for North Dakota. Problems that beset other Americans and midwesterners—racial and ethnic conflict, drug abuse, environmental degradation, violent crime, family breakdown, and so forth—exist in North Dakota, but somehow they are not so intense or serious or intractable there as elsewhere. This fact causes some problems. One is a reluctance to recognize and address difficulties when they occur. Another is the sort of smug, self-satisfied attitude manifested by those who cluck about the problems of others and express relief at living in North Dakota. But for those willing to sacrifice excitement, lower their material expectations, and put up with an unappealing climate, life there can be good. People are friendly, living is secure and comfortable, and public services are of high quality. It is "a good place to raise children," as North Dakotans never tire of saying, or at least a relatively easy place. The state's leading cities—Fargo, Grand Forks, Bismarck, and Minot—score consistently high on quality-of-life surveys done by national organizations. The death rate is low, and life expectancy is high. The farm crisis has eroded the reality of a predominantly middle-class state, though North Dakotans cling to this ideal. Certainly the contrast between the wealthy and the poor is not as dramatic there as it is in many other places. When Zero Population Growth, measuring crime, pollution, cost of living, crowding, and a variety of other negative phenomena, found Fargo the most "stress-free" city in the United States, it was a source of amusement to many North Dakotans, who find Fargo quite stressful relative to their own towns. But the choice said something about the state as a whole—it is a place of relative comfort and security and freedom from stress in many areas. The other side of that is that life there is relatively unexciting and even boring, but most North Dakotans seem happy to be in their present condition.

North Dakota did not realize the future its early boosters had in mind, but it did realize a future that is not without its attractive aspects. To achieve and maintain what they enjoy, North Dakotans have sacrificed much, consciously or unconsciously. They have given up material affluence, a place in the American mainstream, and hundreds of thousands of sons and daughters. They endure a colonial economy, a difficult agricultural situation, and even the humorous jibes of their fellow citizens. They have given much to achieve the life they have, and they will give more. They will endure.

BIBLIOGRAPHY

Readers interested in learning more about North Dakota must begin with Elwyn B. Robinson's *History of North Dakota* (Lincoln, Nebr., 1966). Robinson's book serves as the standard work on the state and compares favorably with the best single-volume studies of other states. Shorter, breezier, more impressionistic, and thoroughly delightful is *North Dakota: A History* (New York, 1977), which Robert P. and Wynona H. Wilkins wrote for the bicentennial series. *North Dakota History: Journal of the Northern Plains* is an outstanding state historical periodical, especially in light of the limited resources of state government, but, like other such publications, it is hampered by contributions of uneven quality.

North Dakota's early years are not completely chronicled, though valuable studies of some particular aspects of the experience exist. For example, political aspects of the territorial period are covered in Howard R. Lamar's classic *Dakota Territory, 1861–1889: A Study of Frontier Politics* (New Haven, Conn., 1956). D. Jerome Tweton's *Marquis de Mores: Dakota Capitalist, French Nationalist* (Fargo, 1972), traces the career of one colorful figure on the ranching frontier. The Red River Valley, and especially the bonanza farms located there, have received fairly extensive treatment. Hiram Drache's *Day of the Bonanza* and *Challenge of the Prairie: Life and Times of Red River Pioneers* (Fargo, 1964, 1970) and Stanley N. Murray's *The Valley Comes of*

Age: A History of Agriculture in the Valley of the Red River of the North, 1812–1920 (Fargo, 1967) address this subject. The "dirty thirties" receive attention from D. Jerome Tweton and Daniel F. Rylance in *The Years of Despair: North Dakota in the Depression* (Grand Forks, N.D., 1973).

Particular aspects of North Dakota life have received some scholarly attention. William Sherman's *Prairie Mosaic: An Ethnic Atlas of Rural North Dakota* (Fargo, 1983), for example, is a masterful and painstakingly executed exploration of ethnicity in the state.

Also instructive is *Plains Country Towns* (Minneapolis, 1985), John C. Hudson's insightful study of railroad town-building activities in north central North Dakota. The Farmers Union, preeminent among North Dakota farm organizations, has produced two histories of its activities, Charles and Joyce Conrad's *50 Years: North Dakota Farmers Union* (Jamestown, N.D., 1976) and Karl Limvere's *Economic Democracy for the Northern Plains: Cooperatives and North Dakota* (Jamestown, 1980). Scholars have done little with the social and cultural ambiance of North Dakota, but popular authors have touched on these areas. Especially evocative fictional and popular treatments include Lois Phillips Hudson's *Bones of Plenty* and *Reapers of the Dust* (Boston, 1962, 1964), Larry Woiwode's *Beyond the Bedroom Wall* (New York, 1965), and Richard Critchfield's *Those Days: An American Album* (Garden City, N.Y., 1986).

In light of the state's turbulent and radical past, it is not surprising that politics have drawn much scholarly attention. Though it is a bit dated, Robert L. Morlan's *Political Prairie Fire: The Nonpartisan League, 1915–1922* (Minneapolis, 1955) remains the definitive work on this organization. Edward C. Blackorby's *Prairie Rebel: The Public Life of William Lemke* (Lincoln, Nebr., 1963) and Wayne S. Cole's *Senator Gerald P. Nye and American Foreign Relations* (Minneapolis, 1963) study the lives of two of the "sons of the wild jackass." The definitive scholarly biography of William Langer has yet to be written. *The North Dakota Political Tradition* (Ames, Iowa, 1981), edited by Thomas W. Howard, includes chapters by distinguished North Dakota scholars on such figures as turn-of-the-century railroad boss Alexander McKenzie, progressive governor John Burke, and Langer, as well as discussions of a number of important political movements in the state's history. Even in the area of politics, though, there are gaps aplenty in North Dakota history and a need for scholars to fill them.

Cullom Davis

ILLINOIS

Crossroads and Cross Section

PERCHED NEARLY FOUR HUNDRED miles apart are two Illinois cities whose different traits and divergent fates epitomize the state's many ironies and contrasts. Cairo and Chicago are the south and north poles of Illinois geography and history; a brief reminder of their story offers clues to understanding the fifty-seven thousand square miles of Prairie State lying between them.

Cairo was settled in 1818, the year Illinois became a state. Strategically located on the narrow and low peninsula where the Ohio River joins the Mississippi, it had seemingly boundless prospects as the commercial center for an agricultural economy. Its latitude (close to that of Richmond, Virginia), magnolia trees, original settlers, and river access gave Cairo an emphatically southern orientation. This point of view took political form in zealous proslavery sentiments before and during the Civil War.

Cairo never realized the growth or prosperity envisioned by its promoters. Other river cities proved better suited for shipping, and its floodplain location proved less strategic than vulnerable. Cairo slowly declined as the state grew, a lingering and socially fragmented remembrance of unfulfilled dreams.

Chicago also sat at a natural transportation point, but its economic prospects seemed far less auspicious to early visitors than Cairo's.

WISCONSIN

LAKE MICHIGAN

• Galena   STEPHENSON   WINNEBAGO   BOONE   McHENRY   LAKE   Lake R.
JO DAVIESS   Rockford •

CARROLL   OGLE   De Kalb •   KANE   Evanston •
    DE KALB   DUPAGE   • Skokie
                            • Chicago
WHITESIDE   River   LEE   COOK   • Cicero

Moline •   Rock   HENRY   BUREAU   LA SALLE   KENDALL   Des Plaines   Joliet •
Rock Island •   ROCK ISLAND   LaSalle •   Morris •   WILL
                            GRUNDY
MERCER   Bishop Hill •   PUTNAM   KANKAKEE   Kankakee R.
    KNOX   STARK   MARSHALL
    WARREN   Galesburg •   PEORIA   LIVINGSTON   IROQUOIS
• Nauvoo   WOODFORD
    Peoria •   El Paso •
HANCOCK   McDONOUGH   FULTON   TAZEWELL   McLEAN   FORD
    SCHUYLER   River   Normal •   CHAMPAIGN
                    Bloomington •   Champaign •
ADAMS   MASON   LOGAN   DE WITT   Urbana •   VERMILION
• Quincy   BROWN   Sangamon   MENARD   PIATT
    CASS   Beardstown •   Decatur •   DOUGLAS   EDGAR
        Springfield ✪   SANGAMON   MACON   • Arthur
    • Jacksonville   River   MOULTRIE
PIKE   SCOTT   MORGAN   CHRISTIAN   COLES   CLARK
    GREENE   MACOUPIN   SHELBY   CUMBERLAND
    JERSEY   MONTGOMERY   CRAWFORD   River
CALHOUN   FAYETTE   EFFINGHAM   JASPER
        Vandalia •   RICHLAND
    • Alton   BOND   River   CLAY   LAWRENCE
    MADISON   MARION   Wabash
    • East St. Louis   CLINTON   WABASH
Cahokia •   • Belleville   WAYNE   EDWARDS   Wabash R.
    ST. CLAIR   Kaskaskia   • Albion
MONROE   WASHINGTON   JEFFERSON
Fort de Chartres •   PERRY   WHITE
    RANDOLPH   FRANKLIN   HAMILTON
• Kaskaskia   JACKSON   SALINE   GALLATIN   • Shawneetown
    Carbondale •   WILLIAMSON   River
        UNION   JOHNSON   POPE   HARDIN   Ohio
    Mississippi   River   MASSAC
        ALEXANDER   PULASKI
            • Cairo   KENTUCKY

ILLINOIS

Miles   0   10   20   30   40   50
✪ State Capital

IOWA   MISSOURI   INDIANA

Situated on marshy ground, it seemed more conducive to mosquitoes and disease than to prosperity. Its main settlers were transplanted Yankees who migrated along the Great Lakes. Situated on roughly the same latitude as Boston, Massachusetts, it naturally assumed an eastern orientation and later an antislavery posture.

Yankee ingenuity and immigrant industry made Chicago one of the world's urban success stories. Adversity in the form of flooding and the great 1871 fire served to stimulate rather than stifle its growth. With an apt city motto ("I Will"), Chicago quickly became a national hub of transportation, manufacturing, commerce, and the arts. Today no longer second in size, it nevertheless remains "second city," a sprawling, vibrant, heterogeneous "City of the Big Shoulders."

North and south, east and west; boom and bust, tolerance and prejudice; agriculture and industry, finance and transportation: Cairo and Chicago symbolize the larger reality of Illinois. The most populous of the heartland states, it also offers the most puzzling diversity. In a national context it is at once both sui generis and typical, the most representative among all fifty states of the national whole.

Natural location and human achievement put Illinois at the nation's crossroads. A hub for water, land, and air transport, it reaches out to all other sections of the country. Geographically and economically it "belongs neither to the North, South, East, nor West, but at a peculiar focal point to all four."[1] Within its boundaries can be found the western border of the eastern woodlands, the northern limits of the southern hill country, a southern projection of the northern lakes and forests, and the easternmost reach of the western prairie. Agriculturally it embraces eastern truck farming, northern dairying, western corn and soybean planting, and southern fruit-farming. To imagine a single state stretching from Boston to Richmond and from the Ohio River valley to the western grasslands is to appreciate the sense in which Illinois belongs not so much to one region as to all regions.

The state's representativeness is more than simply geographic. For most of the twentieth century the nation's population center has stood in or near it. Social scientists and other observers insist that this demographic quirk actually symbolizes much more: that Illinois comes closest among all the states to being a miniature cross section of the Union. Daniel Elazar, in a pioneering study of American political culture, put it this way:

> Illinois . . . is one of the most heterogeneous states in the Union. In its social structure and its patterns of political response it is very likely the nation's most representative state. In the heart of the Middle West, it stands at the geohistorical center of the United States. While its physiographic personality is relatively undistinguished, it combines within its boundaries most of the social, economic, historic, and geographic diversities found in this country.[2]

Anticipating this assertion was the 1939 Federal Writers' Project descriptive guide:

> Across this State have eddied almost all the major currents from both without and within the country. Crisscrossed by railroads from all corners of the country, a steel-maker as well as a wheat-stacker, Illinois in its entirety functions as a working model of the Nation as a whole. Therein the heterogeneity of the State takes on meaning and becomes in itself a symbol burdened with deep significance.[3]

Many writers who share this opinion have chosen to capture it with catch phrases or metaphors. Illinois is "core America," the "microcosm state," a "cultural mosaic," "the fulcrum upon which this country balances," an "historic test-strip for the peopling of the United States," "a vast stretch of modernistic linoleum," "a working model of the Nation," and the "heterogeneous centerpin of the nation."[4]

Centrality, typicality, and middleness—terms commonly associated with the entire heartland region—apply with as much reason and with sharper focus to Illinois. Lighthearted expression of this idea occurs in "Henry Lichenwalner: Living in the Middle," by poet Dave Etter:

> Here in Alliance, Illinois,
> I'm living in the middle,
> standing on the Courthouse lawn
> in the middle of town,
> in the middle of my life,
> a self-confessed middlebrow,
> a member of the middle class,
> and of course Middle Western,
> the middle, you see, the middle,
> believing in the middle way,
> standing here at midday
> in the middle of the year,
> breathing the farm-fragrant air
> of Sunflower County,
> in the true-blue middle
> of middle America,
> in the middle of my dreams.[5]

Another writer, reflecting on his native state, recalled:

> What Chicago and the state of Illinois provided me in my youth was a condition of almost irreconcilable contradiction. . . . We have been tested by extremes . . . the gaps between city and country . . . between generations, races, families, professions. . . . [N]owhere in our culture do these elements stand in starker contrast than here. They are as harsh

as our violent weather. . . . America's heart is schizoid, and here in the heartland I battled that condition.[6]

History and statistics lend strength to these claims. Illinois's presidential preferences, age cohorts, vital statistics, economic activities, and employment ratios, to name just some indices, closely resemble national data. Marketing firms know that how a product or message "plays in Peoria" offers reliable indications of its broader national appeal. "Jonesville," "River City," and "Coal Town" are just three of the fictional-sounding place names of actual Illinois towns. Probably no other state has had so many of its cities selected as microcosms by social scientists. The "community studies" literature in sociology includes major works on Morris, Vandalia, Park Forest, Chicago, Cairo, and Quincy. Fifteen of the nineteen middle-sized cities in Daniel Elazar's study of American metropolitanism are in Illinois.

Pluralism, dissonance, complexity, and diversity are the general qualities that make Illinois so representative. By the shape of her land, the mix of her resources, the makeup of her people, the nature of her economy, and the quality of her politics, Illinois boasts the puzzling honor of being unique for her ordinariness.

The state's natural landscape is generally regarded and remembered as one vast parcel of prairie: level, unending, and fertile. Such imagery is an oversimplification, as there are important unglaciated sections of rolling and heavily wooded land in the Shawnee Hills (Ozark Plateau) of southern Illinois, the Wisconsin Driftless region around Galena in the northwest, and smaller segments along the western or Mississippi River boundary. Even within the Grand Prairie that comprises central and northern Illinois there are such topographic interruptions as river valleys and moraines.

But flat prairie is the Prairie State's dominant vista and her geographic fixation. It occupies a generous preponderance of her total area and is the priceless legacy of four successive glaciers that shaped most of the state.

Flat terrain topped with a deep crust of rich topsoil greeted successive waves of white settlers with symbolic messages of openness, access, movement, and fertility that were an invitation to human ingenuity. Governor Adlai E. Stevenson recognized this message when he welcomed delegates in Chicago at the Democratic national convention that later nominated him for president:

Here, my friends, on the prairies of Illinois and of the Middle West, we can see a long way in all directions. We look to east, to west, to north and south. Our commerce, our ideas, come and go in all directions. Here there are no barriers, no defenses, to ideas and aspirations. We want none; we want no shackles on the mind or the spirit, no rigid patterns of thought, no iron conformity.[7]

Early observers compared the prairie profile to an ocean vista: "outstretched and undulating . . . a vast ocean of meadowland; in some parts . . . dotted with coasts, capes or islands of forest-wood." French missionary and early explorer Père Marquette described Illinois as "God's meadow," and poet William Cullen Bryant thought of it as "the gardens of the Desert." While full agricultural development of the prairie awaited technological advances in plow design and land drainage methods, its easy accessibility and deep topsoil were promising signs.[8]

Long horizons could have psychological as well as economic implications. After his 1842 visit to a prairie site near Belleville, Charles Dickens described the setting as "oppressive in its barren monotony." Illinois Democratic leader Stephen A. Douglas reacted differently:

I have found my mind liberalized and my opinion enlarged when I get out on these broad prairies, with only the heavens to bound my vision.

Expansiveness and a sense of life's limitless opportunities were natural companions to the open horizon of the Illinois prairie.[9]

One early and important consequence of the level terrain was its suitability for overland transport. Numerous buffalo traces and Indian footpaths that antedated white settlement evolved into trails and stagecoach routes for pioneers on the move. Except for occasional streams and rivers that required fording and later bridging, it was relatively easy to travel in all directions by foot, on horseback, or in wagons. Trails evolved into roads, and roads into major overland arteries. The old Saint Louis Trace, which crossed the state from Vincennes, Indiana, to St. Louis, began as a buffalo trail, then became a stagecoach route and a railroad right of way, and finally in the twentieth century became U.S. Highway 50. The final stretch of the National or Cumberland Road ran from Terre Haute, Indiana, to Illinois's second state capital at Vandalia; later its natural alignment made it the route for U.S. 40 and later still Interstate 70.

Second only to prairie flatness among the state's dominant topographic features was her remarkable river network. Illinois is the heart of the interior river system of North America; water from twenty-three states flows through or along her borders. Jointly the Wabash, Ohio, and Mississippi rivers provide most of her territorial definition, and together with Lake Michigan they supply her with access to both the Atlantic Ocean and the Gulf of Mexico.

This arterial dimension of the landscape historically has reinforced the prairie metaphors of welcome, access, and fertility. Over three hundred years ago the state's first white explorers, Marquette and Joliet, discovered the relative ease of traversing this wilderness by paddling on the Mississippi and Illinois rivers and on Lake Michigan. Early pioneers used the Ohio, Mississippi, Wabash, and Illinois to reach choice settlement sites in southern and central Illinois. Emulating their Indian and French predecessors, they chose river banks for such pioneer towns as Kaskaskia, Shawneetown, Galena, Peoria, and Quincy. Subsequent waves of immigrants entered by way of Lake Michigan and down the Illinois and other rivers.

Original settlers stayed close to the water for sustenance as well as transportation. Seven gentle but distinct water basins comprise an elaborate drainage system that serves 87 percent of the state's land. Plentiful water was a mixed blessing; large portions of the Grand Prairie were thus rendered untillable. They remained marshy and unoccupied until drainage efforts released their rich potential as the state's prime farmland.

While settlement and development have dramatically altered the virgin landscape of primeval Illinois, many of the state's most conspicuous and important agricultural, engineering, and architectural practices have augmented rather than diminished the symbolic messages of her prairies and waterways.

First among these developments was the rectangular or grid survey system superimposed upon the Northwest Territory by the 1785 Land Ordinance. This fateful gesture of human ingenuity was designed to efficiently transfer the public lands into private hands. It did this and more. The concept of six-mile-square townships and their sectional components arranged along principal meridians and baselines facilitated settlement, created norms of land ownership, reduced the likelihood of property disputes, imposed geometric uniformity upon an uneven landscape, and established a precedent for public support of education. From it followed the development of townships as political subdivisions as well as survey units, along with county boundaries, roads, and other man-made adjustments to the landscape.

Federal surveyors reached Illinois in 1804, barely ahead of the migrant hordes of the next several decades. Their work, and that of the various federal land offices at Kaskaskia, Shawneetown, Edwardsville, and elsewhere, encouraged rapid land acquisition with a minimum of confusion or dispute. Subsequent government steps to lower the price of land from $2.00 to $1.25 per acre and to permit sales of tracts as small as eighty acres enhanced this process.

Aviation-age travelers can readily observe the consequences of this grid survey system on the checkerboard appearance of Illinois and her sister states. One observer labeled it "Illinoleum"; another concluded, "The whole wide land was a map." To the settlers who bought a section or half section, plowed the land and erected hedgerows or fences, the rectangular survey system simply accentuated impressions of openness and easy access. Like the flat prairie, survey lines stretch unbroken and straight to the horizon. Private land ownership was an attainable dream even for the poorest settlers. Whatever sense of opportunity and welcome the prairie and rivers offered, the grid survey system reinforced. It is, as one observer noted, "a noncentrist and nonhierarchical organization . . . the ultimate expression of Cartesian rationality and Jeffersonian democracy."[10]

Illinois agricultural habits echoed this pattern. Farmers of the nineteenth and twentieth centuries discovered that the land and climate were ideal for row crops such as corn and soybeans, which have become the staples of state production. Unlike smaller grains, row crops mimic and underscore property lines. One writer has noted that driving past Illinois farm fields in late summer is "like speeding through eye-level corduroy."[11] Farmers compete for the neatest and straightest crop rows, which reach as far toward the horizon as the eye can see.

Modern farming practices seek to eliminate natural or man-made vestiges that interrupt this geometric uniformity. Woodlands and hedgerows succumb to tillable acreage and fences; scattered and irregular outbuildings give way to rectangular pole buildings; and ground-hugging ranch homes replace the stately dwellings of the past century.

As if a splendid natural river system were not enough, Illinoisans beginning in the 1830s joined the canal-building craze. The Illinois and Michigan Canal, the first in a proposed series of extravagant internal improvements, sought to connect existing river routes with Lake Michigan. After delays and other problems, it was completed in 1848. A later and more enduring project was the Sanitary and Ship Canal linking the Illinois River and the south fork of the Chicago River. Inspired not by commercial visions but by an urgent need to stop the pollution of Lake Michigan drinking water by Chicago sewage, this engineering marvel was the world's second largest artificial waterway when it was completed in 1900. Its twenty-eight-mile channel succeeded in reversing the flow of the Chicago River, thereby cleansing Chicago's water supply by sending the sewage downstate. Chicagophobes have long accused the city and her political leaders of repeating this practice in figurative as well as literal terms.

Simultaneous with early canal construction was the arrival of steamboating on Illinois waters. Steam traffic further enhanced the state's river commerce by increasing its tempo and tonnage. A steamboat reached Peoria on the Illinois River in 1820; in 1831 there were thirty-two such arrivals at Beardstown, slightly downriver. Among the communities benefiting most from this technological advance were Galena, Rock Island, Quincy, and Alton. Canals and machine-propelled boats combined to reinforce the cheap and far-reaching mobility afforded by Illinois waterways.

Railroad and road construction did for land travel what canals and steamboats accomplished for water transit. The dramatic advent of rail travel was a remarkable Illinois achievement. After several fitful efforts in the 1830s and 1840s, railroad construction boomed at mid-century. In 1850 the state had only 111 miles of track; ten years later the mileage was over 2,700 and by 1890 it had reached 10,000. During the decade of the 1850s Illinois railroading jumped from negligible standing to second rank among the states.

The key to this dramatic boost was construction of the Illinois Central. After several decades of inconsequential planning, the dream of iron rails running the length of the state quickly materialized. Democratic Senator Stephen A. Douglas persuaded Congress to contribute 2.5 million acres of public domain for right-of-way and adjoining land sale or development. Using British and American private financing and plentiful immigrant labor, the Illinois Central took just five years to join Chicago at the state's northeastern corner with Cairo at its southern tip. By 1856 the line boasted seven hundred miles of track in Illinois, making it the longest railway in the world and the nation's largest private venture to date.

Similar if less grandiose construction projects at midcentury created a network of rail lines crossing the state: the Galena and Chicago Union, the Chicago, Burlington and Quincy, the St. Louis, Chicago and Alton, and the Rock Island. Practically overnight Illinois became the keystone of American railroading, and Chicago the world's largest railroad center. Into Chicago the trains brought grain, livestock, immigrants, and settlers; they departed with processed pork and beef, lumber, leather, and farm machinery. The completion of rail lines to the Atlantic seaboard afforded Illinois people and goods modern transit eastward as well as southward.

The railroad revolution in Illinois was another major step in giving the Prairie State its reputation as the nation's crossroads. What nature had generously endowed in the form of level land and convenient waterways, human ingenuity (and pork-barrel politics) accentuated with canals, steamboats, and the iron horse. The easy transit and access that early settlers had appreciated became even more welcoming to succeeding generations of migrants and immigrants in the machine age.

One side effect of the Illinois Central construction boom was the creation of planned towns at regular intervals along the Chicago-Cairo right-of-way. To encourage settlement that would create demand for both its rail service and its booty of federal land, the Illinois Central platted numerous new communities, all laid out with a grid street system along the north-south axis of its route. Unintentionally but no less significantly the railroad thus transplanted the rectangular pattern of the land survey to an urban setting. Like the checkerboard survey, the street grid stood as a practical and efficient land-development plan, a symbol of democratic if not egalitarian impulses, a functional if monotonous contrast to the haphazard street layouts farther east, a boon to city growth and a spur to expansionist visions.

The city street grid developed throughout the state, not just along the Illinois Central line. By ordinance Chicago was platted with square-mile sections, with each section line serving as a major thoroughfare; each section ran sixteen blocks in one direction and eight in the other. Chicago's rare exception to this geometric plan was an occasional diagonal street that had once been an Indian trail. The basics of this plan recur through the state, representing the marriage of a compatible flat natural landscape with the utilitarian and booster spirit of her inhabitants. Thus Illinoleum—the checkerboard face of the state—covers its cities as well as its agricultural countryside.

Building design and construction also contributed to the Prairie State's metaphorical landscape. One relatively unheralded housing innovation born in Illinois was the balloon frame structure. The balloon frame house first appeared in Chicago in 1833, quickly replacing the traditional and cumbersome method of joining heavy beams with mortise, tenon, and pegs. Much cheaper and faster was the use of standardized two-by-four lumber and nails, an achievement of new technology combined with construction ingenuity. Initially known as "Chicago construction," or the basket frame, the balloon frame proved so popular and adaptable that within twenty years it was the standard building method throughout the urban West. By nature it required uniform dimensions and yielded a consistently rectangular house design. Moreover, its practicality both served the housing boom and reinforced the prevailing sense of mobility. Balloon frame buildings could be transported intact with relative ease, or even taken apart and reassembled at another location.

Two generations later Chicago again was the setting for major design and construction breakthroughs that exerted a worldwide influence while also echoing the principles and traditions of the prairie landscape. The skyscraper and the Prairie House were dissimilar in function and profile, but they shared common ancestry, principles, and cultural messages.

Chicago is the undisputed birthplace of the skyscraper. The great fire of 1871 created a massive market and bonanza for city architects and engineers. During the 1880s a remarkable group of architects, with Louis Sullivan in the vanguard, perfected the first era of skyscraper construction, using steel girders, elevators, and novel window treatments that presaged the ever higher and sleeker commercial buildings of succeeding decades. This tradition continued in the twentieth century, with a second surge of modern design led by Ludwig Mies van der Rohe and his disciples. By midcentury the Chicago loop and environs still maintained this leadership, with the skyscraper evolving to its ultimate expression in simple direct lines, dominant window curtains looking outward, and wide-open interior spaces. The Sears Tower, which rises straight and unornamented for more than a hundred stories, stands as a tribute to this tradition and its fulfillment.

At least equal in cultural impact to the skyscraper was the Prairie House concept of Frank Lloyd Wright, an architect of extraordinary genius and influence. A Wisconsin native, Wright lived and worked in the Chicago area during the 1890s and after. In developing ideas that would revolutionize the norms of family residential design, he consciously looked to the Illinois prairie landscape for inspiration:

> We of the Middle West are living on the prairie. The prairie has a beauty of its own and we should recognize and accentuate this natural beauty, its quiet level. Hence, gently sloping roofs, low proportions, quiet sky lines, suppressed heavy-set chimneys and sheltering overhangs, low terraces and out-reaching walls sequestering private gardens.[12]

Wright chose to express these themes using indigenous materials, familiar textures, and natural colors. The result was the Prairie House design that he and his protégés (whom he collectively labeled the "New School of the Middle West") planted throughout suburban Chicago, downstate Illinois, and neighboring states. Approximately 40 percent of the Prairie House residences he designed during this fertile period were in Illinois.

As its name suggests, the Prairie House bore a complementary relationship to the flat regional landscape. Low-pitched rooflines, extended eaves, large windows, indigenous construction materials, and earth colors perfectly suited this popular house design to its natural setting. Like the prairie skyline, the Prairie House emphasized horizontality and openness. Like the grid survey and townscape, its design elements featured rectangular geometric patterns. By replacing narrow interior doorways with wider passageways, Wright further accentuated a sense of openness and adaptability. Here was a trend-setting residential design that once again associated the Illinois landscape with freedom, endless horizons, and creative human enterprise.

The skyscraper and the Prairie House were obviously different in appearance and clientele, but they spoke the same message. Approximately simultaneous in development, each was innovative in seeking to underscore the structure's dominant axis: vertical with skyscrapers and horizontal with Prairie Houses. Both eschewed ornamentation for simplicity, practicality, and clean lines. Both offered linear and rectangular images, and both opened interior spaces for maximum freedom and flexibility. Each was the beneficiary of machine-age technological progress. Finally, by their linear emphasis and unornamental design, both conveyed a potential for virtually limitless extension, growth, and movement. Adding either a new wing to a horizontal Prairie House or several new floors to a modern vertical skyscraper appears feasible both physically and aesthetically. Compared to the conventional styles they rivaled—the Queen Anne house, for example, and the cathedral-shaped office building—these innovations were strong statements for growth and mankind's unlimited potential. These qualities they shared with the natural landscape of prairie and waterway and with the other human contrivances in Illinois that reinforced their message of movement, access, and productivity.

The same flat and fertile landscape that welcomed newcomers became the foundation of a thriving and diversified state economy. Land, water, minerals, and capital were the available resources for a developing economy of workers and entrepreneurs. Illinois quickly and consistently resembled national economic trends through its distinct achievements in agriculture, manufacturing, mining, commerce, transportation, and finance. In modern times the state's diverse output has closely mimicked the national gross product. It also has experienced the familiar stresses of abundance versus poverty, management versus labor, and goods versus services.

Farming was the principal lure for most white settlers, and it has remained an economic mainstay ever since. Enthusiasts marveled at the rich topsoil, which was "ten feet deep . . . fine as buckwheat flour . . . black as gunpowder."[13] The long growing season and generous rainfall were favorable for cash crops like corn and wheat as well as livestock. Even with primitive technology farmers could support their families and also market a crop.

Succeeding farm generations discovered that Illinois also boasted an edge in the mechanical and plant sciences. John Deere of Ogle County revolutionized plowing and opened the prairie to cultivation through his invention of the steel plow in 1837. Cyrus Hall McCormick perfected the mechanical reaper and then began mass producing it at his Chicago plant in the 1840s. The new grain reaper enabled farmers to harvest five times more wheat than had been possible by hand. Mechanical planters and cultivators tripled corn production in the mid–nineteenth century. Later, Joseph Glidden of De Kalb introduced barbed wire to simplify the perennial fencing chore.

There were parallel improvements in seed and livestock quality. Morris Birkbeck and other early English settlers promoted better livestock breeds and farming methods. Agricultural societies and fairs became an important stimulus. Early in the twentieth century Gene Funk of Bloomington and Lester Pfister of El Paso pioneered in the development and distribution of hybrid corn, thereby launching a modern revolution in agricultural productivity.

Rapid prairie settlement in the mid-nineteenth century was accompanied by the advent of large landholders. In eight counties of the Grand Prairie of east central Illinois sixteen landlords accumulated a total of 140,000 acres of fertile land. William Scully acquired enormous tracts in central Illinois as part of the quarter-million acres he eventually owned throughout the Middle West and Louisiana. Such concentrations of land ownership provoked some resistance and made the prototypical yeoman farmer of American history more myth than reality in Illinois. By 1880 nearly one-third of the state's farms were operated by tenants rather than owners, and the figure passed one-half early the next century. Moreover, tenancy was disproportionately widespread on the better lands of central and northern Illinois.

In modern times as in the past, Illinois farming has seen both boom and bust. The bonanza from new commodities like soybeans or advanced technology has also brought the ills of depressed prices and excess tillage. Today three-quarters of the state is still farmland, and three-quarters of that is considered prime soil. Annual production totals for hogs, corn, and soybeans invariably compete for highest among all states. Illinois commodity exports are a multibillion-dollar annual business. Yet serious problems persist, including the enormous waste from unregulated development and topsoil erosion. Man is rapidly depleting the bounty that nature and climate gave Illinois. It has been estimated that Illinois farmers send twice as much topsoil down the Mississippi River as they do corn. Every year an average 100,000 acres of farmland is paved, platted or otherwise removed from agricultural production. Farming still is vital to the Illinois economy, but its future is precarious.

Natural wealth lay beneath the Prairie State surface as well as on it. Lead mining was a major extractive industry in some portions of the young state. Of greater ultimate value were the enormous coal deposits and lesser oil fields, the former lying under nearly two-thirds of the state's area. Coal mining steadily grew in the late nineteenth century, with the principal effort gradually shifting from the relatively thin veins in northern counties to the larger and better-grade deposits in southern Illinois. By 1916 the state was second only to Pennsylvania in annual coal production but slipped thereafter despite increasing output. The pattern was similar with oil-well production, which early in the twentieth century ranked Illinois third among all states.

Coal mining proved a mixed blessing. Fluctuating prices and heightened competition made it volatile for both investment and employment purposes. Underground mining posed constant dangers; between 1900 and 1930 the average annual death toll from mine accidents was nearly two hundred. Strip mining was much simpler and safer, but it left scars on the landscape and destruction of land and surface water. Mining technology and economic forces shifted ownership from individuals to corporations, with resulting labor unrest. In recent years the major problem has been environmental, as Illinois coal's high sulphur content has weakened her competitive position. Today the state still possesses a huge bituminous coal reserve and manages to continue as a leader in production, but its future in this area is as problematic as it is in agriculture. The same is true for oil- and gas-well production, which peaked in the 1930s, plummeted after World War II, and then experienced a brief resurgence during the energy price escalation of the late 1970s.

Manufacturing developed in Illinois much as it did in the rest of the United States. Modest activity in the first half of the nineteenth century largely consisted of mills and other facilities designed to meet local needs. After the Civil War the necessary components merged for a state industrial revolution. Swelling demand, a rail and water network, skilled and unskilled labor, and capital resources were coupled with inventive and entrepreneurial energies to nourish the boom. By 1880 the annual value of manufacturing output exceeded that for agriculture, making Illinois the industrial leader among states west of the Alleghenies. Chicago boasted nearly three-quarters of the state's total production.

Principal industries at the turn of the century included steelmaking, farm machinery, meat-packing, and distilling. In each of these industries and others there were powerful organizers and promoters who built personal fortunes, corporate empires, and legendary reputations. Men like Elbert Gary, Cyrus McCormick, John Deere, Gustavus Swift, Phillip Armour, and George Pullman exemplified the era's robber baron image and rapid growth. A natural corollary to industrial progress was the rise of Chicago as a financial center. Commercial and investment banking prospered to make Chicago's LaSalle Street second only to Wall Street in the nation's financial system. In later decades new industries like printing, automotive manufacturing, and electronics helped sustain the state's ranking position.

Through the first three-quarters of the twentieth century Illinois manufacturing closely resembled national patterns in relative size, distribution by sector, and economic health. Its diversification was remarkably similar to that for the United States in general, and its changing fortunes echoed larger trends. In recent years this relationship has taken a melancholy turn, as plant closings and layoffs in Illinois and other "rust belt" states have foretold a national industrial downturn.

Chicago matched its regional hegemony in manufacturing and finance with similar leadership in wholesaling and retailing. Marshall Field took little time after arriving at midcentury to gain control of a profitable dry goods establishment. His merchandising skills and modern sales ideas helped create a new commercial institution, the department store. Following closely on Field's success were pioneering commercial ventures. Both Montgomery Ward and Richard Sears selected Chicago in the 1880s as headquarters for their respective visions of mail-order retailing. Central location and superior transportation service in all directions were decisive reasons for locating their companies in Illinois.

Shifting economic forces and rapid industrialization proved fertile ground for worker unrest. On the farms and in the factories and stores of Illinois, low earnings and hard times generated organized protest. During the latter decades of the nineteenth century the Granger, Greenback, Anti-Monopoly and Populist movements found vocal but scattered support in the Prairie State. In the early 1900s socialist groups organized and fielded electoral candidates in state and municipal contests. The Industrial Workers of the World was founded and headquartered in Chicago.

Labor upheaval became a familiar counterpoint to the state's industrial growth. Several Illinois cities experienced outbreaks of the nationwide railroad strikes of 1877. Wage reductions and a lockout at Chicago's McCormick harvester plant in 1886 led to demonstrations and the Haymarket Square bombing and trials. A few years later railway union organizer Eugene Debs and others were jailed for their abortive effort to strike and boycott the Pullman Palace Car Company. Throughout these and later years Illinois coal mines were the setting for periodic confrontations. United Mine Workers leaders John Walker and John L. Lewis both actively organized state miners. Earlier outbreaks between strikers and strikebreakers were mild compared with the protracted "mine wars" of the 1920s and 1930s, when rival unions fought each other as well as the owners.

With so many different components, the Illinois economy is practically unmatched in its diversification. Long a leader in agriculture, mining, manufacturing, finance, and commerce, it also has been conspicuous in the annals of worker unrest. Perhaps that explains why its performance so closely corresponds to national data and trends. A comparison of the Illinois and national gross products reveals close correlation in a number of key areas. The most striking parallels are in labor force occupations, the composition of gross product, and the various sectors within manufacturing. Thus there are close similarities between U.S. and Illinois occupational percentages in manufacturing, trade, finance, transportation, mining, agriculture, and government. Also comparable are related social characteristics, such as level of education, race, urban concentration, and wage-earning versus salaried employees.

Illinois therefore has not only a composite economy but also one that probably is more representative of the nation as a whole than any other state. Its historic growth and achievement are a microcosm of America's economic development. Its gross state product of approximately $100 billion makes it the wealthiest of the midwestern states. As in the United States generally, extremes of wealth and poverty coexist in Illinois. Certain Chicago suburbs like Wilmette and Northbrook are among the wealthiest cities in the country, as measured by median family income. Among congressional districts nationwide those with the lowest and second lowest poverty rates both sit in Illinois. On the other hand, the fifth and eighth poorest districts are also there. Extreme poverty exists in scattered areas of southern Illinois and in parts of Chicago and East St. Louis.

The historic correlation between the Illinois and national economies makes the Prairie State both a useful indicator and a troublesome augury. In the past decade the state has lost 200,000 industrial jobs to automation, labor strife, and foreign competition. Efforts have been only modestly successful to incubate new electronics firms and to exploit the considerable assets and expertise at the Fermi and Argonne laboratories. Similar ills in mining and agriculture have weakened the state's economic stature. Organized labor is in disarray. The economic future of Illinois—and by inference that of the nation as well—appears less dynamic and proud than her history.

Nowhere is the Prairie State's diversity and broad representativeness more evident than in the composition of her population. Today eleven million Illinoisans epitomize the "cauldron of American values" that we call cultural pluralism.[14] Moreover, this variety is no recent development; it has been characteristic of the area since the earliest days of exploration and settlement. Pluralism has had its own consequences—factionalism, sectionalism, and occasional violence—since divergent origins meant different value systems, cultural divisions, and dissident voices. Consequently Illinois, like the United States, can point to many episodes of both tolerance and prejudice in its social history.

Ethnic and racial diversity long antedate the great migrations of the early nineteenth century. The area that became Illinois was settled by Indians of Asian origin some twenty-five thousand years ago. Gradually evolving from a hunting to a farming culture, they reached a high point with the Mound Builders of the Middle Mississippian period, who flourished for five hundred years beginning around A.D. 900. Vestiges of their extraordinary achievements remain along the lower Illinois River valley and at Cahokia, near East St. Louis. The extensive mounds at Cahokia are believed to have been part of a capital with forty thousand inhabitants, the largest city in North America at the time. The best known of these mounds, later named Monk's Mound, rises one hundred feet above the prairie and extends over sixteen acres. It was the center of a complex and highly developed culture with transcontinental trading networks.

The first white explorers encountered a diverse Indian population. The confederated tribes—known to the French as the Illini Confederacy—consisted of the Cahokia, Tamaroa, Michigamea, Kaskaskia, and Peoria. Gradually they left under the pressure of white settlement. Later Indian resistance to white encroachments ended on an especially violent note with the short-lived Black Hawk War of 1832. Disagreement over the terms of an 1804 treaty plus a combination of inadequate communication and excessive rumor led to overzealous military action by the whites against remnants of the Sauk and Fox Indians led by Black Hawk. The resulting rout and near-massacre of the Indians concluded the centuries-old history of organized tribal life in the Illinois region.

For ninety years (1673–1763) France claimed the land. French exploration and development proved modest in political or economic terms, but its cultural impact endured. In addition to coining a name that stuck—Illinois: land of the Illini—French travelers provided the first territorial descriptions and planted some roots. Interest in fur and precious metals prompted them to establish military and trading outposts as part of a chain of forts from Canada to the Gulf, with major Illinois sites at Cahokia, Kaskaskia, and Chartres.

British and then U.S. jurisdiction opened Illinois to the successive waves of migrants and immigrants that have given the state her polyglot population. Settlers were induced first by visions of the "new Eden" of virgin land and rich topsoil, made accessible by easy overland and waterway travel. Later migrants—individually, by family, and in groups—were motivated by economic hardship, persecution, or communitarian ideals. Still others beginning in the mid–nineteenth century sought jobs on the railroads and in the coal mines and factories of a rapidly developing state.

So heavy was this influx that cultural heterogeneity became a conspicuous trait of the state's social complexion. In 1856 one of every fourteen immigrants docking at New York City was destined to settle in Illinois. In 1870 nearly a half million immigrants moved to the state, which by then claimed 8 percent of the nation's foreign-born population. In those years jobs were a powerful magnet; construction of the Illinois Central Railroad alone provided employment for ten thousand immigrant laborers.

Nowhere in the state was the population so racially and ethnically mixed as in Chicago. Fort Dearborn, on the site of the future city, claimed in its environs a number of Indian villages comprising several tribes. French and British traders were regular visitors before the

Yankee incursions of the 1830s and after. In 1860 nearly half of Chicago's population was foreign born, and by 1900 the city was a clearly delineated checkerboard of ethnicity. Traveling south on Halsted Street the visitor would encounter a Swedish neighborhood, then German, Polish, Italian, Greek, Jewish, Bohemian, Lithuanian, and Irish. Black migration reached major proportions in the twentieth century, and blacks have been joined in recent years by Latinos (Mexicans, Cubans, Puerto Ricans) and Asians (Chinese, Japanese, Filipinos, Vietnamese).

While Chicago led the state in cultural pluralism, smaller towns also contributed to the diversity. Many Illinois cities still display a singular ethnic complexion. Belleville was a distinctively German settlement, Highland was Swiss, Gillespie Scottish, Galesburg Swedish, Benld and neighboring towns Italian and Slavic.

English control over Illinois was brief, from the end of the Seven Years' War in 1763 to the successful military expeditions of George Rogers Clark in 1778–79. Nevertheless, residents of English birth or ancestry have always been a substantial fragment of the cultural patchwork. An important English colony of the territorial period was Albion, in the southeastern corner of the state.

Irish were among the earliest residents of the new state. In 1818 Congress provided for public lands to be set aside and sold for two dollars an acre to refugees from Ireland's turmoil. By the 1830s Irish immigrants were a major component of Galena, where they had been drawn by the prospect of work in the lead mines, and of Kane County just southwest of Chicago and McLean and Randolph counties in central Illinois.

Germans also were early on the scene. Dunkel's Grove and similar communities near Chicago began appearing in the 1820s. St. Clair County, which lies in the American Bottom of the Mississippi River valley south of St. Louis, rapidly became a center of German population and culture. The county seat of Belleville gained cultural recognition as the home of German liberals and freethinkers, especially after the 1848 revolution. Other Germanic communities included Darmstadt, Warsaw, Teutopolis, and New Trier, while the river cities of Alton, Quincy, Galena, and Peoria also had many German residents. By 1860 they constituted over 7 percent of the state's population and 20 percent of Chicago's.

Intentional communities represented another dimension of the state's heterogeneity. Some were ethnic or regional in origin; others had religious, philosophical, or political coherence. Most were part of the utopian movement of the 1830s and 1840s. In addition to the Albion colony from the English midlands, there was the Fox River band from Norway, the Bishop Hill disciples of Sweden's Eric Jansson, the Mormons and Icarians of Nauvoo, and later the Amish of

Arthur and environs. Jansson led his band of religious dissidents to found the prairie settlement of Bishop Hill in Knox County in 1846. After several difficult years this communal society thrived in the 1850s, only to suffer factionalism and demise in 1861.

Mormons led by Joseph Smith founded Nauvoo on the Mississippi River in 1839. Equipped with a state charter that practically made them an independent city-state and motivated by a powerful theology and a charismatic leader, they quickly built a substantial city of fifteen thousand residents. Soon, however, internal dissension and the hostility of neighboring villagers brought trouble. Vigilantism led to the murder of Smith and several associates in 1844, and the next year state legislators repealed the Nauvoo charter. By 1846 the Mormons had dispersed, with the principal faction following Brigham Young to Utah. On their heels arrived another communal society, the Icarians. Led by Frenchman Etienne Cabet, these economic separatists tried to operate a socialist colony at Nauvoo, but by 1860 they had failed.

While ethnic and communal groups added cultural and ideological spice to Illinois society, the major sources of early nineteenth-century population growth were trans-Appalachian and orthodox rather than transoceanic and unconventional. Several distinct migratory streams accentuated the state's social complexity. The first great surge of settlement came from the South. For several decades after statehood the dominant access to Illinois was along existing river routes (the Ohio, Mississippi, and Illinois rivers) and well-traveled paths (notably the National Road from Wheeling eventually to Vandalia). Filling these migratory avenues were adventurers and restless farmers from the upper South, especially Virginia, Kentucky, and Tennessee. Eschewing the distant and less accessible prairie in the northern two-thirds of Illinois, they established small homesteads in the less fertile rolling land south of the Shelbyville moraine. Hunting and subsistence farming were the focus of their limited but habitual economic aspirations. As a result, the southern third of the state, which came to be known by the nickname of "Egypt," was the first region to welcome substantial settlement. The 1850 census revealed that three-quarters of the residents of southern Illinois were from the upper South.

The opening of the Erie Canal, tales of fertile and tillable land on the Grand Prairie, and mounting migratory pressure from the eastern states created a second wave beginning in the late 1820s. The overlapping of these two migrations tripled the state's population between 1830 and 1840. Newcomers to northern and central Illinois traced their origins to New England and the Middle Atlantic states. These Yankees typically brought more assets and enterprise than their southern precursors, and they enjoyed the additional advantage of richer land more suitable to large-scale farming. They came in great numbers to rapidly occupy the virgin land, as revealed in an 1835 account:

> the emigration from New-York City is immense; they come in companies of hundreds, and pitch their tents in some hitherto wild and uncultivated place, and in a few days make it one of the most considerable settlements in the country.[15]

The differences between southerner and Yankee went beyond place of origin. As already noted, each brought different economic assumptions and aspirations bred by past experience and cultural disparities. Recent studies by social historians have identified religious and behavioral contrasts as well. Southerners brought a traditionalist value system that emphasized loyalty to clan and other leaders, a hierarchical sense of the social order, relative indifference or skepticism toward education, and a fatalistic outlook. Yankees were much more modern in orientation, stressing individualism and ambition, faith in social progress and education, and civic egalitarianism. Such cultural differences expressed themselves in divergent politics, with southerners overwhelmingly Democratic and Yankees typically Whiggish and later Republican. They also took the form of contrasting farming practices and products, as well as different dialects, religious denominations, and housing styles. Such issues as state banking laws, temperance, and observance of the Sabbath tended to divide Illinoisans cleanly along sectional lines.

The state's midsection, comprising a dozen counties, experienced some overlapping of these two cultural orientations. Some cities like Springfield were founded and initially dominated by upland southerners, while nearby villages born a decade later were predominantly Yankee. Vestiges of these different social strains became part of the history and folklore of each such community.

Black settlement antedated statehood by a century. Slaves first appeared in the area during the French era, in the early 1700s. Blacks grew to become both a substantial element in the social fabric and a chronic test of the state's democratic practices. Reconciling the ideals of an open society with its racist realities has been for Illinoisans an especially acute version of the "American dilemma" portrayed a half century ago by Gunnar Myrdal.

Interracial issues and tensions took root in Illinois as soon as blacks took residence. The Northwest Ordinance of 1787 banned slavery in the territory but failed to prohibit its surrogate, registered servitude. Thus began a charade of symbol versus substance that for two centuries has been an emblem of Illinois race relations. The state's first six governors all were slaveowners at one time, and several had registered Negro servants while in office. The new state's original charter

(1818) sustained this double standard, and a slave code enacted the next year imposed harsher constraints and penalties on blacks than similar laws in many southern states. Several thousand Kentucky and Tennessee slaves were leased to work in the lucrative salt wells near Shawneetown.

Intense proslavery views and practices were common among the southern white migrants who swarmed into Egypt and central Illinois in the early decades of the nineteenth century. Evidence of their numbers and determination surfaced in a heated and nearly successful drive to legalize slavery by amendment to the state constitution. The statewide referendum enlisted ardent support, failing in the end because of couragcous resistance by Governor Edward Coles, a former Virginia slaveowner who had grown to despise the institution.

As Illinois welcomed Yankee newcomers and as the national crisis over slavery grew, the state experienced sharper debate and even violence over racial issues. Pioneering abolitionist Elijah P. Lovejoy, who used the pages of his Alton newspaper to attack slavery, was murdered in 1837 by an angry mob of southern sympathizers; his brother Owen espoused the cause during several terms in Congress. In southern Illinois counties free Negroes as well as runaway slaves were fair game. One fugitive reportedly surrendered because four days of fear and threat in Cairo were worse than four years of bondage. The state constitution and statutes denied full citizenship to blacks, and a law enacted in 1853 attempted to prohibit freedmen from moving to Illinois. Copperhead sentiment was a potent minority voice during the Civil War, and a referendum in 1862 revealed overwhelming popular sentiment against Negro suffrage.

The ambivalence, complexity, and contradiction so characteristic of antebellum Illinois views on slavery and race found their supreme embodiment in the life and work of Abraham Lincoln, the state's most famous citizen. Lincoln's ambiguous and changing positions on slavery, Negro rights, abolition, racial differences, and the fate of freedmen are well documented elsewhere. He despised slavery but was willing to permit its survival as the price of union. No disciple of racial equality or social integration, he nevertheless foresaw the advent and justice of civil rights. As senatorial and presidential candidate and later as chief executive, he walked a racial tightrope that at times linked him with racist sentiments common to southern Illinois and at other times resembled abolitionist and egalitarian views associated with Yankee residents farther north. Thus Lincoln epitomized the cacophony of Illinois voices on racial matters, though he also displayed a humanitarian capacity for progressive change.

Illinois became an important destination in the post–Civil War Negro exodus to northern cities. Convenient travel routes, the lure of new mining and factory jobs, and perhaps the lingering image of

Lincoln the Great Emancipator combined to draw a disproportionate share of restless blacks to the state.

The swelling ranks of Negro Illinoisans typically realized a marginal improvement in their economic prospects at the price of hostility and segregation in their social relations. Fueling the existing interracial tension was a practice among mine and factory proprietors to recruit unskilled southern blacks as strikebreakers. It is emblematic rather than coincidental that three of the nation's earliest and worst urban race riots occurred in Illinois. Lincoln's hometown of Springfield erupted in a week of violence in the summer of 1908. At that time the capital city had the state's largest share of black residents. Several lynchings, along with assaults and massive property destruction, left no doubt about the depth of racist feelings. Nine years later another Negro population center, East St. Louis, experienced even bloodier mayhem when dozens of blacks died, some the victims of mob atrocities. In the summer of 1919 it was Chicago's turn when a lakefront incident ignited a week of violence that left twenty-three blacks dead and hundreds injured.

In the years since these outbreaks the black population has continued to grow. Today blacks comprise 12 percent of the population but are unevenly distributed around the state. Some counties have scarcely any blacks while Chicago's proportion is 40 percent. For fifty years the Illinois congressional delegation has included at least one Negro. Today Chicago has a black mayor, many large and successful minority businesses, and the nationwide headquarters of PUSH (People United to Save Humanity), led by Jesse Jackson. Among other prominent black Illinoisans are state comptroller Roland Burris, modern dance pioneer Katherine Dunham, and poet Gwendolyn Brooks.

Generally milder forms of racial stress have prevailed in the past seventy years. Contemporary evidence of the state's dissonance on racial matters is most conspicuous in Chicago. The same city that houses over one million black citizens who include international celebrities in politics, commerce, and the arts also displays unmatched levels of segregation in housing and schooling. Bitter racial divisions pervade municipal politics and neighborhood discourse; some of modern America's ugliest racial incidents have occurred in Cicero and other white enclaves. Thus the double standard survives as a constant in Illinois race relations. There is some irony in the fact that it was an Illinois governor, Otto Kerner, whose presidential Commission on Civil Disorders in 1968 concluded, "Our Nation is moving toward two societies, one black, one white—separate and unequal."[16]

Blacks are not the only social group to have encountered isolation and hostility in modern Chicago. It was largely in response to the plight of recent immigrants that Jane Addams founded Hull House on Halsted Street in 1889. Educational and social programs there sought to ease the cultural adjustment and ameliorate the harsh living conditions of foreign-born residents. Ethnic feelings and antipathies reached fever pitch during World War I, when Balkan émigrés and refugees demonstrated periodically for their respective national causes. In more recent years Jewish survivors of the Holocaust rediscovered virulent anti-Semitism when an American Nazi splinter group sought to march against them in their adopted hometown of Skokie, just north of the city limits. Generational change and acculturation have somewhat softened the vividness of Chicago's polyglot makeup. But race and ethnicity continue to exercise powerful influence from the neighborhoods to city hall.

Pluralism and factionalism thus have been staples of the Illinois experience just as they have helped shape the nation's history. Woven of many different threads, the state's social fabric has managed to remain intact despite occasional stretching and tearing that threaten its fragile integrity. In this respect, too, it resembles the national whole.

Government and politics in Illinois are big business. They also reflect the vivid sectional and factional divisions that have characterized the state's social makeup. Notorious for the flagrant exercise of clout, the abuse of patronage, and some of American political history's most entertaining skulduggery, Illinoisans also have occasionally joined the vanguard of progressive reform. These traits plus some demographic facts probably account for the remarkable partisan balance in modern Illinois politics, and also for the state's extraordinary congruence with national election results.

Government is big in Illinois because there is so much of it. Until recently the state legislature swelled with 236 elected representatives and senators, an unusually high number. Meeting in annual rather than biennial sessions, it is nearly always busy, with thousands of bills crowding its agenda.

Moreover, Illinois enjoys the dubious honor of having more units of local government than any other state. There are 102 counties, 1,300 cities and villages, 1,400 townships, and 1,000 school districts. Overlapping and often battling these basic entities are some 2,500 special governmental districts responsible for libraries, fire protection, airports, colleges, parks, convention centers, water, sanitation, mass transit, and "mosquito abatement." It would appear that the standard response of Illinoisans to a civic task is not just to let government do it, but to create a government to do it.

This proliferation is not surprising in light of the state's heritage of sectionalism, factionalism, and partisan rivalries. Political scientist Daniel Elazar selected Illinois as a microcosm because it accommodated all three of the distinct political cultures—the individualistic, the moralistic, and the traditionalistic—that have blended to produce the American political system. The 400-mile-long state's location astride the principal migratory avenues of the early nineteenth century yielded a healthy transplant of each culture. Traditionalists inhabiting the southern counties emphasized loyalty and hierarchy in their politics and resisted such reform causes as abolition and public education. Moralists were chiefly Yankee and Scandinavian residents of the northern counties who embraced reform efforts for public betterment. Individualists (Richard Jensen combines them with moralists and labels both as "modernizers") were pragmatic and ambitious migrants from the mid-Atlantic states who wanted government to operate like and for business.[17]

The interplay of these three cultures explains not only the shifting agenda of Illinois politics but also the partisan and sectional alignments regarding this agenda. Slavery, public education, internal improvements, prohibition, legislative apportionment, and welfare policy have been reliable litmus tests for such alignments. Sectional differences over slavery gave Democrats the edge over Whigs. Between the Civil War and the Great Depression Republicans generally had the advantage through strength in the northern and central counties plus successful resistance to reapportionment. The New Deal produced another rearrangement, with Democratic strength growing in Chicago and downstate urban centers. Subsequent suburban growth and court-mandated apportionment altered the political equation yet again, producing three approximately equal voting blocs: an overwhelmingly Democratic Chicago and an equally Republican five-county "collar" around the city, which compete for support with a downstate swing region that has pockets of strength for each party. Further complicating this tripartite competition are a popular trend toward voter independence and ticket-splitting, deep rifts among Democrats in Chicago, and certain issues like ERA and regional mass transit that defy and divide party loyalties.

Lurking behind much of this intra- and interparty struggle has been the Illinois tradition of interest-group politics. An unusually diverse economy has given rise to such competing interests as agriculture (small and large scale), finance, organized labor, shipping, merchandising, and manufacturing. Similarly, the cultural mosaic of ethnic, religious, and racial loyalties often overrode party or sectional positions.

For more than a century the Illinois constitution exerted further influence on this complex political drama. The 1870 charter experimented with cumulative voting by creating multimember legislative districts and permitting voters to assign their three votes to one, two, or three candidates. This interesting scheme assured minority representation in even the most lopsided districts and thus produced

unorthodox legislative personalities and complicated intraparty deal-
ings. Abandoned in 1981, cumulative voting nevertheless exerted a
long-standing and important influence on state politics.

Close party balance is a natural consequence of Illinois's political
culture. Party control of the governor's office seesawed eight times
in the half century that began in the Great Depression. During the
same period the state's U.S. Senate seats almost always were divided
between the two parties. Another indicator of equilibrium is popular
vote for congressional candidates. Out of more than nineteen million
votes cast for Illinois congressional candidates between 1972 and
1980, there was a slender twenty-thousand-vote difference between
the Democratic and Republican totals. There are, of course, some
legislative districts that are dependably Democratic or Republican,
but overall the two major parties remain closely balanced; polls of
the state's registered voters report that approximately 30 percent
identify themselves as Democrats and 30 percent as Republicans.

As Illinois goes, so goes the nation. Voter presidential preferences
have paralleled the national results to a remarkable degree for a long
time. In thirty-two presidential elections since 1860 Illinoisans have
agreed with American voters in all but three instances (1884, 1916,
1976). Moreover, the specific popular vote percentages also have
closely corresponded to national returns. The mean Democratic percentages between 1870 and 1972, for example, show only 2.1 points
difference between Illinois and U.S. returns. This congruence places
Illinois at or near the top among all states and thus qualifies it as a
national political bellwether.

It is easier to document this close correlation than to explain it.
It is at least plausible, however, that the state's central location, mixed
economy, heterogeneous society, and crossroads function have made
it peculiarly susceptible to the separate regional and cultural trends
that create the ebb and flow of national political moods. If that is the
case, then Illinois is a political bellwether because it is a political
microcosm.

Political practice in the land of Lincoln is the source of constant
amusement to some and embarrassment to others. Politics is an un-
yielding preoccupation for hordes of party regulars and for many other
citizens as well. It is best known for certain qualities: the exercise of
power (or "clout"), a decided preference for the spoils system, and
a colorful heritage of corruption and malfeasance. The state's unsa-
vory political reputation may be slightly exaggerated, but it is not
basically inaccurate.

Downstate Illinoisans prefer to blame the state's image on Chicago
and Cook County. It is true that clout, patronage, and occasional scandal are conspicuous traits in the modern history of Chicago, but they
existed in Illinois politics long before Mayor Richard Daley's time,

and they are as indigenous downstate as in the big city. Put simply, they constitute the way Illinoisans habitually perform the public's business.

Among heartland states Illinois belongs in the southern tier, where politics is oriented more to patronage and power considerations than issues or ideology. One political scientist has questioned whether any state matches its reliance on money and jobs for political purposes. Others have asserted that most Illinois public officials are motivated by patronage and personal considerations rather than notions about public service. Even within the state's merit civil service system there are sufficient loopholes to permit widespread patronage. Nearly every state elective post, from governor and attorney general to supreme court justice, has been tarnished by criminal conviction or dishonorable resignation.

In such a pervasive statewide system Chicago is but the ultimate expression, not the sole source. For fifty years a powerful Democratic organization exercised tight municipal control, which under Mayor Daley reached a zenith of power and success. Authoritarian and hierarchical, it prospered by dispensing favors and obligations among the thousands of party faithful whose livelihoods depended on it. Ward leaders, each with perhaps five hundred patronage jobs to award, exercised a crucial intermediate role between the party chief and the rank and file. Operating with the efficiency of a successful business and the authority of a well-disciplined army, it not only governed Chicago but also protected its interests among civic leaders and state officials. Former Senator and gubernatorial candidate Adlai Stevenson III, who alternately quarreled and allied with it, described the Daley organization as "a feudal system that rewards mediocrity or worse, with jobs for the blind party faithful, special favors for business, and ineffectual civil service."[18]

During the 1970s a series of embarrassments and setbacks combined to weaken the Chicago Democratic organization. Daley's death in 1976 was a crippling blow. Racial and factional divisions have followed, leaving the machine a warring parody of its former majesty.

With such a heritage it seems almost a miracle that Illinois political history also boasts periodic episodes of achievement, reform, and enlightened statecraft. The state's pantheon of nationally recognized public officials compares creditably with other states: Abraham Lincoln, Stephen A. Douglas, Frank Lowden, Adlai E. Stevenson, Paul Douglas, and Everett Dirksen. During the late nineteenth and early twentieth centuries Illinois was unusually fertile territory for third-party and other reform efforts, from antimonopolists and prohibitionists to socialists. Progressive ferment took root among Illinois politicians both in Springfield and Washington, where Prairie State legislators joined the vanguard favoring woman suffrage, the federal income tax, prohibition, and the direct election of senators. Even wicked Chicago at the turn of the century boasted a remarkable band of high-minded reformers and pathbreakers in diverse fields, including Clarence Darrow, John Peter Altgeld, Jane Addams, Florence Kelley, John Dewey, Thorstein Veblen, and Theodore Dreiser.

One instance of this prouder face of Illinois politics is the state's historic role in the women's rights movement. Illinois women were among the first outside New England and New York to organize for suffrage. Reinforced by parallel crusades for abolition, temperance, and women's educational opportunity, they staged a convention in 1869 that gave birth to the Illinois Woman Suffrage Association. Soon this organization of largely middle-class and Chicago-area disciples was operating with as much energy and effect as its eastern precursors.

The suffrage campaign benefited by example and support from several celebrated Illinois women of high achievement. Jane Addams was the best known and closest ally. Myra Bradwell also inspired women through her long struggle to pass the bar and her national reputation as a legal reporter and reformer. Heroine to a different following was the legendary Mary ("Mother") Jones, who actively participated in nearly every major labor struggle from the 1877 railroad strikes through the miner, steel, and garment worker clashes of the early 1900s.

The cumulative effect of these efforts was an Illinois landmark, the 1913 Presidential and Municipal Suffrage Act, which granted women the vote under broad if selective terms. Following the more progressive models adopted in western states, it earned Illinois the honor of being the first major urban-industrial state and the first state east of the Mississippi to enact woman suffrage. Interestingly, Illinois continued to be an important women's rights battleground. Pioneering feminist Betty Friedan came from Peoria, and arch-opponent Phyllis Schlafly exercises leadership from her home base in Alton. Illinois and its capitol at Springfield were the focus of rallies and counter-rallies during the tortuous battle for ratification of the Equal Rights Amendment. Between 1976 and 1982 massive demonstrations, vigils, civil disobedience, and a six-week fast were reminders of the contest's intensity. It is ironic but altogether consistent with the state's crazy-quilt history that Illinois has been both a pioneer in woman suffrage and a fatal obstruction in women's rights.

Public support for education was a second arena of notable progressive action. In the state's early years public education was one of the issues that divided traditionalist skeptics in the south from their modernist neighbors to the north. Consequently Illinois was slow to adopt compulsory attendance laws or provide generous levels of state support. The first important public school legislation was enacted in

1855; after that progress came more readily. The state's 1970 constitution codified decades of piecemeal action by mandating efficient and high-quality public education for all Illinoisans. It also assigned primary financial responsibility to state government. School consolidation, however, remained a nagging issue. As late as 1942 there were twelve thousand separate school districts in Illinois, a national high. Some counties had more school board members than teachers, and many schools were decrepit, ill-equipped, and poorly staffed. Persistent effort plus the lure of increased state aid cut the number in half by 1948, and it has moved steadily downward thereafter.

By most measures Illinois colleges and universities are a major state asset. As early as 1840 there were a dozen struggling colleges. In the years since, Illinois has developed a strong system of both private and public institutions. At the apex are celebrated universities like Chicago, Illinois, and Northwestern. A dozen robust public universities compete for students with an even larger number of private liberal arts colleges. Following World War II the state established a comprehensive community college system of more than forty institutions. Quality higher education, including advanced and professional studies, is thus widely available throughout the state and at reasonable cost.

The colorful history, partisan flavor, and mixed performance of Illinois government are a faithful expression in political terms of the state's heterogeneity and representativeness. Foreign visitors who pause respectfully at the Lincoln tomb in Springfield and then read of statehouse shenanigans a few blocks away are thereby discovering the state's checkered political life. They also are getting an authentic glimpse of the entire nation's struggle with practical democracy.

"Not without thy wondrous story, can be writ the nation's glory, Illinois . . . Illinois." Such is the claim in the state song, and such is the theme of this essay. The state's very diversity may well defy simple description but nevertheless capture the national experience. To a singular degree among its sister states Illinois embraces the complexity, the confusion, and the conflict of the United States. It is, as noted elsewhere,

> a state half urban, half rural; half northern, half southern; half foreign, half native. It is the state of Adlai Stevenson and the *Chicago Tribune*, Al Capone and Clarence Darrow.

Such diversity helps make Illinois "a passionately political state," with the major parties always contending for advantage and with abolitionists battling copperheads, workers striking the Pullman Company, feminists demonstrating alongside STOP ERA, and Black Power versus the Ku Klux Klan.

Illinois is the Chicago symphony and "Solidarity Forever"; the smell of Lincolnburgers and Portuguese pastry; it is . . . the sounds of a loop El train, a coal mine tipple, the grunting of hogs, the sonorous phrases of Everett Dirksen, the gunshots of violence. It is wooded beauty, hills that roll, prairies that hypnotize, a river that is history; square farm houses, and atomic reactors. It is people who were blighted, men and women who healed them; the desperately poor, the exceedingly rich; reapers and magnolias, writers and musicians; humanitarians and hoodlums; of every color and origin, no two the same, no one different; people, places. That is Illinois, her culture, her legacy.[19]

N O T E S

The author acknowledges the assistance of many people, notably Margie Towery, Robert Howard, James Krohe, and Linda Jett, in developing this essay.

1. Federal Writers' Project, *Illinois: A Descriptive and Historical Guide* (Chicago, 1939), 5.

2. Daniel J. Elazar, *Cities of the Prairie: The Metropolitan Frontier and American Politics* (New York, 1970), 282.

3. Federal Writers' Project, *Illinois*, 6.

4. Ibid., 6, 7; Jane Hood, "Inventing Illinois," *Humanities* 7, no. 1 (Winter 1986), 3–5; Elazar, *Cities of the Prairie*, 20; Asa Baber, "Writing in the Heartland," *Illinois Issues* (September 1984), 24–27; Neal R. Peirce and John Keefe, *The Great Lakes States of America* (New York, 1980), 102.

5. Quoted by permission of the author. Dave Etter, "Henry Lichenwalner: Living in the Middle," *West of Chicago* (Peoria, Ill., 1981), 1.

6. Baber, "Writing in the Heartland," 25–26.

7. Quoted in John Bartlow Martin, *Adlai Stevenson of Illinois* (Garden City, N.Y., 1976), 585.

8. Mark Wyman, *Immigrants in the Valley: Irish, Germans, and Americans in the Upper Mississippi Country, 1830–1860* (Chicago, 1984), 2; Robert C. Bray, *Rediscoveries: Literature and Place in Illinois* (Urbana, Ill., 1982), 14.

9. Wyman, *Immigrants in the Valley*, 3–4; John J. Murray, ed., *The Heritage of the Middle West* (Norman, Okla., 1958), 33.

10. Bray, *Rediscoveries*, 69; Robert B. Riley, "Square to the Road, Hogs to the East," *Illinois Issues* (July 1985), 26.

11. Riley, "Square to the Road," 25.

12. Quoted in Frederick Gutheim, ed., *In the Cause of Architecture, Frank Lloyd Wright* (New York, 1975), 237.

13. Walter Havighurst, *Land of Promise: The Story of the Northwest Territory* (New York, 1946), 203–4.

14. Melvin G. Holli and Peter d'A. Jones, eds., *The Ethnic Frontier: Group Survival in Chicago and the Midwest* (Grand Rapids, Mich., 1977), 9.

15. Quoted in Dan Elbert Clark, *The Middle West in American History* (New York, 1966), 19.

16. The National Advisory Commission on Civil Disorders, *Report* (Washington, D.C., 1968), 1.

17. Richard J. Jensen, *Illinois: A Bicentennial History* (New York, 1978), 34.

18. Peirce and Keefe, *The Great Lakes States of America*, 40.
19. John Keiser, *Illinois Vignettes* (Springfield, Ill., 1977), ii–iii, 2.

BIBLIOGRAPHY

Illinois is as rich in historical attention as it is in history. General and specialized studies cover every cranny of its past. To date, however, it lacks any comprehensive guide to sources. The *Illinois Historical Journal* (formerly the *Journal of the Illinois State Historical Society*) offers book reviews and research notes in addition to its articles.

A good place to begin is with two single-volume studies that are very different in purpose and tone. Robert P. Howard, *Illinois: A History of the Prairie State* (Grand Rapids, Mich., 1972), is a richly detailed and well-informed narrative account that properly remains first on any list. Much shorter, more analytical, and more controversial is Richard J. Jensen, *Illinois: A Bicentennial History* (New York, 1978).

Two recently published collections also merit special attention. One is Roger D. Bridges and Rodney O. Davis, eds., *Illinois: Its History and Legacy* (St. Louis, 1984), which offers eighteen essays on various topics. The other is Ronald E. Nelson, ed., *Illinois: Land and Life in the Prairie State* (Dubuque, Iowa, 1978), which is particularly useful on natural history and geographical topics. Another general volume that has remained useful for nearly fifty years is Federal Writers' Project, *Illinois: A Descriptive and Historical Guide* (Chicago, 1939).

Statehood anniversaries have spawned two multivolume efforts at historical stocktaking. One is *The Centennial History of Illinois*, under the general editorship of Clarence Alvord. Its first three titles, which are still useful, include Clarence W. Alvord, *The Illinois Country, 1673–1818*; Theodore C. Pease, *The Frontier State, 1818–1848*; and Arthur C. Cole, *The Era of the Civil War, 1848–1870* (Springfield, Ill., 1917–20). Two volumes in a sesquicentennial series have appeared: John H. Keiser, *Building for the Centuries: Illinois 1865 to 1898* (Urbana, Ill., 1977), and Donald F. Tingley, *The Structuring of a State: The History of Illinois, 1899 to 1928* (Urbana, 1980).

Politics is a favorite among the more specialized histories. One major contribution is a continuing series, Daniel J. Elazar, *Cities of the Prairie: The Metropolitan Frontier and American Politics* (New York, 1970), and Elazar et al., *Cities of the Prairie Revisited: The Closing of the Metropolitan Frontier* (Lincoln, Nebr., 1986). Similar in their comparative and ethnoreligious approach are Paul Kleppner, *The Cross of Culture: A Social Analysis of Midwestern Politics, 1850–1900* (New York, 1970), and Richard J. Jensen, *The Winning of the Midwest: Social and Political Conflict, 1888–1896* (Chicago, 1971). Also revealing is James Przybylski, "As Goes Illinois . . . The State as a Political Microcosm of the Nation," in *Illinois Government Research* (Urbana, Ill., 1976).

In economic history the best work has dealt with agriculture, though there also are many good articles on labor. For the former, see Allan G. Bogue, *From Prairie to Corn Belt: Farming on the Illinois and Iowa Prairies in the 19th Century* (Chicago, 1963), and Margaret Beattie Bogue, *Patterns from the Sod: Land Use and Tenure in the Grand Prairie, 1850–1900*, vol. 34, in *Transactions of the Illinois State Historical Library* (Springfield, Ill., 1959). Particularly helpful for comparative purposes is Robert N. Schoeplein and

Hugh T. Connelly, "The Illinois Economy: A Microcosm of the United States?" in *Illinois Government Research* (Urbana, 1975).

The state's social complexion receives thoughtful attention in several studies. Excellent on racism in the nineteenth century is V. Jacques Voegeli, *Free but Not Equal: The Midwest and the Negro during the Civil War* (Chicago, 1967). For ethnic history during the same period, see Mark Wyman, *Immigrants in the Valley: Irish, Germans and Americans in the Upper Mississippi Country, 1830–1860* (Chicago, 1984). Melvin G. Holli and Peter d'A. Jones have coedited two interesting collections: *The Ethnic Frontier: Group Survival in Chicago and the Midwest* (Grand Rapids, 1977), and *Ethnic Chicago*, rev. ed. (Grand Rapids, 1984).

For the arts and letters a key reference is Robert C. Bray, *Rediscoveries: Literature and Place in Illinois* (Urbana, 1982). Chicago's literary flowering in the early 1900s is the subject of Bernard I. Duffey, *The Chicago Renaissance in American Letters: A Critical History* (Lansing, Mich., 1954). On architectural matters, see H. Allen Brooks, *The Prairie School: Frank Lloyd Wright and His Midwest Contemporaries* (Toronto, 1972).

Biographies too numerous to mention trace the lives of such notable Illinoisans as Abraham Lincoln, Stephen A. Douglas, Adlai E. Stevenson, Richard J. Daley, Clarence Darrow, Frank Lloyd Wright, Samuel Insull, Edgar Lee Masters, and others. One interesting collective portrait is Ray Ginger, *Altgeld's America, 1890–1905: The Lincoln Ideal Versus Changing Realities* (New York, 1958).

Peter T. Harstad

INDIANA

and the Art of Adjustment

THE REPORTER KNEW full well that the top qualifying speed for the 1986 Indianapolis 500 was 216.828 miles per hour. Yet he asked fifth-generation Indianan Thomas Binford, chief steward of the Indianapolis Motor Speedway, whether speeds of three hundred miles per hour were attainable at the two-and-a-half mile track. "It depends," Binford replied, "upon whether the technology of safety can keep up with the technology of speed."[1]

Indianans think instinctively about the interplay and adjustment of forces and have developed traditions, skills, and mental processes for doing so—even a dialect for expressing themselves. The purpose here is to explore this theme in order to understand Indiana, its role in the American heartland, and its place in the nation. No claim of uniqueness is advanced to explain why or to what ends Indianans adjust social, economic, and political forces or to what ends. Yet, some patterning has developed in the way people of the state go about the process, particularly when they are acting collectively and when they must answer to the public.

The Indianapolis 500 involves the interplay of natural, technological, and human complexities within a defined (but not a controlled) environment. There are both similarities and differences between Indiana's premier sports event and the course of its history.

LAKE MICHIGAN

M I C H I G A N

I L L I N O I S

O H I O

K E N T U C K Y

INDIANA

Miles 0 10 20 30 40

⭐ State Capital

Like the 500, the state's history involves a specific environment—
Indiana as it has been defined since statehood. But there is no track
with an assigned direction for historical developments to run upon.
George Rapp of Harmony and Robert Owen, who bought out the
Harmonists, may have tried to establish tracks for their followers, but
experiments wherein adults are expected to proceed in prescribed
ways, within highly structured environments, generally have not fared
well in this state or nation. Moreover, Indiana history is a continuum
with many more variables than any automobile race. Despite its limitations, the race metaphor will be used occasionally in the ensuing
discussion.

States are difficult to explain to American schoolchildren, who
take them for granted, and they baffle foreign visitors, who have
difficulty understanding that they are not subdivisions of the national
government. What are the American states? A century ago an Englishman, James Bryce, traveled and studied in this country to answer
this question and related ones. At the outset of his two-volume *American Commonwealth*, Bryce likened the nation and the states to a large
building erected over a number of smaller ones as, had been the case
with the Church of the Holy Sepulchre at Jerusalem. "First the soil
is covered by a number of small shrines and chapels, built at different
times and in different styles of architecture, each complete in itself.
Then over them and including them . . . is reared a new pile with its
own loftier roof, its own walls, which may perhaps rest on and incorporate the walls of the older shrines, its own internal plan."[2] The
simile works well enough for the original thirteen states, but its chro-
nology is incorrect for Indiana and the other states of the heartland.
Here the foundation of the Union and much of its superstructure
predate the smaller units—a basic consideration in understanding nationalism in the Midwest. Indianans may, at times, be smug, but they
do not think of their state as "complete in itself."

When Bryce wrote, the states were unequivocally within the Union
and "subordinate to it." The Civil War had settled that. Yet Bryce
saw the Union as "more than an aggregate of States," and the states
as "more than parts of the Union." He perceived "two loyalties, two
patriotisms," with the lesser jealous of the greater. "There are two
governments, covering the same ground, commanding, with equally
direct authority, the obedience of the same citizen." Understanding
this double organization was, for Bryce, the "first and indispensable"
step in understanding American institutions (I, 14–15).

In addition to functioning as political institutions "the states have
cultures," insists Jon Margolis. In the epigrammatic world of popular
culture, "Iowa is clean and wholesome. Wyoming is empty. Oregon
is snobbish and proud of it. Rhode Island is full of larceny. Pennsylvania is tough. Ohio only thinks it is. North Dakota, perhaps, does

not exist." Margolis searches for reasons for contrasting traits of some neighboring states. "Wisconsin is known for clean and open politics. Illinois isn't." The explanation may relate to origins, he suggests; "perhaps Scandinavians simply will not tolerate certain practices the Irish find acceptable, even admirable."[3]

Whether tongue-in-cheek or not, the latter observation leads to the truism that the culture that emerges in a state is, in large measure, determined by its people. Attention will therefore be devoted here to how Indianans have adjusted to one another, to their environment, and to the main forces they have confronted. In counterpoint, the Indiana environment has responded to its inhabitants and some inanimate forces have been modified by people. To paraphrase Ralph Waldo Emerson, "things" have not always been in the saddle and do not always ride mankind.

Using the classic definition of thirty years per generation, six generations have lived in Indiana since statehood. The turn of the century is therefore the midpoint of Indiana history and the fulcrum for this chapter. Third-generation Indianans were then in leadership roles. Apprehensive of what the new century would bring, old-line Indianans tended to look to the past for virtue and stability. Their forebears had built farms and towns, had fought Indians and secessionists, and had founded Indiana's basic institutions. At least in retrospect, their purposes seemed resolute and clear.

By 1900 some members of old-line families were accumulating wealth and some had the leisure and inclination to reflect. Elements of historical and cultural consciousness were congealing. The Indiana Historical Society, long dormant, emerged as a viable cultural institution. That, Lana Ruegamer explains, "coincided with and was part of a wider flowering of midwestern letters in which Hoosier literati and Indianapolis played a prominent part." A "golden age" of Indiana literature resulted, featuring such luminaries as James Whitcomb Riley, Meredith Nicholson, and Booth Tarkington. Not widely known beyond the state, historians William H. English, Daniel Wait Howe, and Jacob Piatt Dunn, Jr., studied the Indiana past and wrote about it. What motivated these turn-of-the-century writers and historians? According to Ruegamer, it was the perception that rural ways were changing and that "something valuable and definitively Hoosier was disappearing in the wake of the dramatic new prosperity fostered by the natural gas boom and the concomitant forces of urbanization and industrialization."[4]

Thomas R. Marshall (1854–1925) is a genial guide to the middle period of Indiana history. Master politician, governor, raconteur of Indiana history, and interpreter of its culture, he was also influenced by what happened elsewhere in the heartland. Moreover, he went on to play a role on the national scene.

Born in North Manchester, Marshall was a third-generation Indianan whose paternal grandfather arrived from Virginia in 1817. Whether the latter "belonged to the first families, the second families, was just well spoken of, or was downright white trash," Marshall could not determine.[5] The family had manumitted the few slaves they had owned in the Old Dominion, but a great-uncle had scurried off to Missouri with some of the blacks before they knew they were free. On the eve of the Civil War this relative owned a plantation and three hundred slaves. "God does not pay at the end of every week," Marshall inserted at this point in his recollections, "but He pays" (19). Hard-working people, the Indiana Marshalls made the most of their opportunities. Thomas's father became a doctor.

His maternal ancestors, Pennsylvanians who came to Indiana via Ohio, were Presbyterians. "That does not necessarily make a good man," Marshall quipped, "but it makes a religious one" (14). He might have added that in the Indiana setting it also tends to make a political man with a "trustee" disposition. Although the Presbyterian church has never attracted a large percentage of Indianans, its members tend to seek and be elected to public office out of all proportion to their numbers. In state General Assemblies from 1816 to 1851, for example, Presbyterians ranked second only to Methodists (who consistently ranked first), and they continued this ranking until they were nosed out by Roman Catholics in 1931. Since then, Presbyterians have stood third on the list.[6] In searching for reasons for the persistence of Presbyterian political strength one would do well to examine the missions, roles, and alumni of two colleges founded early by members of this denomination: Hanover on the Ohio River (1827) and Wabash at Crawfordsville (1832).

Malaria plagued Indiana in the 1850s. Marshall spun a yarn in which this disease explained why he became a Democrat. One man of "domineering character and predatory wealth" lived in North Manchester, Marshall wrote. When summer came and malaria seized the townspeople, this man took sick with third-day ague. "He was an aristocrat. The rest of us shook every other day. We were democrats" (25).

For reasons of health, the Marshalls went west to Illinois when Thomas was a toddler and stayed long enough for the elder Marshall to take his son to a political debate at Freeport in 1858. A "suggestive memory" led Thomas to believe that he "sat on Lincoln's lap while Douglas was talking, and on Douglas' lap while Lincoln was talking." Although the youthful Marshall liked "the tall man," it pleased the aged raconteur to think that "something of the love of Lincoln and of Douglas for the Union, the constitution and the rights of the common man flowed into my childish veins" (52–53).

Again for reasons of health, the family moved to Kansas (but stayed only long enough to conclude that it was "a dark and bloody ground"), then to Missouri (where Dr. Marshall got into a scrape with a secessionist), and finally returned to Indiana. Thomas attended public schools and then went off to Wabash College. He graduated with honors, studied law under a judge in Fort Wayne, and settled down to thirty years of practicing law in Columbia City. Although he took an active interest in the Democratic party, Marshall refused to run for Congress on grounds that he might be elected, then hinted that he would like to be governor.

In 1908 the Democratic party nominated Marshall for governor and he was duly elected. Four years in this office gave him perspective on the state and its people. He agreed with those who said that "the Hoosier is and always will be different from other people" and illustrated what he observed to be a common characteristic of Indianans: self-consciousness. He wrote that some people were sitting in a New York club telling stories about their backgrounds. One man gazed into the fireplace while one after another spoke. At last someone asked him where he came from. "I came from Indiana," he replied. "Now, dog-gone you, laugh!" (33).

Marshall observed that "the Hoosier did not come from another planet, nor even from another continent." In asserting that the "vast majority of them, up to 1850, came from the older states of the Union," he is in agreement with the census returns and with modern scholarship. Whereas James Bryce observed two sets of loyalties in the United States, Marshall saw Indiana as two states with the National Road (U.S. 40) as the dividing line between them: "South of that line the vast majority of people who came in were from Virginia, the Carolinas and Kentucky." Largely "southern in thought," Indiana below the National Road "was quite inclined to let well enough alone," Marshall concluded. This attitude carried implications for education. One of the few exceptions to the mellowness of Marshall's published recollections is his indictment: "There is, or was, in a graveyard in southern Indiana, a tombstone bearing the inscription, 'Here lies the enemy of the Public School System of Indiana'" (34–36).

In contrast, northern Indiana "was very largely settled by New Englanders, New Yorkers, Pennsylvanians, people from Ohio, to which were added, after the Revolution of 1848, vast numbers of liberty-loving Germans, who came with Carl Schurz to this country." Indiana above the National Road "was always experimenting" (35–36). Caleb Mills, father of the common school system in Indiana, was Marshall's hero. A native of New Hampshire and an indefatigable advocate of causes to enlighten and uplift, Mills taught Marshall Greek at Wabash College.

Marshall, who labeled the midcentury arrivals from Germany as "sturdy, industrious, honest and honorable," concluded that Indianans had drafted the constitution of 1851 to make it easy for these people to become citizens and to vote. Suspicious of the twentieth-century immigrants from eastern Europe who streamed into the industrial region of northwest Indiana and partisan enough to want to reserve the stereotype image of these newcomers being herded to polling places to vote for Democrats, Marshall claimed that twenty-seven hundred men who had passed through Ellis Island in the spring of 1908 voted illegally and almost unanimously for Republicans that fall at Gary. The "ignorant, hungry horde" somehow came to believe that by voting for Taft they were voting for president of the steel works in Gary! Later in life, Marshall confessed that he ought to have been more patient with the "hundred tribes and tongues" that went into the making of this new city. He even retracted a gubernatorial statement that it would "afford me very great relief if some night Gary would slip into Lake Michigan" (36, 177, 185).

One area where Marshall did not relent was in his criticism of United States Steel Corporation for acting high-handedly, and on one occasion even confiscating a trainload of coal that it did not own. Corporate existence troubled America, he observed: "It seems to be unable to dissociate itself from the idea that it possesses sovereign power" (185).

As governor, Marshall worked to reverse such trends. Archaic labor laws and the machinery of state government needed adjustment to the realities of twentieth-century industrialism and urban life. Marshall concluded that the 1851 constitution was an obstacle to progress. When Democrats gained majorities in both houses of the General Assembly in 1911, he made his move. Since amending the constitution was exceedingly difficult, he proposed an entirely new one. Bills embodying much of the reform thought of the day (including authority to institute the initiative, referendum, and recall) passed both houses with ease. Did the General Assembly have the power to draft a new constitution and to submit it to the people? Negative answers came back from the Circuit Court of Marion County and from the Indiana Supreme Court. The United States Supreme Court ruled that it had no jurisdiction in the matter; therefore the decision of the Indiana Supreme Court held.

Indianans' penchant for gradualism had surfaced and had caught off guard a progressive governor who had been moving too fast for his own political safety. Marshall could not steer around the impasse imposed by the courts and closed out his statehouse career convinced that reform must continue "to avoid socialism," but with a reputation as a "liberal with the brakes on."[7] In 1912 Marshall's name came before the Democratic national convention as Indiana's favorite son for president. The nomination went to Woodrow Wilson with Marshall as his running mate. The two were elected that year and reelected in 1916. Within the range of opportunities provided by the vice-presidency, Marshall did quite well as an adjuster of forces on the national level and may have been the most popular vice-president the country has ever had.

Had Marshall countenanced the idea, he might have taken over as president after Wilson became ill and unable to function. No communications issued from President Wilson's sickroom when the Treaty of Versailles, including the League of Nations, was hanging in the balance in the Senate. Senators needed executive response to their criticisms. People urged Marshall, "for the good of the country," to seize the reins of power on the constitutional grounds of the president's "inability to discharge the powers and duties of the said office." Marshall would have none of it. "I never have wanted his shoes," he wrote in his recollections (368). No evidence to the contrary has been found. Marybelle Burch of the Indiana State Library contends that Marshall was acting in a manner consistent with his Indiana background, "with restraint." She generalizes: "When greatness is thrust upon an Indianan, the tendency is to thrust it back again."

While presiding over the Senate Marshall dropped his most frequently quoted remark: "What this country needs is a good five-cent cigar." Ordinarily classified as political humor, this quip might just as well be regarded as a pragmatic Indianan's use of humor to adjust political forces. Marshall's quaint Indiana humor and ways won people over. Even James Bryce, raised to the British peerage, appreciated it. Along with his contemporary James Whitcomb Riley, Marshall did much to bring Indiana favorably into the consciousness of the nation.

After eight years in Washington, Marshall took up residence in Indianapolis and worked on a manuscript for a flourishing publishing house in the city, Bobbs-Merrill. In 1925 he offered to the public *Recollections of Thomas R. Marshall, Vice-President and Hoosier Philosopher. A Hoosier Salad*—"in the hope," as he explained in the front matter, "that the Tired Business Man, the Unsuccessful Golfer and the Lonely Husband whose wife is out reforming the world may find therein a half hour's surcease from sorrow." He died the same year.

Many questions arise about how Indiana got to be the way it was in Marshall's day. Consideration of five topics suggests some answers: Indiana's window on the Great Lakes, the "southernness" of Indiana, adjustments to the natural environment, Indiana's place in the union, and the natural gas boom as a stimulant to industrialization.

Drafters of the Northwest Ordinance of 1787 intended to provide Great Lakes frontage for each of the "not less than three nor more than five" states to be created out of the area north of the Ohio River and east of the Mississippi. Eastern, southern, and western boundaries for the area that became Indiana are strongly suggested in the ordinance, but the northern boundary is mentioned only in reference to the possible subdivision of territory to its north: "Congress . . . shall have authority to form one or two States in that part of the said Territory which lies north of an east and west line drawn through the southerly bend or extreme of Lake Michigan."

By 1848, enabling acts had created five states out of the Northwest Territory, each of which had a window on the Great Lakes. It would have been easy enough to create one "horizontal" state with no Great Lakes outlet from what is now southern Indiana and the "Egypt" portion of southern Illinois. The lawmakers of 1787 headed that off in article five of the ordinance when they drew an interior line within the territory from "the Wabash and Post Vincents, due north to the territorial line between the United States and Canada." State-makers followed their lead. The southern extremity of this line became the Indiana-Illinois boundary when Indiana was admitted to statehood in 1816. The language of the ordinance urged vertical shapes for the southern subdivisions of the Northwest Territory (if it did not mandate them); the same is true of Great Lakes frontages. If, as historian Justin Winsor suggested, the lawmakers of 1787 envisioned windows on the Great Lakes to encourage settlers of the southern reaches of the Northwest Territory to look northward, the scheme worked. Along with the prohibition of slavery in article six of the ordinance, Indiana's and Illinois's windows on the Great Lakes deserve consideration as palliatives to southernness in those regions.

Although neither large nor blessed with a good natural port, Indiana's shoreline has had a continuing influence on the economy, history, and culture of the state. Without a Great Lakes port, it is unlikely that ore from the iron ranges of Minnesota would have been smelted on Indiana soil with Indiana coal beginning in 1908. Without iron and steel plants within its borders, there would have been less inducement for other heavy industries to locate in Indiana and less ethnic and cultural diversity in the state. Had Gary arisen on the other side of the Illinois border, developments in that state and in Indiana would have been different.

The result of a geographical legacy of the ice age and of a political adjustment of 1787 (upheld in 1816), Indiana's window on the Great Lakes provided perspectives and opportunities that were not inevitable.

As for Indiana's southernness, when William Henry Harrison looked out over the Wabash River from the veranda of his spacious

Grouseland in Vincennes, he was at the latitude of the nation's capital—
from whence came his appointment as governor of Indiana Territory.
When he traveled the Ohio River along Indiana's southern border he
reached the approximate latitude of his ancestral home, Berkeley, on
the James River in Virginia. The social structure of tidewater Virginia
is what Harrison had in mind for Indiana.

For a brief period after the Louisiana Purchase, Vincennes became
the seat of government for the District of Upper Louisiana as well as
for Indiana Territory, then consisting of the original Northwest Territory minus Ohio, which had become a state in 1803. Harrison wrote
in his 1839 autobiography that "for one year I was Governor of two
Territories, embracing what are now the States of Indiana, Illinois,
Michigan, Missouri and Arkansas, and the Wisconsin and Iowa Territories."[8] In this dual capacity, Harrison came as close as any person
has come to imposing political unity upon the particular region dealt
with in this volume. As expected, this temporary hegemony soon
yielded to the dynamism of the westward movement and the state-
making process.

Southern influences predominated in the 1816 Indiana constitution. That was hardly accidental because thirty-four of the forty-three
members of the constitutional convention had previously lived below
the Mason-Dixon line. But try as they might, neither Harrison nor
anyone else before or after Indiana statehood could rescind the antislavery article of the Northwest Ordinance. Thomas D. Clark sees
in the Indiana Constitution the "outline and details" of the second
Kentucky constitution (minus slavery), a bill of rights from Ohio, and
some general principles from the Declaration of Independence.[9] Thus
the art of adjustment was already working at the time of statehood.

Through close demographic studies, modern scholars are providing more accurate insights into the nature and extent of Indiana's
southernness than were previously possible. Whereas Marshall saw
the old National Road as the northern extremity of southern preponderance in Indiana, Gregory S. Rose in a 1985 article finds the division
to be "a transition zone across the state's middle section where counties were either slightly above or below the average nativity percentages." In 1850 southern-born settlers in Indiana "comprised 44.0
percent of the population that was born in the United States exclusive
of Indiana, far above the average of 28.3 percent for the Old Northwest as a whole."[10] Illinois came closest to this level with 34.8 percent. Here, then, is a sharp contrast between Indiana and the remainder of the Old Northwest: Indiana's population as of the middle
of the nineteenth century was decidedly more southern in origin.
Some of the people who migrated northward into Indiana did so,
however, to escape certain features of southern civilization. That is
most emphatically the case with the fugitive slaves, recently eman-

cipated slaves, and free blacks who sought refuge in Indiana. The 1850 census indicates that of 11,000 Negroes living in Indiana, 1,426 were born in North Carolina, 1,172 in Virginia, 1,116 in Kentucky, 600 in Tennessee, 826 in Ohio, and the rest in Indiana or a scattering of other states and countries. Abraham Lincoln said that his family moved to Indiana from Kentucky "partly on account of slavery; but chiefly on account of the difficulty in land titles" in Kentucky.[11] Other people who had no use for the institution of slavery were the Quakers from North Carolina who concentrated in east central Indiana.

Rose found south central Indiana to be the most heavily southern region of the state, "reaching a maximum of 91.5 percent of the non-native Hoosier, United States-born population in Monroe and Orange counties" (214). He plotted out concentrations of people from particular southern states. In his doctoral dissertation, he builds a case from sources other than the federal census that "most Southerners living in Indiana by 1850 had been born in and left from some place within the Upland South region." As the demographic data base improves, historians will shed new light on Indianans' attitudes toward slavery, the Copperhead movement, dialect, and, as Rose expresses it, "character traits that combine to form the 'Hoosier experience.' "[12]

The Caucasians who came into the new state of Indiana from the southern uplands and elsewhere were predominantly farmers. As Indian title was extinguished (sometimes before) they swarmed out obliquely over the land in a general pattern from the southeast toward the northwest. By 1850 they occupied the entire state except the Kankakee Swamp with a population of at least six people per square mile.

These people altered forever the natural community of living plants and animals by felling centuries-old trees, plowing the earth, and replacing the native fauna with bovines, swine, horses, and sheep of European origin. They planted a mixed bag of seeds and tubers that plant geneticists had developed over a period of centuries on both sides of the Atlantic. At first their tools were simple, their power muscle—animal and human. But they had a proclivity toward mechanization. By the end of the century they were plowing, planting, cultivating, and harvesting with increasingly efficient implements manufactured in the region by such men as James Oliver of South Bend. The steam-powered threshing machine was their most complicated machine.

One common practice was to breed swine (Eurasian animals that bear large litters), feed them maize (a New World plant that can yield more than a thousandfold), and apply the latest mechanized techniques to the plant's cultivation. Especially in the fertile soil of central and northwestern Indiana, the results were prodigious.

From early in Indiana history farmers and townsmen alike could benefit from access to cash markets beyond the state and region. What could be more logical in a state located between the Ohio River and the Great Lakes than construction of canals to link the major waterways? There appeared to be no greater hindrances than those already overcome with the completion of the Erie Canal in New York.

The Mammoth Internal Improvements Act of 1836 called for the alteration of Indiana's drainage system with canals, locks, aqueducts, and dams to make the major river systems navigable and to provide outlets to Lake Michigan and Lake Erie. The scheme, financed by a ten-million-dollar loan to the state, bogged down after the Panic of 1837. In the words of Paul Fatout the plan was "conceived in madness and nourished by delusion."[13] Interest alone on borrowed money was ten times the state tax revenue. This time men and money succumbed to the environment.

The resulting political and fiscal embarrassment affected Indiana permanently. When Indianans adopted their second constitution in 1851 the document prohibited the state from contracting any debt except "To meet casual deficits in the revenue; to pay the interest on the State Debt; to repel invasion, suppress insurrection, or, if hostilities be threatened, provide for the public defense." An 1873 amendment prohibited the General Assembly from recognizing any liability or paying to redeem any stock of the Wabash and Erie Canal. These principles prevail to this day, a legacy from an attempt to alter the environment. If a visionary legislator forgets the debacle, a fiscally conservative colleague can promptly usher him or her to a Statehouse window and point to a segment of the never-completed Central Canal, which now serves as part of the water system of Indianapolis.

The process of changing the environment took its toll on the citizens. Physicians who examined men for military service during the Civil War generated narrative and statistical informaton on this subject. Dr. E. P. Bond, who examined four thousand men at Greensburg in southeast Indiana, reported a shift in the pattern of disease from the early period of settlement to 1860; malaria declined and diseases of the lung increased. Clearing and draining still required great physical exertion, as did the leading occupation of farming. "Injuries, cuts, wounds, sprains, and fractures are quite numerous," Dr. Bond reported, and so were cases of hernia, strained muscles, and varicose veins.[14] The people who so drastically changed the environment were themselves affected by the process.

Dr. Bond found the "colored race," numbering 11,428 in Indiana in 1860, to be adapting to its changing role. The 1816 constitution prevented blacks from voting and that of 1851 was designed to prevent them from entering Indiana. For the first two years of the Civil

War blacks could not serve in Indiana's fighting units. After the ban was lifted Dr. Bond wrote:

> I do not see why they may not make good soldiers. They have sufficient strength, activity, and endurance. They are rather quick of apprehension and are imitative. They bear up under injuries, and their wounds heal readily. Their sensibility, moral strength, and self-reliance have been somewhat diminished by long years of servitude; but with the prospects of liberty and the elevation of their race, with their habits of obedience, and with worthy and skillful officers to lead them, they will doubtless make very good soldiers (429).

And they did, particularly near Petersburg, Virginia, late in the war.

Indianans reacted in various ways to health problems that they believed to be related to the environment. Many coped the best they could and were rewarded when malaria eventually disappeared. Unbeknownst to them, they were diminishing the breeding places for the carrier of the malaria parasite, the anopheles mosquito, when they drained and plowed. Some people, such as Edward Eggleston and Thomas R. Marshall's family, left Indiana for a time and returned. Still others left the state permanently. One such person was W. W. Mayo, an 1850 graduate of Indiana Medical College at La Porte, who practiced medicine at Lafayette. Each summer a stiff case of malaria plagued the doctor. One day in 1854 he "shouted to his startled wife as he drove off westward, 'Good-bye, Louise. I'm going to keep on driving until I get well or die.' "[15] He kept going until he reached Minnesota, where he settled permanently and where he and his wife became the parents of Charles H. and William J. Mayo, founders of the Mayo Clinic.

National and state patriotisms have been present in Indiana since 1816, but the "lesser patriotism" has always remained just that. There has been no inclination on the part of Indiana to call a midwestern version of a Hartford Convention and no reason for Congress to pass a Force Bill to keep Indiana in line.

It was up to a son of the heartland to steer the Union through its greatest crisis. Abraham Lincoln's early "textbook" on American history and government, *The Revised Laws of Indiana* (1824), is prefaced by ten key documents that trace the legal foundations of Indiana from the Declaration of Independence through to the constitution of 1816. Lincoln mastered and digested these documents and returned to them time and again, particularly the Northwest Ordinance and the United States Constitution. The mature Lincoln coupled these two documents in a manner that bore directly upon the nature of the Union and gave his nationalism the flavor of the Old Northwest. He explained to an Indianapolis audience on September 19, 1859:

The ordinance of 1787 was passed simultaneously with the making of the Constitution of the United States. It prohibited the taking of slavery into the North-western Territory. . . . There was nothing said in the Constitution relative to the spread of slavery in the Territories, but the same generation of men said something about it in this ordinance of '87, through the influence of which you of Indiana, and your neighbors in Ohio, Illinois, Wisconsin and Michigan, are prosperous, free men. That generation of men, though not to the full extent members of the Convention that framed the Constitution, were to some extent members of that Convention, holding seats, at the same time in one body and the other. . . . Our fathers who made the government, made the ordinance of 1787.[16]

A subtle mind was telling Indianans that they were prosperous and free because the men who wrote the nation's constitution also prohibited slavery in Indiana. This argument he developed more fully and reasoned more closely at the Cooper Institute in New York City on February 27, 1860. He argued that the new congress under the constitution clinched his point in 1789 when it reaffirmed the ordinance. There was no question about the intent of the founding fathers—the central government was supreme and could impose conditions upon the territories and states.

After the Civil War broke out, some Indianans who accepted the supremacy of the national government challenged the Lincoln administration on other points. Governor Oliver P. Morton, a powerful executive, clashed frequently with the War Department about military leadership and support for Indiana troops in the field. Morton vexed his fellow Republican in the White House and strained the ties between Indianapolis and Washington. Yet there is little doubt that majorities in both political parties in Indiana supported Lincoln's concept of an indissoluble union.

This support can be quantified and compared with data from other states. Indiana is first in Robert Dykstra's ranking of states by percentage of military population furnished to the Union armed forces. Fifty-seven out of every hundred Indiana males of military age served the Union cause, followed in the Midwest by Illinois, 56.6 percent; Ohio, 49.8 percent; Iowa, 48.8 percent; Michigan, 46.7 percent; Wisconsin 46.4 percent; and Minnesota, 45.0 percent. (Except for Missouri, which was war torn, none of the other heartland areas had yet attained statehood.) Dykstra's ranking also shows that a greater percentage of the military-age population of Indiana than of any other Northern state was among the white Union soldiers who died in the war.[17]

Even with majority agreement on the basic issue of preservation of the Union, Indiana leaders did not practice the art of political adjustment very gracefully during the Civil War. A bitter division separated "those who wanted 'the Union as it was' and those who wanted to break with the past and build a new nation functioning upon new economic principles," explains Kenneth M. Stampp. Fierce party battles, bitter hatreds, and rapid changes led to the collapse of representative government "and to the establishment of Governor Oliver P. Morton's personal dictatorship."[18]

Indianans welcomed the end of the Civil War, observed John T. McCutcheon, because "it gave the inhabitants more time for politics." The state then became "a political flapjack, first on one side and then on the other. At one election she is blond, at the next she is brunette."[19] In 1872 it was the Republicans' turn to be "down," and Thomas A. Hendricks became the first Democratic governor of a Northern state after the war.

For nine presidential elections in succession (1880 through the first election of Wilson and Marshall in 1912) Indiana's presidential vote went the same way as the national results. Three gentlemen from Indiana served as vice-president during these years and one, Benjamin Harrison, as president, from 1889 to 1893.

The art of political adjustment, American and Indiana style, that brought Harrison to the White House fascinated James Bryce. While traveling in 1883, Bryce fell in with two Indiana journalists. When conversation turned to presidential politics the newspapermen spoke of chances for the nomination of their man, "a comparatively obscure person." Bryce expressed surprise that "their man," presumably Benjamin Harrison, should be in contention. He asked why they would not come out for someone "of more commanding character" and suggested "Senator A." The journalists concurred with the assessment, then added, "But you see he comes from a small State, and we have got that State already. Besides, he wasn't in the war. Our man was. Indiana's vote is worth having, and if our man is run, we can carry Indiana" (I, 78). Harrison had to wait for another presidential cycle, but he was in the White House when Bryce went to press with the American edition of *The American Commonwealth*. Diplomat that he was, the Englishman tailed off the subject of the making of presidents with a safe quotation about the role of time and chance in human affairs.

Ohio, also a political "swing" state, produced an inordinate number of presidents between the Civil War and World War I. Like Harrison, the Ohioans tended to be "minority presidents," meaning they were elected without receiving majorities of the popular vote. Thus the two eastern states of the heartland shared similar roles within the nation during an era when a small adjustment could tip a national election.

The discovery and use of natural gas, because of its timing, stimulated Indiana's industrial development out of all proportion to its long-term importance. The Civil War had accelerated forces of economic change, but industrialization had not progressed very far in Indiana by the mid-1880s. The biggest changes from the prewar years probably involved the greater use of steam power in small factories in the river towns and the replacement of animal power with steam power in some farm functions. Coal, a useful commodity in the age of steam, was in ample supply in southern and western Indiana, where it was mined as early as the territorial period.

The natural gas phenomenon was quite different and more dramatic. The events unfolded north of the Old National Road in that part of the state where Marshall claimed people were "always experimenting." As explained by State Geologist John B. Patton: "Discovery of natural gas in 1886 in what was to become the famed Trenton Field of northwestern Ohio and northeast-central Indiana triggered an industrial expansion that transformed sleepy county seat towns throughout the area into manufacturing centers that are still vital parts of Indiana's (and Ohio's) economy. . . ."[20] Drillers found natural gas in 1876 at Eaton, near Muncie, but they did not know what to do with it. By 1886 that had changed; Ohioans had demonstrated its utility and had learned how to handle it in the eastern reaches of the Trenton Field.

A boom was on in Indiana by late 1886. The bringing in of a well was a spectacular event, especially when it was accomplished by dropping nitroglyccrin down the drilled-out hole and igniting it. When the result was a roar of pressurized gas, belches of smoke, and flames taller than elms, Sunday afternoon audiences went home delighted. More than five thousand wells drilled in Indiana between 1886 and 1897 marked out the largest natural gas field then known in the United States. Burning fumes dotted the midnight landscape.

At Anderson a flaming archway spanned the street near the train depot. Gas was also pumped into the White River and ignited so that a gigantic flambeau appeared to burn out of the water. In November 1887 a geologist estimated that fifteen billion cubic feet of gas had been wasted during the preceding six months in Indiana. Boom books and publicity campaigns attracted potential industrialists and investors. Towns vied with each other by offering various combinations of free factory sites, free fuel in perpetuity, and cash. Not since the flush times of the Mammoth Internal Improvements Act had there been so much optimism in Indiana.

In 1880 a few over 4,000 people were living in Anderson; in 1890 10,741. By Lamont Hulse's count, twenty-five new factories located there between 1887 and 1892 producing twenty-three hundred jobs. The boom was good for laborers and other city dwellers too because the towns offered free or very cheap gas for home heating, cooking, and lighting.

The Ball brothers, manufacturers of containers in Buffalo, New York, sought a good source of natural gas for manufacturing fruit jars. Before the days of pipelines, it was necessary to locate near gas wells. By offering five thousand dollars, free fuel, and free land, Muncie promoters induced the Ball brothers to locate there. Between 1890 and 1920 the Balls and other users of silica leveled Hoosier Slide, a 200-foot-high dune near Michigan City, by removing 13.5 million tons of sand. Manufacturers of plate glass, ceramic tile, and pottery located in Indiana; so did foundries, wire works, and metal fabricating plants.

Natural gas production peaked in 1900 with an estimated thirty-six billion cubic feet coming from the Trenton Field. It dropped off precipitously thereafter because of dwindling supply. Gas for domestic heating failed in Muncie in the winter of 1905. By 1906 production in the field declined to less than a quarter of that of 1900. The "down" side of the cycle is significant in the history of Indiana industrialism because it illustrates how Indianans adjusted to new circumstances.

Ralph D. Gray's *Alloys and Automobiles: The Life of Elwood Haynes* is about a science teacher caught up in the gas boom at Portland, Indiana. Haynes invented a meter to measure the flow of gas through pipes as well as other items useful in the gas industry. In 1890 he became involved in "the nation's first long-distance, high-pressure natural gas pipeline," which was to run from the Trenton Field to Chicago. He felt the need for a faster and more dependable means of transportation along the pipeline than a horse and buggy could supply. That motivated Haynes to build what he claimed to be "the first automobile" in 1893–94. In 1898 he incorporated the Haynes-Apperson Company for manufacturing "Motor Carriages, Gasoline Motors and gearing for motor vehicles" and began manufacturing cars at Kokomo. That, in turn, led to experiments with metals and the patenting of alloys. Haynes carried on with an active and useful life as Kokomo's foremost industrialist until his death in 1925.[21]

The natural gas boom stimulated Haynes and other able Indianans while orienting them for roles in twentieth-century industrialism. The fact that a solid Indiana Presbyterian occupied the White House from 1889 to 1893 may have accelerated Indiana's industrial takeoff. But conservationist that he was, Harrison put no damper upon waste in the Trenton Field. Geologists estimate that much more of Indiana's precious natural gas was wasted than was judiciously used.

To prepare for the hundredth anniversary of Indiana statehood in 1916, Meredith Nicholson brought out a new edition of *The Hoosiers*, his turn-of-the-century assessment of the state's cultural heritage. In the first edition, Nicholson had called attention to new heroes emerging from the novels of Booth Tarkington—urban natives of Indiana who, like Tarkington, had gone to college elsewhere and had returned with outside influences. These heroes had little kinship with the lovable, indigenous, dialect-speaking rustics inhabiting the pages of Edward Eggleston and James Whitcomb Riley. In his "Centennial Postscript" to *The Hoosiers*, Nicholson went a step further and openly regretted that "the State is losing—indeed, has lost—much of its tang and native flavor."[22] He attributed this loss to the trolley and the automobile. Proud of younger Indiana writers then beginning to make their mark, Nicholson praised Theodore Dreiser, born in Terre Haute, who held up a mirror to industrial America and shocked many Americans with what his mirror reflected.

The centennial of Indiana statehood (December 11, 1916) and American entry into World War I (April 6, 1917) stimulated the "two patriotisms" articulated by Bryce. Their near convergence and double impact upon nativistic tendencies warrant further study. Was anti-German sentiment stronger in Indiana than in Nebraska or Wisconsin? Were there different ingredients in it from state to state?

The war made life no easier for Mathilde and Jacob Reinhardt, German American Lutherans of rural Evansville. Well before American entry, old-stock neighbors protested against women's relief activities on behalf of wounded German soldiers. After America declared war on Germany, local pressures resulted in suspension of publication of the Evansville *Demokrat*, cancellation of German worship services at St. Paul's Lutheran Church, dissolution of the Turnverein and the Perry Township Volksbund, and the dropping of the German language from the curriculum in the Vanderburgh County public schools. The Reinhardts witnessed the public humiliation of Friedrich Lauenstein, who, "after having his newspaper shut down, was compelled to become a bond salesperson."[23] On occasion, hooliganism encouraged people to conform to community norms.

For the most part, the Reinhardts acquiesced to the pressures. Prosperity came. They bought more farmland and a tractor at about the time that manufacturing surpassed agriculture as the leading occupation in Indiana. After the fall harvest in 1917, Jacob paid cash for a Model-T Ford. A few years later the Reinhardts moved away from Mathilde's parents, whose "stubborn insistence on speaking only German" was, Mathilde and Jacob believed, "harming their children" (173).

A darker theme in the drive for conformity involved the Ku Klux Klan. Until recently, scholarship tended to focus on Klan leaders, particularly D. C. Stephenson, the World War I Army lieutenant from Texas who came to Indiana in 1920. A spellbinder and showman, Stephenson joined the Klan in Evansville and rose meteorically through the ranks to become grand dragon of Indiana. From his headquarters in downtown Indianapolis Stephenson wielded power over high elected officials, and his empire also extended into other states. In the mid-1920s, at the pinnacle of his power and wealth, the state convicted Stephenson of murdering a young Statehouse secretary, Madge Oberholtzer, whom he had sexually assaulted. Indignation similar to that which the grand dragon had used in his rise now brought him and his empire down.

Using quantitative methods and sources that have become available only recently, Leonard J. Moore demonstrates in his 1985 study "that over a quarter of all native-born white men in the state joined the Klan in the early 1920's; that Klansmen represented a general cross-section of Indiana's white Protestant society; that in individual communities, the Klan sought primarily to revitalize community institutions and values; and that the Klan's dominance in the state election of 1924 resulted from high levels of support across a wide spectrum of social groups."[24] Here, then, is a framework for understanding why the Klan became so integrally involved in politics during the 1920s and why it engaged in such an activity as the building of a hospital in Kokomo. Ironically, the Sisters of St. Joseph eventually acquired and operated this hospital. When its cornerstone was opened in 1986 no hint of Klan wizardry was found among its contents.

The Klan flourished during years of rapid industrialization when gaps widened between job and family, city and country, rich and poor, educated and ignorant, labor and capital. Industrialization frustrated Indianans because many of the resulting problems were more easily seen than understood or remedied.

Big industry and organized labor have now been part of the Indiana scene for three generations, yet they still obtrude. They have brought unprecedented prosperity, but at a price. This price has often been loss of local autonomy, abrupt changes that do not synchronize with Indiana gradualism, and disruption of lives. Even after the passage of eighty years, the Gary Works of the United States Steel Corporation seem out of place against the bright blue of Lake Michigan and the verdant green of the nearby swamps. Gary's older residential and commercial areas, once the showcase of American capitalism, now stand decrepit, mute evidence of a noble plan either abandoned, interrupted, or gone wrong.

Each new blast furnace fired up on the shores of Lake Michigan early in the century required an influx of labor. Gary, a company-sponsored town that did not exist in 1905, had a population of 55,378 by 1920. The first wave of blacks from the South arrived just before and during World War I. A few seasons brought more blacks to one Indiana city than the number inhabiting the entire state on the eve of the Civil War. Federal laws restricting immigration encouraged even greater reliance on blacks to make the steel to put America on wheels. By 1930, 17,922 blacks lived in Gary (17 percent of the population), plus fifteen nationality groups numbering five hundred or more persons. European tongues blended with "the soft-spoken Spanish of the Mexicans and with the slow drawl of the Southern Negroes. . . ."[25] To the public school system fell the responsibility of educating the daughters and sons of the working class. For three decades under the leadership of William A. Wirt the system received high marks.

Prior to World War I, Gary experienced the first of many economic shocks it has since come to expect. The year after the armistice, organized labor proved that it could make an impact even on U.S. Steel. The Great Depression initially diminished the power of labor, lowered steel production to 15 percent of capacity in Indiana's steel region by 1932, and idled thousands of proud workers. Local relief organizations had exhausted their finances by the time Governor Paul V. McNutt negotiated a loan to Lake County from the Reconstruction Finance Corporation. Thereafter, New Deal programs lightened the welfare obligations of local government. The Democratic landslide of 1932 carried two blacks to the General Assembly, Robert L. Stanton from Lake County and Henry J. Richardson, Jr., of Indianapolis—the first of their race to serve in the twentieth century (four had served earlier). Richardson (1902–83) gained attention as the author of one of the earliest fair employment practices laws in the country. In the 1950s he teamed up with Thurgood Marshall and won a pivotal lawsuit concerned with the integration of public housing.

Through boom and bust, strife and harmony, Gary and the "Calumet Region" of which it is a part have come to epitomize heavy industry for the nation if not for the world. The area may have had its finest hour delivering on supply contracts during World War II. In more recent years American steel producers have not been able to meet foreign competition effectively, nor has Congress been willing to enact tariffs high enough to revitalize the "rust belt." Yet the Calumet Region is not without optimism. In the 1960s Bethlehem Steel began building a gigantic, fully integrated, and highly automated facility at Burns Harbor that employed 6,250 people in 1987 and enabled Indiana to become America's number one steel-producing state. Many whites have been moving from homes near the mills to the suburbs. Merrillville, not even incorporated in 1970, registered a population of 27,677 in 1980. Meanwhile, Richard C. Hatcher, the black mayor of Gary, brought federal funds to the downtown area to build a huge convention center and, more recently, an ultramodern physical-fitness facility. But he went down to defeat in the 1987 primary elections, some contend, because he diverted too much of his energy to national politics.

In the General Assembly and elsewhere, Indianans regard Gary and the other industrial towns of the Calumet Region as atypical municipalities more closely akin to Chicago than to the rest of Indiana. Indeed, the cities of Indiana's northwest corner use Chicago's street numbering system.

Because of the convictions and persistence of one of its citizens, Terre Haute occupies a unique place in the American labor movement. Of the same generation as Thomas R. Marshall, Eugene V. Debs (1855–1926) used his native town on the Wabash River as his lifelong base of operations. A railroad worker and founder of the American Railway Union, Debs turned socialist when he concluded that other approaches to reform were doomed to failure. He ran for the presidency five times between 1900 and 1920. What is unusual about his last attempt is that he received nearly a million votes while in a federal penitentiary. What landed him there was a speech he delivered in Canton, Ohio, during the summer of 1918. "The speech was merely a restatement of what Debs had said for years with only one vague statement about capitalists declaring war for profits while the workers fought them and died." For that he was found guilty of violating the recently amended Espionage Act and given a ten-year prison term. When President Harding released Debs from prison in 1921 following the "Red Scare," Marshall likely expressed the sentiments of many Indianans who simultaneously respected Debs while disagreeing with his economics and his politics: "So long as ten million Fords are driven by ten million Americans, God's in His Heaven, and the government at Washington will continue to live" (77). In 1975 Indiana senators Birch Bayh and Vance Hartke introduced a resolution to the United States Senate to restore Debs's citizenship posthumously. Bayh noted that "many of Debs' goals such as social security, unemployment compensation, public works for the unemployed, and disability insurance had been achieved."[26] Members of Indiana's radical tradition are generally tolerated while they are alive; a few of them are even honored when dead.

If there is a common denominator to the economies of Indiana towns in the twentieth century, it is the automotive industry. On the eve of World War I Indianapolis stood second only to Detroit in the production of automobiles. During the early decades of this century many towns in the northern half of the state could boast of locally produced automobiles, the Studebaker of South Bend being the longest survivor among them. Although the last Haynes came off the production line in Kokomo in 1925, plants there illustrate how integral to the American automobile industry Indiana is sixty years later. The transmissions for rear-drive Chrysler Corporation automobiles are made there. A Delco Electronics Corporation plant located in Kokomo makes electronic components for all General Motors vehicles. "At times, Delco has acted more like a Silicon Valley computer concern than a Rust Belt auto plant," said the *Indianapolis Star*. Because of a "just in time" inventory concept borrowed from the Japanese to cut costs, these components are manufactured hours before they are needed in plants in Michigan and five other states. What happens in Kokomo impacts within hours upon the well-being of General Motors.[27] Dozens of other Indiana towns, even small ones in the southern part of the state, have their niches in the automobile parts industry.

Indianapolis is not only the state's capital but also its nucleus and its metropolis. Its strong influence on the state is, in part, attributable to scale. Indiana, the smallest of the contiguous states west of the Appalachians, is less than half the size of Kansas, Nebraska, South Dakota, or Minnesota. People from all parts of the state can drive to Indianapolis for business or shopping and return home the same day (although they will be tired if they live in Evansville). Created as a "paper town" by the state legislature at the center of the state in 1821, Indianapolis became a transportation hub when the National Road and the Michigan Road intersected there. It has maintained this function through a succession of dominant transportation modes (wagon roads, an uncompleted canal system, railroads, and motor highways) down to the present, when four interstate highways intersect in the city. By a close call, Indiana is a northern state and Indianapolis qualifies as a northern city. The Statehouse, constructed of native Indiana limestone quarried south of the National Road (U. S. 40), symbolically stands a few rods north of the time-honored dividing line. So do the leading financial institutions and the City-County Building.

Indianapolis is a bustling, pragmatic, patriotic city (national headquarters of the American Legion), where Acapulco Joe displays a huge "God Bless America" sign in the window of his restaurant, where Kelly & Cohen's Delicatessen features "party trays for wakes and bar mitzvahs," and where it would surprise few if that establishment were to take in a partner and add a line of soul food. A highly diversified, steady economy (including the headquarters of one Fortune 500 firm, Eli Lilly & Co.) stabilizes the city. Community pride, private enterprise, philanthropy, and a unique form of government have seen to it that the city does not "rot out at its core."

The "Unigov" act of 1969 can be understood only in the context of Indiana's conservative political institutions and traditions. The still-operative constitution of 1851 does not allow easy remedies to urban problems through alteration of city charters or popular referenda. Significant change must come through the General Assembly. That is difficult because neither of the two major political parties long dominates the legislature, and two other branches of state government serve as checks upon it. Further, party rivalries run rampant at the county, municipal, and township levels. Potential changes, therefore, involve four levels of government, two political parties, a variety of special-interest groups, and—in Indianapolis, the Calumet Region, Evansville, and a few other communities—two races. (The 1970 census showed that 13 percent of the population of Marion County, where Indianapolis is located, was nonwhite, with the heaviest concentration in the central city.)

When the General Assembly passed the Unigov act in 1969 and the governor signed it, Richard Lugar, then mayor of Indianapolis, received more credit than any other individual for explaining the concept and for threading it through a political labyrinth. Unigov merged most agencies of the City of Indianapolis and Marion County under a mayor and a City-County Council elected by the voters of the entire county. Effective January 1, 1970, the law brought Indianapolis from twenty-sixth to ninth place in the ranking of American cities by population (from 476,258 to 793,590). The six Unigov departments are Parks and Recreation, Public Safety, Transportation, Administration, Metropolitan Development, and Public Works.

Although people opposed Unigov both before and after passage, there has been no serious attempt to "unscramble the egg." Citizens and journalists alike report that the system is effectively delivering countywide public services, including transportation. Substantial federal funding has been forthcoming, attributable to eligibility because of the city's increased size and to changes of heart on the question of whether to accept federal funding by Lugar and other leading Republicans. The voters have indicated their approval of Unigov by "promoting" Lugar to the United States Senate. Lugar's successor, Mayor William H. Hudnut III, a Presbyterian clergyman, claims that the city "has grown in its capacity to deal effectively with the problems of modern urban-center employment, safety, health and welfare needs, the environment, metropolitan planning, etc."[28]

Unigov left some functions of local government alone, most notably the eleven public school corporations in Marion County. Many blacks criticized that as a means of keeping suburban schools predominately white. In 1971 the U. S. Court for the Southern District of Indiana ruled that de jure segregation was indeed being practiced. After unsuccessful appeals all the way to the Supreme Court, and after delays and redefinition of the issues, "one-way busing"—of central city blacks to outer perimeter schools—commenced during the 1981–82 school year. Families of some of these students objected. The district court provided relief to one set of their objections by ordering that these families have the right to vote for school board members where their children are bused.[29] It is too soon to tell whether Indianapolis's version of Unigov will go down in history as a positive contribution to municipal government (as did the "Des Moines Plan" of the early years of this century), or whether it will be regarded as a means of sidestepping pressing social issues.

In the late 1980s Indianans have become increasingly sensitive about their public education system. Measured in terms of both inputs (expenditure per pupil) and outputs (pupil performance on standard tests), Indiana ranks on the lower end of many national scales. Here Indiana stands apart from the other heartland states. It is a vexing problem with no easy solution, but one which Governor Robert D. Orr and other leaders are not ignoring. Indiana needs a latter-day Caleb Mills to carry the banner for public education.

As is true of the geological structure of the heartland, the historical strata differ from place to place. Much of Indiana has been affected by the agricultural frontier, the Civil War experience, the process of industrialization, and a postindustrial present. These layers are distinct. For the most part they occurred in that order and with different generations furnishing the prime participants for each stratum. Not so in the Minnesota River valley, for example, where the first two occurred simultaneously and where the Sioux seized upon the national confusion to reverse, temporarily, the direction of the agriculturalists. Vast areas in the northern and western reaches of the heartland remain untouched by industrialization.

The layer of political progressivism so clearly visible in several of the heartland states is thin or nonexistent in Indiana. To this day Indiana has none of the cardinal marks of progressivism—the initiative provision for state legislation, the referendum provision for same, or the recall of state officials. Each of the other heartland states (except Minnesota) has at least one of these principles. Indianans do not want direct democracy, nor do they want their government to be predisposed toward change: "Thank you, balanced government, of the type in vogue during Indiana's infancy, will do." The "spoils system," also prevalent during the early American republic, is hard to defend in the latter years of the twentieth century. Only in 1986 did the Indiana General Assembly take steps to dismantle a system wherein the governor appoints managers to operate offices where motor vehicle licenses are sold. These managers run their license branches from fees charged to motorists for handling transactions, pocket any profits, and normally donate part of these sums to their party's coffers. It is also common for departments of state government to deduct party contributions from employees' paychecks. When the state auditor unilaterally halted the practice in 1986, a circuit court judge ordered him to resume the deductions from the checks of forty-one hundred workers.[30]

All who practice the art of political adjustment in Indiana must reckon with substantial inertia in the machinery of state government and resistance to change on the part of the Indiana citizenry. Nevertheless, the closest student of the middle period of Indiana history, Clifton J. Phillips, rejects as unfair the designation of Indiana as "the original lair of the stand-patter in the United States." Positive changes came then and later. Phillips's assessment of Indiana's political mood during the first two decades of this century as a compound "of nearly equal parts of conservatism and cautious liberalism, neither dominant for long and each force acting as a check upon the other," applies in a broader context as well (128).

Jacques Barzun wrote that "whoever wants to know the heart and mind of America had better learn baseball."[31] A corollary may follow that to know Indiana one must also understand both basketball and the Indianapolis 500. For reasons that defy analysis, for many years high school basketball has been played with greater intensity in Indiana than anywhere else, but the principles are similar to those operating throughout the heartland wherever small, vulnerable towns dot the landscape. From December through March, a minimum of five adolescent males or females (six of the latter in Iowa) have the potential of bringing victory and pride to their schools and towns. The game is played in a manner suggesting that individual and community destinies are being settled on the spot. "Hoosier hysteria" it is called in Indiana—an exciting and inexpensive celebration of youth, dexterity, and locale.

In contrast, the Indianapolis 500, a heavily capitalized sports event, is carried out with experienced, professional contenders. Its traditions date from the day Thomas R. Marshall laid the last brick (a gold one) in the track at Speedway. Some of these traditions stem from an older sport popular in the neighboring state to the south. While Kentuckians visit the paddocks to size up horses and to talk to the grooms and jockeys, the fans at Speedway visit the pits to view the machines and to talk to the crews and drivers. After time trials come Carburetion Day (another vestige of a bygone era), a huge parade, and finally Race Day itself, replete with celebrities, pageantry, pretty girls, and patriotism. The crowd joins in the singing of the "Star Spangled Banner." Then state patriotism gets its due with the strains of "Back Home Again in Indiana."

"Gentlemen, start your engines," comes the traditional command. After parade and pace laps, the race begins in earnest. The drivers know that, to win, they must respect the traditions of the track and push for the limits while adjusting the technologies of safety and speed to ever-changing situations. Bankers, housewives, and laborers—a cross section of the state and nation a third of a million strong—look on. All lose their cares during this Indiana rite of spring while men and metal compete for high stakes. Laborers who spend their lives in repetitive tasks such as cutting metal for the front supports of auto transmissions get particular satisfaction from observing the totality of the latest high-performance machines put to the test of the track. Few if any of the machines will be back next year because technology moves on. But the track will be here and so will many of the drivers. Three hours pass quickly while spectators discuss the race with friends, snack on fried chicken, and sip beverages. Something decisive is soon to take place. After two hundred laps the checkered flag comes down as the winner crosses the finish line—a narrow row of bricks left in place from the early years of the century. When the officials award trophies and purses amid network news coverage, Indianans know they have witnessed a world-class event in the heart of their state. Hoosiers love a good show and thrive on outside recognition.

On the way home spectators see a barefoot inebriate in the infield—an angular Anglo—beer in hand, smile on his face, mud up to his knees, and a red shirt on his back bearing the words, "It ain't bad to be a Hoosier."

But many perceive a deeper meaning to the events of the day. The Indianapolis 500 involves the accommodation of the technology of speed to that of safety. On the track, as well as in life, where men and women are put to the test and where conditions constantly change, there is need for continuity with what has gone before. Indiana is a state in the American heartland where this truism is widely understood and appreciated.

NOTES

1. *Indianapolis Star*, May 24, 1986, 58.

2. James Bryce, *The American Commonwealth*, 2 vols. (Chicago, 1890), I, 14. Subsequent quotations from this source are cited by volume and page number in the text. Where there is no ambiguity, this method is also used to identify other sources.

3. John Margolis, "Natural States," *New Republic*, April 11, 1981, 11.

4. Lana Ruegamer, *A History of the Indiana Historical Society 1830–1980* (Indianapolis, 1980), 77.

5. Thomas R. Marshall, *Recollections of Thomas R. Marshall, Vice-President and Hoosier Philosopher. A Hoosier Salad* (Indianapolis, 1925), 19.

6. From studies conducted by Justin E. Walsh and the staff of the Centennial History of the Indiana General Assembly project.

7. Quoted in Clifton J. Phillips, *Indiana in Transition: The Emergence of an Industrial Commonwealth, 1880–1920* (Indianapolis, 1968), 110.

8. William Henry Harrison to James Brooks, July 20, 1839. Transcript in files of Harrison Papers Project, Indiana Historical Society.

9. Thomas D. Clark, *Frontier America: The Story of the Westward Movement* (New York, 1959), 323.

10. Gregory S. Rose, "Hoosier Origins: The Nativity of Indiana's United States-Born Population in 1850," *Indiana Magazine of History* 81 (September 1985), 212–14.

11. Roy P. Basler, ed., *The Collected Works of Abraham Lincoln*, 8 vols. (New Brunswick, N.J., 1953–55), IV, 61–62.

12. Gregory S. Rose, "The Southern-ness of Hoosierdom: The Nativity of Settlement Groups in Indiana by 1850" (Ph.D. dissertation, Michigan State University, 1981), 263; Rose, "Hoosier Origins," 232. See also his "Upland Southerners: The County Origins of Southern Migrants to Indiana by 1850," *Indiana Magazine of History* 82 (September 1986), 242–62.

13. Paul Fatout, *Indiana Canals* (West Lafayette, Ind., 1972), 76.

14. Quoted in J. H. Baxter, *Statistics, Medical and Anthropological, of the Provost-Marshall-General's Bureau . . .*, 2 vols. (Washington, D.C., 1875), I.

15. Helen Clapesattle, *The Doctors Mayo* (Minneapolis, 1941), 32.

16. Basler, III, 465.

17. Robert R. Dykstra, "Iowa 'Bright Radical Star,' " in James C. Mohr, ed., *Radical Republicans in the North: State Politics during Reconstruction* (Baltimore, 1976), 170, 172.

18. Kenneth M. Stampp, *Indiana Politics during the Civil War* (Indianapolis, 1949), ix–x.

19. Kin Hubbard, ed., *A Book of Indiana* (n. p., 1929), 22.

20. John B. Patton, "Mineral Resources in Indiana's Economic Development," *Indiana Business Review* (March-April 1976), 22. This section is also based on G. L. Carpenter, T. A. Dawson, and Stanley J. Keller, *Petroleum Industry in Indiana* (Bloomington, Ind., 1975), and on papers by Patton, Lamont Hulse, and Dan M. Sullivan at the Indiana Historical Society's Spring History Conference, May 17, 1986.

21. Ralph D. Gray, *Alloys and Automobiles: The Life of Elwood Haynes* (Indianapolis, 1979), 51, 81, 89.

22. Meredith Nicholson, *The Hoosiers* (New York, 1915), 273.

23. Quoted in John G. Clark, David M. Katzman, Richard D. McKinzie, and Theodore A. Wilson, *Three Generations in Twentieth Century America*, rev. ed. (Homewood, Ill., 1982), 138.

24. Leonard Joseph Moore, "White Protestant Nationalism in the 1920's: The Ku Klux Klan in Indiana" (Ph.D. dissertation, University of California at Los Angeles, 1985), xi–xii.

25. Powell A. Moore, *The Calumet Region: Indiana's Last Frontier*, reprint of 1959 edition with an Afterword by Lance Trusty (Indianapolis, 1977), 342.

26. Miriam Z. Langsam, "Eugene Victor Debs, Hoosier Radical," in Ralph D. Gray, ed., *Gentlemen from Indiana . . .* (Indianapolis, 1977), 271, 285, 290.

27. *Indianapolis Star*, November 23, 1986, 1, 25, and February 17, 1987, 21, 24.

28. York Willbern, "Unigov: Local Government Reorganization in Indianapolis," in *The Regionalist Papers* (Detroit, 1974). Quotation from material distributed by office of Mayor William H. Hudnut III, dated May 1985.

29. Emma Lou Thornbrough, "The Indianapolis School Busing Case," in *We the People: Indiana and the United States Constitution* (Indianapolis, 1987), 68–92.

30. *Indianapolis Star*, November 23, 1986, 1, 25.

31. Quoted in *Newsweek*, October 20, 1986, 62.

BIBLIOGRAPHY

The best and most recent one-volume history of the state is James H. Madison's *The Indiana Way: A State History* (Bloomington, Ind., 1986). Madison's thesis, that Indianans tend to reject the radical and the extreme, "preferring to savor the comfort and security that comes from a respect for tradition and for the achievements of preceding generations," was frequently in mind while writing this chapter.

Four volumes have been completed to date in the sesquicentennial history of Indiana series: John D. Barnhart and Dorothy L. Riker, *Indiana to 1816: The Colonial Period* (1971); Emma Lou Thornbrough, *Indiana in the Civil War Era 1850–1880* (1965); Clifton J. Phillips, *Indiana in Transition: The Emergence of an Industrial Commonwealth 1880–1920* (1968); and James H. Madison, *Indiana through Tradition and Change: A History of the Hoosier State and Its People 1920–1945* (1982). Published jointly by the Indiana Historical Bureau and the Indiana Historical Society (except the fourth volume, which was published by the society alone), these volumes are "must" reading for serious students of Indiana history. Through the years the bureau, the society, and Indiana University Press have published a great number of worthwhile books about the history and culture of Indiana, many of which remain in print.

Patrick J. Furlong, *Indiana: An Illustrated History* (Northridge, Calif., 1985); Howard Peckham, *Indiana: A Bicentennial History* (New York, 1978); John D. Barnhart and Donald F. Carmony, *Indiana: From Frontier to Industrial Commonwealth*, 4 vols., (New York, 1954); and Logan Esary, *A History of Indiana*, 2 vols., 3d ed. (Fort Wayne, 1924) all contain much that is useful. So does Ralph D. Gray's anthology, *The Hoosier State: Readings in Indiana History*, 2 vols. (Grand Rapids, Mich., 1980).

A Guide to Manuscript Collections of the Indiana Historical Society and Indiana State Library by Eric Pumroy with Paul Brockman (Indianapolis, 1986) will lead researchers to many untapped sources at the two institutions. John W. Miller's *Indiana Newspaper Bibliography* (Indianapolis, 1982) is indispensable for newspaper users. Since 1905 the *Indiana Magazine of History*, now owned by Indiana University, has published a great wealth of articles and book reviews. Cumulative and annual indexes provide access. In recent years bibliographies of Indiana historical materials appearing elsewhere are also printed in the magazine. The Indiana Historical Bureau has recently published two useful items about Indiana blacks: Alan F. January and Justin E. Walsh, *A Century of Achievement: Black Hoosiers in the Indiana General Assembly, 1881–1986* (Indianapolis, 1986) and Darlene Clark Hine et al., *The Black Women in the Middle West Project: A Comprehensive Resource Guide, Illinois and Indiana*. More accessible than the items cited in the notes about Unigov is C. James Owen and York Willbern, *Governing Metropolitan Indianapolis: The Politics of Unigov* (Berkeley, 1985).

During the preparation of this chapter I had at my disposal the text of a guide to travel in Indiana, patterned after the WPA guides, which is currently in the editorial offices of the Indiana Historical Society. I traveled extensively in the Calumet Region to verify a portion of that text and I attended the Indianapolis 500 in 1986 and 1987—experiences that defy conventional citation.

Finally, all who think seriously about Indiana history and the role of this state in the regions of which it has been part must acknowledge the standard of excellence which R. Carlyle Buley set in *The Old Northwest*, 2 vols. (Indianapolis, 1950).

Herbert T. Hoover

SOUTH DAKOTA

An Expression of
Regional Heritage

SOUTH DAKOTANS HAVE many things in common with neighboring state groups in the Upper Mississippi and Missouri River basins. All were the homeland of the Sioux Indian federation, and all evolved through similar territorial procedures. Their social habits and political tendencies have common roots. Their land-based economies are affected by similar climatic cycles and economic trends. Many members of each state group in the region have family ties that extend from the western Great Lakes plains to central Montana.

Yet South Dakotans have always been different from neighboring groups. Their forebears claimed the most complicated network of streams and provinces in the Missouri River basin. The resident Arikaras and Sioux attracted more attention from outsiders than did other tribes of the region. Both Indians and whites in South Dakota suffered more than their neighbors from climatic cycles and excessive reliance on land-based industries. Diverse ethnic enclaves have been shielded more from change by isolation.

The distinctive characteristics of people in this state are understood best in the contexts of physiography and history. The natural setting was created when prehistoric glacial action formed the Missouri River basin on approximately 580,000 square miles of sloping terrain. As the ice cap receded, new topographic provinces appeared.

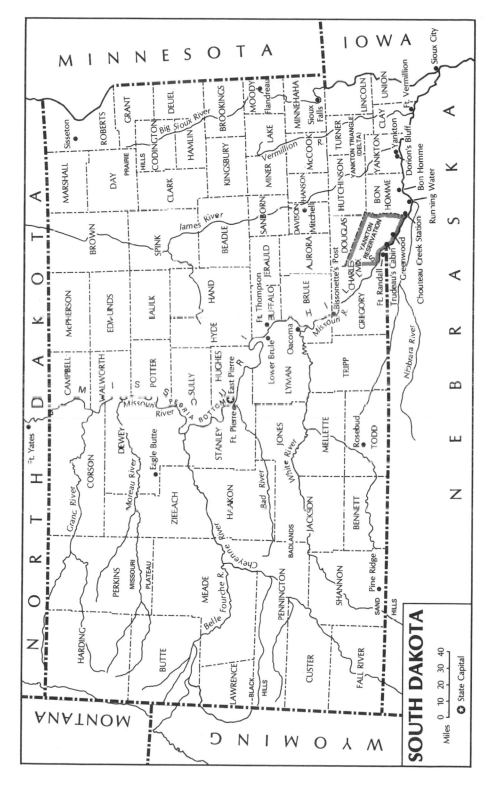

SOUTH DAKOTA

Miles 0 10 20 30 40

⊕ State Capital

The Missouri mainstem drained them through a crooked channel more than twenty-seven hundred miles long. Between present-day Bismarck, and Sioux City, runoff swelled sharply from the issues of substantial tributary streams. The Cannonball, Grand, Moreau, Cheyenne, Bad, White and Niobrara rivers rushed down from the Missouri Plateau, Black Hills, Sand Hills, and Badlands. The James, Vermillion and Big Sioux rivers flowed more gently out of the spacious James River basin, and from the sprawling Missouri and Prairie Hills.

The drainage system in this melange of topographic features created hazards as pronounced as those of any other river system on the continent. Excessive silt loads poured down from western tributaries into the "Big Muddy" and brought shifts in its channel, formed obstructions to navigation, and at flood times made the water practically useless for human needs. Floods around ice gorges in early spring destroyed settlements and sent valley residents scurrying to high ground for safety. Erratic weather and serpentine river channels were responsible. Every few years an early thaw high on the Missouri mainstem or a principal tributary loosened great slabs of ice, which jammed in sharp turns and narrows downstream to create dams as high as forty feet. Sometimes a cold snap held a jam in place as long as two weeks and formed a lake that covered the valley upstream as far as twenty miles. On the mainstem, nine major overflows occurred between 1851 and 1952, including the Great Floods of 1881 and 1907. Along the lower White River, jams brought eighteen destructive floods through the years 1905–78, including two of major consequence in 1907 and 1978. On other tributaries, gorges and floods were not that severe but ever a threat to valley residents.

The construction of earthen dams on the mainstem between 1954 and 1966 curtailed siltation downstream, to be sure, while it eliminated floods along the Missouri channel and produced other benefits. Spokesmen for the U.S. Army Corps of Engineers boast that in two decades an initial investment of $1.1 billion saved approximately $1.6 billion in flood damages between Fort Peck, Montana, and New Orleans and generated more than $1.2 billion from the sale of hydroelectric power. They point to how the four dams and Great Lakes in South Dakota enhanced its recreational opportunities, tourist industry, trans-state communication, wildlife habitat, and reclamation works. Yet they offer no solutions to the worst of problems. Silt lodes that give a milky texture to western tributaries gradually fill in the lakes and threaten the dams. Gorges and floods continue to damage property throughout the network of tributary rivers and creeks.

Added to hazards caused by the rivers have been others due to a cyclical pattern of climatic extremes. Dry spells have threatened the survival of inhabitants with droughts, grasshoppers, and fires. Wet cycles have brought killing blizzards, torrential rains, and floods from late spring to midsummer.

Unpredictable weather and complicated topographic features have caused problems as far back as collective memory goes, but the network of capricious rivers has been a lifeline, too. In early chronicles, passersby recorded the dependence of Caddoan Arikaras upon the mainstem for wood, water, protection, transportation, arable land, and other essential bounties. For nearly a century after initial contact in 1743, non-Indian explorers and traders recorded the capacity of these riverine farmers to produce corn of eleven varieties plus other vegetables in excess of local needs for trade with neighboring Indians and with merchants from St. Louis and Montreal. During the same era, travelers and traders described the relocation of Sioux people from prairie village sites around Mille Lac to their traditional hunting ground in the central Missouri River basin, where they dislodged Arikaras and other Indian occupants and marked large areas of use for bands by natural landmarks. At their villages near the mainstem and its tributaries, Sioux residents enjoyed access to wood and water and blended farming with gathering, trading, and hunting big game that grazed on natural grasslands across the region.

Soon after the Sioux spread out in band encampments, non-Indians began to settle nearby. The year around, small groups of traders lived at Dorion's Bluff, Trudeau's Cabin, Bissonette's Post, Fort (Tecumseh) Pierre, Fort Vermillion, and a site on the floodplain near the mouth of the Big Sioux River. In appropriate seasons, others camped to barter at Running Water, the forks of the White, Cheyenne, Moreau, and Grand rivers, and several advantageous points across a triangle of lush prairie between the Missouri and the upper Big Sioux. Living in close proximity to each other, traders and their Indian hosts engaged in cultural interchange, and through intermarriage created a society designated "half-breed" in federal nomenclature.

Subsequent arrivals formed yet another group to thrive on business from Sioux encampments, trading posts, and traffic up the mainstem. "Missouri Valley society" comprised venturesome men and women who raised food crops for sale, marketed goods at steamboat docking places, and supplied services on demand. They did wood cutting and storage for steamboat lines and supplied meals and lodging for traveling officials and tourists. They provided recreational opportunities both within and outside the law, including oyster feeds, community socials, spiritous beverages at numerous "whiskey stations," gaming at card tables and farrow wheels, and companionship with prostitutes who shuttled from place to place. Valley residents gathered mainly at Fort Vermillion; lower Choteau Creek Station, known also as William Shakel's Honolulu Ranch; Oacoma near the mouth of White River; Fort Pierre, which evolved from a trading post into a licentious entrepôt for Black Hills commerce; East Pierre, a whiskey station across the Missouri from the Fort; Peoria Bottom, along the east bank of the mainstem upstream from Pierre; and numerous islands large enough to survive inundation as the Missouri channel shifted from flood to flood.

The vice-ridden components of Missouri Valley culture, added to the undesirable elements in half-breed society, had deleterious effects on tribal life. Commercial operatives sold alcoholic beverages, ran gambling tables, and rented prostitutes to Sioux people. At the same time, valley residents and mixed-bloods buffered many abrasive aspects of Indian-white relations. They served as bilingual spokesmen in diplomacy, maintained communications through a succession of wars, and gave instruction to either side on the ways of the other. Through their efforts, cross-cultural relations were tempered by tolerance and seldom upset by violence until midcentury.

Valley residents and mixed-bloods also lent assistance to newcomers who showed up in the 1850s. Most of them were land speculators and prospective settlers from Wisconsin, Minnesota, and Iowa who coveted a tract between the Big Sioux and Missouri rivers—called the Yankton Triangle or Yankton Delta—which contained more than eleven million acres suited to farming or ranching. Yankton tribal occupants seemed confident in their ability to fend off encroachment. They had aboriginal claim and possessed military potential that non-Indians had feared for half a century. They gained assurance from the 1851 Fort Laramie Treaty, which enhanced their rights of use on land west of the Missouri. Most outsiders thought the cession of the Yankton Triangle for public entry to be inevitable, however, because federal officials had "quieted" Indian title to valuable tracts many times before under circumstances like these. Demand increased as an exodus from western Europe swelled the movement of whites out of eastern states to trans-Mississippi provinces. Easy access to the area was available overland or up the Missouri waterway. Service communities evolved near the center and the mouth of the Big Sioux, named Sioux Falls and Sioux City (Iowa).

Land-hungry pioneers who assembled at these and other staging places knew about the agricultural potential of the Triangle. Its tribal occupants had succeeded as vegetable gardeners for a century or more. Federal officials had operated a U.S. government farm at Fort Vermillion with marginal success in the 1830s. Traders had raised garden truck near their homes at the Fort. Mormons had stopped by to plant a crop as they fled from Nauvoo in the mid-1840s.

The Triangle seemed safe enough, too. Traders Theophile Bruguier and Henri Angé had acted in concert with Yankton chiefs Mad Bull, War Eagle, and Struck-by-the-Ree to carry on cordial relations with outsiders for approximately twenty-five years. General William

Harney added military presence with the founding of Fort Randall in 1856 and diminished the probability of trouble from Tetons or Yanktonais if Yanktons ceded their Triangle to the United States.

There was some resistance within the tribe. Two band chiefs ordered settlers out of Sioux City, for example, and followers of Smutty Bear and Mad Bull evicted squatters from the lower edge of the Triangle. But non-Indians were correct in their assumption that chiefs and headmen preferred negotiation to a bloodbath. In 1858 cession came easily in the terms of the Treaty of Washington, whereby Yankton leaders exchanged aboriginal claim to 11,155,890 acres for half a century of annuities and benefits, plus recognized title to both a 430,000-acre reservation near Fort Randall and the Pipestone Quarry site. During the summer of 1859 most Yankton people assembled near an "agency mile square" later named Greenwood, where they remained as the only tribal group of Sioux that never made war against the United States. By 1860 the expansive Triangle was available for survey and settlement. In 1861 it became the main center of activity for Dakota Territory, whose officers at Yankton city offered governmental services to settlers and began preparations for statehood.

No land boom ensued during early territorial years. The Civil War and the Minnesota Sioux War went on simultaneously through the early 1860s. Blizzards, floods, droughts, dust storms, prairie fires, grasshopper invasions, and early autumn frosts stifled agrarian interest until 1868. An "Indian scare" was a deterrent from the beginning of Red Cloud's War in 1866 to the end of Sitting Bull's Great Sioux War in 1877. Financial panic accompanied another cycle of droughts, prairie fires, dust storms, grasshopper plagues, and floods through the mid-1870s. For nearly two decades only small contingents arrived. Norwegian, Irish, Swedish, Dutch, Danish, and British immigrants joined older residents to enlarge a thin line of settlement that reached from the upper Big Sioux River down to Sioux City and up the Missouri Valley to the territorial capital. As early as 1869, eastern European Czechs began to occupy the area between Yankton city and Bon Homme.

Gradually, major obstacles to settlement disappeared, troubles in continental Europe enlarged the wave of immigrants, and by 1878 the Great Dakota Boom was under way. Most prominent among new arrivals were people of German descent. Those escaping problems in central Europe spread out among residents of British and Scandinavian heritage who filled the east end of the Triangle, while others formed new communities farther west. Most unusual were the Hutterites, who purchased a ranch near Bon Homme from former Yankton agent and delegate to Congress Walter Burleigh in 1874 and created the mother colony for a line of communes up the James River basin. More numerous were the Mennonites, who settled north and west of Yankton, and the Bohemian, Slovakian, and Moravian Czechs, who occupied land from the lower James River basin to the Yankton Reservation. Most curious were the smaller groups that failed at farming and moved to towns nearby: Jewish settlers near Mitchell, for instance, and black rural colonists in the Missouri Hills.

The main elements of "East River" culture were in place by 1889, as the boom ended in another cycle of economic dislocation and adverse weather conditions. By then leaders had gone through procedures of empire prescribed by the amended Northwest Ordinance and had transformed southern Dakota Territory into the State of South Dakota with East Pierre as its capital. In addition, resident prospectors had initiated the settlement of land west of the Missouri River, most of which opened for entry under the terms of the congressional Great Sioux Agreement of 1889.

"West River" South Dakota had a legacy of its own. Place names and early records indicate that Cheyennes ranged eastward across the Black Hills region until Tetons and Yanktonai moved out from Minnesota to settle. Crossing the Missouri by 1750, these western Sioux spread out and adjusted to conditions on the northern Great Plains. For approximately a century their contacts with non-Indians were limited to barter with hinterland traders, periodic talks with federal negotiators, and occasional visits with explorers, artist-ethnographers, adventurers, and other tourists. But in the 1850s immigrants streamed across the southern edge of their land. Armed conflict began with the Grattan Affair and Ash Hollow Battle along the Platte River basin in Nebraska. It went on intermittently until the Wounded Knee Affair close to Pine Ridge and the death of Sitting Bull in 1890 near his birthplace on the lower Grand River. Sitting Bull and Red Cloud stood out among numerous leaders who rallied forces to keep white people out. Recognition of futility in the effort came under duress, however, with acceptance of the 1889 Agreement. Three decades of warfare and diplomatic resistance ended in the confinement of western Sioux people on reservations similar to those created for East River Indians following the Washington Treaty of 1858.

Most of the Sioux in South Dakota were segregated from non-Indians on nine reserves and subjected to federal acculturation procedures fashioned to prepare Indians for citizenship in the United States. East River reservations surrounded Greenwood, Flandreau, Sisseton, and Fort Thompson. West River reserves headquartered at Rosebud, Pine Ridge, Lower Brule, Fort Bennett replaced by Eagle Butte, and Fort Yates. Most half-breeds joined their relatives on reservations, while others remained in the settlements of Missouri Valley society, which blended into the burgeoning mass of non-Indians.

Until the outset of the twentieth century, most white people who entered West River country engaged in activities related to Indian affairs. Some arrived in military units to fight the wars or keep the peace. Many worked at the distribution of annuity goods provided by Indian treaties or agreements. Steamboat operators dropped manufactured items and supplies at points of distribution along the Missouri, for example, while herdsmen drove cattle up from the south for use as annuities on issue days and as foundation herds for an infant livestock industry.

As in West River, so in East River, others came to reservations as regular employees of the United States Indian Field Service. The typical agency staff comprised an agent, chief clerk, assistant clerk, physician, several U.S. farmers bearing various labels and obligations, many educators, cattle tenders, issue clerks, teamsters, and artisans imported to practice and teach carpentry, blacksmithing, and tinsmithing. Later came field matrons, field nurses, expert farmers, stockmen, and extraneous others to help U.S. farmers with the establishment of agrarian industries. Attached to agencies were mission groups, mainly of Catholic, Presbyterian, Congregational, and Episcopal denominations. With support from eastern benefactors and federal officials, they built churches and schools to spread the gospel as they gave instruction about the ways of white people.

The immigrants involved with Indian affairs had diverse impacts. While imposing policies formulated by federal officials and eastern reformers at agencies, albeit with lofty intentions, they did considerable harm to the Sioux. As overlords charged to expunge the ways of Indians quickly, they nearly ruined tribal economies, drove ancient cultural practices underground, and further distorted reciprocal images of Indians and whites already twisted by three decades of war. At the same time they bolstered the economy of non-Indians, which faltered after the heyday of the fur trade. Men and women who operated military and agency units purchased goods and services with federal and mission funds; spent salaries drawn from congressional allocations or eastern benefactors; paid for carrying services by steamboat, wagon, stagecoach and railway; and hired as irregular agency employees hundreds of mixed-bloods and non-Indians dependent on part-time jobs for survival.

As agency personnel scattered on reservations, miners entered the Black Hills province. Their arrival in the 1870s forced a showdown between the western Sioux and the United States over possession. Prospectors bought supplies and spent proceeds from "diggins" briefly through flush times. Industrial operators followed with heavy equipment, employing workers of international heritage to extract precious metals from quartz. Deadwood, Lead, Rapid City, and smaller mining towns became centers of service and trade for the Black Hills.

Close behind those who arrived to work in Indian affairs or mining came participants in a final surge of land seekers, who nearly filled out rural society across the Missouri Hills and West River provinces between 1890 and 1920. Taking advantage of rapid change in federal policies on Indian land ownership and management, new arrivals leased, homesteaded, or purchased the lion's share of arable acreage both off and on the reservations. Many relocated from East River communities or neighboring states. Others came from troubled spots in eastern Europe: a large contingent of German-Russians, mainly from the Volga River basin, and numerous refugees from the decaying Austro-Hungarian Empire. Markers in cemeteries at Deadwood and Philip, for example, comprise names of national origin from all parts of Europe and even the Orient.

An aggregate society struggling with austere conditions was in place by 1920. From its historical development evolved some internal divisions. On every Sioux reservation, separation existed between mixed-bloods and full bloods for their different responses to reservation life. In East River non-Indian society, people differed from those of West River. In every tribe and major rural white settlement, South Dakotans were unique for their ethnic attachments.

The opportunity to defend these distinctive ways in relative isolation from mainstream society was one of several things nearly all South Dakotans held in common. Approximately a third of the non-Indian population was foreign born at the time of statehood, and many new arrivals came from eastern Europe before the onset of the 1920s. Groups that stood out for size and ethnic character included Lutheran German, Mennonite, Hutterite, German Russian, Dutch, Norwegian, Swedish, Danish, Finnish, Czech, French, Irish, Polish, and Welsh. In most of their communities, noteworthy percentages did not use English as a first language, if at all. Settlers in white enclaves retained "old country" ways by reading foreign language newspapers, and through like behavior in church affiliations, food preparations, social values, family practices, and cultural activities on solemn or festive occasions.

In aggregate, their ethnicity and regional perspective gained reinforcement from provincial emphasis in the contents of such newspapers as the *Dakota Republican, Yankton Press and Dakotaian, Sioux Falls Argus Leader, Vermillion Plain Talk,* and *Rapid City Journal.* Their diverse cultural ways were transmitted through educational systems. Denominational primary schools, academies, and colleges that featured regional developments were accessible to Lutherans, Presbyterians, Congregationalists, Methodists, and Catholics. Public educational service, established with federal land grant assistance to nurture learning with provincial focus, was available in district primary schools, a professional university at Vermillion, and the College of Agriculture and Mechanic Arts in Brookings. State-supported high schools and colleges were within the reach of nearly every settlement.

South Dakotans had many vehicles and institutions available to transmit ethnic and provincial ways from generation to generation.

Intellectual focus on regional heritage was encouraged, too, by the rich body of literature available to educators and general readers alike. Natural splendor, economic opportunity, and Indian affairs had long attracted authors. Jean Baptiste Trudeau wrote the first in a substantial list of worthy sighting reports and chronicles that focused on the central Missouri River basin. George Catlin and Karl Bodmer created the first of many art and ethnographic collections on the region. Pierre Jean DeSmet, Stephen Return Riggs, Thomas and John Williamson, and William Hobart Hare were foremost among distinguished clergy who wrote from here to benefactors in the East. Riggs, James Owen Dorsey, Alice Fletcher, Marie McLaughlin, and Charles Eastman headed the list of those who recorded information about Indian ethnology. Ole Rolvaag and Doane Robinson stood out among scores of popular writers, journalists, biographers, and tourists who described the evolution of non-Indian culture. Along with lessons from *McGuffey's Readers*, Mason Locke Weems's biographies, *Webster's Spellers*, and *Clark's Grammar*, South Dakotans drew from this literature and their oral traditions reinforcement for ethnic and provincial life. The only pressure for Americanization came to non-Indians of German heritage during World War I, when briefly they concealed their ways or went into exile in Canada.

Sioux people experienced greater exposure to mainstream values and more intense pressure to accept them. Some went on relocation for employment. The others were exposed to Anglo-American ways through news organs, educational materials, and practical training on reservations designed to prepare them for citizenship. Reservation progressives were more amenable than were traditionalists. Yet, majorities in both groups clung to ancient legacies through activities that foiled acculturation efforts by agency personnel and missionaries, who relied mainly on social pressure and job opportunities for leverage. Only the Sun Dance, the giveaway, and for a brief period the Peyote religion were forbidden here by official edicts. In the absence of federal proscriptions, reservation residents preserved their own values and practices. Medicine men carried on the Sacred Pipe religion in spite of ridicule. Road men conducted Peyote meetings at isolated locations. Indians redesigned Christian teaching and philosophy to their liking. Reservation residents participated in traditional activities at dance halls and learned from their elders at least as much as they heard from schoolteachers and missionaries. Like the people in white ethnic enclaves, the reservation Sioux were successful in their resistance to mainstream Americanization.

For whites and Indians alike, cultural concerns were not related as much to ethnic change as to self-image or group identity. Non-

Indians fell victim to a trend in national history. Down to the mid-1850s, with representatives of farmers in charge of the United States, virtue in agrarian life was honored according to a tradition that reached back in literature to ancient Greece. After the Civil War, politicians beholden to urban-industrial society took over, and country folks became members of a shrinking minority maligned as "hayseeds," "sodbusters," and the like. A Vermillion editor warned Dakota readers that industrial salesmen regarded them as "convenient menials" to be duped.[1] In self-defense, they reaffirmed their noble heritage. The land they occupied was "part of God's estate on the globe," wrote the editor; people with title went "into partnership with the Original Proprietor of the earth."[2] Yet, self-esteem eroded steadily as industrial society grew proportionately larger in size and political strength.

Reservation residents experienced an identity crisis of a different sort. As Indian Office employees and mission personnel applied pressure to change them in preparation for citizenship, they responded in ways that created factions. A substantial number acceded to official pressure and went away for either boarding school education or employment. Many did not return, but some came back to join those classified as reservation progressives, who followed the example of earlier mixed-bloods. Called half-breeds by other Indians as well as by whites, they strove for smooth adaptation and improvement in the economies of their tribes. Others clung more tenaciously to ancient practices and beliefs. Persecuted or shunned by agency personnel, missionaries, and progressives as "full blood," "blanket," or traditional Indians, they viewed cultural survival as their central cause. One's designation as half-breed or full blood was determined by attitude and behavior more than blood quantum. Some who were largely white by blood lived as traditionalists. Others who were nearly all Indian joined the progressives. Many achieved cultural adaptation without substantial loss of traditional ways. Nevertheless, there emerged in every tribe three general factions: relocatees, progressives, and traditionalists. With their ancient form of government now supplanted by reservation business committees under the control of agency superintendents, political power was vested mainly in progressive spokesmen. Deep divisions were the inevitable result as people struggled for employment and acceptance.

Along with problems of identity among South Dakotans came economic hardship that drove many to bankruptcy and others to the verge of starvation. Rural non-Indians faced double jeopardy most of the time. As citizens of a trans-Mississippi state group doing colonial service for the industrial East, they sold raw materials at prices fixed by purchasers, bought manufactured goods and essential services at costs established by suppliers, and paid transportation fees as high as the traffic would bear. Ever at the mercy of outsiders, they went through cycles of distress imposed by droughts, grasshoppers, ice gorges, summer floods, hail storms, prairie fires, killing frosts, blizzards, and economic depressions.

Reservation residents fell into greater economic distress. Late-nineteenth-century policymakers arranged the allotment of communal land in individual subsistence acreages and the sale of surplus tribal domain for funds to help allottees gain self-sufficiency as farmers or ranchers. In theory, all had farms or ranches large enough to accomplish this. In practice, their land-based economy let them down. Reasons included the termination of treaty annuities before the transition was complete, a disinclination by many to take up farming or ranching full time, the infertility of acreages on allotments, land hunger among whites, adverse climatic conditions, and discouragement resulting from bureaucratic paternalism on the reservations. Federal surveys in the 1920s revealed that only three Yankton Reservation families drew total support from their own land. Other tribal groups fared little better. Most reservation residents fell into dire straits as many searched for seasonal work among white farmers and ranchers or went on relocation into urban communities and wild West shows as wage laborers.

The inevitable result of economic distress was growing dependence on governmental agencies for help. To hinterland non-Indians, this was hard to accept. Occupational individualism coupled with religious commitment and belief in the nobility of farming ran counter to collective action, but there was no alternative. After brief engagement in the social, educational, and cooperative programs of the Granger movement, they accepted the liberal posture of the Farmers' Alliance. Then many gave their support to the People's party, whose 1892 platform called for federal intervention and socialism. Like their Populist neighbors, South Dakotans were disappointed by successive losses at the polls from 1896 to 1904 and turned to Progressive Republican leaders in state government to accomplish similar ends. Governors Coe Crawford, Peter Norbeck, and William McMaster joined state legislators to challenge forces that sapped rural profits; they officially intervened in service practices and socialized vital industries.

In addition, Progressive leaders worked to diversify the economy. Previously, a precarious farm base had been supplemented by a livestock industry that produced feeders from foundation herds in West River for fattening on corn and grains in East River and export to packers in Sioux Falls, Sioux City, and Omaha. After statehood, miners began the production of industrial materials as well as precious metals. Investors started a forestry business. Yet there was need for greater diversification, and state officials led the way in the development of tourism. It was already nearly as old as white society in

Dakota. George Catlin was one of the sightseers who competed successfully for passage on the *Yellowstone* in 1832. Thereafter, countless wayfarers on steamboats purchased food, lodging, and entertainment from Missouri Valley residents as they paused to visit the tribes and view the landscapes. Business picked up with the coming of stagecoaches and railroads and grew still more with the appearance of automobiles and buses. Partly to entice more tourists, Progressive state leaders initiated the development of parks and created a highway department. Road crews drew on matching funds available under the Federal Highway Act of 1916 to build concrete thoroughfares. Attractions were little different from those of the nineteenth century, but by 1920 the commitment of state officials in South Dakota to exploit tourism made it an industry of value second only to farming and ranching.

The growing dependence of Indians on public officials for the management of their economic lives grew out of treaty terms and surplus land sale agreements, which provided payments from tribal funds held in the U.S. Treasury. Dependence increased because of individual Indian money accounts, which contained earned increments accrued to individuals in local bank deposits that could be drawn out a few dollars at a time only with agency approval. Dependence became still more pronounced as these funds were depleted and Interior Department officials supervised the lease and sale of individual allotments. Federal officials kept the books as Sioux people used up most of their individual resources, then paid out in per capita sums nearly all that remained in tribal accounts by the early 1920s. A few years later, industrial survey reports indicated that economic self-sufficiency from the land was no longer feasible. Tribal members became dependent on federal programs for education, health care, relocation, social services, and supplies of essential items. Faulty and scarce as these things tended to be, they became the mainstay to reservation residents. By 1920 most of them were in some degree victims of a paternalistic system from which there was no obvious escape—except for those who surrendered Indian affiliations and went on relocation into mainstream society.

With so much in common because of conditions beyond their control, white and Indian South Dakotans should have felt empathy if not sympathy for each other, but in the main they shared mutual contempt instead. Back when non-Indians appeared on Indian turf only for trade, diplomacy, and exploration, relations were cordial most of the time. After settlers arrived in the 1850s, that changed abruptly. In thirty-five years of armed confrontation over land and cultural differences, the image held by each side about the other deteriorated into disdain if not hatred. A surveyor dispatched in 1870 to mark boundaries for homesteads of the Santee Sioux near Flandreau expressed an attitude common to whites when he protested against his assignment because he "hated an Indian so much that he did not want to have anything to do with them."[3] More than twenty-five thousand of his Indian contemporaries demonstrated similar feelings when they joined Sitting Bull's movement to keep non-Indians out of Sioux and Cheyenne country by force of arms if necessary. At length Sioux people grew bitter about conditions on reservations. Their white neighbors had little sympathy because of tales about wartime atrocities and ethnic peculiarities. Agency and mission personnel might have ameliorated tension had they not been preoccupied by their attempts to modify Indian behavior and culture. By 1920 the majority of non-Indians came to view Sioux people as rural vagrants thriving on the federal dole at the expense of taxpayers while drinking, stealing, and avoiding gainful employment. In fact, most Indians were living on the last of tribal funds derived from treaties or land sale agreements, drank little if at all, went without things they could not afford, and accepted meager help from the federal government as a last resort. Conversely, Indians thought no better of whites. They appeared to be selfish, callous, arrogant, land-hungry bigots bent on seizing Indian land. In fact, most whites bought or homesteaded tracts acquired earlier from tribes by eastern politicians and refrained from cordial relations more because of language barriers and fear than racism. Non-Indians inherited a twisted image of Sioux people through tales about wars in which few had taken part. Misunderstanding born of ignorance and fear on both sides twisted reciprocal images into intercultural conflict as severe as any in the history of the United States.

Main features in the aggregate society of South Dakota underwent modification without drastic change during the twentieth century as the population increased by less than 8 percent, from 637,000 in 1920 to slightly more than 687,000 in 1985. The best efforts of the Corps of Engineers only modified hazards related to complex natural conditions. In exchange for a fertile valley along the Missouri River flooded by lakes, the engineers offered no more than flood control on the mainstem, reclamation potential, and the other benefits already mentioned. Problems with siltation, ice gorging, and flooding on the tributaries were not addressed. Hardships related to a weather pattern that cycled every fifteen or twenty years, parching the northeastern counties, most of the Missouri Hills, and the West River provinces and then drenching floodplain settlements and inundating crops, did not abate. Complex physiography and capricious climate remain a primary concern to this state.

The quality of ethnic composition did not change appreciably. It only eroded moderately as a result of school consolidation, mobility, the appearance of modern media, and a scarcity of non-English publications. Indeed, a 1980 study indicated that nearly nine thousand persons still spoke Sioux dialects and more than sixty-five thousand still used German dialects as first languages. To stave off further loss of ethnicity, in the 1960s South Dakotans began to offer instruction in Sioux dialects and culture at reservation schools and in off-reservation colleges and universities, European dialects through the Czech Heritage Society in Tabor as well as in the Hutterite colonies, Norwegian culture studies at Augustana College, and increasing participation in ethnic practices during festivities—Czech Days at Tabor, Swedish Midsommar at Dalesburg, Nordlandfest in Sioux Falls, frequent religious ceremonies and powwows on Indian reservations, and other such affairs.

Concern about the loss of ethnicity evolved not only out of community interest but also through the influence of a national propensity to celebrate ethnic diversity and the local desire to preserve a salable commodity. Since the visit of George Catlin in 1832, outsiders have been fascinated by cultural anomalies in this region. South Dakotans have shown increasing inclination to accommodate visitors who are willing to pay for food, lodging, travel service, and entertainment. Midsommar at Dalesburg brings an annual return of several thousand dollars to keep community facilities in operation, while Nordlandfest strives for profit through admission fees and ethnic merchandise fairs. Sioux people rely for summer income on prizes derived from admission fees and contributions for dancing and work year-round on arts and crafts to sell.

While South Dakotans have been prone to market the outward symbols of ethnicity for profit, they have shielded from national view the dynamics of culture and withheld from outsiders the environmental and ethnic treasures they have cherished. Most tourists rush through on Interstate 90 to get faint glimpses of East River prairie, Lake Francis Case at Chamberlain, fringes of the Missouri Hills and Badlands, and things in the Black Hills region that interest most residents very little, including carnival atmospheres at Wall and Keystone, Reptile Gardens, Mount Rushmore, and erroneous images of Sioux people. Only South Dakotans and sensitive visitors who move slowly on secondary roads enjoy the more interesting features. They include pink rock palisades in the Prairie Hills that connect underground to the Pipestone Quarry, a continental divide at Brown's Valley, the pinnacle of the Prairie Hills at Summit, magnificent wildlife from Waubay to the lower James River basin, the open grandeur of the Missouri Valley and Hills, a Sand Hills sanctuary at LaCreek where white swans and great Canada geese hide away, Spearfish Canyon, Bear Butte, sacred Green Grass, and a host of others. South Dakotans have even withheld from general access their primary historical sites and arranged the construction of a heritage center in relative isolation at Pierre. This behavior is sometimes expressed as a desire that neither tourists nor population in excess of a million should soon spoil the treasures of the state.

Concealment of cultural habits also stems from lingering problems with self-image or identity. Without much grasp of historical causes, many non-Indians hide daily attachments to ethnic ways and provincial focus from scrutiny by outsiders. "Dumb Norwegian" humor, "Pride in Farming" bumper stickers, hayseed caricatures, erroneous presentations of past events in tourist literature, and illiteracies on road signs all reflect the causes for self-consciousness. Indignant denial of the problem only underscores its depth. As hinterland people, South Dakotans are at ease with peers but unsteady when exposed for long to visitors. Even "snowbirds" who flee to Arizona for comfort in wintertime live in communities occupied mainly by South Dakotans.

This trait persists because of a colonial status in national life and a provincial education that values strategies for survival and regional mores more than exposure to national humanities and arts. It also reflects satisfaction with provincial contributors. To the list of important authors already presented have been added such names as Siouxland novelists Frederick Manfred and Herbert Krause, popular author Robert Karolevitz, literary contributor John Milton, and historian Herbert Schell. Following nineteenth-century painters came the distinguished Yanktonai Indian artist Oscar Howe and a score of other able painters, including the Indians Arthur Amiotte and Robert Penn, prairie artist Harvey Dunne, and Missouri Hills artist laureate James Pollock. There are also many others who express ethnic heritage through crafts and fine arts—none more distinguished than the Yankton Sioux beadworker Clarence Rockboy and the Teton musician and dancer Kevin Locke. In addition, there is the calligrapher Benedictine sister Leonarda Longen; several prominent quilters, weavers, and potters; and others supported in part by dynamic humanities and fine arts councils.

Sioux people may flaunt the symbols of Indianness before visitors, but like rural whites most are reluctant to share the dynamics of ethnic life. Obviously this results from the ridicule they still endure for Indian ways. Perhaps it also reflects a concealment of laments about factionalism in tribes. Friction among urban, progressive, and traditional groups has been exacerbated by reservation unemployment estimated in recent years at more than 80 percent on every reservation in the state. While there is unity in defense against outside pressure, there is abiding internal division through competition for limited opportunities available to growing tribal populations. The inward focus of Sioux South Dakotans stems, too, from pride in the great variety of humanities and art forms available through tribal performers.

Economic distress remains as severe for all South Dakotans as it was through the 1920s or 1930s. Farming, ranching, and urban agribusiness among non-Indians suffered greater difficulty in the 1980s than at any time since the Great Depression. Employment for wages and salaries paid by federal and tribal funds is more scarce on reservations than at any time since their establishment.

Trends in history that rendered both whites and Indians dependent on governmental agencies for economic survival continue. Among non-Indians, these trends have been visible in several ways. One has been the call for federal assistance through rural organizations. To be sure, the Livestock Growers Association and Farm Bureau chapters have promoted a free-enterprise credo that rejects any official involvement in rural economies. But the United Farmers League of the parched northeastern counties became a Communist affiliate during the early 1930s, and the American Agriculture Movement represented ranchers of West River in the demand for parity at 90 percent through direct federal subsidy during the tractor protest in Washington through the spring and summer of 1979. Speaking for a majority between these extremes, the Grange, Farmers Union, and National Farmers' Organization all have taken a liberal posture to promote cooperative purchase of essential commodities and services, collective marketing strategies, and federal crop subsidies and price supports.

Another symptom of dependence has been a voting tendency in times of stress. Although enrolled mainly as Republicans, South Dakotans suffering from hard times in the 1920s and 1930s sent Progressive Peter Norbeck to the U.S. Senate and Democrat Tom Berry to the governorship as they sacrificed pride in independence for help from Franklin Roosevelt's New Deal programs to save themselves. Responding to distress over limited federal assistance following a dry cycle in the Eisenhower era, they elected Democrats George McGovern, James Abourezk, and Tom Daschle to Congress to solicit federal aid. In 1986 they moved Daschle from the House of Representatives to the Senate and elected Democrat Tim Johnson to the lower house.

Yet another barometer of dependence has been increasing reliance on federal resources for state expenditures since World War II. Without going far into debt, the legislature has elevated annual expenditures as high as $953 million while never collecting state revenues in amounts half this size. Along with program subsidies from federal agencies, South Dakotans have received help through the presence of the Corps of Engineers along the Missouri and the armed forces at Ellsworth Air Base near Rapid City. Without federal assistance of many kinds, an economy reliant upon agriculture, tourism, mining, and service industries could not keep the books of state government in balance.

Out of necessity, people of Sioux extraction (in 1980, 6.25 percent officially, but some 9 percent realistically, of the total population) have followed a similar course. New Deal Indian programs helped the Sioux through the Great Depression. Federal support diminished during World War II as they left reservations to enter the armed forces or to take wartime jobs. Governmental assistance was further curtailed in the Eisenhower era, when federal relocation officers labored to move reservation Indians to cities for industrial or service job employment. Great Society programs of the 1960s lured many back in the belief that federal support would at last be sustained. Since the election of Richard Nixon, however, the needs of growing reservation populations have been answered not by federal assistance but by official encouragement of tribal "self-determination" and a plan to withdraw federal program assistance as soon as possible.

Escape from poverty either on reserves or in off-reservation communities has been futile for most Indian residents of the state. Mechanization and economic stress in agriculture have all but eliminated seasonal work. Lingering social distance between Sioux people and whites has made urban jobs very scarce. Most members of Indian populations in excess of 5,000 at Rapid City, 2,000 in Sioux Falls, and 750 at Yankton, for example, have searched in vain for employment even at menial tasks. Hundreds if not thousands of tribal members shuttle back and forth between reservations and urban communities without finding help at either end. Prospective employers recite tales of faulty performance as an explanation and conceal the fear of losing white customers as the underlying cause. All progressive tribal leaders, most clergymen, and some businessmen strive to correct misconceptions about job performance and to combat discrimination, while Sioux people wait for better times.

It should now be possible to see that South Dakotans are not to be distinguished from their neighbors by a few particular characteristics but by the degree to which historical trends and environmental conditions of the region have affected their lives. In physiographic diversity and adverse weather cycles, abiding commitment to ethnicity, economic hardships, self-image or identity crises, reliance on governmental assistance, and even race relations they can find common ground with other state groups around them. But in the degree to which these things affect them, they are not like their neighbors.

South Dakotans stand out, too, for the consequences of failure to diversify their economy since the 1920s. Except in scattered light industries and the credit system of Citicorp at Sioux Falls, there has been no sign of substantial improvement through private investment.

That is evident in the retention of rural culture. Until 1960 more than half the population lived on farms or ranches or in towns of less than 2,500. Since then, even the largest urban centers—Sioux Falls with less than 100,000 and Rapid City with fewer than 50,000 people—have remained principally service units for land-based industries and visitors. Neither bears much resemblance in purpose or temperament to Minneapolis or even to Omaha.

More than any state groups of middle America except perhaps those in Wyoming, North Dakota, and Montana, South Dakotans retain characteristics explicable only through the examination of events and trends in the past. Theirs has been from its formation and remains an aggregate population that endures the hazards of natural conditions and colonial economics along with dependence on federal assistance and other adversities for the privilege of a gratifying life in provinces and enclaves protected by distance from mainstream America.

NOTES

1. *Dakota Republican*, February 26, 1874.
2. *Dakota Republican*, January 16, 1873.
3. Governor John A. Burbank to Indian Commissioner E. S. Parker, August 20, 1870, M234, roll 766, National Archives.

BIBLIOGRAPHY

Several guides to published sources on South Dakota history have appeared since 1979. Herbert T. Hoover, *The Sioux: A Critical Bibliography* (Bloomington, Ind., 1979), annotates some two hundred books and articles on Sioux culture and relationships with non-Indians. Jack W. Marken and Hoover, *Bibliography of the Sioux* (Metuchen, N.J., 1980), contains more than thirty-three hundred items that pertain not only to Sioux history but also to the fur trade of the region and to the establishment of white culture prior to territorial times. Sue Laubersheimer, ed., *A Selected Annotated Bibliography: South Dakota* (Brookings, S.D., 1985), includes approximately twelve hundred entries in bibliographical essays on general history by Hoover, natural resources by Bob Carmack, ethnicity by Marken, and literature by Ruth Alexander. A supplement describes the holdings of thirty-five libraries in the state. Hoover, ed., *Planning for the South Dakota Centennial: A Bibliography* (Vermillion, S.D., 1984), analyzes published sources in eleven subject areas and recommends ethnic composition as a subject for special emphasis at the observance of the hundredth birthday of South Dakota, and of the Great Sioux Agreement, in 1989.

Topical selections in the latter publication support the use of ethnicity and images as central themes in this chapter, and numerous collections of original sources are employed to give them substance. The Pierre Choteau, Jr., and Company Papers (Missouri Historical Society in St. Louis) supply material to supplement secondary sources on the early years to 1860. The

Territorial Governor's Papers (North Dakota Historical Society in Bismarck), together with the newspapers mentioned in this chapter, provide contexts as well as details to expand contents drawn from books and articles on themes down to 1920. The experiences of the Sioux are drawn mainly from Letters Received by the Office of Indian Affairs and the Indian Office Central Decimal File (National Archives in Washington), Sioux Agency files (Federal Archives in Kansas City, Denver, and Seattle), various documentary collections preserved by the Minnesota Historical Society (in St. Paul), and the Bureau of Catholic Indian Mission Records (at Marquette University Library in Milwaukee). Many smaller collections have been useful, too, and will soon receive recognition in a bibliography on original sources by the author.

The writing of South Dakota history must still be accomplished mainly through the use of materials contained in documents, but there exists a condensation of substance on non-Indian political, economic, and cultural histories in four vital publications: Herbert S. Schell, *History of South Dakota*, 3d ed., rev. (Lincoln, Nebr., 1975); Howard Roberts Lamar, *Dakota Territory, 1861–1889* (New Haven, Conn., 1956); John Ronald Milton, *South Dakota: A Bicentennial History* (New York, 1977); and the South Dakota Historical Society *Collections*.

R. *Douglas Hurt*

OHIO
Gateway to the Midwest

O HIO IS MAINSTREAM AMERICA. Politically , economically, socially, it is at once North and South as well as East and West. At the same time the Buckeye state is both urban and rural, and like the Midwest in general it is industrial and agricultural—a place of rolling fields, small towns, and sprawling cities. Because Ohio has more metropolitan centers than any other midwestern state, it also has an urbane sophistication and a sordid ugliness that contrast sharply with the tranquillity and beauty of the countryside. If a key exists to explain the cultural distinctiveness of Ohio, it is that Ohioans always have revered pragmatism, political traditionalism, Jeffersonian agrarianism, and the Puritan ethic. The resulting adherence to these philosophical ideals has created a people who exhibit the naiveté and the canniness that is characteristic of many midwesterners. The fruits of these guiding principles also have been the creation of a culture that has thrived on economic conservatism and political moderation.

That does not mean, however, that Ohioans have been unwilling to take risks. While supporting Henry Clay's American System, for example, the state embarked upon an ambitious if not reckless program of canal building that left it nearly hopelessly in debt. Ohio also has had its outspoken political reformers. Only Elijah P. Lovejoy in Missouri and Illinois vied with Ohio's John Rankin, whose biting "Let-

ters on Slavery," together with Benjamin Lundy's appeal for the universal emancipation of slaves, helped change the focus of American politics. Moreover, Ohio shared the messianic and filibustering John Brown with Kansas and helped set the nation on the road to Civil War.

Still, Ohio has been ambivalent. During the antebellum period, most residents opposed slavery as well as abolitionism while at the same time supporting a host of black codes that were among the harshest in the Midwest. Ultimately, however, they feared disunion more than they opposed racial equality. In the twentieth century, Ohioans welcomed the New Deal and the Great Society while preaching the merits of hard work and economy in government. They also have been a peace-loving but sometimes violent people. The fire still burns in the Straitsville mine where labor and management fought bitterly over the right of workers to earn a living wage more than a century ago. Nor has substantive political change come without sharp division. Only in Ohio, for example, during the height of the student protests over the Vietnam War, did the National Guard fire on and kill students engaged in a lawful protest over a matter of principle. Yet for all these contradictions, the state has enjoyed political and economic stability. Both of these features have contributed to material progress and social harmony and to the development of a typically midwestern state with its own special characteristics.

Early in the state's history, immigrants, whether native or foreign born, came to Ohio primarily in search of land. Their dream was little different from that of other frontiersmen in the Midwest. They did not stay for long, however, if they were burdened by "great, impossible dreams." Ohioans, of course, had inventive minds and skillful hands, as the work of the Wright brothers, Charles F. Kettering, and Thomas A. Edison clearly attests. But the vast majority of the men and women who created the state were not like those who painted "Pike's Peak or Bust" on their wagons, nor did they shout "California, here I come." Instead, they were the people who came to stay—farmers, shopkeepers, miners, and factory workers. They did not expect miracles but only the opportunity to work hard and to prosper.

The early pioneers of New England and southern heritage were not disappointed in the faith which they placed in the Puritan ethic. Their spirit, energy, and labor quickly created a leading agricultural state with a decidedly Jeffersonian philosophical foundation. Eventually, their work ethic led to the creation of an industrial economy that was slow to shed both the Jeffersonian tradition and the Puritan ethic. The resulting tug and pull between the agrarian past and the modern industrial state has shaped the main features of Ohio's development since the mid–nineteenth century. Rapid economic change fostered by science, technology, and new business practices, however, created a state that exemplifies the best and the worst of American agricultural and industrial life.

In contrast to other midwestern states, however, Ohio did not develop a genuine provincialism. That is not to say that cultural distinctiveness did not emerge; indeed, it did. New Englanders commonly settled in the Western Reserve in northern Ohio. They built whitewashed Greek Revival homes around neat town squares and established a host of private academies to educate their children. In contrast, Virginians entered southern Ohio and brought the agrarian features of the rural South with them, while German immigrants developed bountiful farms and built solid stone churches in the northwest. The cultural uniqueness which these settlers transferred to each of these areas remains today, if only architecturally or linguistically. Even so, culture determined how the immigrants adapted to their new environment, and it has left an indelible imprint on the development of Ohio. Still, a particular statewide provincialism did not emerge, primarily because Ohio is situated on a major line of immigration between the East and the West. Although tens of thousands of individuals passed through Ohio or stopped temporarily, each contributed to a cultural amalgamation which, if not a true melting pot, fostered social harmony while preserving local color.

The abundant life came slowly. No one ever spoke of Ohio as the land of milk and honey, only as a land of opportunity, if you worked for it. Ohioans always have known that prosperity and comfort came with a price, whether it is paid in the fields, factories, or mines. From the beginning of statehood until the present, they have been willing to pay it. Today, however, Ohioans are becoming increasingly uncertain about the hallowed values and truths of the past, particularly Jeffersonian agrarianism and the Puritan ethic. Economic events that are beyond the control of the family farmer have forced a host of foreclosures and a decline in agriculture as a way of life. Moreover, a sagging industrial economy has made an increasing number of Ohioans question the value of the Puritan ethic. Hard work no longer is the absolute key to success; nor is the family farmer the epitome of independence and self-reliance or the guardian of democracy. If any cultural features of Ohioans remain intact as the state approaches the twenty-first century, they are those of pragmatism and political traditionalism.

The pragmatism of Ohioans clearly is evident in relation to commercial agricultural development during the early nineteenth century. Until the completion of the Erie Canal in 1825, inadequate markets and insufficient transportation restricted Ohio's agricultural development. Buckeye farmers had little choice but to send their commodities to market over difficult roads and distant mountains or down the Ohio and Mississippi rivers to New Orleans for transshipment to the ports beyond. Either method involved time and expense. Moreover, once Ohio's farmers had money in their pockets, they had little access to the consumer goods that would enable them to improve their standard of living.

In 1827, after considerable political maneuvering, Ohioans responded to this economic isolation in a pragmatic fashion by building canals. Eventually, these canals linked Lake Erie with the Ohio River and created an interlocking network across the state, thereby providing access to the markets that farmers desperately needed. When the digging stopped in 1847, state and private canals stretched across more than a thousand miles of Ohio. Even before they finished digging the canals, however, Ohioans turned to a new form of transportation— the railroad. By the end of the 1850s, the canals and railroads had opened the state's fields, forests, and mines to the outside world. Only Indiana caught a similar "canal fever," although the railroad mania affected all midwestern states.

The canals and railroads also stimulated manufacturing. These new forms of transportation encouraged farmers to produce surplus crops for sale, and merchants were quick to buy, process, and ship agricultural commodities as well as to purchase the goods that farm families needed. As a result, trading centers sprang up across the state. At the same time Ohioans were distrustful, even fearful, of industrialization, which many believed would corrupt society and, in turn, ruin the rural way of life. The first industries were, however, more necessary than threatening. By 1840 extractive industries, such as agriculture and mining, created the basis for an urban industrial network that extended from Cleveland in the north to Cincinnati in the south.

While this economic transformation occurred, Ohio, of course, did not exist in isolation. The state, like the others in the Midwest, stumbled through the Panics of 1819, 1837, and 1857. During each economic depression, the working class became more severely affected, in part because it grew in number. In 1837 members of the working class frequently sought refuge in soup kitchens, and the state's unemployment corresponded with the national average of between 6 and 8 percent. Clearly by this time Ohioans felt the ramifications of major economic change on a national level. Whether this change would be for better or for worse, they were increasingly tied to a manufacturing economy.

Ohio, like the other emerging industrial states in the Old Northwest, experienced divisions between skilled and unskilled workers as manufacturers relied more and more on outside capital, distant markets, and volume production to ensure economic gain. Impersonal and adversarial relationships among skilled and unskilled workers and between labor and management further stratified society and made the attainment of the American dream harder to achieve. Still, workers as well as farmers remained politically conservative. Radicalism was not part of their lives. In contrast to many states, for example, Ohio as late as 1835 had not yet embraced the movement for a ten-hour day.

Although manufacturing increased prior to the Civil War, Ohio became the leading agricultural state in the nation. By the mid–nineteenth century, Ohio resembled Iowa today. Buckeye farmers led the nation in the production of cereal grain, and they were among the leading producers of wool, pork, and dairy products. Much of this production was the basis for the state's major manufacturing industries—flour, meat-packing, and distilling. The 1850s, however, were seminal, transitional years for Ohio as manufacturing superseded agriculture in importance. The rapid increase in population, coupled with the development of regional markets, enabled Ohio to maintain a high ranking among the manufacturing states between 1850 and 1870. The value of manufactured goods quadrupled during this time, while the work force nearly tripled. The dual economic development of agriculture and industry, however, was symbiotic. In 1870 Ohio ranked first in the production of agricultural equipment and second in iron. Flour and gristmill products contributed the most value in dollars to the state's economy, followed by rolled and forged iron. The faith Ohioans placed in hard work and the Jeffersonian tradition remained firm.

By the last quarter of the nineteenth century, the growth of industry and the expansion of the railroad network effectively fostered the concentration of population in cities with more than five thousand inhabitants, twenty-six of which existed in Ohio by 1870. This growth gave Ohioans new concerns that were far removed from daily life on the farm—police and fire protection, sanitation, housing, lighting, water supply, street maintenance, and vice. Once in the city, an individual necessarily gave up a great deal of self-reliance and personal freedom. There, the communal needs of society superseded those of independent rural inhabitants.

After the Civil War, Ohio rapidly moved into the age of big business. By 1900 it epitomized all that was both good and bad about corporate, industrial America. As Ohio became more dependent on industry, agriculture continued to decline. Although approximately 75 percent of the work force held agricultural jobs in 1840, only 50 percent remained in farming by the Civil War. The industrialization and urbanization of labor continued to increase at a pace that far exceeded the national average. While the national work force engaged in nonagricultural pursuits did not reach 51 percent of the population until 1880, by that time 60 percent of Ohio's workers were employed in off-the-farm activities. Indeed, by 1880 the transformation of Ohio from an agricultural to an industrial state was complete. Even so, pragmatism, political traditionalism, Jeffersonian agrarianism, and the Puritan ethic remained basic features of Ohio's cultural distinctiveness.

Although agriculture declined as a way of life, most residents still believed that hard work and frugality eventually would provide a better living. That does not mean, however, that a great unity of purpose existed among the working class. Indeed, it often did not. The division of labor in the factory system, hostility to immigrants, and religious and ethnic differences, together with competition for jobs, inhibited the solidarity of the work force needed to build strong craft or industrial unions. In Cleveland, for example, squabbles among German, French, and Irish Catholics over the governing of their parishes carried over into the work place. The Poles in Toledo also were divided among themselves over religious issues. At the same time, white, native-born males frequently refused to work with immigrants, women, or blacks and openly discriminated against foreigners and Catholics. A high rate of geographic mobility among workers further hindered working-class cohesiveness and hampered the establishment of strong unions.

In addition, prosperity, coupled with periodic economic depressions, hindered the efforts of workers to unite. The independent proclivities of labor, together with Horatio Alger dreams of success, also prevented it from developing a working-class consciousness that soon would lead to unionization. The unity among workers that existed was ethnic, religious, and racial. It was not that of working men and women in general. Even so, by the last quarter of the nineteenth century, those barriers began to crumble as workers realized that they faced common problems that only cooperative action could solve. It was not by accident that Columbus hosted a convention of workers in 1886 that organized the American Federation of Labor.

Increased migration from the farms to the cities, coupled with the immigration of the foreign born, accelerated competition for jobs, kept wages low, promoted overcrowding, and changed the landscape of life in Ohio. Nativism and immigration, however, contributed to the development of isolated ethnic communities, such as German Village in Columbus, Over-the-Rhine in Cincinnati, and the Kossuth Colony in Dayton. Although the foreign born never exceeded 14 percent of the population between 1860 and 1920, ethnic communities fostered segregation rather than acculturation and assimilation. By the early twentieth century, Italians, Poles, Hungarians and other southern and eastern Europeans increasingly settled in the industrial cities of Cleveland, Toledo, Youngstown, Akron, Dayton, and Middletown. In 1920, Germany, Hungary, Poland, and Italy contributed the most foreign born to Ohio. This new ethnic mix had a major cultural effect on the composition of the cities. These immigrants and their descendents strengthened the Catholic parishes, established vibrant branches of the Eastern Orthodox Church, and built Jewish synagogues. The Greeks introduced their coffeehouses while the Slovaks transplanted their social halls to Ohio's urban scene.

As industrialization and immigration combined to create a new urban landscape, Cincinnati self-consciously attempted to build an elite, sophisticated city far removed from the industrial grime that blighted most urban centers in the state. After the Civil War, for example, some people talked about moving the national capital from Washington to protect the federal government from another Southern insurrection. Although Chicago quickly bid for this relocation, Cincinnati sniffed that she would rather not be considered for the honor. The editor of the Cincinnati *Gazette* wrote: "Cincinnati offers all the beauties of site, climate and civilization, but Cincinnati does not need the capital. If the country desires to put it here . . . we shall acquiesce as a patriotic duty." This self-assurance and independence caused one reporter for a Louisville newspaper to refer to the Queen City as "our clever but rather vain sister up the river." If Cincinnati worried about its image, however, the other industrial-based cities did not. The city fathers of Toledo, Cleveland, and Youngstown, among others, welcomed industrialization, immigrant workers, and the political power that each helped create.

While Ohio underwent a major transformation from an agricultural and rural to an industrial and urban state, it remained politically consistent and moderate. Ohioans always have been practical and traditional in politics. Although Democratic-Republicans dominated Ohio's early politics, between 1832 and World War I the major political parties roughly shared the spoils of office and more commonly the vote. During this time, the size and composition of the two major political parties were remarkably stable. Indeed, continuity was the preeminent characteristic of political affairs within the state. Between 1832 and 1855, for example, the Whig party won eight and the Democratic party nine of the seventeen presidential and gubernatorial contests. Although Democrats were ardent supporters of Andrew Jackson, the Whigs represented two cultural entities. The New England tradition of John Quincy Adams characterized the first group, and settlers from the Northeast chose the Western Reserve for their homes. Southerners composed the second group. They settled in the Virginia Military District and southern portions of the state. These Whigs followed the banner of Henry Clay. Democratic strongholds centered in areas with a large German population, such as northwestern Ohio.

In 1855 the Republican party replaced the Whig and antislavery parties on the ballot. It did so, however, without upsetting the two-party system, because the Republicans essentially garnered the votes that formerly had been cast for their predecessors. Political continuity remained strong even during times of national crisis. In 1860, for example, when the Democratic party splintered, the Republicans garnered only 49.4 percent of the vote while the Democrats polled 46 percent. The tally for the Democratic party was only three percentage points less than it usually totaled when the Whig party was its major competitor. Although Stephen A. Douglas, the nominee of the northern Democrats won 43 percent of Ohio's vote in 1860, the other Democratic candidates garnered 5.5 percent of the vote to give the collective party nearly a 49 percent share of the total vote. This tally was the best showing for the Democrats since the organization of the Republican party. Although the Republican party maintained large margins of victory during the war years, the Democratic party soon reasserted itself once the war ended. By 1870 a strong, vigorous, two-party system had returned to the Buckeye state.

Between 1870 and 1892, presidential elections remained closely contested. Even though the Republicans won all six presidential elections and seven of eleven gubernatorial contests, their average share of the vote was only 49.3 percent. During this time the Democratic party averaged 47.4 percent of the vote. Clearly, both the Republican and Democratic parties survived the disunion of the Civil War with their constituencies intact. The Panic of 1893, however, began a decade-long decline for the Democratic party. Between 1893 and 1904, the party averaged only 43.6 percent of the popular vote in eight gubernatorial and presidential elections. That was the worst showing for the Democrats in twenty years. Still, with the exception of the aberrations caused by the Civil War and the most serious economic crisis yet experienced in the nation's history, the Republican and Democratic parties were evenly divided. After the Civil War, many Ohioans voted as they had shot, but nearly as many voters gave their traditional support to the Democratic party. The differences between the two parties were less matters of substance or ideology than of emphasis and methodology. During the late nineteenth century, then, Ohio's voters responded to culture and traditional habits. No matter whether these customs were based on social class, ethnicity, or occupation, tradition remained supreme.

In addition to being traditional in politics, Ohioans remained eminently Jeffersonian. Indeed, if Jefferson believed that the nation could profit from a revolution every twenty years, Ohioans provided for this possibility. In 1851 a new constitution enabled the voters to determine every twenty years whether the state should call a new constitutional convention. This Jeffersonian concept of democracy reveals that Ohioans still believed that government should remain close to the people. Moreover, it indicates that Ohioans maintained the assumption that the public was capable of determining whether systematic, constitutional revolution was necessary to safeguard personal freedom and the democratic tradition. Still, this constitutional provision and ideological concept are inherently conservative. Ohioans were not afraid or reluctant to change the mechanics of their government in order to provide needed social, political, and economic reform, but the change would come through an established, traditional process. While the results might be revolutionary, the process would be conservative. Ohioans cherished liberty and self-government, but they also favored law and discipline. They would maintain their liberty, but it would be an ordered freedom.

Thus a stable but growing economy and a conservative political system that provided for substantive reform tempered the public reaction to the changing conditions of the industrial age. Ohioans preferred the safe, known approach to social, political, and economic reform. Radical ideas, voiced through third-party politics, were anathema to most of them. Populism, for example, not only had no charm, it was dangerous. Jacob Coxey's call for major economic reform based on the federal government's issuance of non-interest-bearing bonds and support for a good-roads program was Ohio's weak answer to the slashing rhetoric of Jerry Simpson and Mary Elizabeth Lease and to the sharply honed, intellectual reasoning of John Davis in Kansas. In Ohio the Populists met scorn, ridicule, and neglect. With a diversified agricultural economy and few of the problems Populists experienced in the Great Plains, Ohio farmers marched to the drummers of their traditional political parties.

By the turn of the twentieth century, Ohioans retained their cultural distinctiveness in relation to pragmatism, political traditionalism, Jeffersonian agrarianism, and the Puritan ethic. They were hard working, ambitious, and optimistic in their daily affairs. Many believed that the agricultural life was the foundation of freedom and democracy. In contrast to other midwestern states with the exception of those in the Old Northwest, most Ohioans pursued the American dream in the factories and shops of the towns and cities. Corporate insensitivity to the needs of the worker, however, coupled with a blatant disregard for the consumer, stimulated a major reform movement in the early twentieth century. In Ohio this Progressive movement differed little from elsewhere in the Midwest and the nation, with the exception of North Dakota, where the Nonpartisan League convinced many that the Flickertail state was home for all sons-of-the-wildjackass. With the leadership for reform coming from such individuals as Tom L. Johnson and Samuel M. ("Golden Rule") Jones, the Progressives swept away machine politics. They also improved social conditions through the political process by winning increased governmental regulation of corporate enterprise while gaining an expansion of public services. Although Democrats charged that Republicans could not serve as agents of reform, considering their past record, both political parties supported the Progressive movement.

Progressivism, however, increasingly restrained the individualism of the past and by so doing revealed the struggle Ohioans had adjusting to the industrial and urban world. This cultural realignment can be seen in relation to the constitutional convention of January 1912. This convention, the fourth for Ohioans, did not produce a new document, but the delegates drafted forty-one prospective amendments for submission to the voter. The electorate responded in part by rejecting woman suffrage and by refusing to eliminate the word *white* from the qualifications for male voting rights—which, of course, placed the state constitution in violation of the Fifteenth Amendment to the Constitution of the United States. Ohioans, however, adopted the provision of the initiative and referendum for state matters. Other amendments permitted workmen's compensation, minimum wages, maximum hours legislation and an eight-hour day on public works, the abolition of prison contract labor, and the conservation of natural resources. The voters also approved amendments requiring the merit principle in the state's civil service as well a stricter governmental regulations of banking. Despite the setback for women and a perpetuation of the mentality of racism, these constitutional provisions enabled Ohioans to meet rapidly changing economic and social conditions in a practical fashion.

The Progressive movement did not radically upset the traditional response of the voters to the two major parties. The Democratic party, however, dominated the gubernatorial office by winning five of the six elections between 1905 and 1918. It also carried the state for Woodrow Wilson in 1912 and 1916. But in 1920, when James M. Cox and Warren G. Harding, both Ohioans, held the presidential nominations for the Democratic and Republican parties, respectively, a shift in voting behavior occurred. Although Harding won the presidential election by a vote of 58.5 percent to Cox's 38.6 percent, the large gap resulted from the abandonment of the Democratic party by many German voters because of its wartime policies.

Although party contests remained evenly divided on the state and national levels until the election of 1936, the age of Ohio's supremacy in national politics ended with the election of Harding to the presidency. Not since the Virginia dynasty dominated national government during the early years of the Republic had a state made such a mark on national political affairs. Between the Civil War and 1920, seven Ohioans were elected to the presidency, and many others came close to winning the nomination of either of the two major parties. During this same time, six Ohioans sat on the Supreme Court and two served as chief justice. The state also sent nineteen men to hold cabinet positions. Moreover, several Ohioans, including John Sherman, George H. Pendleton, Marcus A. Hanna, and Joseph B. Foraker wielded substantial power in the Senate. Others in the House of Representatives also played instrumental roles in setting the course of national politics.

Ohioans dominated national politics for seventy years primarily because of the diversity of the people, the strength of the industrial and agricultural economy, and the balance between rural and urban populations. The individuals who played major roles in national affairs appealed to broad national constituencies because they learned their skills in Ohio, where political success required candidates to reconcile wide differences among the electorate. Ohioans were both northerners and southerners as well as easterners and westerners, depending on family background, economic interest, and the way an individual interpreted geographical location. Consequently, Ohio's politicians addressed constituencies at home that generally were the same as those across the nation. Because Ohio ranked third in population during much of this time, it also had great numerical strength in Congress, political conventions, and party caucuses. Moreover, in a leading industrial state the parties could find individuals who were willing to support candidates financially or could choose wealthy individuals, such as Marcus A. Hanna, who would run for office themselves.

Continuity and traditionalism remained major features of Ohio's political contests through the presidential election of 1932, when Franklin Delano Roosevelt carried 49.9 percent of the vote while Republican incumbent Herbert Hoover garnered 47 percent. In 1936, however, voters responded favorably to the New Deal policies of the administration by giving Roosevelt 58 percent of the vote to Alfred M. Landon's 37.4 percent. The Democrats made the largest gains in industrial and urban areas where the working class greatly appreciated the New Deal programs, particularly the National Labor Relations Act of 1935, which recognized the right of labor to organize and bargain collectively.

Certainly, the New Deal substantially affected party alignment, but it also influenced economic structure and altered the views Ohioans held sacred concerning the relationship of government to the individual. When the stock market crashed in 1929, Ohioans faced an economic and social crisis of unprecedented magnitude. Like other Americans, they tried to solve it by political means. They recoiled from laissez-faire governmental policies and the capitalist economics that Hoover championed by giving Roosevelt a plurality and the Democratic party control of the state. The spirit of the New Deal soon permeated public affairs in Ohio. The legislature responded to the economic crisis by providing increased regulation of the state banks, creating a board of arbitration to establish minimum wages for women and children, providing old-age pensions, granting relief from foreclosure, and reducing property taxation. Ohioans also participated in a host of New Deal programs, such as those provided by the Agricultural Adjustment Administration, Works Progress Administration, and Public Works Administration. By so doing they were little different from other citizens. Indeed, most midwesterners allowed the federal and state governments to regulate their lives in a remarkably un-Jeffersonian manner.

The New Deal also injected a mild dose of socialism into the lives of most Ohioans. In 1935, for example, Roosevelt created the Rural Electrification Administration (REA) by executive order to provide long-term, low-interest loans to local cooperatives to help provide electricity to rural homes. At that time only 20 percent of the farms in Ohio had electric service. Consequently, farm men and women could not use a wide variety of electrical appliances and implements that would make their farms more efficient and productive while at the same time easing the burdens of their daily lives. Because they needed electricity, Ohio farmers greeted the REA with open arms. By May 1936, Ohio led the nation in the number of farmers and rural residents who contracted for electric service. At first some farmers believed that the REA was socialistic, and they hesitated to give their support to the agency even though they desperately wanted electricity. Once their farms were wired, however, and the lights turned on, their misgivings quickly disappeared. With REA service, the long trip to the windmill or the outhouse in subzero temperatures came to an end, along with the Saturday night bath and cooking over a wood stove in the summertime. Electric pumps, hot-water heaters and stoves now became common features throughout rural Ohio.

If the REA represented socialism, no farmer cared. This attitude, however, reflected not so much a change in political, social, or economic ideology as it did the reaffirmation of the practicality of Ohioans. Because the utility companies failed to furnish adequate, equitable service at a reasonable price, rural Ohioans assumed the responsibility of organizing independent cooperatives and, with the aid of the federal government, provided electric service for themselves. In 1936 the president of the Lorain-Medina Rural Electric Co-Operative exhibited this practical and independent spirit when he remarked that farmers had "begged" Ohio Edison for electric service but that the utility company always refused to provide it because of the alleged high cost; with access to REA support, "We just told them to go to hell." By 1938 REA lines were a common feature of the landscape. A year later the electric co-ops helped provide power to 43 percent of Ohio's farms while only 25 percent of the farms nationwide had electric service. The reception that Ohio farmers and other rural residents gave to the REA also reaffirmed their continued belief in the Jeffersonian concept of agrarian self-sufficiency, democracy, and cooperation.

The New Deal also affected voting habits in Ohio. Indeed, in 1934 the traditional voting patterns began to shift as the Democratic vote moved from the rural to the urban areas. This realignment occurred because of the New Deal's influence and because large numbers of the foreign born were employed in the steel and rubber industries. The industrial, ethnic vote has remained with the Democratic party ever since. Still, not all cities are inherently Democratic, nor are rural areas naturally Republican. Cincinnati, for example, remains a Republican stronghold while the Democrats are influential in northwestern Ohio, where the political behavior of the German-Americans resembles that of the Russian-German-American population in western Kansas. Even so, traditional Republican areas such as southeastern Ohio retain strong Republican links while the central counties still lean toward the Democratic party. In short, the current voting patterns are historic—that is, traditional—and they involve settlement patterns. The old New England Whig areas generally are Republican while the locales settled predominantly by southerners are Democratic. In this respect Ohio's political makeup resembles that of Indiana and Illinois, and for the same reasons. In contrast, few southerners settled in Michigan or Wisconsin, and an early Democratic political heritage is missing from these states. As a result, the Republican party virtually dominated their politics between the Civil War and the New Deal, much in contrast to Ohio. After the New Deal, the Democratic party in Minnesota, Wisconsin, and Michigan inherited the agrarian reform movement and a viable two-party system developed. These generalizations, of course, have exceptions. Northwestern Ohio, which traditionally was Democratic and German in heritage, has increasingly shifted into the Republican camp, spurred by its relative prosperity and the ideological affinity of its residents with the latter-day Republican party.

Today, Ohio remains a viable two-party state. Both Republicans and Democrats must appeal effectively to urban and rural constituencies to win elections. The close traditional balance between the major parties can be seen in relation to the national and statewide elections between 1940 an 1970. Although the Republican party captured six of eight presidential races during this time, it won only six of thirteen gubernatorial elections. The propensity of Ohio's voters to send Republicans to the White House and Democrats to the governor's mansion during this time primarily resulted from the popularity of Democrat Frank J. Laushe, who won gubernatorial election five times between 1945 and 1962. Laushe, however, was a conservative and little different from most Republicans. His personal popularity and ideological principles enabled him to cut across party lines, and many traditional Republicans supported him. Many Democrats, particularly those of German heritage, also opposed the liberalism of Adlai Stevenson on the national level. During the 1970s the Republican party again dominated the governorship because James A. Rhodes had wide appeal to many Democrats. A decade later the Democratic party recaptured the gubernatorial position.

The elections since 1940 also have been based on conservative principles. Moreover, organized labor has remained fragmented among Ohio's many cities, and it has been more concerned with local issues than with statewide unity. As a result, urban, organized labor has not built a strong political organization with a liberal, issue-oriented base, much in contrast to Chicago, Detroit, Milwaukee, and Minneapolis–St. Paul, places where the working class has associated economic interest with politics and the ballot box. Nor has the ethnic vote responded favorably to issue-oriented campaigns. Both groups tend to support only bread-and-butter issues. Thus, Ohio remains a job-oriented rather than issue-oriented state in contests between the major parties. As such, it is similar to Indiana and Illinois. In contrast, Michigan, Wisconsin, and Minnesota are issue-oriented states at election time. Consequently, job-oriented states like Ohio are more traditional and conservative in their political response to problems, and they spend far less for government services. Ohio, for example, customarily has been more interested in good roads than in public support for education, aid to dependent children, or old-age assistance.

In many respects, then, Ohio remains the "great, Middle-class state." Job-oriented politics, together with a continued reverence for the virtues of hard work and political conservatism, govern daily affairs. Moreover, self-reliance and independence remain defined in terms of freedom from government. This Jeffersonian traditionalism in politics helps explain the caution which the state's politicians use when dealing with economic and social issues. Bold action or the advocacy of major alternatives might divide the electorate, hence the preference for meeting the traditional expectations of the people. Consequently, few differences exist among candidates. The public tends to favor rectitude rather than reform from its candidates and representatives. The requirements of the postwar world, however, not only caused Ohioans to adjust their political loyalties or to reaffirm them, but it also led them to question, for the first time, the values and beliefs of the Jeffersonian tradition. Ultimately, the postwar economy would destroy any lingering hope for the perpetuation of this traditional way of life in Ohio, the Midwest, or the nation. It also would seriously jeopardize Ohioans' faith in the Puritan ethic.

During the Second World War, for example, many farmers reared in the agricultural depression of the 1920s and 1930s experienced the first prosperity they had ever known. The postwar years also were a time of milk and honey for most Ohio farms. But while science and technology contributed to higher productivity, it also dramatically changed the emphasis and number of Ohio farms. Agriculturalists, for example, became increasingly specialized and mechanized. Yet specialization and technological change contributed to the continued decline of the farm population and to the number of farms. Moreover, while production remained high, prices were insufficient to enable many Ohio farmers to maintain full-time operations. More and more agriculturalists sought employment off the farm to make ends meet. By the mid-1950s about 37 percent of Ohio's agriculturalists worked away from their farms for a hundred or more days each year. Thus, by the late 1950s part-time farming no longer represented a period in which an individual worked in outside employment to build the capital to begin full-time farming. Now part-time agriculture was essential to preserve the family farm.

Despite the necessity to seek off-the-farm employment, many farmers remained on the land because they believed the values of rural living were superior to those of an urban environment. The family farm, like the church, the local school, and the Supreme Court, remained a symbol of freedom and democracy, and Ohio farmers strongly defended it. Throughout the 1950s, then, the Jeffersonian tradition remained strong. Nevertheless, the reality of its continued validity was open to question. Indeed, agriculture in Ohio, as elsewhere in the Midwest, could not escape the influence of science, technology, new management practices, and government policy. By the 1950s farming had become more than a way of life. It was a business where only the most efficient survived. The days of the small-scale farmer were gone, and many of them went bankrupt or quit.

By 1960 only 8 percent of Ohio's population were farmers. Three years later only 6 percent remained. More and more agricultural land was lost to cultivation each year, due in part to urban expansion. Despite the decline of agricultural population and good cropland, however, Ohio's farmers became more productive than ever. But increased productivity lowered prices and forced more farmers from the land. Thousands left the farms for the more economically secure life offered in the cities and towns, where the service industries expanded rapidly. By 1970 farmers represented only 3 percent of the state's population. Ohio farmers frequently felt helpless. No single farmer could change the economy by acting alone, and farmers were too independent, too conservative, and too diverse in their needs to act collectively.

Despite these problems, Ohio's farmers remained convinced that farming provided the good life. They continued to believe that the farm was the best place to raise their children and that it provided the foundation for democratic government. Despite sentimental attachments and nostalgic views of farm life, however, most agriculturalists regarded agriculture as a business. Nonetheless, by the late 1970s Ohio's farm income lagged far behind the national average. More farmers sought off-the-farm employment and nearly half of their income came from outside jobs. The Jeffersonian tradition remained, but it had less credibility than ever before. By the early 1980s Ohio had more part-time farmers than full-time farmers. Only the most productive and efficient farmers were able to marshal the resources needed to maintain operation in an economy where they did not control the prices that they received. As a result, more and more young men and women fled the farms. Their parents frequently encouraged them to go, and many parents left as well. No one can yet say with certainty what effects this upheaval will have on life in Ohio.

By the last quarter of the twentieth century, Ohio was known more for being part of the "rust belt" than the corn belt. Like other industrial states, Ohio's economy suffered hard times as cheap, foreign competition, rampant inflation, and rapid technological change decimated manufacturing and heavy industry. As the cities withered economically, the American dream also faded for many Ohioans. Most, however, continued to show a pragmatic flexibility. A select few, those with advanced education or access to retraining programs, adjusted to the new age by entering such fields as computer science and robotics technology. Many shifted from industrial and manufacturing jobs to the service industry. Other workers in the Midwest and nation followed the same trend. Between 1975 and 1980, however, more than 900,000 people fled the state in search of opportunities elsewhere. Since 1980 Michigan and Iowa also have suffered population losses and the resulting economic decline. Many of those who have left Ohio have been among the young and the well-educated. Only Michigan lost more people in this category than Ohio between 1978 and 1984. By mid-1986 only Illinois had a higher unemployment rate than Ohio. Those who left the state did not relocate in the Midwest but rather sought employment and refuge in California, Texas, or Florida. The loss of population had serious political as well as economic consequences—the potential loss of two congressional seats and a corresponding reduction of political power and favor.

The social costs of the decline in Ohio's industrial base also are serious and incalculable. Unless a majority of the displaced industrial workers can be retrained for jobs in the growing service and light-manufacturing industries, more and more families will fall beneath the poverty line. Moreover, with the loss of high-paying industrial jobs and the shift of workers to lesser-paying positions in the service industry, declining personal income will require an increase in taxation of some sort and the expansion of the state's bureaucracy to meet a host of social problems ranging from malnutrition to crime. Certainly, Ohio's future, both on the farms and in the cities, involves mastering new forms of science and technology. The brawn of the past no longer is sufficient to build new or to sustain old agricultural- and industrial-based economies.

The triple plagues of industrial decline, agricultural depression, and flight to the Sun Belt will not soon end, and the stigma of the "rust belt" will continue to mar the state's reputation as a pleasant place to live. Moreover, economic decline has widened the gap between the haves and have-nots. The increasing number of poor whites and poor blacks also is creating an underclass that is unified by economic plight rather than by race. Continued economic recession, high unemployment, and inadequate education may in time create a solidarity within the underclass that will have political, economic, and social ramifications for all Ohioans. Just what these ramifications may be are, of course, as broad and ill-defined as they are potentially dangerous.

Ohio is in the process of major cultural adjustment caused by economic factors beyond the control of the people. Farmers are no longer certain that they are working to gain a better living, and many doubt that agriculture ensures the best quality of life. Moreover, the laboring community no longer strives to gain new rights but rather works to preserve past gains. The strength Ohio drew from its natural resources also has waned. Coal, which once supported the state's heavy industry, now causes difficulties for others beyond Ohio's borders in the form of acid rain. For many, the American dream has escaped them. With a sluggish industrial and agricultural economy, people now speak of downward mobility on the social scale as a certainty. Children no longer expect to live more comfortably than their parents. The rapidly growing service industry that replaced heavy industry, manufacturing, and mining as the chief employer pays far less than union-protected jobs. By 1980 the service industry employed approximately 67 percent of the work force. Consequently, the Jeffersonian tradition essentially is gone and the future of the Puritan ethic remains very much in question.

Ohioans, however, remain a practical people. And, despite the demise of the Jeffersonian tradition and the waning of the industrial state, they continue to be an optimistic people. Although Ohioans hold many of the same opinions held by other midwesterners, they are a moderate people in the heartland. If, as Woodrow Wilson proclaimed, the voice of the Midwest is the "voice of protest," then Ohioans stand alone. If the Midwest is generally against something rather than for it, or if it is the home of the native radicalism of the Right and the Left, then Ohioans are different. Although they have flirted with conservatism and liberalism, they are predominantly middle-of-the-roaders. Ohio is not, as one writer noted of the heartland, "a bizarre and uniquely American mixture of Rotarians and Wobblies."

In the waning years of the twentieth century, however, Ohioans are suffering an identity crisis. Located on the eastern edge of the Midwest and on the western edge of the East, Ohioans are not sure where they belong. Although they are certain that eastern effetism is not for them, they admire the cultural, economic, and political vibrancy of the eastern seaboard. The people of Ohio, like other midwesterners, also feel a sense of being under seige. They frequently are portrayed as naive, unsophisticated, bland hicks, particularly by easterners. At the same time Ohioans are certain that people with talent only come from the Great Plains, they do not go there. Still, Ohioans have a cultural affinity, forged over nearly two hundred years of common experience, with the other people of the heartland.

Today, Ohio faces all the industrial, agricultural, and urban problems that plague the Midwest and the nation. Ohioans also enjoy the benefits of being part of the heartland—a moderate life-style, a pace that permits reflection, and a bountiful land. If the heartland is indeed the most American region of the United States, then Ohio is the key to the Midwest, economically, politically, and socially—that, is culturally. As such, the Buckeye state remains the epitome of midwestern distinctiveness.

BIBLIOGRAPHY

The best single-volume survey of Ohio remains Eugene H. Roseboom and Francis P. Weisenberger, *A History of Ohio* (Columbus, 1976). This study includes an excellent bibliography, but Roseboom and Weisenberger's analysis of Ohio's twentieth-century history is not comparable to their review of the nineteenth century. Indeed, a synthesis of Ohio's twentieth-century history has not yet been written. The best study of nineteenth-century Ohio can be found in volumes two through five of the *History of the State of Ohio*, edited by Carl Wittke and published by the Ohio Historical Society between 1941 and 1944. This series consists of William T. Utter, *The Frontier State 1803–1825*; Francis P. Weisenberger, *The Passing of the Frontier, 1825–1850*; Eugene H. Roseboom, *The Civil War Era, 1850–1873*; and Philip Jordan, *Ohio Comes of Age, 1873–1900*.

Raymond Boryczka and Lorin Lee Cary have written the best study of organized labor in Ohio, *No Strength without Union: An Illustrated History of Ohio Workers, 1803–1980* (Columbus, 1982). This study also includes valuable information about the industrialization of the state. A more specific study of the working class and its cultural influence can be found in Steven J. Ross, *Workers on the Edge: Work, Leisure, and Politics in Industrializing Cincinnati, 1788–1890* (New York, 1985). For political change, much of which emphasizes the twentieth century, see John H. Fenton, *Midwest Politics*

(New York, 1966); John J. Gargan and James G. Coke, eds., *Political Behavior and Public Issues in Ohio* (Kent, Ohio, 1972); James Reichley, *States in Crisis: Politics in Ten American States, 1950–1962* (Chapel Hill, N.C., 1964); and two articles by Thomas A. Flinn, "Continuity and Change in Ohio Politics," *Journal of Politics* 24 (August 1962), 521–44, and "The Outline of Ohio Politics," *Western Political Quarterly* 13 (September 1960), 702–21. Andrew R. L. Cayton provides a survey of early politics in *The Frontier Republic: Ideology and Politics in the Ohio Country, 1780–1825* (Kent, 1986), while John Clayton Thomas gives a contemporary look at political structure in *Between Citizen and City: Neighborhood Organizations and Urban Politics in Cincinnati* (Lawrence, Kans., 1986).

Robert Leslie Jones furnishes a topical history of agriculture in *History of Agriculture in Ohio to 1880* (Kent, 1983). This study, however, is mistitled because it emphasizes agriculture only through the Civil War. R. Douglas Hurt has written a number of articles on Ohio's agriculture, including "Dairying in Nineteenth Century Ohio," *Old Northwest* 5 (Winter 1979–80), 387–99; "The Sheep Industry in Ohio, 1807–1900," *Old Northwest* 7 (Fall 1981), 237–54; "The Ohio Grange, 1870–1900," *Northwest Ohio Quarterly* 53 (Winter 1981), 19–32; "Pork and Porkopolis," *Cincinnati Historical Society Bulletin* 40 (Fall 1981), 191–215; "The Vineyards of Ohio, 1823–1900," *Northwest Ohio Quarterly* 55 (Winter 1982–83), 3–16; "A Is for Apple: By the Bushel, By the Barrel," *Timeline* 2 (October–November 1985), 2–9; "REA: A New Deal for Farmers," *Timeline* 2 (December–January 1986), 32–47; and "The Farmer's Alliance and People's Party in Ohio," *Old Northwest* 10 (Winter 1984–85), 439–62. Two recent studies dealing with important aspects of Ohio's social history are Jed Dannenbaum, *Drink and Disorder: Temperance Reform in Cincinnati from the Washingtonian Revival to the WCTU* (Champaign, Ill., 1984), and Zane Miller, *Suburb: Neighborhood and Community in Forest Park, Ohio, 1935–1976* (Knoxville, Tenn., 1981).

Frederick C. Luebke

NEBRASKA
Time, Place, and Culture

M ORE THAN A DECADE AGO, as the United States was preparing
for its bicentennial celebration, the federal agency charged with
the commemorative responsibility decided that one appropriate way
to celebrate national history would be to commission the publication
of histories of each of the fifty states. Despite efforts to impose certain
standards of concept and method, the results were on the whole disappointing. Few of the fifty authors effectively addressed the question
of what forces or combination of circumstances made the history of
their particular state distinctive. To put the matter plainly: why should
we bother with the history of Nebraska or any other state? What
makes its history distinctive or different, let us say, from that of Iowa
or Kansas? A skeptic might well argue that while the superficialities
of names and events change from Nebraska to its neighbors, truly
significant historical trends are not encompassed by the artificial
boundaries of a state.

The author of the Nebraska entry in the bicentennial series attempted to explain the distinctiveness or uniqueness of her state by
describing what she called "the Nebraska psyche." In her view, Nebraska was founded by "ordinary men who possessed a vision of freedom, independence, and the chance to make a living for themselves
and their families through their own labor." Through the exercise of

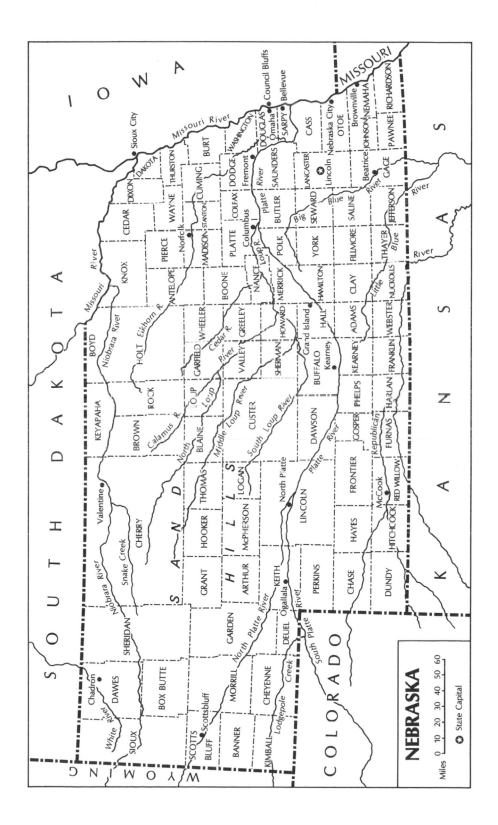

IOWA

SOUTH DAKOTA

WYOMING

COLORADO

KANSAS

MISSOURI

Missouri River

Sioux City

Council Bluffs
Omaha
Bellevue

Lincoln
Nebraska City
Brownville

Beatrice

Norfolk

Columbus

Fremont

Grand Island

Kearney

North Platte

Ogallala

McCook

Valentine

Chadron

Scottsbluff

DAKOTA
DIXON
CEDAR
KNOX
BOYD
HOLT
ANTELOPE
PIERCE
WAYNE
THURSTON
BURT
CUMING
MADISON
STANTON
COLFAX
DODGE
WASHINGTON
DOUGLAS
SARPY
CASS
SAUNDERS
BUTLER
PLATTE
BOONE
WHEELER
GARFIELD
GREELEY
VALLEY
NANCE
MERRICK
POLK
YORK
SEWARD
LANCASTER
OTOE
JOHNSON
NEMAHA
PAWNEE
RICHARDSON
GAGE
JEFFERSON
SALINE
FILLMORE
THAYER
NUCKOLLS
CLAY
HAMILTON
ADAMS
KEARNEY
HALL
BUFFALO
SHERMAN
HOWARD
CUSTER
BLAINE
LOUP
THOMAS
LOGAN
McPHERSON
ARTHUR
GRANT
HOOKER
KEITH
DEUEL
GARDEN
MORRILL
CHEYENNE
BANNER
KIMBALL
SCOTTS BLUFF
BOX BUTTE
SHERIDAN
DAWES
SIOUX
CHERRY
KEYAPAHA
BROWN
ROCK
FRANKLIN
WEBSTER
HARLAN
FURNAS
RED WILLOW
HITCHCOCK
FRONTIER
GOSPER
PHELPS
DAWSON
LINCOLN
HAYES
FRONTIER
CHASE
DUNDY
PERKINS

SAND HILLS

Missouri River
Niobrara River
Elkhorn R.
Platte River
Loup R.
Big Blue
Little Blue
River
River
River
Cedar R.
River
North Loup
Middle Loup River
South Loup River
Calamus R.
Snake Creek
Niobrara River
White River
Lodgepole Creek
North Platte River
South Platte River
Republican
Platte River

NEBRASKA

Miles
0 10 20 30 40 50 60

✪ State Capital

"imagination, dogged perseverance, and continual optimism" in the frontier period, Nebraskans evolved qualities of determination, friendliness, generosity, stoicism, and daring to create "a breed of forceful, energetic, free-ranging souls." Nebraskans, she wrote, are audacious, honest, creative, imaginative, frugal, practical, and so on.[1]

Upon reflection one realizes that such charming statements are meaningful only if Missourians, Iowans, Dakotans, and Kansans, among others, do *not* possess these same characteristics, at least in the same order of magnitude. Conversely, if Kansans and South Dakotans *do* share these heroic qualities equally with Nebraskans, there is nothing special about "the Nebraska psyche" and therefore that which may be distinctive about the history of the state can hardly be attributed to its influence. In the place of such an approach, I suggest that noteworthy or unique aspects of Nebraska's history may be identified and described in terms of the interplay of culture with environment over time and that distinctiveness is revealed through appropriate comparisons in time and space.

This formula emerges from a desire to coordinate two rich traditions in American historical thought—one that has concentrated on the powerful altering or disrupting influence of physical environments on cultural forms and another that, conversely, has emphasized the tenacity, the persistence, or the enduring qualities of cultural forms over many generations and under difficult circumstances. The most celebrated exponent of the first of these two traditions is Frederick Jackson Turner, the father of the frontier thesis, who described an environment that transformed the traditions and behaviors of European culture and stimulated individual strength, ingenuity, inventiveness, practicality, buoyancy, and exuberance—qualities that in his view distinguished the American character and hence American history from the European. But other scholars, among them historians, geographers, folklorists, and linguists, traced the persistence of cultural forms—speech patterns, architectural styles, customs of all kinds, food preferences, agricultural methods, political behaviors and practices, and many more—over great distances and many decades. In their books and articles the influence of place or physical environment is all but ignored; their interpretations have tended to slight the influence of unique physiographic features of given regions in much the same way that environmentalists have tended to ignore the persistence of culture in the same place.

It should be obvious, however, that wide variations in culture may exist within one environment, just as surely as physical environments impose certain limits on human activity. Therefore fruitful studies of a state should focus on the complex relationships that exist between people and the land they live on in order to discover the manifold ways in which men and woman have modified their environment;

conversely, they must also analyze the ways in which the physical characteristics of a given place tend to limit and condition human behavior.

It is true, of course, that the land Nebraskans live on is not entirely unique. It is part of the Midwest, even though it has a western character not found in Iowa, Missouri, or even Kansas. It straddles much of the Great Plains with a roughly rectangular space of about 77,500 square miles. Stretching westward from the Missouri River at Omaha for 430 miles, it separates Kansas from South Dakota by another 210. Patterns of rainfall, temperature, soils, and topography in the eastern third, where two-thirds of the people live, resemble those of Iowa. Although Nebraska is naturally almost treeless and without significant mineral resources, its deep, rich, and humous soil made it highly attractive to both American and European immigrants seeking new lands to farm. But as one travels west across the state, the physical environment changes in important ways. Rainfall decreases from thirty-six inches a year in the southeast to fifteen in the northwest, and soils begin to vary greatly in quality. They are generally rich in the eastern third and in the southern counties, but the north central portion of the state consists of the grass-covered Sand Hills, an area of twenty thousand square miles that is nearly equivalent in size to West Virginia. Almost devoid of human inhabitants (less than one person per square mile), the Sand Hills region is ideal cattle country. It separates the eastern third of the state from the Panhandle, which is a lightly populated, semiarid area that has strong affinities with Wyoming, which it resembles as much as the east resembles Iowa.

Rivers are crucial to understanding Nebraska, which lies entirely within the drainage basin of the Missouri. Most secondary streams— the Niobrara, the Loup, the Republican, and the Platte—form a ladder of rivers that flow eastward to the Missouri, which, before the railroad era, provided the transportation link to well-settled, older parts of the United States. But only the two branches of the Platte rise in the Rocky Mountains and have the plenteous flow such origins afford. It alone runs the length of the state from west to east—from Scottsbluff to a few miles south of Omaha—and fixes Nebraska's east-west orientation. The Platte valley provides a ribbon of fertile, irrigated soil and a spinal cord of transportation and communication. It forms a sturdy backbone for the state, offering trade and services; it attracts tourist dollars, a few modest ventures in manufacturing, and people displaced from nearby farms by an agricultural economy in decline. Appropriately enough, the Platte has even provided the state with its name, for in the Omaha and Otoe languages Nebraska means "flat water."

The Platte valley has always been central to Nebraska history. It was America's first great highway to the West; in the mid–nineteenth century it funneled several hundred thousand people along the Platte's banks across the Great Plains to South Pass in Wyoming and on to new homes in Oregon, California, and Utah. It was the natural route for the first transcontinental railroad. Later, with the advent of the automobile, the first band of concrete to stretch across America paralleled the Platte's course, as does much of Interstate 80 in our own times. Even the airlines seem to trace this natural highway as they leave contrails high in the sky, six miles above the Platte's shallow and interwoven channels. Kansas has nothing quite like it; the Arkansas River, similar though it is in many ways, only led pioneers to the impenetrability of the Colorado Rockies; and instead of flowing to the metropolitan northeastern quadrant, it veers off to Oklahoma. South Dakota is divided rather than united by the Missouri, which leads only to North Dakota; no great highways follow its course through the northern plains. But the Platte is Nebraska's Nile. Perhaps the comparison is overdrawn, but it is nonetheless instructive.

The modern character of Nebraska was partly shaped by a fierce political struggle in the territorial and early statehood periods. When Congress created the territory in 1854, the only place bearing any resemblance to a town was Bellevue, a few miles north of the mouth of the Platte. The first territorial governor, a political hack from South Carolina named Francis Burt, apparently intended that Bellevue should become the capital. But he died suddenly, just two days after he had taken his oath of office. Into his place as acting governor strode the territorial secretary Thomas Cuming, a young, aggressive Iowan who was determined to make Omaha the capital. Located across the river from Iowa's Council Bluffs, Omaha was the direct beneficiary of this man's schemes. Cuming drew legislative districts that grossly overrepresented the country north of the Platte, and he appointed to the territorial council men who shared his views of development in Nebraska.

There were two main consequences of his connivance. The first is that Omaha was destined to become the metropolis of the state, bearing a relationship to the rest of Nebraska not unlike that of Chicago to Illinois. Possessing a favorable location that gave access to the hinterland tapped by the Platte, Omaha became a major industrial and transportation center with an ethnically diverse population, and like Chicago it later came to specialize in meat-packing.

The second product of Cuming's intrigue was unintended. Once statehood was achieved, the long-suffering anti-Omaha factions coalesced sufficiently to remove the capital from Omaha to someplace—any place—south of the Platte. Unable to unite on an existing town as an alternative to Omaha, the founding fathers of the state agreed on an undistinguished rural site south of the Platte that was to be named Lincoln. Rather than distributing the institutional functions of state government among various cities of the now-dominant anti-Omaha coalition (as was customary in the practice of nineteenth-century state politics), they put them all—capitol, state university, penitentiary, and asylum for the insane—on neutral ground, a place where in 1867 there was no town.

Thus today Nebraska has two large cities: Omaha and a capital that is to Nebraska what Madison is to Wisconsin or, for that matter, what Washington is to the nation. This precedent further encouraged Nebraska, again like Wisconsin, to focus its land-grant resources available under the Morrill Act of 1862 in one state university, rather than to diffuse limited strength between two institutions, as did neighboring Iowa, Kansas, South Dakota, and Colorado.

For countless numbers of persons in both the nineteenth and twentieth centuries, Nebraska was merely a transit area—a place to be crossed. Yet many people came to stay, especially in the 1870s and 1880s, when the number of inhabitants increased by nearly a thousand percent. But all population groups came to this place from somewhere else.

Even the Indians were relative newcomers. None of the tribes traditionally identified with Nebraska, with the possible exception of the Pawnees, inhabited the area before Columbus set foot on the West Indies in 1492. Others, such as the Teton Sioux, had scarcely begun to cross the Missouri when Washington crossed the Delaware in 1776. As for other Nebraskans, virtually none predate 1854, the year the area was opened to settlement. That is not to say that there were no white men in Nebraska before this auspicious date but rather that their numbers were exceedingly small and their imprint upon the landscape insignificant.

The people of Nebraska must therefore be thought of as immigrants who brought their culture here from somewhere else in the United States or Europe. In any case, the first groups that effectively settle an area will mark it with their culture more strongly than later, possibly more numerous, groups. Early patterns of settlement therefore must be examined carefully because they establish the essential form and structure of culture, which later groups can only modify.

Most of Nebraska's inhabitants of the 1850s and 1860s arrived by steamboat on the Missouri River; others came by ox-drawn wagons across Iowa. They huddled in hastily constructed villages strung along the west bank of the river. Omaha, Nebraska City, and Brownville, among others, were all founded within days or weeks of each other in the summer of 1854, following the enactment by Congress of the law establishing the territorial governments of Kansas and Nebraska. Here as elsewhere, towns were the spearheads of the frontier. In 1860, when the population nudged thirty thousand, more than 60 percent of the gainfully employed were engaged in urban-type occupations—speculators, entrepreneurs, lawyers, merchants, clerks, construction workers, teamsters, unskilled laborers. Almost everyone hoped to get rich fast and with minimal regard for the niceties of law. Farmers were in a minority, and many of them were not seriously engaged in agricultural pursuits. Most came from states directly east—Iowa, Illinois, Indiana, Ohio, and Pennsylvania. Some came from slave states such as Missouri, Kentucky, and Arkansas, but relatively few came from New England or upstate New York.

In all of this Nebraska was not much different from Kansas. But because it was farther upstream and hence more distant, Nebraska was settled rather more slowly. Because Kansas began a mere fifty miles west of a major concentration of slave-based, hemp-producing plantations in Missouri, it attracted a band of abolitionists from New England and elsewhere, small in number but powerful in influence, who bitterly fought the extension of slavery into the territories and who, victorious in the battle for statehood, remained in Kansas to flavor its politics with puritanical values. But Nebraska had no experience that was the equivalent of "Bleeding Kansas." It did not inherit a comparable cadre of politicians whose Yankee moralism and commitment to commonwealth principles led to the enactment of prohibition and other forms of state regulation of personal behavior in the post-Civil War decades. Kansas thereby acquired an early reputation for political moralism that attracted pietists of all kinds, including Swedes and Germans of such tendencies. But this identity also deflected to Nebraska more numerous immigrants who preferred a place where there was less interference with European traditions, customs, and manners.[2]

Nebraska, like other Great Plains states, was clearly shaped by its railroads. The territory itself was organized to provide a modicum of government for the area through which the projected transcontinental railroad was to be laid. But a decade passed before serious construction work began in 1864, extending west from Omaha. During the 1850s and 1860s many of the towns of eastern Nebraska, especially the county seats, were founded before the network of railroads was built. Consequently, in their spatial relationships they resemble scores of other midwestern county seats. The courthouse is placed in a square surrounded on all sides by a variety of business enterprises; the railroad with its depot is located as close to the heart of the town as its late arrival permitted.

But farther west in Nebraska, in areas penetrated by the railroad before substantial settlement occurred, the transportation system dictated the location and physical layout of the towns. Instead of coming to the people, the railroad caused the people to come to it. The depot, normally placed on land granted to the railroad by the federal government, thus displaced the courthouse square as the center of activity. If grain elevators were on one side of the tracks, then stores, hotels, saloons, livery stables, and the like would line the other side on a street running parallel to the tracks. Other commercial ventures would be placed on a thoroughfare stretching away from the depot and leading to the courthouse. In this arrangement of urban space, the courthouse was usually located, not on a square in the middle of the business district, but at the edge of town on cheap land donated by the railroad for this purpose.[3]

The internal spatial relationships of towns in central and western Nebraska (like much of Kansas and the Dakotas) was thus influenced by technological culture as it existed in the late nineteenth century. The same may be said for their placement. Sidings with stations (the nuclei of small towns platted by the railroads) were placed every six to ten miles, a distance governed by the number of miles a farmer could drive his horse-drawn wagon to town, loaded with grain or hogs, and return home on the same day, which meant a maximum round trip of fifteen to twenty miles. It also meant that, if the farming population was to be served effectively, about twenty miles would separate one railroad line from another. The lightly populated countryside could not support more development than that.

Railroad companies even decided the names of towns. Sometimes, to keep these nondescript places straight in their minds, railroad officials named them alphabetically. For example, stations on the Burlington route west of Lincoln were named Asylum, Berks, Crete, Dorchester, Exeter, Fairmont, Grafton, and so on to Kenesaw, Lowell, and Newark before coming to Kearney and the Union Pacific. Long since rendered obsolete by a new transportation technology, some of these places have disappeared without a trace. Others barely hang on but are doomed in the long run unless rescued by some new combination of economic and technological forces. In any case, however, there are today no Nebraska towns or villages exceeding 250 inhabitants that are not now or once were located on a railroad.

The railroad was not the only technological advance that made the rapid development of Nebraska possible. Its settlement period coincided exactly with a series of dramatic technological developments in eastern states. Railroad expansion itself was possible because of other basic advances, such as the expanding capacity of American industry to mass-produce steel by means of the Bessemer process (1856) and the open-hearth system (1866). At the same time railroads were central to the development of the range cattle business on the Great Plains that emerged in the late 1860s. Simultaneously, Philip Armour developed mass-production techniques for processing the huge numbers of cattle and hogs transported by rail to Chicago. Refrigerator cars appeared in 1868 to carry dressed beef to distant markets in the East. Five years later J. F. Glidden perfected barbed wire, about the same time that windmills made of steel became available to homesteaders on the plains. Farm machinery was also evolving at a rapid pace in the 1870s. To cite only one example, the twine binder used in wheat harvesting was patented in 1874. All these technological advances, plus others too numerous to describe here, combined to stimulate the settlement and early growth of Nebraska in a way that was impossible for midwestern states located farther east.

At the same time that railroads were creating strings of towns across the plains, the state legislature responded to local pressures and began to proliferate counties in central and western Nebraska. Upon the completion of their handiwork the politicians had created ninety-three counties where less than half that number would have sufficed. But they did their work in the 1870s and 1880s, when the plains was experiencing a drought followed by a period of ample rainfall. Speculators called "boomers" endlessly and perhaps mindlessly repeated the slogan that "rain follows the plow," in the naive belief that the introduction of agriculture in a subhumid environment would alter the climate favorably for this enterprise. Counties were thus organized on such ill-founded optimism about future growth. The Sand Hills region, too, was divided into the standard grid of square or rectangular counties based on the congressional survey system; some even consisted of the standard sixteen townships embracing thirty-six square miles each—and very few people. Today exactly one-third of Nebraska's counties have fewer than five thousand inhabitants; nine fall below one thousand. McPherson County, with a population of 593, is served by an elected official who, much like Pooh-Bah in Gilbert and Sullivan's *Mikado*, combines the functions of county clerk, election commissioner, registrar of deeds, assessor, and clerk of the district court–all for an annual salary of $13,000. Another county official, the highway superintendent, serves two neighboring counties in the same capacity.[4] Loath to part with the county as a symbol of identity, Nebraskans prefer to retain institutional inefficiency rather than to consolidate or reorganize these relics of frontier optimism.

The school system presents a similar problem. Before the advent of the automobile and its virtual annihilation of rural space, the one-room country school was a necessity. Such institutions certainly were improvements over no school at all. Like most states, Nebraska had a compulsory school attendance law and had adopted a system of school districts intended to serve the needs of rural children who usually walked to school. By 1883 the law specified that a school district could not be smaller than four square miles in size or have less than fifteen children of school age. Permitting such a small size had the effect of proliferating school districts until they numbered 5,664 in 1888. That prompted the state superintendent of public instruction to complain that "there are too many small school districts, with the inevitable result of small schools, low standards, low wages and poor teachers, with poor local supervision or none at all." Corruption was another by-product. The superintendent reported that, left to the direction of persons with little or no interest in public education, some "school districts were formed for no other reason than to defeat the levying of taxes and the maintaining of a school."[5]

But such complaints and warnings went unheeded and the number of school districts continued to increase until 1920, when more than seven thousand had come into existence. Then the automobile began to have its effect and the consolidation movement began. The number is now reduced to 955, but that still is more than any other state has, except heavily populated Texas, California, and Illinois. When the data are expressed in terms of a ratio of school districts to population, Nebraska is solidly in first place. Why Nebraska should so tenaciously retain its inefficient rural schools, in contrast to the neighboring states of Kansas, Iowa, South Dakota, and Colorado, remains a mystery.

The rapid growth of Nebraska's counties and towns was most pronounced in the 1880s. During this decade the population grew from about 450,000 to more than a million persons. This profound increase, which was similarly experienced by other Great Plains states, was due to a confluence of temporal, environmental (i.e., ample rainfall), and technological forces. The settlement of the plains occurred at the same time that steam-powered trains and transatlantic ships were transforming spatial relationships around the world, and agricultural expansion in the Midwest, stimulated by improvements in farm machinery, was helping the United States capture a large share of the world grain market. This development, in turn, had the effect of disrupting agricultural economies in Europe, especially in Sweden, Denmark, and northern Germany, and causing hundreds of thousands of displaced farmers and agricultural day laborers to emigrate to the United States. Some of these persons found new homes and farms in Nebraska, which was in its period of most dramatic growth.

But the influx of European immigrants was by no means uniform in the plains states. From the time of earliest settlement in the 1850s, Nebraska regularly had twice as high a proportion of foreign-born persons as Kansas had. At the same time, Dakota Territory doubled Nebraska's percentage. By 1900 first- and second-generation immigrants constituted 45 percent of the total population of Nebraska, compared with 26 percent in Kansas, 58 percent in South Dakota, and 71 percent in North Dakota, the highest proportion of any state in the Union.

Germans were by far the largest single group of foreign-born immigrants in Nebraska, where in 1900 they and their children accounted for 18 percent of the total population. The Swedes were a distant second at 5 percent and the Irish third at 4 percent. Czechs and Danes also formed important colonies in Nebraska; numerically they equaled the totals for these two groups in the entire tier of states from Texas to North Dakota. Germans from Russia were also important, but both Kansas and South Dakota doubled Nebraska's contingent. Today the descendants of German-speaking immigrants constitute more than 40 percent of the state's population.

The ethnic composition of the state's population had important political ramifications. During the late nineteenth century, prohibition became a potent symbol of the cultural clash between a substantial part of the native-born population and many of the newcomers, for whom the use of alcoholic beverages was an integral part of their culture. Throughout the Midwest and much of the Northeast, prohibition and attendant issues of woman suffrage, public school education, and Sabbatarian regulations dominated state and local politics. Nebraska's immigrants included many Catholics of German, Irish, Czech, and Polish origins, plus numerous German Lutherans, all of whom were attracted to the Democratic party as the champion of the fullest measure of personal liberty consistent with law and order. For them, typical Republican tendencies to support prohibition and other coercive cultural measures (usually defined in terms of morality, progress, and reform) had to be opposed as intolerable efforts to inject governmental authority into personal and spiritual affairs and to impose Anglo-American Protestant values on a reluctant immigrant population.

Because of the political strength of these ethnocultural groups, the complex of issues symbolized by prohibition did not fare well in Nebraska, compared to Kansas, which was the first state to write prohibition into its constitution. Drawing upon its New England traditions, Kansas achieved this dubious distinction in 1880 with a 4 percent margin in a popular vote. Enforcement was difficult, however, even under the best of circumstances, and since the amendment permitted the sale of liquor for medicinal purposes, the proportion of sickly Kansans increased dramatically. Even so, Kansas went on to enact in 1909 what was considered to be the most stringent prohibitory law in the nation. Iowa behaved much like Kansas, but with less success. In 1882 its electorate approved a prohibition amendment 55 to 45 percent, only to have the Iowa Supreme Court declare it unconstitutional on a technicality.

But it was a different story in Nebraska, where in 1881 the prohibition forces could not even get their measure through the legislature, presumably because of the political clout of its ethnoreligious groups. Instead, the so-called advocates of temperance had to be satisfied with the enactment of a high-license law. The next year they sought to strengthen their hand by means of a woman suffrage amendment, which was generally thought of as a halfway house to prohibition. The Nebraska electorate responded by rejecting the measure by a two-to-one margin; in strongly German precincts the rejection rate spiraled to ten to one. A prohibition amendment finally appeared on the Nebraska ballot in 1890; it failed, 58 to 42 percent. Not until 1916, when the possibility of war with Germany altered the shape of state politics, did prohibition succeed in Nebraska.

None of this is to suggest that Nebraskans were liberal in their attitudes toward racial and ethnic minorities. A national map showing Indian reservations provides a clue: Nebraska, like Iowa and Kansas, has almost none, whereas South Dakota has one of the largest areas set aside for this purpose in the entire nation. Time relationships provide the explanation: even as Congress was debating (and finally approving) the admission of Nebraska as a state in 1867, the territorial legislature memorialized Congress to remove the Otoe and Missouria Indians so that their lands could be made available to white Nebraskans, who, unlike the Indians, would effectively cultivate the fertile soil. During the next decade the state legislature repeatedly and successfully demanded that Congress extinguish Indian titles and remove the Pawnees to Oklahoma and the Sioux agencies to Dakota Territory. By the time the states of North and South Dakota were organized in 1889, the Indian policy of the federal government had long since created the huge Rosebud, Pine Ridge, and Standing Rock reservations, where the environment effectively limits the possibilities for successful farming.

The study of ethnic groups in Nebraska returns us again to the fact that the state's physical environment dictates that small numbers of people be thinly spread over vast spaces. The kinds of personal interactions that occur and the variety of institutions that can be maintained efficiently are directly related to population density. Concentrations of large numbers of people in relatively small spaces (i.e., cities) obviously permit activities and institutions that are virtually impossible to sustain in sparsely populated areas. If ethnocultural forms are to be sustained over time, they must have the support of institutions such as churches, schools, immigrant-language newspapers and periodicals, social and cultural associations of all kinds, and businesses that cater to the ethnic trade. In the sparsely populated plains of Nebraska, churches were the easiest of immigrant institutions to create; often they were the only ones to survive the disappearance of the immigrant languages. Because the churches frequently functioned as substitutes for the array of social and cultural societies that were available in large cities, they assumed special importance in Nebraska for the formation of personal identity.

The level of population density is also related to the internal cohesion of an ethnic group and its homogeneity, or sense of peoplehood.

In Nebraska the clusters of German Mennonites who originally emigrated from Russia have a keen sense of identity. Even though Swedes far outnumber Czechs in Nebraska, they have a weaker sense of cohesion and hence their assimilation has been more rapid. The Germans, by far the largest ethnic group in the state, have today what may be the weakest sense of peoplehood, possibly because of the enervation of two world wars in which Germany was the prime enemy and in which German language and culture were denigrated.

Nebraska has not been without incidents of racial and ethnic conflict. Such disturbances are usually identified with teaming, heterogeneous cities. So it has been in Nebraska, where Omaha experienced a violent anti-Greek riot in 1909 and, worse, an antiblack disorder that resulted in the lynching and mutilation of an innocent black victim, destruction of property in the black neighborhood, and the burning of Omaha's new county courthouse in 1919. Even smaller cities had occasional problems. For example, in 1929 a racial incident occurred in North Platte in which, following the murder of a white policeman and the subsequent death of his black assailant, the small black community of the town, which numbered about thirty-five persons, fled from the city for fear of their lives. In many Nebraska communities, large and small, fears and suspicions engendered by the war with Germany in 1917 and 1918 led to numerous minor acts of prejudice and oppression against German-American fellow citizens. Although Americans have often suggested that all such outbreaks are manifestations of our heritage of frontier violence, this relationship is tenuous in these cases, unlike the instances of prejudice Nebraskans sometimes have displayed against the state's small Indian minority.

Despite these occasional manifestations of tension, racial and ethnic discord is not a deep-seated characteristic of Nebraska history. Agricultural discontent is. From the earliest times, when railroads received huge subsidies and grants of some of the best land in the state, farmers have tended to see themselves as victims of distant and oppressive economic forces. They naturally turned to politics as a means to relieve their distress. At first they perceived the Greenback party as congenial to their interests. In 1880 and 1882, the Anti-Monopoly party exercised a brief flash of power in some counties. By 1890 agricultural discontent had mushroomed into what soon became known as the Populist party. Like the earlier 1870s and the later 1930s, the 1890s were years in which severe drought combined with economic depression to produce much misery in rural areas. Like voters in the other states of the Great Plains but unlike those farther east, many Nebraska farmers and their sympathizers in the towns turned to Populism as a vehicle for radical reform, including government ownership of the banking, transportation, and communication

systems. They elected governors, congressmen, judges, and state legislators, but they never gathered enough power to enact their program. Instead, the impulse for reform languished until the Progressive
era, when, starting in 1907, it had a brief life under the gubernatorial
stewardship of Republican George Sheldon, followed by Democrat
Ashton Shallenberger. Even though the reforms of the Populist and
Progressive eras did little for the farmers, the character of politics
as practiced in Nebraska was transformed from a unidimensional,
symbolic system best understood in terms of ethnocultural conflict
to a multiple-issue system in which political loyalties were weakened
but professional leadership was strengthened.

Agrarian discontent rooted in Populism emerged again in the early
1920s, especially under the banner of the Non-Partisan League, an
organization founded on socialistic principles in North Dakota. Roundly
denounced as a subversive organization, it found its greatest strength
in the northeastern quarter of Nebraska, where German farmers, still
chafing from the injustices of the World War, were especially numerous.

But the NPL was unable to dislodge public attention from the
progressive reforms of Republican Governor Samuel McKelvie, who
was eager to streamline state government in the image of the modern
businessman. Preoccupied with efficiency through centralized administration, McKelvie sought to strengthen gubernatorial authority
by the drafting of a new, "modern" state constitution and the enactment of an "administrative code." Although he technically failed
to achieve the first goal, he got much of what he wanted in the form
of forty-one constitutional amendments and a series of laws. They
remain in force today, though in a much altered form.

McKelvie also realized a second, more monumental, goal—the
construction of a new state capitol to house his modernized government. Erected on a pay-as-you-build plan, Nebraska's new capitol,
often characterized as an extraordinary architectural achievement,
was finally dedicated in 1934. It quickly became the preeminent symbol of the state to its citizens. Now more than a half-century old, this
magnificent structure is perceived by Nebraskans as a symbolic link
between the state's pioneer history, a progressive present, and a hope-
ful future. That the symbol belies an ultraconservative reality is beside
the point.

The dedication of the capitol was only one of a series of momen-
tous events in the 1930s that fix upon Nebraska certain unique qualities. Like other states of the Midwest, Nebraska suffered severely
from the Great Depression and the Great Drought. The rural exodus,
already under way, accelerated as farmers moved to town, if not in
Nebraska, then in California, Oregon, or elsewhere. Agricultural discontent flared again and even threatened to burst into violence in

some communities, as farm strikes, penny auctions of farms and farm equipment, and a moratorium on mortgages were undertaken. But when real help arrived, it came from the federal government, not the statehouse.

More important for the state's history was the adoption of the nonpartisan, one-house legislature by constitutional amendment in 1934. Usually called the Unicameral by Nebraskans, this unique body, which is a major departure from American political tradition, was approved in the depths of the depression as a way of reducing the "baneful influence" of lobbyists and the special interests they represent. The idea of a one-house legislature was not new to Nebraskans in 1934; it had been proposed frequently since 1913 but had failed just as often to be placed before the voters of the state. Although it has frequently been described as a liberal or progressive innovation designed to inject a new measure of responsibility and accountability into state government, it was also a conservative device to reduce state expenditures. The proposed amendment to create the Unicameral was linked with two others, one to repeal prohibition in the state and another to legalize pari-mutuel betting; both were expected ultimately to revitalize the state's treasury. Regardless of its merits, the amendment probably would not have been adopted without the herculean efforts of its chief sponsor, Senator George Norris, a man of great personal prestige who campaigned tirelessly for it for more than a decade.

In its half century of operation, the Unicameral has generally proved its worth, even though it has failed utterly to curb the power of lobbies. Its nonpartisan character has weakened, rather than strengthened, popular democracy. Partisanship continues but in a disguised and enervated form, and party responsibility in the legislature has disappeared. Yet most informed Nebraskans regard the Unicameral highly; they are proud of the fact that their state is the only one to recognize the obvious virtues of such a legislative system. Frequent attempts have been made to remove the nonpartisan feature, but all have failed. The Unicameral has repeatedly demonstrated its ability to reflect the strong conservatism of the people. Nebraskans like it and intend to keep it.

The hard times of the 1930s introduced a second unique feature to Nebraska: it is the only state in the Union with public ownership of its entire capacity to produce electricity commercially. Like the Unicameral, it is part of the legacy of George Norris, its chief sponsor. Although public power is often denounced by its opponents as socialism, Nebraska acquired the ownership of its power plants through a confluence of many economic and political factors, most of them pragmatic if not conservative in character. Ideological questions were never part of the debate; farmers were at the heart of it. Eager to increase their income in the drought-stricken thirties, farm leaders pushed for the construction of a major irrigation dam to be built on the North Platte River north of Ogallala, in accordance with a federal law passed in 1932 permitting the Reconstruction Finance Corporation to make loans to public organizations for hydroelectric and irrigation projects. The legislature thereupon allowed for the organization of public power districts with certain governmental powers, but not including the authority to levy taxes. The project was subsequently approved by the Public Works Administration in 1935 and construction of Kingsley Dam proceeded. It began the production of electric power in 1941. Meanwhile, four public power districts were created, the last in 1945, which led to the purchase of the final remaining investor-owned utility a year later. Since then the system has been expanded and developed and now includes two major nuclear power plants.

The adoption of the Unicameral and the statewide system of public power reflect the workings of Nebraska's political culture. Although they appear to be radical innovations, they spring from conservative, nonideological concerns about economic relationships that date back to the Populist and Progressive struggles against the railroads, banks, and monopolistic tendencies of private enterprise at the turn of the century. They reflect what Daniel Elazar has characterized as the "marketplace orientation" that strongly marks Nebraska's political culture, in contrast to the "commonwealth" conception that is dominant in Wisconsin, Minnesota, and North Dakota. The former, according to Elazar, views public policy as emerging from bargaining among political groups and leaders acting in terms of self-interest; the latter conception refers to the belief that all citizens should cooperate to create and maintain the best possible government on the basis of moral principles. Moreover, the former orientation provides the foundation for "individualistic" politics and calls for efficient government action to enhance economic opportunity and the pursuit of private goals; the latter holds that government is the means to achieve "the good society" through social and economic programs that are in the public interest generally.[6]

When analyzed in these terms, the western tier of midwestern states reveals a pattern in which North Dakota is clearly the most radical, South Dakota somewhat less so, Nebraska generally conservative but productive of progressive reforms consonant with private interests, and Kansas like Nebraska but even more conservative. In Elazar's view, the marketplace orientation is strongest in Nebraska; similarly, it is the only midwestern state west of the Mississippi that mixes individualistic and moralistic tendencies, but with individualistic elements dominant.

How are these differences to be explained? The answer lies in the patterns of migration. Whereas North Dakota, like Minnesota and Wisconsin, was settled by persons with cultural roots in New England and upstate New York, supplemented strongly by streams of pietistic Scandinavians, Nebraska received a large flow of Americans from the "Midlands," as geographer John Hudson has described it,[7] plus substantial reinforcements of Germans, Irish, Czechs, and other Europeans whose preference for individualistic politics was clear. Highly dependent in its frontier period on its Missouri River connection with the Mississippi and Ohio river valleys, Nebraska received a more heterogeneous population than its immediate neighbors north and south. Thus, while Nebraska's political history has not been without a moralistic flavor, it has been more individualistic, more oriented to the marketplace, than either Kansas or the Dakotas, the states with which it shares a similar physical environment.

Because Nebraska has received little in-migration during the past century, the original pattern of ethnic and religious group settlement continues to help explain contemporary political behavior. Where German, Swedish, or Czech farmers broke the sod a century ago, there their descendants continue to farm today. Where Democratic voters motivated by ethnoreligious issues were concentrated in the late nineteenth century, there Democratic majorities are still to be found. The most recent voter registration lists reveal that counties largely settled by Catholic immigrant groups continue to record Democratic pluralities, if not majorities, as they did in the nineteenth century. In 1986 only twelve of Nebraska's ninety-three counties registered more Democrats than Republicans. Each Democratic county is presently inhabited largely by the descendants of ethnic or religious groups with historic attachments to the Democratic party of the nineteenth century. They include disproportionate numbers of voters of Irish, Polish, Czech, and Italian origins, many of them Catholic in religion, plus Danes and American Indians. Only the German Lutherans have abandoned their nineteenth-century ties to the Democratic party as the party of personal liberty.[8]

Politics on the state level since the Great Depression have not been distinctive. Nebraska is basically a Republican state, though Democrats are strong enough to win important offices occasionally, provided their candidates are appropriately conservative. Party identification generally does not inhibit crossover voting. Although the constitutional grant of gubernatorial powers is substantial compared with that in many other states, Nebraska's governors have tended to view themselves primarily as administrators rather than as political leaders with powers to shape public debate and to influence the legislature in the enactment of their policies. The nonpartisan character of the Unicameral makes it difficult for the governor to provide effective, positive leadership, but the example of Republican Norbert Tiemann, who served from 1967 to 1971, demonstrated the possibilities. Tiemann repeatedly exercised the powers of his office to restructure the state's tax base, improve higher education, introduce state aid to local school districts, and push economic development. As one observer put it, "Tiemann pulled Nebraska kicking and screaming into the twentieth century." He was also dismissed by the voters after one term in favor of a Democratic candidate, J. James Exon, who denounced him as a "blank-check spender."[9]

In any case, political leadership is always difficult in times of retrenchment resulting from structural changes in the economy, such as Nebraska and other midwestern states have experienced in recent years. Agriculture continues as the foundation of the state's economy; and agriculture, long addicted to support programs of the federal government, is suffering severe stress as aid is reduced or withdrawn. Only 9 percent of the work force in this agricultural state is still directly employed in agriculture, compared with about 2 percent nationally. The number of farms in the state has decreased by half in forty years; during the same period the average farm has nearly doubled in size to more than seven hundred acres.[10] The contemporary history of this state is thus influenced profoundly by the federal government and its ever-changing policies. State governments are forced to adapt to such variables just as much as to the exigencies imposed by the physical environment.

Inevitably such drastic economic changes have far-reaching demographic consequences. Internal migration is redistributing the population of the state. Seventy percent of the counties lost population in the 1970s; the rate has accelerated in the 1980s, when out-migration has exceeded 10 percent in sixteen counties. The median age of the population exceeded forty years in six counties (compared with the state figure of 29.7 in 1980) as young people fled the farms. Meanwhile, rural poverty has increased dramatically, especially in Sand Hills counties. Almost all population growth in Nebraska is occurring in counties located along Nebraska's Nile, its section of Interstate 80, or its railroads carrying coal from Wyoming. When, in 1961, President John Kennedy's chief aide, Ted Sorensen, made a bitterly resented speech in McCook in which he said that his home state of Nebraska was "a place to come from or a place to die," he was reflecting upon demographic realities. His facts were correct; his explanation less sure.[11]

It has been my purpose in this essay to demonstrate that distinctive features of Nebraska's history emerge from the interaction of time, place, and culture. Nebraska is a place that is warmer than the Dakotas, colder than Kansas, drier than Iowa, and wetter than Wyoming.

It is a grassland, not forested naturally like Michigan and Wisconsin. Its topography is more varied than that of Illinois, but like Kansas it has nothing to compare to the Black Hills of South Dakota. Like Iowa and Kansas, Nebraska has great beauty, but little of the kind that appeals to the modern romanticism that idealizes mountains and seashores. One of the state's illustrious sons, Alvin Johnson, wrote that Nebraska's "magnificent plains" would have delighted the classical Romans, who detested the Alps as "horrid and miserable" but loved verdant fields along "sluggish streams exuberant with harvests."[12] Such an environment, beauteous or not, decrees that Nebraska's economy rest squarely on agriculture—in an era when fewer farmers can produce more food than an exploding world population can buy.

How a people responds to stress is the stuff of history. Environmental variables merely set the limits for the history that is transacted in a given place; how a society orders its affairs over time is governed more by the culture its members have brought to the land they inhabit. To this place came Americans mostly from states directly east. They were accompanied by immigrants mostly from northern and central Europe—Irish, English, Swedes, Danes, Germans, Czechs, and Poles, plus Germans from Russia, but fewer blacks than any midwestern state except the Dakotas (the place where it sent its Indians) and still fewer Asians. Religious beliefs have conditioned their political attitudes and behaviors, even though Nebraska, like every other state, has a large minority of persons who admit no church affiliation. Nebraskans are individualistic, self-reliant, and conservative, but they have been willing to consider the use of radical means to achieve their conservative goals. They cherish their nonpartisan, unicameral legislature; they do not hesitate to elect to high political office women, Jews, and members of ethnic minorities. And their football heroes at the University of Nebraska are usually black.

Because Nebraska occupies a unique space and because it has been populated by a unique mixture of cultural groups, its history is also unique. This history inevitably bears many similarities to that of its neighbors; Nebraskans naturally have conducted their affairs in ways much like those of other midwesterners. But the distinctive qualities of Nebraska's history emerge from the interaction over time between the environment and the culture brought to this place by its people. These differences are most readily discerned through appropriate comparisons with the histories of other states in America's heartland.

NOTES

1. Dorothy Weyer Creigh, *Nebraska: A Bicentennial History* (New York, 1977), 6; but see also 5–13.

2. This relationship was first impressed upon me by a quotation from the distinguished Kansas journalist and Progressive William Allan White, who observed that Kansans "still have in [their] veins the blood of the New England settlers who came in with the immigrant societies in the fifties and filled the first eastern tiers of counties. Following the first settlers in the fifties came the young soldiers of the Civil War and their wives seeking free homesteads. They were Union soldiers. They came from the North. They pushed the Yankee blood westward in one great impulse, three hundred miles from the Missouri border. Then being puritanical, Kansas in 1880 adopted prohibition. More than that, Kansas advertised its prohibition, and in advertising its prohibitory law erected a barrier against the beer drinking, liberty loving immigrants from northern Europe which Kansas needed so badly to enrich her blood as these people have enriched the blood of the population of Minnesota, Wisconsin, Iowa, Nebraska, and the Dakotas." Quoted in Neal R. Peirce, *The Great Plains States of America* (New York, 1973), 223–24.

3. This analysis is developed by John C. Hudson, "The Plains Country Town," in Brian W. Blouet and Frederick C. Luebke, eds., *The Great Plains: Environment and Culture* (Lincoln, Nebr. 1979), 103–5.

4. *Sunday Journal-Star* (Lincoln, Nebr.), July 6, 1986, 1D.

5. *The School Laws of Nebraska, As revised and amended in 1881 . . .* (Lincoln, 1881), 15; *Twentieth Annual Report of the [Nebraska State] Superintendent of Public Instruction, 1888* (Lincoln, 1888), 71, 74.

6. Daniel J. Elazar, "Political Culture on the Plains," *Western Historical Quarterly* 11 (July 1980), 267–68, 277–79.

7. John C. Hudson, "Who Was 'Forest Man?' Sources of Migration to the Plains," *Great Plains Quarterly* 6 (Spring 1986), 74.

8. The counties, in order of Democratic strength, are Sherman (Polish), Greeley (Irish), Butler (Czech), Saline (Czech), Thurston (American Indian), Nance (Polish), Cedar (German Catholic), Howard (Poles and Danes), Saunders (Czech), Colfax (Czech), Douglas (metropolitan Omaha with large numbers of Italians, Czechs, blacks, and other minority groups), and Dakota (Sioux City metropolitan area). Data supplied by the office of the Nebraska Secretary of State.

9. Peirce, *The Great Plains States of America*, 205–9.

10. Much of the data in this and the following paragraph is from various issues of *Business in Nebraska*, a publication of the College of Business Administration, University of Nebraska–Lincoln.

11. The relevant portion of Sorensen's speech is quoted in Peirce, *The Great Plains States of America*, 198.

12. Alvin Johnson, *Pioneer's Progress: An Autobiography* (1952; reprinted Lincoln, 1960), 169.

BIBLIOGRAPHY

The standard reference for the history of Nebraska in the nineteenth and early twentieth centuries is Addison E. Sheldon, *Nebraska: The Land and the People* (Chicago, 1931), published in three volumes, two of which are biographical. A huge work based on both personal experience and on the learning its author acquired as superintendent of the Nebraska State Historical Society, it is also rambling and idiosyncratic, though nonetheless valuable. More concise and balanced is James C. Olson, *History of Nebraska*, 2d ed. (Lincoln, Nebr., 1966). It is also regrettably out of date and has little value for the decades since World War II. Dorothy Weyer Creigh, *Nebraska: A Bicentennial History* (New York, 1977), is an engaging, well-written study, but it is fragmentary and lacking in a systematic exposition of the state's historical development. Easily the most useful introduction to contemporary Nebraska is Bradley H. Baltensperger, *Nebraska: A Geography* (Boulder, Colo., 1985). As one would expect, this geography says nothing of politics, a subject that is effectively introduced in Robert D. Miewald, ed., *Nebraska Government and Politics* (Lincoln, 1984). The richest source of information about the state's history, though not its interpretation, are the hundreds of articles in *Nebraska History*, published since 1918.

The physiography of Nebraska is introduced in Nevin M. Fenneman, *Physiography of Western United States* (New York, 1931), and its climate in Merlin P. Lawson et al., *Climatic Atlas of Nebraska* (Lincoln, 1977). For materials that help to relate Nebraska to the Great Plains region, see Brian W. Blouet and Merlin P. Lawson, eds., *Images of the Plains* (Lincoln, 1975); Brian W. Blouet and Frederick C. Luebke, eds., *The Great Plains: Environment and Culture* (Lincoln, 1979); and Merlin P. Lawson and Maurice E. Baker, eds., *The Great Plains: Perspectives and Prospects* (Lincoln, 1981).

Several important recent studies relate the state's political history to its social characteristics. Among them are Frederick C. Luebke, *Immigrants and Politics: The Germans of Nebraska, 1880–1900* (Lincoln, 1969); Stanley B. Parsons, Jr., *The Populist Context: Rural versus Urban Power on a Great Plains Frontier* (Westport, Conn., 1973); and Robert W. Cherny, *Populism, Progressivism, and the Transformation of Nebraska Politics, 1885–1915* (Lincoln, 1981). Also important for understanding the modern political history of the state is James F. Pederson and Kenneth D. Wald, *Shall the People Rule? A History of the Democratic Party in Nebraska* (Lincoln, 1972).

For the great epic of migration on the so-called Oregon Trail, see Merrill J. Mattes, *The Great Platte River Road* (Lincoln, 1969), and John D. Unruh, *The Plains Across* (Urbana, Ill., 1979). Settlement is treated anecdotally in many books, among them Everett Dick, *The Sod-House Frontier* (Lincoln, 1937). The role of the railroad in settlement history is examined in Richard C. Overton, *Burlington West* (Cambridge, Mass., 1941). Addison E. Sheldon, *Land Systems and Land Policies in Nebraska* (Lincoln, 1936) continues to be especially valuable, despite its age. Settlement propaganda is effectively analyzed in David Emmons, *Garden in the Grassland* (Lincoln, 1971). Howard Ottoson et al., *Land and People in the Northern Transition Area* (Lincoln, 1966), continues to be valuable. A particularly useful study for a limited area in Nebraska is Richard G. Bremer, *Agricultural Change in an Urban Age: The Loup Country of Nebraska, 1910–1970* (Lincoln, 1976). An essential source for the modern agricultural history of the state is James H. Williams and Doug Murfield, eds., *Agricultural Atlas of Nebraska* (Lincoln, 1977). The agricultural sector of the state's economy is surveyed in Richard E. Lonsdale, ed., *Economic Atlas of Nebraska* (Lincoln, 1977).

The urban history of Nebraska remains largely unexplored. The most useful volumes in this field are studies by Howard P. Chudacoff, *Mobile Americans: Residential and Social Mobility in Omaha, 1880–1920* (New York, 1972), and Lawrence H. Larsen, *The Urban West at the End of the Frontier* (Lawrence, Kans., 1978), and *The Gate City: A History of Omaha* (Boulder, Colo., 1982), the latter written with Barbara J. Cottrell.

For an introduction to various racial and ethnic groups in Nebraska, see the essays in *Broken Hoops and Plains People* (Lincoln, 1976). Several articles in Frederick C. Luebke, ed., *Ethnicity on the Great Plains* (Lincoln, 1980), are limited to Nebraska.

The history of the development of public power is treated in great detail in Robert Firth, *Public Power in Nebraska: A Report on State Ownership* (Lincoln, 1962). Nebraska's one-house legislature is best studied in a series of articles and dissertations, but a useful introduction is Adam C. Breckenridge, *One House for Two: Nebraska's Unicameral Legislature* (Washington, D.C., 1957).

Leo E. Oliva

KANSAS

A Hard Land
in the Heartland

K ANSAS, LIKE MOST STATES, is an artificial geographic entity without natural boundaries. While geographic conditions affect significantly such factors as living conditions and the economy, the people and their culture provide each state with additional distinctive characteristics. Identification with a state is based on residence, popular images, and history. Kansans have traditionally thought of their state as a hard land because of its fickle climate, which forced many who tried to live in Kansas to leave and try their luck elsewhere, and because of constant struggles against real or imagined social evils, which often became contests between individualism and conformity. Those who endured the challenges developed an intense pride in their accomplishments and a love-hate relationship with their state.

The heritage of Kansas is closely tied to struggles and survival, and some writers have observed that Kansans like nothing better than the challenges of hard times. Kansas-born novelist Paul Wellman wrote in *The Bowl of Brass* (1944):

No Kansan likes to do anything easy. He raises his crops hard. He takes his religion hard. To be able to get licker easy would jest be contrary to nature for him. So he makes laws to keep him from gettin' it . . . which makes it harder, which give mo' of a point to drinkin' it, and behold, yo' Kansan thereby derives greater satisfaction of soul out'n it.

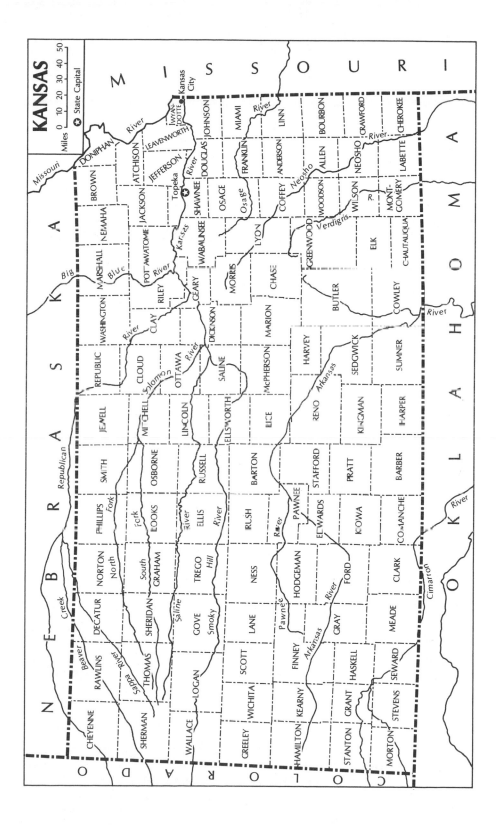

Kansas is a state of diversities, some of which appear incongruous or outright contradictory, and all of which make it difficult to categorize the people and their history. For each generalization that has been made about Kansas, an opposite example may be found. The state has a long-standing image problem; it has too often been viewed as barren, hot, and dry with furious tornadoes that can sweep innocent children and their pets into beautiful places far away from home. In addition, it has been viewed as a place where personal morality and behavior are constantly scrutinized by a code designed to prevent anyone from having fun.

Kansas has a variety of images; some are controversial. The image problem is part of the heritage. There is an oft-told joke about a quiz contest in which first prize is a week's vacation in Kansas and second prize is two weeks' vacation in Kansas. Kansas has been thought of as puritanical, conservative, rural, barren, backward, and, strange as it may seem, radical (abolition, prohibition, Populism, and the struggle for woman suffrage). Many have wondered why the Kansas legislature has spent so many sessions discussing and cussing such issues as prohibition and liquor by the drink and bingo, leaving little time to deal with education, highways, and social problems. Others have wondered why Kansans promote pious, self-righteous ideals while their daily habits are just as human as those of other Americans. Obviously there are more than a few myths about Kansas. Even one symbol of Kansas (the Jayhawk) is a mythical bird.

Fred Trigg, Kansas correspondent for the *Kansas City Star*, declared in the 1920s that

> Kansas has always been different from any other state. God just dropped Kansas out here on the plains and the next morning it organized a constitutional convention. . . . Even historians don't understand Kansas; I wonder sometimes if anybody except God understands Kansas and sometimes I think Kansas even has Him fooled.[1]

Kansas was named for the Kansa Indians, a Siouan-speaking people who once lived along the river also named for them. The Kansas River, tributary to the Missouri, is one of two major rivers in the state; the other is the Arkansas. The word *Kansas* has been translated as "South Wind" or "People of the South Wind." The meaning is appropriate, for Kansas is known for its proverbial winds. Dodge City, in the southwestern part of the state, has the highest average wind speed in the nation.

Kansas has a reputation for being flat, and portions of it are, but it has a greater range in surface altitude (from a low of 680 feet to a high of 4,039 feet above sea level) than all other midwestern states but two (Nebraska and South Dakota), and the Flint Hills exhibit a rugged terrain and natural beauty surpassed only by the Black Hills of South Dakota. The largest remnant of tall grass prairie, which once dominated the landscape of most of the Midwest, is found in the Kansas Flint Hills, some of the finest grazing land in the world.

Except for the southeast corner of Kansas, contained within the Ozark Plateau, the state lies within two of the major physiographic provinces of the conterminus forty-eight states: the Central Lowland and the Great Plains. Despite the flat reputation, the names of half of the subprovinces refer to hills. The portion of Kansas within the Central Lowland includes five subprovinces: Cherokee Lowland, Chautauqua Hills, Osage Cuestas, Glaciated Region, and Flint Hills. The Great Plains Province in Kansas also is divided into five subprovinces: Great Bend Prairie, Wellington Plain, Red Hills, Smoky Hills (also called Blue Hills), and the High Plains. Good soils in most of these regions make Kansas a leading agricultural state in the Midwest, the nation's breadbasket.

Kansas has the image of a dry state, referring to precipitation and liquor. It ranks lowest in average annual rainfall of all midwestern states, but the averages are not nearly so important as the annual variations and the periodic and unpredictable wet and dry cycles. Kansas has seemed like a garden during the former and a desert during the later. The desert and the garden have been themes in Kansas history, literature, and folklore. Kansas has few natural lakes, but man-made lakes abound for flood control and recreation. A few provide limited irrigation. Most irrigation water is pumped from underground.

Kansas has been dry in other ways. It was the first state in the Union to enact constitutional prohibition in 1880, a reform method that swept other states and the nation, leading to the Eighteenth Amendment to the U.S. Constitution in 1920. When the pendulum swung the other way, Kansas resisted. Constitutional prohibition was sustained in Kansas following national repeal in 1933 and lasted until 1948, and a constitutional prohibition of the "open saloon" remained in Kansas until 1986. Despite the restrictions, however, Kansas produced and consumed alcoholic beverages. Package liquor was sold for "medicinal" purposes through drug stores during the late nineteenth and early twentieth centuries. During national prohibition, some of the highest quality corn liquor served in midwestern speakeasies as far away as Chicago was distilled in Kansas. Bootleggers, bottle clubs, and legal private clubs mocked the self-proclaimed purity of Kansas.

Kansas has a rural heritage, although the majority of its people live in urban communities in the late twentieth century, when the economy is more diverse than ever before, although still based to a large extent on agriculture and its related industries. Wichita, largest city in Kansas, is the airplane manufacturing center of the nation. Ironically, the most famous city associated with Kansas, Kansas City, is mostly in Missouri (Kansas City, Kansas, second largest city in the state, is only a shadow of its neighbor across the imaginary line). Topeka, third largest city, is the state capital; government accounts for its size and strength. Although Kansas is generally thought to have much more agriculture than culture, the fine arts are alive and well in the cities, many small towns, and the college and university communities.

Kansas has had a remarkably successful system of education. It has ranked at or near the top among all states in literacy since it entered the Union. In general, quality of and opportunities in education have been good in Kansas, but many of the trained young people have had to find employment in other states. A major export of Kansas has been its talented youth. The ongoing out-migration is more typical of plains states than the rest of the Midwest.

Kansans have a pride in their state and history that may be exceeded only by that of Texans. The Kansas State Historical Society, founded by newspapermen in 1875, ranks high among such institutions, the peer of outstanding societies in other midwestern states, and most county historical societies in Kansas have been active and strong. Unlike many other states, however, Kansas does not require the teaching of its history in public schools nor require a competency in Kansas history of its teachers.

Kansas is the largest midwestern state in area but one of the smallest in population (Nebraska and the Dakotas have fewer people). Kansas was the first part of the Midwest to be visited by European explorers, when Coronado sought the fabled gold of Quivira and strangled the Indian guide who led him there with false tales of mineral wealth in 1541, but it was among the last of the midwestern states to be settled (again, Nebraska and the Dakotas were later). Although gold was not found in present-day Kansas, mineral wealth was later discovered in the form of coal and petroleum, and the fertile soils, about which Coronado commented favorably, turned out to be the most valuable natural resource.

The pattern of westward settlement leap-frogged from Missouri to the Far West (Oregon and California) and dropped back later to fill in the gaps in the middle of the continent. During the interim Kansas was the "dumping ground" for Indians removed from several midwestern states, a part of what was proclaimed to be the "permanent Indian frontier." Soldiers and missionaries came to the area to protect and aid the reservation Indians and, as the Indian frontier was breached, to protect and aid travelers heading farther west.

Because of the state's geographical position at the center of the contiguous United States, Kansas was a crossroads for almost everyone and everything heading west. It was a crossroads for the overland trails to the Southwest, Oregon, and California. It was a crossroads for the railroads (although the first transcontinental went through Nebraska), eventually having more miles of railroad track in service than any other state. The same was true of modern highways, with only Texas having more miles in service.

For most people in the Midwest and elsewhere who have occasion to be in the state, Kansas remains a crossroads (something that must be endured to get someplace else, such as the Colorado Rockies). Living in a state where most people are (sometimes reluctantly) passing through and seldom stopping, Kansas residents have been affected by the crossroads image as well as the reality. Some have felt shame that their state has such a negative image beyond its borders; others have expressed a smug pride that their unnoticed land (with its prairie beauty and healthy climate) and people (with their industriousness and sense of responsibility) were free from the crowds of tourists and sightseers.

Kansas is a border state of the Midwest, divided in orientation toward the rest of the Midwest and toward the Great Plains region. The eastern one-third of the state, from the Flint Hills east, contains most of the population and is tied most closely to the Midwest (geographically, economically, socially, and culturally). The western two-thirds (lying west of the Flint Hills or the Sixth Principal Meridian used for the geographical survey of the land or, most popularly, west of U.S. Highway 81, which runs north-south through Concordia, Salina, and Wichita) is tied to the Great Plains. Western Kansas is a land of large farms (some irrigated), cattle feedlots, meat-packing plants, pockets of petroleum production, small country towns with populations of less than two thousand, and occasional regional centers with ten thousand to over twenty thousand offering medical and educational facilities, other services, and large retail businesses. Despite orientation, both regions within the state are clearly heirs of New England and midwestern rural traditions.

In all its diversities, Kansas has been, perhaps, the least typical midwestern state. Yet, as a reservoir of middle-class, midwestern rural values, Kansas is one of the more typical parts of the region. From a national perspective, Kansas was most important and creative during the nineteenth century. It tended to fall behind during part of the present century, deserving at least in part the view of outsiders who saw Kansas as backward and stagnant in its conservatism. Since World War II or the 1950s, however, when much of the rest of the nation seemed to lose moral direction and social stability, these qualities were exemplified and recognized in Kansas. Thus, as with many other things that can be said about Kansas, it has been a land of contrasts.

During at least the first half century of statehood, Kansans often believed there was a higher purpose or ideal cause, a mission, in their behavior, which made the lives they lived and the work they did more than just ordinary lives and work. Although they were thirteen hundred miles and two centuries removed from New England Puritans, Kansans were direct heirs of the Puritan desire to improve the world and serve as examples to change others who had not yet seen the truth. When Kansans had a cause, be it free state, abolition, prohibition, Populism, or woman suffrage, they enjoyed the feelings of superior ideals and improving the lives of those less fortunate and less informed. At the same time, however, there were Kansans whose primary motives were materialistic greed, who had no interest in reform and considered the do-gooders to be cranks and troublemakers who interfered with the enjoyment of life. They found enough challenge trying to wrest a living from a hard land. Interestingly, Kansas pioneers had this struggle in common with New England colonists, too.

The New England influence in Kansas is difficult to explain. In 1860 less than 4 percent of the Kansas population was of New England origin and over 30 percent of the residents were immigrants from the Midwest, particularly Ohio, Indiana, and Illinois. Despite their small numbers, however, New Englanders held a disproportionate share of public offices and positions of community leadership, and they exerted political and social influences far beyond their numbers. Seldom have so few influenced so many. Perhaps they were among the first on the scene and established positions which later arrivals followed, although such midwesterners as James Lane from Indiana challenged New England primacy in Kansas with some success. Perhaps they were better informed, some have said more intelligent, and continued to educate themselves and their neighbors. They established several early newspapers to promote their causes. Kansas has had more newspapers established than any other state, and it may be that the power of the press played a more decisive role there than in other states. It was impossible to provide financial support for so many papers, and more of them failed than survived.

Whatever the reasons, the power of the middle-class, self-righteous, democratic, individualistic, conformist, and reformist Puritan influence, clearly present in the free state, abolition, prohibition, and Populist movements of the nineteenth century and a force behind some of the reactionary activities of the early twentieth century, remained part of the Kansas heritage. The New England influence may be found throughout the Midwest, but it permeated Kansas more than any other state. This reform spirit did not always gain the support of the majority, but a significant part of the population embraced a vision of higher purposes while sharing with those who did not the common struggle to make the land productive.

Most settlers came to Kansas Territory to obtain land, the prime force in the settlement of the Midwest and the nation, but many came, too, to settle the moral question of whether it would be a slave or a free state. In this situation, economic and moral issues were joined because economic opportunity was believed to be better in a nonslave economy. Making Kansas a free state was a political endeavor, inseparable from the economic and moral issues. This made the struggle for statehood in Kansas different from that of any other state, and the issues affected national politics in a unique way. The Kansas question of letting the people there decide the fate of slavery (the first real test of popular sovereignty) forced a reorganization of national parties, created the Republican party, gave midwesterner Abraham Lincoln an essential boost toward the presidency, and split the Union into two sections between which a civil war became inevitable. Believing their cause was just, Kansans interpreted a Union victory as confirmation of their self-righteous ideals and mission.

The spiritual and the temporal interests were not mutually exclusive among those pioneers. Nineteenth-century Kansans wanted land to farm so they might improve their economic welfare and better contribute to the needs of their children and grandchildren. They wanted land for commercial agriculture and for a way of life that was considered almost sacred in the popular mind. They wanted land to produce wealth and provide freedom, sometimes contradictory expectations at the center of the persistent mythology of the value of the family farm. Farms not only produced commodities but they shaped the characters of men and women. The essential ingredient was land.

Many early settlers were frustrated to find a large part of the fifty million acres of Kansas occupied by Indian reservations, held in trust for Indians who had been removed from Kansas, or held in large quantities by railroads and speculators. Land in the western portion of the state that was eligible for entry under the Homestead Act could not be settled successfully until the Indians were cleared out and railroads were built. Kansas, with less opportunity for river transportation than the other midwestern states, was more dependent on railroads for economic development.

Without rail transportation most of Kansas could not develop beyond self-sufficient agriculture (a Jeffersonian dream destined to fail because of the power of commercial farming). Except for the corner bordering the Missouri River and the region along the lower Kansas River, Kansas could not depend on water transportation. The growth and settlement of most of Kansas accompanied the post–Civil War expansion of railroads, and the location and future of every Kansas city and every small town that maintained a population of more than 250 people was dependent on at least one railroad connection. Towns that did not get a railroad either moved to a railroad or withered and died, and only a few small villages survived without a rail line. The railroad had more impact on town planning in Kansas than did any regional pattern familiar to settlers, be it the central-square or elon-

gated main-street orientation. Townsite locations and names were
often determined by the corporations that built the lines. Settlement
and economic growth followed the rails across Kansas.

Economic well-being was important to Kansans, but they, like
other midwestern settlers, carried to the land a strong religious faith
and a strong desire that their children receive a good education. Faith
was an item of considerable importance to those who left everything
to start life anew in what was often a harsh environment. They saw
education as essential if their children were to have a better opportunity than they had. And, although less was said about this, they
understood that freedom and democratic institutions (ideals of the
Midwest and the nation) required informed citizens if they were to
govern themselves successfully and preserve the precious heritage of
human rights established with the founding of the nation. The state's
high literacy rate testifies to the general effectiveness of Kansas education.

Kansans often exemplified the neighborly cooperation that was
typical of rural communities. Life in Kansas, as in other rural areas,
was closely related to the seasons and the life cycles of plants and
animals. The values of the people were midwestern rural values with
New England roots, the middle-class ideals of family loyalty, hard
work, frugality, savings, honesty, steadfastness in the face of adversity, neighborly cooperation, democracy, and the right to enjoy what
one had earned. These ideals, like all ideals, were more closely followed in practice by some than others, but they remained goals with
which few, if any, were in theoretical disagreement. There was a
sense of responsibility that extended beyond home and family to embrace neighbors and even strangers who were in difficulty. At the
same time there was little respect for privacy and for the noncon-
formist (someone who did not pursue rural values).

While Kansas reformers typically turned to government to implement and enforce desirable social programs, there was also fear
of governmental economic power. This distrust of government seemed
to increase in proportion to the distance the government was from
the community in which one lived, apparently the result of a feeling
that local units of government (school districts, townships, cities, and
counties) were more democratic than were state and national units.
There has been little understanding in Kansas that the state was and
remains largely dependent on the federal government for its economic well-being. The federal government has provided much of the
land, aided the railroads and other transportation improvements, aided
education, provided military protection, supported the postal service,
and subsidized agriculture and selected industries (especially since
the 1930s) and, thereby, the rest of the economy. Unlike most of the
Midwest and like most of the Far West, Kansas has received more

economic benefits from the federal government than it has paid in federal taxes. Yet the image of independence survived, another of those contradictions that cannot be readily explained.

Although Kansas has a lower proportion than the rest of the Midwest of foreign-born population (a trait shared with Iowa) and exhibits less social pluralism than the region or most of the rest of the nation, Kansas has a rich ethnic heritage. But the state and the region are better described as a salad bowl than a melting pot, since the ingredients have not lost their identity while contributing to the whole.

The German heritage is present throughout the state, and the Germans from Russia (Volga Germans) brought their culture and religion (Catholic, Lutheran, and Mennonite) to several Kansas counties. A colony of Pennsylvania Dutch River Brethren Germans settled at Abilene, and one of their descendants named Eisenhower became president. Dwight D. Eisenhower, though born in Texas, was the most popular Kansan in the nation's history. He was known as the general and the president from Abilene, and his remarkable career is exhibited there at the Eisenhower Museum, the records of his life and times serve scholars at the Eisenhower Library, and his remains rest in the chapel near his boyhood home.

The Swedish heritage may be seen at Scandia and Lindsborg. Bethany College at Lindsborg, opened in 1881, continues to perpetuate the heritage of the Swedes, including the art of Birger Sandzen and the annual production of the *Messiah*. The city of Lindsborg has promoted its ancestral connections so successfully that a Swedish newspaper proclaimed it the most Swedish community in the world.

The black heritage is found at Nicodemus and in Topeka, Leavenworth, Lawrence, and Fort Scott. A Nicodemus citizen, E. P. McCabe, became Kansas state auditor, the first black elected to a major state office in the North. Nicodemus produced an outstanding musician and composer, Lorenzo Fuller. The U. S. Supreme Court decision designed to end segregation in public schools resulted from a case originating in Topeka.

The Mexican heritage is closely associated with the railroads and migrant farm workers. There is a Croatian heritage on Strawberry Hill in Kansas City. There is an English heritage at Victoria and Runneymede. There is a Bohemian heritage at Wilson, Munden, and Cuba. There is a Jewish heritage. More recently there is a Vietnamese heritage in several Kansas communities. All of these groups and others, too, have preserved some of their traditions and cultures, which enrich Kansas society.

The Mennonites brought hard red winter wheat and the milling processes to use it, making Kansas the breadbasket of the nation in the twentieth century. In most years Kansas leads the nation in wheat production and its nickname is "the Wheat State." The major contribution of Kansas in the great wars of the present century was food production (and aircraft manufacturing during World War II and after). Ironically, Mennonite pacifists, descendants of those who introduced the Turkey red wheat, were imprisoned for refusing to bear arms during these wars.

Kansas leads the nation in wheat production, contains two of the best known military installations, Leavenworth and Riley, one of the largest aircraft industrial areas in the world, Wichita, and yet is best known among people outside the state as the gray place where Dorothy lived before she and Toto were transported to the Land of Oz, which was everything that Kansas was not.

Kansas attracts national attention for its sometimes bizarre weather. There have been many tornadoes, including one of the most destructive in history, which hit Topeka in 1966. Newsworthy blizzards occurred in 1886, 1912, 1958, and 1987. Droughts periodically brought attention and aid from other states, including the most notable droughts of 1859–60, 1879–80, 1888–95, 1910–12, 1933–37, and 1952–56. Major floods occurred in 1903 and 1951.

National attention has also focused on violent incidents in Kansas, including the destruction of Lawrence by William C. Quantrill's raiders in 1861 and the death of Notre Dame football coach Knute Rockne in an airplane crash on a Kansas Flint Hills ranch in 1931. The same is true of bizarre crimes. Two examples from the nineteenth century were the multiple murders of innocent guests at the table of the John Bender family near Parsons during the 1870s and the destruction of the Dalton gang at Coffeyville in 1892 after they brazenly robbed both banks there. Two more recent examples were the murder of the Herbert Clutter family by Perry Smith and Richard Hickock near Holcomb in western Kansas in 1959, which was detailed in Truman Capote's *In Cold Blood* (a best-selling book and movie), and the sordid affair of an Emporia clergyman with a woman of his congregation, including the murders of their spouses, which was portrayed in a television miniseries.

Other factors influenced the image of Kansas. Prior to settlement, much of Kansas was classified as the "Great American Desert." For a time this image made it all the more reasonable to assign the region to displaced Indians. The concept of a permanent Indian frontier flourished briefly, destroyed by the irreversible push of a nation moving west. Following the acquisition of Oregon, Texas, and the Southwest in the 1840s, sectional issues (including the expansion of slavery, development of a homestead law, and tariffs) threatened to split the nation in two while pressures for a transcontinental railroad built up a head of steam. The passage of the Kansas-Nebraska Act in 1854 was designed by Senator Stephen A. Douglas and others to help resolve some of the sectional disputes and provide organized territory for railroad expansion.

The struggle for Kansas statehood in the 1850s was a prelude to a Civil War that threatened to destroy the Union. Kansas was the focal point of the westward expansion of slavery and slave versus free states in the 1850s, and a bitter contest popularly dubbed "Bleeding Kansas" required the intervention of federal troops to keep order and oversee elections. The outcome was determined by the large migration of free-staters from the Midwest and the few from New England, and Kansas entered the Union in 1861 as a free state under a constitution based on that of Ohio. Before that, however, a drought in 1859–60 showed Kansans how hard the land could be, and many citizens returned East (some never to return). Those who stayed survived with aid sent mainly from the Midwest. The motto adopted by the new state, *ad astra per aspera* (to the stars through difficulties), had special meaning to those who struggled and survived.

Before the new state government was organized and functioning, there was a call for troops to preserve the Union. Kansas furnished more troops per capita and her troops suffered more casualties per capita than any other state during the Civil War. Many Kansans saw the war as a continuation of the struggle they had endured to become a part of the Union.

As in the rest of the Midwest, antislavery in Kansas did not automatically mean problack, however, and discrimination was sanctioned. After the Civil War, Kansas was touted as a haven for freed slaves, but the realities of second-class citizenship remained evident in the black communities of Lawrence, Leavenworth, Fort Scott, Topeka, and other cities well into the twentieth century. The landmark school desegregation case, *Brown vs. Topeka Board of Education* (1954), was filed in Kansas. Famous black Americans with Kansas roots included George Washington Carver, Langston Hughes, and Gordon Parks. The latter two wrote novels about growing up black in Kansas.

Kansas was a major issue in the birth of the Republican party, with its platform including free soil, free land, and free men, and the Republican political persuasion has dominated the state since the state's birth in 1861. At times, especially during the two decades after the Civil War, Kansas politics exhibited the problems usually associated with a one-party state, including corruption in high places. While some Kansans exhibited their share of the greed associated with the "Gilded Age" (Kansas provided the historical basis for a novel, *The Gilded Age*, by Mark Twain and Charles Dudley Warner), there was a reform persuasion at work to build a better society in what was seen as a hard land.

The struggle for woman suffrage, a democratic ideal brought by some early settlers, began with a group of women attending the Wyandotte constitutional convention in 1859, hoping to persuade the delegates to omit the word *male* from the franchise clause. It ended over fifty years later, after several major campaigns, with the adoption of a constitutional amendment in 1912. Women achieved the right to vote in stages in Kansas. They could vote in school elections after 1861 and in municipal elections after 1887, the year that Susanna Madora Salter of Argonia became the first woman to be elected to the office of mayor of any town in the United States (by 1987 Argonia had not had another woman mayor). The right of Kansas women to vote in state and national elections came eight years before the Nineteenth Amendment to the U.S. Constitution was adopted in 1920. Because of that and the traditional loyalty of the state to the Republican party, it was fitting that Kansas novelist Margaret Hill McCarter was the first woman to address a Republican national convention (1920).

In no other state was liquor control of more concern than in Kansas, and the controversial issue between the "dry" and "wet" factions began before statehood and was not dead in 1987. Legal prohibition was another part of the cultural baggage brought from New England, where Maine passed the first enforceable statewide law in 1851. The first territorial legislature in Kansas adopted a local-option "dramshop" law in 1855, and many cities banned the sale of intoxicants. An attempt to write prohibition into the state constitution was withdrawn for lack of support.

Following the Civil War, Kansas temperance societies increased in number and membership during the same years that the infamous cattle towns exhibited their saloons, gamblers, and prostitutes. The Murphy movement, Good Templars, WCTU, and Kansas Temperance Union heightened awareness and helped make prohibition a political issue. It was written into the state constitution by amendment in 1880. Enforcement was another persistent struggle. The smashing career of Carry Nation and her hatchet reflected on the image of Kansas, but her cause was the cause of many Kansans and others throughout the nation. Enforcement improved with tougher laws in 1909 and 1917, and the era of national Prohibition followed. Another Kansas crusade for morality had achieved victory, albeit temporary. As already noted, national repeal in 1933 was followed by repeal in Kansas in 1948, and a heated contest was fought in 1986 with the repeal of constitutional prohibition of the "open saloon." With a number of dry counties, liquor control remained a Kansas issue in 1987. Other reform movements in Kansas were just as intense but less persistent.

Reform politics in Kansas gained regional and national recognition during the Populist era, a response to another era of hard times, although the results were largely disappointing. An agricultural depression and drought in the late 1880s and early 1890s led hard-pressed farmers and those who depended on them to seek reforms of a system they viewed as unconcerned and unresponsive to their economic needs. With roots in earlier farm organizations, Populism was also a moral crusade against social Darwinism and the "gospel of wealth." The reformers wanted to protect the weak from the strong, and they wanted a government to benefit the many rather than a few. All this was in keeping with the democratic spirit of reform in Kansas.

The People's party platform included banking reform, an increase in the supply of money, prohibition of alien ownership of land, an agricultural subtreasury program, a graduated income tax, adoption of the secret ballot, direct election of senators, and government ownership of the means of transportation and communication. Later, some Populists embraced woman suffrage and free and unlimited coinage of silver at a favorable ratio to gold. Populists were divided over the vote for women and "fusion" with the Democrats.

Kansas was at the center of Populism and elected more People's party candidates to office in the 1890s than any other state, including a U. S. senator, two governors, several national congressmen, several judges, and a majority in each of the state houses for a time. Women, including Mary Elizabeth Lease and Annie Diggs, were active in the campaigns. Lease was an effective orator who advised farmers to "raise less corn and more hell." Diggs was active in the prohibition and woman suffrage movements, and she wrote newspaper columns and lectured for Populism. In 1892 Kansas gave its electoral votes to Populist James B. Weaver, the first time the state had not supported the Republican presidential candidate. But Populism was temporary, and most of its programs were unfulfilled during the 1890s, in Kansas as in other parts of the Midwest, although most of the platform was enacted nationally during the Progressive Era in the early twentieth century. Kansas participated in this later reform movement but did not provide the kind of leadership that it had for the People's party.

Kansas Populists had come together in opposition to what existed, but they divided over solutions, a division that prevented enactment of many proposals into law. They were not, however, failures. They enacted new laws affecting labor, banking, agricultural inspection, and elections. They wrote an antitrust law and adopted the secret ballot. More important, perhaps, was their long-term effect on public opinion and political reform. They contributed to the spirit of reform that bore fruit in the early twentieth century, and they proposed solutions that were adopted then. They may have been, as some scholars concluded, men and women ahead of their time. They also represented a typical Kansas response to another era of hard times.

Kansans had always thought of themselves as something special because of their struggle to survive in a hard land and because of their brand of morality. The first scholarly analysis of the Kansas character was provided during the Progressive Era when Carl Becker, seeking an understanding of Kansas, declared in a penetrating essay in 1910 that Kansas was a "state of mind." Becker was professor of history at Kansas University and reported his experience upon entering the state by train:

> I rode out of Kansas City and entered for the first time what I had always pictured as the land of grasshoppers, of arid drought, and barren social experimentation. In the seat just ahead were two young women, girls rather, whom I afterwards saw at the university. As we . . . entered the half-open country along the Kansas River, one of the pair . . . , turning to her companion with the contented sigh of a returning exile, . . . said, "*Dear old Kansas!*" I had supposed that Kansas, even more than Italy, was only a geographical expression. But not so. To understand why people say "Dear old Kansas!" is to understand that Kansas is no mere geographical expression, but a "state of mind," a religion, and a philosophy in one.[2]

After reciting what he found making up this "state of mind," Becker concluded:

> The Kansas spirit is the American spirit double distilled. It is a new grafted product of American individualism, American idealism, American intolerance. Kansas is America in microcosm: as America conceives itself in respect to Europe, so Kansas conceives itself in respect to America. Within its borders, Americanism, pure and undefiled, has a new lease of life. It is the mission of this self-selected people to see to it that it does not perish from off the earth. The light on the altar, however neglected elsewhere, must ever be replenished in Kansas. If this is provincialism, it is the provincialism of faith rather than of the province. The devotion to the state is devotion to an ideal, not to a territory, and men can say "Dear old Kansas!" because the name symbolizes for them what the motto of the state so well expresses, *ad astra per aspera*.[3]

Kenneth Davis, who wrote the history of Kansas for the bicentennial histories of the states, stated that he knew "of no other state, save Texas, whose citizens are as strongly, intensely, personally identified with it as Kansans are with Kansas."[4]

John J. Ingalls, a leading Kansas Republican and soon-to-be U.S. senator, wrote in 1872 that people from other states "can remove and never desire to return. . . . But no genuine Kansan can emigrate. . . . He may go elsewhere, but no other State can claim him as a citizen. Once naturalized, the allegiance can never be forsworn."[5] In seeking why that is so, Davis suggested that the landscape and climate of Kansas, or its geography, had a psychological impact on the people.

The psychological effect has been, I think, to encourage in Kansans a somewhat greater reverence for eternal verities, a somewhat greater concern for the fundamentals of life and conduct, a somewhat more strict and conscientious regard for moral right and wrong, than is common elsewhere. Also environmentally encouraged has been a fluctuating blend of seeming contradictions—a blend of self-assertion and self-abnegation, of rugged individualism and a passion for conformity, of strong insistence that the human person is free and an equally strong insistence that he act in certain prescribed ways—that even his private tastes and personal conduct are fit subjects of legislative action.[6]

Life was not easy in Kansas, and those who survived its extremes became attached to it, even self-righteous about it, and felt superior to others who had not been so sorely tried. The frontier experience, with its wet and dry cycles, boom and bust cycles, conflicts with Indians and grasshoppers, county-seat wars, struggles for and against the railroads, and adaptations of agriculture to a treeless and hostile environment, was another major force in shaping Kansas. The sodhouse frontier was a struggle, with grasshoppers, droughts, hail storms, and blizzards on the outside and snakes, rodents, fleas, and bedbugs on the inside.

Equally important as shaping forces were the immigrant farmers from Europe who reinforced the ideals already associated with Kansas: industry, frugality, independence, self-reliance, Christianity, law-abiding, and generally democratic. The mixture was productive and lasting. Kansas developed through struggle and turmoil, and the struggles shaped the character of the people. They had a cause, the cause was just, and the rest of the world could learn from what Kansas accomplished. Kansans had great pride in what they had accomplished.

Davis concluded that this pride led to some exaggeration, but it showed an unusual attachment to the state:

There was immense pride and delight in Kansas authors, Kansas painters, Kansas journalism, colorful and erudite Kansas politicians, like Ingalls—in any Kansan who distinguished himself in any field. Always he was identified *as* a Kansan in the public mind of this state. There was pride in the beauty of the Kansas countryside, which was alleged by prominent Kansans to be as fair as any on the surface of the globe; and pride in the Kansas climate, which was proclaimed the healthiest in the nation.[7]

Interestingly, the physical examinations of soldiers inducted into the military service during World War I bore out the latter claim, when it was found that men from Kansas were, indeed, the healthiest in the nation.

The Kansas pride and determination to reform gave meaning and degrees of success to both the Populist and Progressive political movements in the state. Social reforms, including abolition, prohibition, and woman suffrage, were other achievements. This creative Kansas was the "state of mind" about which Becker wrote in 1910.

John J. Ingalls expressed the creative turmoil of Kansas this way:

Kansas has been the testing-ground for every experiment in morals, politics, and social life. Nothing has been venerable or revered merely because it exists or has endured. . . . Every incoherent and fantastic dream of social improvement and reform, every economic delusion . . . every political fallacy nurtured by misfortune, poverty, and failure, rejected elsewhere, has here found tolerance and advocacy. . . . There has been neither peace, tranquility, nor repose. The farmer can never foretell his harvest, nor the merchant his gains, nor the politician his supremacy. Something startling has always happened, or has been constantly anticipated.[8]

It was expressed another way by William Allen White in 1922:

When anything is going to happen in this country, it happens first in Kansas. Abolition, prohibition, Populism, the Bull Moose, the exit of the roller towel, the appearance of the bank guarantee, the blue sky law, the adjudication of industrial disputes as distinguished from the arbitration of industrial differences—these things come popping out of Kansas like bats out of hell. Sooner or later other states take up these things, and then Kansas goes on breeding other troubles.[9]

But Kansas had changed even before White wrote this statement, and it ceased to be innovative and became concerned with a moral fervor that led to all kinds of petty prohibitions, such as those described by Paul Wellman in The Walls of Jericho (1947):

The Kansas Seven were: dancing, cards, the theater, non-attendance at church, tobacco, drinking and profanity. To the peculiar mental bent, the chief zest of which is the regulation of the lives of others, not even theft, murder, or adultery seemed somehow so important as these seven sins.

The image of a reactionary Kansas, a rural state that lagged behind a nation becoming rapidly industrialized and urbanized as well as more worldly, was given credence in the 1920s with the creation of the antilabor Court of Industrial Relations, the antitobacco campaign of State Superintendent of Public Instruction Lizzie Wooster, the rise of the Ku Klux Klan, and the abolition of the venereal disease program of the state board of health headed by Samuel J. Crumbine, M.D.

The new Klan began in the South during World War I and spread through much of the nation during the 1920s. Kansans were especially attracted to its antiforeign, anti-Jewish, anti-Catholic, and anti-Negro prejudices because they needed someone to blame for the failure of their moral experiments; not only had the rest of the nation failed to join the crusade but many Kansans had fallen, too. Just as the Puritans turned to petty prohibitions and a hunt for witches when they saw their holy experiment fail, Kansans reacted in similar fashion when it became clear that they could not achieve the impossible; morality could not be enforced by passing a few laws.

The Klan's threat to democracy in Kansas was perceived as serious by many critics, and the state's most famous newspaperman, William Allen White, ran as an independent candidate for governor in 1924 for the sole purpose of opposing and discrediting the Klan. He brought the secret society into the open. In 1925 the Klan was officially stopped; the secretary of state refused to issue the organization a charter and the state supreme court ruled it could not function in the state without one. Local Klansmen continued their activities for a while.

The reactionary temper of the era caused at least one outstanding professional to leave the state. Dr. Crumbine had achieved national fame for his public health and sanitation program in the early 1900s while serving as executive secretary of the state board of health. His "swat the fly" and "don't spit on the sidewalk" campaigns, along with admonitions against the use of the common drinking cup, helped stop the spread of diseases, inspired the invention of the fly swatter and the disposable paper drinking cup, and raised public awareness of the close relationship of sanitation and health. Crumbine produced a food and drug bill that was adopted in Kansas in 1907 and served as a model for other states and for the nation. Crumbine's pioneering program to increase awareness of and to control venereal diseases, however, fell victim to the political reactionaries who gained office after World War I, and Crumbine left Kansas to work in New York.

The Kansas economy faced hard times in the 1920s when the post–World War I agricultural depression forced farmers and those who depended on them into a new struggle for survival. The typical farm reaction to low prices was to produce more, and the mechanization of agriculture toward this end led to increasing surpluses and lower prices for products of the land while farmers' costs increased (a situation best known as the cost-price squeeze). Farmers and others were provided a form of escape from their toil and struggle by the radio.

Dr. John R. Brinkley at Milford, Kansas, a quack of goat-gland sex-rejuvenation-surgical notoriety, was the founder of a radio style mostly associated later with airwave evangelists, and he was a pioneer in the use of radio for political campaigning (he was denied the governor's office as an independent candidate in 1930 even though more people voted for him than for either of the major party candidates).

Brinkley lost his licenses to practice medicine and operate a radio station in Kansas, and he was the founder of the first high-powered "border-blaster" radio station just across the U.S. border in Mexico.

A major scandal occurred in Kansas during the administration of Governor Alfred M. Landon (1933–37). The infamous Finney bond fraud involved friends of the governor and officers of his administration. To his credit, Landon dealt admirably with the situation. He became the Republican candidate for president and was defeated in the Franklin D. Roosevelt landslide of 1936, failing to carry his home state. Landon never sought public office again, but he remained one of the most honored statesmen in America as he approached the century mark in 1987. And Landon's daughter, Nancy Kassebaum, was the first woman elected to the U.S. Senate on her own record (1978).

The major trauma for Kansas during the 1930s was not the depression that affected the entire nation and much of the world, for Kansas had been depressed for almost a decade when the great crash occurred. Kansans struggled through another drought and the Dust Bowl, the most difficult challenge yet provided by the hard land. For those who remained, the 1930s were forever associated with this calamity. An oral history project in western Kansas during the 1970s, in which elderly citizens were interviewed about life during the 1920s and 1930s, made that clear. Almost any question about the depression elicited answers about the dust storms, the main thing still associated with the "dirty thirties." One woman said her family had often remarked during those terrible days that someday they would probably look back and think of them as "good old days" or at least find something good about them. She quickly explained they never did. No one who survived the era was ever the same again.

The combination of lagging behind in economic development, reactionary restrictions on individual freedom, and the image of a dust-blown, God-forsaken land caused many Kansans to be ashamed rather than proud of their state between the world wars. Yet this shame made them just as attached to the state as had the earlier pride, but it was a defensive attachment. They began to think of Kansas as backward. Clearly, wrote Davis, Kansas "was no longer in the vanguard of social progress."[10] A possible explanation for this difference from the nineteenth century may have been a general disillusionment after World War I and a decline in the belief in progress, a belief that had sparked most of the great reform efforts of the previous century.

In another place, Davis declared that the inferiority complex that came over Kansas was debilitating: "The disparity between what was possible and what was actually achieved was tragic, the former being so immensely greater in every respect than the latter." Describing the entire era, Davis lamented: "Seldom has a community with so much vibrant idealism in its soul, so much creative potential in its mind, become so thickly incrusted with petty bourgeois mediocrity."[11]

Davis saw a new spirit of pride in Kansas after World War II, a pride in a rich heritage, a pride in a Kansas product named Eisenhower, a recognition that Kansas was inseparably linked with the larger world which needed its food, and the promise of a better future, a future with renewed "emphasis upon moral concerns, a renewed insistence upon individual moral responsibility. Surely such renewals are required if we as a nation are to reaffirm in action, amid the long and dreary aftermath of Vietnam and Watergate, the divine and human purposes for which, 200 years ago, this Republic was founded."[12]

Becker and Davis made suggestions about the attachment of Kansans to Kansas, but there are probably many other possible explanations. The poetry, folk songs, fiction, and other writings about Kansas often include strong feelings that depict what might best be called a love-hate relationship with the state that are part of the contradictions. The state song, "Home on the Range" (originally written by Dr. Brewster Higley as "My Western Home") is a love song to Kansas. A reporter for the *Dodge City Times* wrote in 1885: "Whatever man has done man may do, and the Kansas man can do lots of things that no man has ever done before." William Allen White declared: "These things—the air, the water, the scenery and we who fill these scenes— hold many and many a man to Kansas when money would tempt him away. . . . Here are the still waters, here are the green pastures. Here, the fairest of the world's habitations."[13]

But in addition to the love of Kansas there was hate and scorn. Wichita novelist Earl Thompson wrote in *Garden of Eden*: "Love a place like Kansas and you can be content in a garden of raked sand. For ground it is the flattest. Big sky, wheat sea, William Inge, bottle clubs, road houses—Falstaff and High Life, chili and big juke road houses—John Brown, Wild Bill Hickok, Carry A. Nation, cockeyed Wyatt Earp, Pretty Boy Floyd, and shades of all those unspoken Indians."

A soldier stationed at Fort Larned in 1864 wrote home: "This is the poorest country I ever saw. The land we passed over this side of Saline is not worth one cent an acre." Another soldier at the same post declared that he could not understand why the army was going to so much trouble to clear the area of Indians, "as we thought it only fit for the Indian."[14] John Ise wrote in *Sod and Stubble*: "When we have rain and crops, we don't want to go, and when there ain't no crops we're too poor to go; so I reckon we'll just stay here till we starve to death." L. Frank Baum gave a bleak picture of Kansas in *The Wizard of Oz*:

When Aunt Em came there to live she was a young, pretty wife. The sun and wind had changed her, too. They had taken the sparkle from her eyes and left them a sober gray; they had taken the red from her cheeks and lips, and they were gray, also. She was thin and gaunt, and never smiled now. When Dorothy, who was an orphan, first came to her, Aunt Em had been so startled by the child's laughter that she would scream and press her hand upon her heart whenever Dorothy's merry voice reached her ears; and she still looked at the little girl with wonder that she could find anything to laugh at.

The close attachment Kansans felt for their state, whether they loved it or hated it, was also found in *The Wizard of Oz*, where this conversation between Dorothy and the Scarecrow was recorded:

"Tell me something about yourself and the country you came from," said the Scarecrow, when she had finished her dinner. So she told him all about Kansas, and how gray everything was there, and how the cyclone had carried her to this queer Land of Oz.

The Scarecrow listened carefully, and said, "I cannot understand why you should wish to leave this beautiful country and go back to the dry, gray place you call Kansas."

"That is because you have no brains," answered the girl. "No matter how dreary and gray our homes are, we people of flesh and blood would rather live there than in any other country, be it ever so beautiful. There is no place like home."

The Scarecrow sighed.

"Of course I cannot understand it," he said. "If your heads were stuffed with straw, like mine, you would probably all live in the beautiful places, and then Kansas would have no people at all. It is fortunate for Kansas that you have brains."

The people of Kansas, just like the characters in the story, are proud of their brains, heart, and courage, all of which are necessary to deal with the rigors of the hard land. As Becker declared:

With Kansas history back of him, the true Kansan feels that nothing is *too much* for him. How shall he be afraid of any danger, or hesitate at any obstacle, having succeeded where failure was not only human, but almost honorable? Having conquered Kansas, he knows well that there are no worse worlds to conquer. The Kansas spirit is therefore one that finds something exhilarating in the challenge of an extreme difficulty.[15]

The provincial orientation of Kansas, be it geographical or a state of mind, was changed dramatically as the result of a major economic depression and the Dust Bowl, the Second World War, and other international conflicts that caused Kansans and other midwesterners, who had enjoyed life in apparent splendid isolation from the rest of the world and its problems for so long, to become aware of the larger world and their role in it. The movement from the farm to the city continued, and so did the out-migration. Many rural areas of Kansas showed a fairly steady decline in numbers after the early twentieth century; the resources were not present to sustain a dense population. There were townships in western Kansas that had a population of four hundred or more at the beginning of the twentieth century but had fifty or fewer people in 1987, including several with zero population. While numbers went down in rural areas, Kansans enjoyed an increase in their material standard of living; average per capita income in Kansas compared to the national average rose from less than 72 percent in 1940 to over 100 percent four decades later.

Kansas farmers realized that they produced for a world market over which they had no control. The world market was not new, but the realization was. It was difficult for Kansas farmers to comprehend that there had been only two eras of sustained agricultural prosperity since statehood: one just before and during World War I and the other during and just after World War II.

It is interesting to note that prosperous Kansas farmers during the first era erected large barns, buildings soon made obsolete by the change from horses to tractors. During the second era prosperous farmers erected metal buildings (inspired by and often patterned after the Quonset building) to house livestock, store grain, and protect equipment and machinery, establishing a style that was dubbed "tin-can architecture" and adapted to commercial and industrial uses throughout the nation.

Since the 1920s agricultural leaders and organizations in Kansas, as in other parts of the Midwest, have known that farming is a business as well as a way of life, a business that has needed a smaller and smaller proportion of the population to produce the food and fiber needed in the United States and abroad. They have often been forced to choose whether it was to be a business or a way of life, especially with the trend toward larger farms, exploitation of the soil, and pressure to pursue quantity rather than quality. The conflicting values weigh heavily on the farming minority that remains in Kansas, the Midwest, and the nation.

The Kansas population has not kept pace with that of the more populous states of the Midwest or the nation, indicative that the out-migration is ongoing. Meanwhile, the family farm became part of the myth perpetuated in the popular mind and the policies of governments. It was the major ingredient in forging the Kansas character.

There is a Kansas character, and its roots are found in the midwestern rural traditions of hard work, struggle in the face of adversity, frugality, practicality, individualism, democracy, and environmental irresponsibility. It is also rooted in puritanism—that is, individualism, democracy, conformity, dissent, middle-class ideals, and a feeling that a way of life based on truth with a capital T is superior—which some might call an intolerance for other ways. Becker's description of the "Kansas spirit" as "the American spirit double distilled" is probably accurate. Kansans are, as Becker stated many years ago, devoted to the ideals for which the state stands. They may not say "Dear Old Kansas" very much any more, but the state motto is still a fitting description of the heritage of the people in a hard land: *ad astra per aspera*.

The economic history of Kansas has seen a virtual revolution in agricultural production and a diversification of industries and services. Kansas, more than any other midwestern state, was ideally situated for the production of hard red winter wheat, a crop that supplanted corn in Kansas in the early 1900s. Like farmers throughout the Midwest, Kansas farmers have benefited from the rise of scientific agriculture (a general term that includes, among other things, soil management, pest controls, improved crop varieties and livestock breeds, and improved farm equipment). Scientific agriculture was primarily a product of the land-grant universities, including Kansas State University and its extension service and several experiment stations (the Fort Hays Experiment Station on the former military reservation near Hays is the largest dryland experiment station in the world).

The most obvious change in agriculture was the application of machine power to farming. Mechanization changed farming from a labor-intensive to a capital-intensive industry. Other developments included more reliable credit facilities and the rise of farm organizations. Kansas farmers have been active supporters of farm organizations since the Patrons of Husbandry (Grange) was organized in the state in 1872. Major farm organizations have included the Farmers' Alliance, Farmers Union, Farm Bureau, National Farmers' Organization, and the American Agricultural Movement. The cooperative movement has been widely accepted in Kansas.

All these groups have promoted education, business techniques, unity of action, and various degrees of political action. None has been able to find a solution to the persistent cost-price squeeze that has forced many out of farming. During the 1930s and since the 1950s, most Kansas farmers who survived did so with aid from the federal government. The requirements for farming have changed. Many farmers like to point out that in the old days, if a farmer's son was not smart enough to get a job in town, he could always farm; while now, if he is not smart enough to farm, he can always get a job in town. The "farm problem" remains the largest unsolved domestic economic issue in Kansas, the Midwest, and much of the nation. It is also an international problem.

To a considerable degree, the economic well-being of nonfarmers depends on how well the farmers are doing, for many services and industries are part of the largest American industry, agribusiness, and nonagricultural segments are often indirectly affected by what happens to agribusiness. Almost every business on the main streets of country towns and cities is affected by farm conditions. Kansas has been fortunate to have mineral wealth and a few industries not tied to farming, giving it a degree of diversification, although Kansas has not developed industry on a scale comparable with much of the Midwest (only Nebraska and the Dakotas have less industrial production than Kansas).

Kansas industries have been ranked throughout the twentieth century in order of economic contribution: (1) food and food products, (2) chemicals and allied products, (3) transportation equipment, (4) petroleum and coal products, (5) machinery, and (6) printing and publishing. Much of Kansas manufacturing is done in small enterprises, and most of it is contained within an industrial triangle bounded by lines connecting Kansas City, Wichita, and Hays. Major services in Kansas, many of which are affected by the prosperity of agriculture, are merchandising, transportation, utilities, banking, insurance, and savings and loan associations.

In 1987 the first nuclear power plant in Kansas was nearing completion in the east central part of the state near Burlington, while a nearly new coal-fired power plant near Holcomb in western Kansas was an economic failure because of insufficient demand for its electricity. For the immediate future Kansas had overbuilt its generating system—which, contrary to the law of supply and demand, made electricity more instead of less expensive to consumers.

Most change in Kansas since statehood has been technological in origin. Just as the railroad made possible the settlement of much of Kansas and barbed wire made stock farming feasible in a treeless state in the nineteenth century, much of the distinctiveness of Kansas and midwestern culture disintegrated in the face of twentieth-century technological developments, particularly the mass availability of electricity, the automobile, radio, and television. These things, plus the airplane, destroyed the isolation that helped preserve local and state traditions. Almost everyone became influenced by the same news reports, advertisements, fads, and entertainment. Families and neighbors spent less and less time together talking about and preserving traditions.

Today the people of Kansas and the Midwest may still be identified by their speech patterns and postal service addresses, but most of them could exchange places with their counterparts in any other state in the nation without noticing much difference. The farmers of all midwestern states have more in common with each other, sharing the same problems and dependent on the same government programs, than they do with the industrial workers in the cities of their own states, and vice versa. Cities, regardless of location, are similar and share the same problems of revenue, fire and police protection, public housing, safe water, sewage disposal, support of the arts, and the like. Their differences are found in identifiable industries (such as aviation at Wichita) and in their histories. The distinctions that remain among states of the Midwest and the remainder of the nation, distinctions that are being preserved and promoted, are primarily historical differences.

Abilene, Caldwell, Dodge City, Ellsworth, Newton, and Wichita were all cattle towns during frontier days, and this heritage makes them unique, but only one, Dodge City, is still a cattle town (it remains the cattle-trading center of Kansas). Abilene has its Old Town, Dodge City its Front Street and Boot Hill Museum, and Wichita its Cowtown, capitalizing on a heritage that has captured imaginations of young and old for a century.

Kansas is no longer a prohibition state, but its prohibition heritage sets it apart. The Santa Fe Trail has been inactive for over a century, but its heritage affects the land through which it passed. Kansas remains predominantly an agricultural state, although only a minority of its population has a direct connection with farming. For the majority of nonfarmers, however, this agricultural heritage gives their state unique, distinctive qualities. State and regional identity depend more and more on historical evaluation, and therein lies the significance of the essays in this volume.

The ability of people to establish an identity as individuals and with communities, states, regions, and nations is important, and as traditional distinctions become inoperative in the everyday lives of ordinary people, the more important the rich heritages become. Perhaps the blurring of provincial lines and the need for everyone to identify with the human condition in general will have positive results for the future, but preservation and promotion of local, state, and regional traditions will continue to make life more meaningful.

Today Kansas and the Midwest have the most common denominator in rural traditions and agriculture; the Midwest remains a breadbasket. Kansas is a major contributor. In 1985 (latest figures available), Kansas ranked first among all states in the production of wheat, grain sorghum, and sorghum silage; in flour milling capacity and wheat flour milled; and in cattle slaughtered. It ranked second in acres of cropland, cattle and calves on farms, and red meat production. It was third in grain storage capacity, cattle and calves in feedlots, and number of trucks and combines on farms. It was sixth in total exports of farm products and all hay production, seventh in farm cash receipts and alfalfa production, tenth in hogs on farms, and eleventh in sheep and lambs on farms.

Agricultural issues are not just state and regional issues, and federal farm policies and conservation programs are critical. From the Kansas viewpoint, the state, the region, and the nation are bound together most closely by the agricultural thread. Federal aid for social programs and urban problems is another common bond. Kansas has special connections with the federal government through its aviation industry, military installations, transportation network, and continued dependence for help with education, health care, credit, welfare, and other segments, including agriculture. Kansas farmers may represent the most evident contradiction that remains, declaring their independent status while decreasing in numbers and with many that remain surviving on welfare.

The rural traditions remain strong in the towns and countryside communities, where people care for each other's welfare, help their neighbors when they are sick or disabled, and miss them when they die. Typical of rural midwestern culture, Kansans generally possess a sense of decency, friendship, democracy, moral integrity, community responsibility, and personal trust, all admirable qualities of long tradition that are missing or suppressed in large, impersonal, urban concentrations and in the lives of too many of the economically and politically powerful. This reservoir of genuine concern for human welfare, provincial as it appears, may serve the nation well when the need to draw upon it to build a better life is perceived.

Life in Kansas may not be any more trying than elsewhere in the Midwest or the nation, but many Kansans think they are challenged more and are a better people for surviving and enduring. At the same time, in their minds, this challenge and their endurance make Kansas a better place to live, and they maintain an ongoing pride in the hard land in the heartland. To think otherwise would be contrary to the Kansas heritage.

NOTES

1. Quoted in Robert Smith Bader, *The Great Kansas Bond Scandal* (Lawrence, Kans., 1982), 79.

2. Carl Becker, "Kansas," *Essays in American History Dedicated to Frederick Jackson Turner* (New York, 1910), 85.

3. Ibid., 111.

4. Kenneth S. Davis, "Portrait of a Changing Kansas," *Kansas Historical Quarterly* (Spring 1976), 27.

5. Quoted in Daniel W. Wilder, *Annals of Kansas* (Topeka, 1875), 563.

6. Davis, "Portrait of a Changing Kansas," 33.

7. Ibid. 42.

8. Quoted in Robert W. Richmond, *Kansas: Land of Contrasts* (St. Louis, 1980), 308.

9. *Emporia Gazette*, April 25, 1922.

10. Davis, "Portrait of a Changing Kansas," 43.

11. Kenneth S. Davis, *Kansas: A Bicentennial History* (New York, 1976), 192–93, 195.

12. Ibid., 217.

13. Quoted in "Kansas: A State of Mind," typescript program funded by Kansas Committee for the Humanities, 1981, 5.

14. Quoted in Craig Miner, *West of Wichita: Settling the High Plains of Kansas, 1865–1890* (Lawrence, 1986), 38.

15. Becker, "Kansas," 91.

BIBLIOGRAPHY

Any evaluation of the state should begin with Carl Becker's "Kansas," in *Essays in American History Dedicated to Frederick Jackson Turner* (New York, 1910), 85–111. Kenneth S. Davis has provided the best recent interpretive study, *Kansas: A Bicentennial History* (New York, 1976), and the essence of Davis's thinking in this book was distilled into his "Portrait of a Changing Kansas," *Kansas Historical Quarterly* (Spring 1976), 24–47. Also helpful are Emory Lindquist, "Kansas: A Centennial Portrait," *Kansas Historical Quarterly* (Spring 1961), 22–66, and Dudley T. Cornish, "Carl Becker's Kansas: The Power of Endurance," *Kansas Historical Quarterly* (Spring 1975), 1–13.

The standard textbook is Robert W. Richmond, *Kansas: A Land of Contrasts*, 2d ed. (St. Louis, 1980). Homer Socolofsky and Huber Self provided maps and historical geography in *Historical Atlas of Kansas* (Norman, Okla., 1972). A fine collection of articles is found in John D. Bright, ed., *Kansas: The First Century*, 4 vols. (New York, 1956). More recent articles are in *Kansas and the West: Bicentennial Essays in Honor of Nyle H. Miller* (Topeka, 1976).

Several scholars have treated a variety of topics in recent years. Craig Miner and William Unrau analyzed the treatment of Indians in *The End of Indian Kansas: A Study of Cultural Revolution, 1854–1871* (Lawrence, Kans., 1978) and *Tribal Dispossession and the Ottawa Indian University Fraud* (Lawrence, 1985). James Rawley analyzed *Race and Politics: Bleeding Kansas and the Coming of the Civil War* (New York, 1969). Robert Smith Bader dealt carefully with two controversial topics, *The Great Kansas Bond Scandal* (Lawrence, 1982) and *Prohibition in Kansas* (Lawrence, 1986). Robert Dykstra applied modern scholarship to an old topic and came up with the analytical *Cattle Towns* (New York, 1968). Paul Wallace Gates's *Fifty Million Acres: Conflicts Over Kansas Land Policy, 1854–1890* (Ithaca, N.Y., 1954) remains a classic study, as does James C. Malin's *Winter Wheat in the Golden Belt of Kansas* (Lawrence, 1944).

Political biographies include Donald R. McCoy, *Landon of Kansas* (Lincoln, Nebr., 1966); Homer Socolofsky, *Arthur Capper* (Lawrence, 1962); Michael J. Brodhead, *Perserving Populist: The Life of Frank Doster* (Reno, Nev., 1969); A. Bower Sageser, *Joseph L. Bristow: Kansas Progressive* (Lawrence, 1968); Burton J. Williams, *Senator John J. Ingalls, Kansas' Iridescent Republican* (Lawrence, 1972); and Don Wilson, *Governor Charles Robinson of Kansas* (Lawrence, 1975). Populism is also treated in O. Gene Clanton, *Kansas Populism: Ideas and Men* (Lawrence, 1969), and progressivism is covered in Robert S. LaForte, *Leaders in Reform: Progressive Republicans in Kansas, 1900–1916* (Lawrence), 1974.

One of the finest studies of a region within Kansas is Craig Miner, *West of Wichita: Settling the High Plains of Kansas, 1865–1890* (Lawrence, 1986). Another is Grace E. Muilenburg and Ada Swineford, *Land of the Post Rock, Its Origins, History, and People* (Lawrence, 1975). A classic on its subject is Everett Dick's *Sod-House Frontier* (Lincoln, 1954), which should be supplemented with John Ise's *Sod and Stubble: The Story of a Kansas Homestead* (reprinted Lincoln, 1967). Another part of Kansas is treated in John G. Clark's *Towns and Minerals in Southeastern Kansas: A Study in Regional Industrialization, 1890–1930* (Lawrence, 1970).

An introduction to the arts is Jonathan Wesley Bell, ed., *The Kansas Art Reader* (Lawrence, 1976). William Koch's *Folklore from Kansas* (Lawrence, 1980) is a fascinating collection. William Allen White's *Autobiography* (New York, 1946) contains much about the state.

Ethnic studies include Robert G. Athearn, *In Search of Canaan, Black Migration to Kansas, 1879–1880* (Lawrence, 1978), James C. Juhnke, *A People of Two Kingdoms: The Political Acculturation of the Kansas Mennonites* (North Newton, Kans., 1975), and Emory Lindquist on the Swedes, *Smoke Valley People* (Lindsborg, Kans., 1953).

Dorothy Schwieder

IOWA

The Middle Land

IN 1930 A RELATIVELY unknown artist painted a rather stark portrait
of two Iowans entitled *American Gothic*. The portrait captured first
prize that year at the Chicago Art Institute and Grant Wood's art
career was launched. For the next decade, Wood produced painting
after painting in which he depicted his native state. His characteri-
zations of Iowa with its velvety smooth, softly rounded hills, its fat
globular trees, its 1930s-vintage farmhouses, and its fastidiously neat
rows of corn came to be widely recognized around the region and
around the world. Through his paintings, Wood proclaimed to the
world that Iowa was a state of natural beauty, a state with great agricultural bounty, and a state of rather staid, conservative folks who
tolerated little nonsense.

At the same time, whether intended or not, Wood presented a far
wider view of the state. Wood's paintings depicted a state filled with
modest farmhouses, hard-working people, and neat, well-kept towns.
His *Spring in Town* captured Iowans dutifully performing a multitude
of tasks associated with the rituals of spring. In a mural, *Dinner for
Threshers*, he depicted an important but typical summer activity in
Iowa when farm wives prepared robust meals for threshing crews.
Through lithographs, he documented the seasonal rhythm of agricultural work performed throughout the year. His paintings of farm-

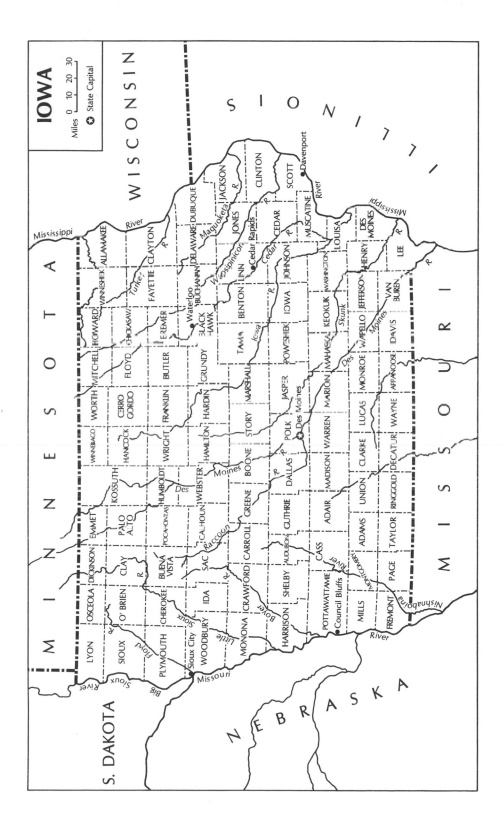

steads, rural countrysides, small towns, and ordinary people presented
a view of a state and a people that could be described with a variety
of adjectives: moderate, stable, regular, and consistent. Certainly he
portrayed a land isolated from the cities, far from the East and West
coasts, a land devoid of excesses or extremes, yet a land of beauty
and a land of plenty. Out of these images and impressions perhaps
the term *middle land* might best capture the mood as well as the
subject matter of Wood's work.

The term has infinite applications to Iowa's location, to its people,
and to its history. In a physical sense, Iowa is indeed the middle land,
lying at the center of the Middle West and therefore at the center of
the nation. If the Middle West is the nation's heartland, then perhaps
Iowa is the heart itself, pulsating quietly, slowly, and evenly, blending
together the physical and social features of the entire region. Iowa
itself is very much a homogeneous region, both in landform and in
population. While the topography of the northeastern part of the state
is uneven, the remainder of Iowa is mostly composed of gently rolling
terrain, crisscrossed with many rivers and streams. Every section of
the state is under cultivation, and agricultural interests permeate Iowans' thinking.

Iowa's population, too, is fairly homogeneous, still composed mostly
of the descendants of nineteenth-century settlers. In fact, according
to the 1980 census, three out of every four Iowans are natives. With
only a few large urban centers and less industry than states of the
Old Northwest, Iowa has not developed the same degree of ethnic
pluralism. During the nineteenth century Iowa attracted large numbers of people from the northeastern United States and immigrants
from northern and western Europe. After the Civil War several thousand blacks migrated from the South, and after 1900 a limited number
of southern and eastern Europeans arrived, all to work in coal mining.
Even with these additions, however, the great majority of Iowans trace
their roots to the British Isles or to northern and western Europe.

Iowa achieved statehood in 1846, and the society that later emerged
in many ways reflected New England influences. Although mostly
moderate, Iowans in the nineteenth century had strong commitments
to education, religion, and numerous social and political causes, particularly the prohibition of alcohol and the abolition of slavery. By
1900 Iowans had come to embrace Protestantism, prohibitionism,
McGuffeyism, and Republicanism, four conditions that had great significance for the state's people and their institutions.

Grant Wood's most consistent theme, rural life, has been and
continues to be the most important and pervasive element in Iowa.
Known in the 1800s for its rich agricultural land, the state came to
be shaped in its economic and the social order by this resource. The
land originally attracted settlers to the state, and the resulting farm

economy in turn shaped most political issues in the nineteenth and early twentieth centuries. Farm people tended to be sober and hard working, with a strong work ethic, and they took their work and families seriously, attended church on Sunday morning, spoke out against the social evils of liquor, and resided very much in the middle of the social and political spectrum. Although Iowa's farm families have had their belief in the superiority of farm life severely tested, the belief has always been retained.

For the most part, then, Wood's image of a comfortable people living in the middle of the nation has correctly portrayed Iowans through the years. Blessed with some of the best agricultural land in the nation, Iowans have labored long and hard to make the land produce. Moreover, Iowans have been fortunate to experience a relative freedom from a harsh environment and capricious climate, so common in the plains states, a freedom that has given them more time and energy to be concerned with issues beyond mere survival. Although Iowa has always had a few large cities, the politics and social concerns of its urban areas would not come front and center until after World War II. Today, Iowa retains a strong nineteenth-century legacy in its views on education, morality, and the value of rural society. The state, it seems, has aged gracefully, remaining true to its early roots while absorbing and adjusting with a minimum of difficulty to new trends and conditions. Continuity is a fact of life in the Hawkeye state.

The land that Grant Wood painted so gracefully in the 1930s was home first to at least seventeen Native American groups, including the Potawatomi, Santee Sioux, Oto, Missouri, Sauk, Mesquakie, and Ioway. (The latter three tribes were the most visible in the Iowa region in the eighteenth and nineteenth centuries.) These Native Americans were a part of the prairie and plains culture. Tribes moving into the Iowa region from the northeast brought along a woodland culture, including a partial reliance on agriculture; the Plains Indians, who by the 1600s were dependent on the horse and buffalo, embraced a nomadic way of life. In the Upper Mississippi Valley, of which Iowa is a part, these two cultures blended together, combining farming and hunting to produce the basis for a seminomadic existence. For all these tribes, Iowa was a bountiful place to live, providing the opportunities to hunt, fish, pursue agriculture, and gather the natural produce of the land.

By the mid-1800s, however, the Native American phase of Iowa history had essentially ended. In 1830 the federal government concluded treaties with the Missouri, Oto, and Omaha Indians, removing them from the western portion of the Iowa region. The most prolonged removal process was with the Sauk and Mesquakie Indians, who finally left Iowa in 1845. The Santee Sioux relinquished their land in Iowa in 1851. In effect, Indian tribes in Iowa did not retard white settlement. In each section of the state, Indians had officially been removed before whites began settlement. A brief encounter between a small band of Santee Sioux and white settlers in northwest Iowa in 1857, known as the Spirit Lake Massacre, marks the only violent confrontation of any importance between the two groups in Iowa.

Not all Indians left Iowa in 1845, however, as some Mesquakie managed to elude government officials. About a decade later, after convincing Iowa's governor James Grimes to act as their trustee, the Mesquakie began to buy back land that had originally been held jointly by themselves and the Sauk. This land, located in Tama County, became known as the Mesquakie Settlement and eventually included about three thousand acres. Today the Mesquakie hold an annual powwow, where they interpret their history and culture to outsiders. The Mesquakie Settlement is the only Native American location in the state; there are no Indian reservations. As a result, the history of Indian tribes in Iowa—and the interaction between Indians and whites— is quite different from that in other midwestern states, particularly South Dakota.

One year after the Sauk and Mesquakie were removed from extreme eastern Iowa, federal officials opened the area for white settlement. On June 1, 1833, frontiers people hurried across the Mississippi River to stake out their land claims. The first settlers moving into extreme eastern Iowa encountered an environment similar to what they had known in the Northeast. Most importantly, the area included sufficient timber for newcomers to build log cabins and to provide themselves with fuel and fencing. Once they moved farther into the region, however, timber was not sufficient to sustain this lifestyle. In central Iowa only the earliest settlers found adequate timber along the rivers and streams; others had to find substitutes to provide the basic essentials of settlement. People who later located in northwest Iowa encountered an area that approximated the Great Plains to the west: fewer trees, a more level terrain, and rainfall averages ten inches less than in the southeastern part of the state. Because of these physical and climatic conditions, Iowa provided the transitional zone for people moving from the woodland regions into the Great Plains. In effect, settlers in the prairie region were forced to modify their farming techniques and settlement practices. For those moving beyond Iowa into the Great Plains proper, adjustments would be of a far more radical nature.

Like settlers in other midwestern states, Iowa's nineteenth-century settlers were a mix of native- and foreign-born people. Before the Civil War most settlers migrated from Pennsylvania, Indiana, and

Ohio, along with substantial numbers from the South. By 1870 the southern-born element had declined considerably and taking their place were more northeasterners and immigrants from northern and western Europe. By 1890, when the number of immigrants reached its highest point, 19 percent of Iowans were foreign born. Germans constituted the largest immigrant population, but Irish, Swedes, Norwegians, and English also settled in substantial numbers.

Settlement in Iowa proceeded in methodical fashion from east to west. In the 1830s the extreme eastern portion of Iowa was settled; by the 1850s newcomers had moved into central Iowa; and by the 1870s extreme northwestern Iowa, the state's last frontier area, was attracting native-born and foreign-born alike. Newcomers took advantage of cheap federal land and also purchased land from Iowa's four land-grant railroads. The Homestead Act of 1862, so significant in states to the west, accounted for only 2.5 percent of Iowa's total land sales. As in other midwestern states, surveyors moved from east to west, marking off uniform sections and townships in preparation for the first land sales. Perhaps of all midwestern states, Iowa with its more uniform terrain and its somewhat rectangular shape—324 miles long and 210 miles wide in its greatest distances—best displays the regularity of the township system.

Given the rapidity and compactness of settlement, Iowa's frontier experience approximated that of the Old Northwest more than that of the midwestern plains states. In the Great Plains families often settled some distance apart, leading to isolation and loneliness, especially for pioneer women. Iowa's early settlers did not experience the degree of isolation described so ably by Middle Border writers Hamlin Garland and Mari Sandoz. In the Hawkeye state, with many farmsteads of eighty acres and with rapid contiguous settlement, isolation or long-term separation from others was not typical.

The rapidity of settlement—in effect, the state was settled in less than forty years—was possible mainly because there were no physical features to disrupt the steady, methodological movement of people. Only one part of the state, a small area in the northwest, was avoided temporarily. That resulted not from irregular terrain or the presence of land barriers but because the area was so level that it remained wet much of the year. In contrast, some midwestern states' dominating physical features slowed settlement and left indelible marks on their later social and economic institutions. Missouri, for example, has its Ozarks, Nebraska its Sand Hills, and South Dakota its East and West River areas. Richard Power, in *Planting Corn Belt Culture*, points out that very real physical differences exist between the northern and southern parts of Ohio, Indiana, and Illinois, resulting in differences also in population and economic enterprise. By contrast, Iowans in nearly every part of the state exhibit a commonality of interests and concerns that reflects the lack of sharp physical differences throughout the state.

Of particular importance to Iowans' shared experience is the role played by the native prairie, the state's most dominant physical feature. Early nineteenth-century explorers recorded that the prairie, with its gentle, undulating surface, its tall grass, and its general absence of trees, covered roughly four-fifths of the region. Iowa was not unique, since the states on all sides also contained prairie land, but the Hawkeye state was blessed with the largest amount, prompting one expert to call Iowa the truest of the prairie states. The large expanse of original prairie, moreover, has determined to a large degree Iowa's eventual preeminence as an agricultural state.

The society that evolved in Iowa was clearly the product of earlier developments in the Northeast. Some historians have used the term *New England belt* to describe a wide path made by New Englanders or their descendants as they migrated across the northern half of the United States. Iowa lay within this belt and soon came to include institutions and values that New Englanders believed to be important. Religious and educational institutions developed quickly in Iowa, both strongly influenced by Protestant church groups and their clergy. In general, Iowa fits the same religious pattern as other middle western states in that it was settled primarily by Protestants whose influence remained dominant throughout the nineteenth century.

Along with a plethora of Protestants, Catholics also became active in Iowa at an early date. Bishop Mathias Loras, a priest from France, established Iowa's first Catholic diocese in Dubuque. Bishop Loras's work paid excellent dividends; by 1850 the Dubuque area served as the center of Catholicism in Iowa and contained two colleges and several sister orders. The bishop was also instrumental in attracting an Irish Trappist monastery to the Dubuque area in 1849. Unlike the Protestant clergy, who were typically native born, Catholic priests and sisters were usually from foreign countries.

All religious groups in Iowa, Protestant and Catholic alike, quickly erected colleges. The Catholics set up separate colleges for men and women throughout eastern Iowa. By 1880 the Methodists had created five colleges, conveniently located so that Methodist young people in almost every part of the state could attend a Methodist institution of higher learning. Other Protestant groups followed suit, establishing colleges everywhere in the state, including Des Moines, Wartburg, Oskaloosa, Fairfield, and Lamoni. By 1900 church colleges numbered more than twenty-five while state institutions of higher learning numbered only three.

Iowa's nineteenth-century educational system developed simultaneously with religious institutions. Like other midwesterners, Iowans quickly erected common schools in rural areas and towns. Believing strongly in the need to provide youngsters with both formal learning and proper moral guidance, Iowans hired teachers not only for their ability to teach but also for their suitability as moral examples. Iowans' concern about both education and morality went hand in hand with the views expressed by William Holmes McGuffey in *McGuffey's Readers*. Countless generations of nineteenth-century Iowa schoolchildren learned to read from one of the many editions of this reader. McGuffey used the device of "constant open moralizing" whereby he continually advised students about proper moral behavior. McGuffey's stories especially admonished children to love God, their parents, and their country. No doubt most Iowa parents would have nodded approvingly when McGuffey observed: "Little children, it is better to be good than to be wise."[1]

Some people who advocated proper moral behavior were even closer to home. Henry Wallace, commonly known as Uncle Henry, wrote innumerable columns of advice for Iowa's rural children in the late nineteenth and early twentieth centuries in which he further expounded on McGuffey's main tenets. Wallace, a native of Pennsylvania and a former Presbyterian clergyman, had moved to Iowa in the 1870s and taken up farming. He soon started writing agricultural columns for the state's farmers. Later he and his son, Henry Cantwell Wallace, a professor at Iowa State College, established a farm publication, *Wallaces' Farmer*. With his own publication under way, Uncle Henry had advice for everyone. In his column, "Letters to Farm Folks," Wallace wrote articles with such titles as "Getting the Boy Started Right," "The Proper Brain Food for Farm Folks," and "Girls for the Scrap Heap." Wallace cautioned young people about the dangers lurking in cities and specifically warned about the evils of alcohol and tobacco. Like so many of his midwestern contemporaries, Wallace believed that the farm was the cradle of democracy and decency while the city was a place of sin, corruption, and sloth.

Nineteenth-century Iowa children were also thoroughly imbued with the Protestant work ethic. But beyond that, attitudes toward different kinds of work filtered through. In his classic study *Main Street on the Middle Border*, Lewis Atherton insightfully described the "Cult of the Immediately Useful and Practical" that dominated the Middle Border. The cult proclaimed that behavior was judged by whether or not it had "immediate, practical utilitarianism." The belief had a corollary related to income: "Every art and profession must justify itself financially." Therefore lawyers, bankers, and businessmen were obviously justified in making substantial incomes. Teachers and preachers were accepted because they "buttressed law and order," but unfortunately for them, although respected, their work did not justify a good remuneration. A second corollary stated that if an action was not immediately useful and practical, it would be tolerated if practiced by women but not by men. Music and art were therefore fine for daughters but unacceptable for sons. Atherton points out that young men who were inclined to follow the fine arts or even a writing career "escaped to the cities" because they found little support or acceptance in the rural areas or small towns of middle America.[2]

By the end of the nineteenth century, Iowa's social, moral, and educational mentality was firmly in place. Its public school system had earned a national reputation, based to a large extent on a high literacy rate. But in addition to receiving a solid basic education, Iowa schoolchildren had absorbed the values and morals inherent in both McGuffey's constant open moralizing and the Cult of the Immediately Useful and Practical. Iowans viewed hard work as good, but along with this perception went a value-laden system that included strong gender distinctions and an implied social and economic class structure resulting from the degree of practicality of one's work.

The society which nineteenth-century Iowans constructed, however, went beyond evangelical Protestantism, McGuffeyism, and the admonitions of individuals like Uncle Henry Wallace. This society also contained a strong impulse toward social reform that became evident as early as the 1840s. Before the Civil War Iowans passed their first prohibition law and took a strong stand against slavery. After the war the reform impulse reasserted itself as Iowans resumed their war on alcohol, moved to grant full constitutional rights to black men, and labored to create various institutions that reflected reformist thinking. An integral part of these changes was the fact that in the 1850s Iowans left behind the party of Andrew Jackson and embraced Republicanism.

The controversy over slavery, so evident in the 1840s, strongly influenced the young state. Given the state's northern location and such laws as the Missouri Compromise and the Northwest Ordinance, there was never any question that Iowa would remain a free state. Although Iowa contained some southern-born individuals in the 1840s and 1850s—a small minority that might have favored slavery—in general Iowans strongly supported abolition. Quakers and Congregationalists were especially active in the abolitionist crusade and in supporting the underground railroad. Quakers created many communities in central and eastern Iowa, including West Branch, Salem, New Providence, and Springdale, that served as centers for their antislavery work.

While Quakers, Congregationalists, and others favored the abolition of slavery, Iowans were of a different mind regarding legal and constitutional rights for blacks. Opposing slavery with its profoundly degrading consequences was one thing, but accepting blacks as social, political, or economic equals was quite another. Iowa followed along the path trod by most northern states before the Civil War in repudiating slavery but withholding constitutional rights from blacks. Iowans, moreover, erected many barriers to keep free blacks out of the state.

In the 1850s Iowa underwent political change. From 1846, when Iowa achieved statehood, to 1854, Iowans had consistently voted Democratic. This habit was broken in 1854 when James Grimes, a bright, energetic easterner who had recently settled in Burlington, was elected governor on the Whig ticket. Like many Whigs, Grimes soon aligned himself with the Republican ticket and was reelected in 1856 as a Republican. Iowans fiercely embraced Republicanism, finding the party's programs of free soil, free labor, and free men much to their liking. At the same time the Democrats seemed to do nothing right. The national leadership of the party did not respond to westerners' requests for free land and money to make internal improvements. Party leadership, moreover, seemed tired and lacking in new ideas. The result of the switch in political parties was long term: with a few temporary lapses, Iowans remained safely within the Republican fold for a century, until the 1950s.

During the latter half of the nineteenth century, the Republican party considered a series of important reform measures that reflected the social concerns of Iowans. Not least among them was the question of a prohibition on alcohol. Iowa contained many Methodists who were increasingly insistent that the state adopt a prohibition law. Responding to this pressure, Republicans in 1855 passed the state's first antiliquor legislation. While Methodists may have approved, however, German immigrants in eastern Iowa reacted with anger. Quick to sense an impending loss at the next election if the Germans deserted them, Republicans negated their action, changing the law to one of local option. The legislation put the Republican party in the difficult position of trying to please several opposing constituencies. On one hand, the ever-growing Methodist denomination strongly supported total abstinence, as did Congregationalists, Presbyterians, Baptists, and Scandinavian Lutherans. On the other hand, the state's German Lutherans, Catholics, and Episcopalians opposed prohibition. From 1855 until national prohibition was adopted in 1920, Iowa Republicans vacillated, usually unsuccessfully, between strong and weak prohibition measures in an effort to placate all their constituents.

While Iowans debated the prohibition issue and state Republicans enjoyed their newfound power, the nation entered its most cataclysmic period. Caught up in this national crisis while part of the state was still undergoing settlement, Iowans responded to Lincoln's call for troops, and most Iowans supported the Union cause. While the Civil War signaled major economic change for the state, social change

was less consistent. Continuity characterized many social movements, including prohibition. In at least one area, however, that of
black rights, Iowans repudiated their prewar stance. In 1868, perhaps
responding to the national leadership of the Republican party, the
Iowa General Assembly approved an amendment to strike out the
word *white* from the state constitution—in effect granting suffrage to
black men—and voters later approved the measure in a popular referendum. In the process Iowa became one of only two states in the
1860s to take such action. State officials also opened the public schools
to black children as a result of three state supreme court decisions
between 1868 and 1875. By 1880, moreover, black men had been
given the right to serve in the state legislature.

After the Civil War Iowa continued to display progressive action
in higher education. The University of Iowa, which had opened its
doors in the decade before the Civil War, is recognized as the first
state university to admit women. Iowa State College (now Iowa State
University) held its first classes in 1869, also admitting women on
an equal basis with men. Iowa had been one of the first states to take
advantage of the Morrill Act, which granted land for the creation of
a land-grant institution. Carrie Chapman Catt (then Carrie Lane) was
a product of Iowa State's coeducational policy. Grinnell College (then
Iowa College) was one of the first private coeducational schools in
the country.

Reform efforts also affected the political sphere. At the turn of
the century the Progressive Era influenced Iowans as well as other
midwesterners. Republican governor Albert Cummins was especially
influential in pushing through legislation to regulate railroads and
lessen the railroads' influence in the state. Moreover, the Cummins
administration successfully worked for a pure food and pure drug bill
and a direct-primary law. Iowa's Progressive movement filtered down
to the city level as well. In 1907 Des Moines changed its form of city
government, initiating the Des Moines Plan, which eventually was
adopted by several other cities.

While the Civil War only temporarily disrupted social development, it affected the state's economy in quite a different way, signaling
the end of Iowa's total domination by agriculture and the beginning
of significant industrial development. Railroads served as the necessary prerequisite for this development. Railroad construction had
started in eastern Iowa before the war, but not until 1870 did all four
major railroad lines reach Iowa's western border. With year-round
transportation assured, Iowans began to develop larger and greater
numbers of industrial operations.

Coal mining serves as an excellent example of a major industry
beholden to railroads for both its initial development and its continued
well-being. As railroads expanded in the state, Iowans began to open

coal mines to supply the railroads with fuel. By 1900 Iowa contained approximately four hundred underground mines, placing the state fifteenth in terms of national production. Iowa's coal industry remained fairly prosperous until the early 1920s, when the state's railroads began to buy coal out of state. The railroads had originally brought about the growth of the industry in the 1870s and 1880s, and their failure to support the industry in the 1920s led to its decline.

While Iowa's coal industry filled a major economic need, the mining industry also brought considerable social change in its effect on Iowa's ethnic composition. Before 1900 most Iowa coal miners had emigrated from the British Isles and Sweden, but after that date southern and eastern Europeans moved into the industry. Once an Italian or Croatian arrived, money was soon going back home to finance the trip of another family member or friend to the United States. Through this chain migration, many members of one European village ended up living in the same coal camp in central or southern Iowa. The result of the continual need for additional mine workers and the response of people in southern and eastern Europe was that Iowa contained at least a small number of Italians, Croatians, Hungarians, Austrians, Poles, and Russians.

Railroads also acted as an impetus to expansion in other areas. Shortly after the Civil War, meat-packing plants began to open in Iowa. In the 1870s John Morrill and Company located in Ottumwa, while Sinclair Meat Packing opened its doors in Cedar Rapids. In the western part of the state, Sioux City quickly became a major meat-packing center. In effect, Iowa's industrial development centered on its main activity of agriculture. Along with meat-packing, farm implement industries also appeared in several Iowa cities and Quaker Oats began production in Cedar Rapids. Through the years most industrial production has taken place in the eastern half of Iowa, which has the heaviest concentration of population.

After 1900 the state developed greater industrial diversity. In 1909 Frederick Maytag, apparently disappointed with other manufacturing pursuits, began producing washing machines. The company developed a number of innovations such as the seamless tub that quickly made its product the best-selling washer in the country. A short time later the Sheaffer Company began selling fountain pens. Another product that gained a national reputation was Amana refrigeration, first developed in the 1930s. Also in the depression years, Collins Radio began operations in Cedar Rapids, later being bought out by Rockwell International. A more recent development is Winnebago Industries, makers of recreational vehicles. Products from Iowa's factories, like products from Iowa's farms, soon earned a reputation for quality and dependability. Today, product names like Amana and Maytag are recognized around the world. Along with quality products,

Iowa has also been recognized for a quality work force. A manufacturer who recently opened a small factory in eastern Iowa explained that he preferred to locate his business there rather than in a city like Chicago for two reasons: Iowans' willingness to work hard and their low rate of absenteeism.

Because of the relatively early development of industry in the state, Iowa has never been viewed as a hinterland, subservient to large cities in other states in the Middle West. Through innovation and quality production, and through the good fortune of having an extensive railroad system and a central location in the nation, Iowa has competed equally in some production areas and gained a reputation for excellence in others. Iowa seems to stand midway between the region's more industrialized states to the east and the region's agricultural states to the west.

Throughout the nineteenth century as Iowans created churches and schools, fought a Civil War, and campaigned to close saloons, agriculture dominated the state, economically and politically. By the 1870s, after some thirty years of agricultural experience, Iowa's farmers had developed an agricultural pattern that would have long-term implications. Soon after the Civil War, state agriculturalists like "Tama Jim" Wilson urged Iowa farmers to diversify, planting a variety of crops rather than just wheat. By the seventies, given this advice and some experimentation, Iowa farmers concurred: they could raise corn and hogs more profitably than other crops. This view produced the corn-hog complex which, along with soybeans, still describes most Iowa agriculture today.

Even with some of the best soil in the world, however, Iowa farmers experienced difficult times between 1870 and 1900. For farmers who wished to expand, interest rates were high. Farmers, moreover, faced high transportation costs and low prices for their products. Like farmers in other parts of the Middle West, Iowa farmers blamed their troubles on the railroads and sought ways to curb the railroads' power. While some Iowa farmers registered their unhappiness in the 1870s by joining the Grange and forming the Anti-Monopoly party, overall Iowa's agriculturalists displayed little militancy and avoided joining the more radical farm organizations. Even in the 1880s, when the Greenback party selected Iowan James B. Weaver as its presidential candidate, Iowa farmers did not desert the Republican party in any appreciable numbers. In the 1890s, when Weaver again was selected as a presidential candidate, this time by the Populists, Iowa farmers tended to look the other way. Even though they were hard hit by the depression in the 1890s, the difficulties of Iowa farmers were considerably less than those suffered by farmers in the Great Plains or in the South. Iowa's farm people were able to blunt the harsh impact of the farm depression through their diversified farming practices. The advice given by "Tama Jim" Wilson and other Iowa agriculturalists in the 1870s had served the state well.

After 1900 and continuing through World War I, Iowa farmers, like their counterparts elsewhere in the nation, experienced the "golden years" of agriculture. Exports increased, prices rose, and during the war farmers received federal guarantees of fair prices. Many farmers expanded by purchasing land on credit. The future for agriculture looked bright, indeed, as farmers reflected on their recent prosperity. A nagging concern, however, was the "flight to the cities" whereby high numbers of people left the farm and headed toward urban areas, often outside Iowa. The 1910 federal census reflected this movement; the state's population was 7,082 less than it had been in 1900.

By the end of World War I the state had reached another major watershed. Before then, Protestantism, McGuffeyism, Republicanism, and prohibitionism had largely shaped and defined the state's predominantly rural social order. After 1918 these influences, particularly Republicanism, were still present, but they were more and more muted. The prosperity of the war years, moreover, quickly faded, placing agriculture among the nation's sick industries in the 1920s. A crisis of faith in rural life resulted, only to be followed by the Great Depression. The twenties, in effect, marked the end of the old order in which rural values and concerns dominated the state.

In the 1920s many of Iowa's rural residents seemed to have reservations about the advisability of remaining on the farm. While the ideas of agricultural superiority espoused by Thomas Jefferson were still widely accepted, on a more practical level farm people could see little cause for optimism. The prosperity of the war years had been short-lived and everywhere farm life was negatively compared with town and city life. *Wallaces' Farmer*, the Midwest's leading farm journal, ran advertisements galore proclaiming that farm people should rid themselves of the isolation, monotony, and dreariness of farm living by buying the modern products advertised in the journal. When farm people visited relatives and friends in nearby towns, they could not avoid contrasting their own unmodernized dwellings with town homes, often complete with electricity, indoor plumbing, and other comforts. Town residents, moreover, had a wide range of social activities to attend. To many farm people in the 1920s, farm life might be good, but it was not good enough.

Farm life in the 1920s was still labor intensive, with most members of the family working from dawn to dusk. The men certainly labored long and hard, but they had opportunities to socialize with neighboring farmers and to handle business matters in town. Farm women, tied down to caring for home, children, chickens, and garden, often had little time or opportunity to socialize with outsiders. The Country Life Commission had recognized this problem as early as 1909, urging farm people to develop more social outlets for farm women. The commission was particularly concerned because it recognized that if farm women were unhappy, they often urged their children to leave the farm and seek other work. One Iowa author, Herbert Quick, called the exodus to the cities a "woman problem" because of women's general unhappiness with farm life.

The 1930s brought greater difficulties for Iowa's farm economy, and for a brief time some Iowa farmers reacted militantly. They first took exception to a mandatory program of testing cattle for bovine tuberculosis, and that led to a brief encounter between farmers and state authorities known as the Cow War. The major outburst came a year later in northwest Iowa, where some farmers had joined the Farm Holiday Association. In responding to a high rate of mortgage foreclosures, farmers first tried a withholding action, urging everyone to keep agricultural products temporarily off the market in an effort to raise prices. When this tactic did not work, members resorted to another approach: interference with legal proceedings to stop foreclosures. The most dramatic incident took place in LeMars when farmers pulled Judge Charles Bradley from his courtroom and threatened to hang him if he did not stop issuing foreclosure notices. While the two actions produced little economic relief, they certainly foreshadowed a political revolt by Iowa's rural population. In November 1932 Iowans voted in large numbers for Franklin Roosevelt. As the temporary militancy of the 1930s indicates, Iowa's farm population has never displayed the same radicalism as farmers in the plains states. In effect, strong reaction has always been blunted by the fairly short-term nature of economic dislocations and the return of stable, consistent weather and production patterns. Although Iowa might produce a James B. Weaver, the typical quick return of "dependable agriculture" would soon lead the farming population back to their traditional political alignments and away from radical reaction and third-party candidates.

By the 1930s, even though economic dislocations had become more severe in some ways, the quality of farm life was improving, particularly for farm women. Of considerable importance were changes that made farm living more comfortable. Iowa's transportation officials began to gravel and hard surface more country roads so farm families could get to town more easily and even begin to take short vacations. The Cooperative Extension Service at Iowa State College, initiated in World War I, had become more and more visible throughout the Iowa countryside, providing farm women with both social outlets and information on how to improve the quality of rural life. Of great importance, farm families began to get electricity, made possible by passage of the Rural Electrification Act of 1935. One farm woman described the electricity as a wonderful fairy who came into her home and transformed her life. By the end of the 1930s, though the state had been through the most devastating depression in history, the quality of life for many rural Iowans had improved.

Even with the changes, however, the flight to the cities continued. Curtis Harnack, raised on a farm in northwest Iowa, wrote about his youth in *We Have All Gone Away*. The title captures a terrible contradiction in the Harnack family: farm life had served them well during their developing years, but when they reached maturity the city held out more promise. Harnack's mother, college-educated and a former teacher, frequently told her four children: "Farm life can kill you."[3] She sacrificed much to send her children to college so they might leave the farm far behind. Like countless other rural Iowans, Harnack speaks lovingly and nostalgically about his childhood on the farm, but he never entertained the idea of remaining there. In effect, *We Have All Gone Away* serves as a poignant testimony to Iowa's rural past. Like Harnack, many Iowans pay tribute to the moral and physical advantage of being reared on the land but look to the cities for a fuller social life and greater monetary rewards. The Cult of the Immediately Useful and Practical is still alive and well in the Hawkeye state.

World War II brought great prosperity to Iowa farm families, as it did to farm families throughout the nation. With greater profits, however, came expansion and greater debts. Until the late 1970s, even though there had been some dislocations, Iowa's farm population seemed secure. After all, with land prices rising rapidly, how could anyone go wrong by purchasing more land and enlarging one's operation? Nevertheless, by the early 1980s many things had gone awry and the farm economy had fallen on hard times. Perhaps the most visible evidence of changing times was the decline in farm units. In 1935, the peak year for farms in Iowa, the state contained 221,986 farm units. By 1985 the number had fallen to 115,000, even though almost 94 percent of the state was still under production.

Since World War II Iowa has become a state with a more visible urban population and more ethnic pluralism. Today the state has three cities with populations over 100,000 (Des Moines is close to 200,000) and a total population of 2,913,387. The cities symbolize Iowa's change from a state once totally dominated by agriculture to a state where industry now generates about three times as much revenue as agriculture. At the same time it should be stressed that Iowa is still a state filled with small towns. Since 1930 there has actually been an increase from 123 to 154 in towns with a population range of one thousand to twenty-five hundred. There has also been only a small decrease in towns of under one thousand population, from 713 in 1930 to 669 in 1980. In effect, Iowa's rural society has not been replaced, but rather must now share center stage with an ever-growing urban society.

Since the turn of the century, the number of minority groups has gradually been growing, with most minorities now residing in cities. Before World War I Iowa had a limited number of southern and eastern Europeans, most of whom worked in the coal mines. Around World War I Mexicans came to work in industries in the Quad Cities area and for the railroad in West Des Moines. Since World War II the number of Hispanics in Iowa has risen slowly. Responding to this increase, the General Assembly in 1978 created the Spanish Speaking Peoples' Committee to provide an advocacy agency for the group. Moreover, in the 1970s Iowa became home to several thousand Southeast Asians. The population of blacks in Iowa has gradually increased, and today they number about 1.4 percent of the population.

In keeping with the trend toward urbanization, Iowa has become a state that can no longer be taken for granted by one political party. Republicans reasserted their domination in the later New Deal years and continued this domination into the 1950s. But by the end of the decade, the Democratic party had picked up considerable strength, particularly in the cities, and successfully challenged the Republicans for both state and national offices. One political scientist, Charles Wiggins, believes that as early as 1955 Iowa had become a two-party state. The reapportionment of Iowa's legislature in 1972 to conform with the "one man, one vote" principle brought rural and urban areas into better balance and in the process gave Iowa the most equitably apportioned legislature in the nation.

Even with considerable change, however, Iowa of the eighties retains characteristics of an earlier time. It is still possible to define Iowa as the middle land where rural and urban values blend together. More and more farmers have taken jobs in nearby cities and towns, often necessary not only to aid in supporting families but to avoid losing the land altogether. Iowans still are a remarkably homogeneous people in regard to cultural values. In keeping with its rural legacy, Iowa is still a state where kinship networks are greatly valued, where family ties are strong, where family members often settle close to one another, and where most social events revolve around members of the family. In small towns across the state, invitations to bridal showers are often printed in local newspapers; in other words, come one, come all. Iowa is still a state with numerous rural churches, many of which are attended by the third or fourth generation of the same families. Families gather to celebrate the rites of passage for the young, including baptisms, birthdays, graduations, confirmations, and marriages. In Iowa, like other parts of the Middle West, summer is filled with family reunions, some attracting two or three hundred people.

Through the years Iowa has been a relatively stable state, with few upheavals or dramatic changes. Like its physical features, which are quite uniform, and its climate, which is fairly consistent, Iowans politically, socially, and economically have tended to display moderate qualities. Extremity in any form is usually not a fact of life in Iowa. There has rarely been either great wealth or great poverty. Moreover, Iowans have retained many traits first apparent in the nineteenth century. They still place great emphasis on quality education for their young people. In 1985–86, for example, nearly 55 percent of the state's budget went for education. Iowans are a people, moreover, who expect high moral conduct and the exercising of good, common sense on the part of their public officials. Iowa has always had a "squeaky clean" reputation concerning its public officials and state institutions and there is little reason to think that these practices will not continue.

At the same time, the state's rural legacy can have negative as well as positive connotations. For people who live here as well as away, Iowa often conjures up a rather bland image. On a recent popular comedy show, the main character announced that he was going to Des Moines on his vacation. After the looks of disbelief had passed from his associates' faces, one asked: "I hope you've had your shots." This implication that Iowa is in the middle of nowhere has long been apparent. Perhaps it rests partly on the fact that Iowa is indeed the middle land and therefore has no sharply distinguishing physical features. While Iowans themselves often perceive a beauty in the land, others may view it as a region of sameness. Perhaps the negative image rests partly on the state's rural character. Hamlin Garland's *Main Traveled Roads*, published in the 1890s, served as the first realistic portrayal of midwestern farm life. For some, this image remains firmly in place, portraying rural life as still devoid of cultural, economic, or social diversity.

These views of the state have naturally had an impact on Iowans as well as other Americans. Older Iowans seem to accept this situation in a rather stoic manner, but the state's young people are perhaps more vulnerable. Even today, when Iowa's young men and women repeatedly score at the very top of the standardized college entrance exams, they are often reticent about applying to the country's top educational institutions and pursuing the widest range of vocations. Surprisingly, with all its natural gifts, its high quality of life and its greatest resource—its well-educated, hard-working people—Iowa is still a place where some people tend to deprecate themselves and have less than a positive self-image.

As part of the Middle West, Iowa continues to share many similarities with other midwestern states. As something of a microcosm of the region, Iowa has characteristics—topographical, climatic, social, and political—of states located on all four sides. Perhaps once again Iowa is the transition zone between East and West. States to the east have undergone more social and economic change, while states to the west have retained more of their rural agricultural flavor.

Because of its location within the Middle West, Iowa really has two faces. One face looks to the East, responding to the industrial-urban world, tempted to move in that direction. At the same time, one face looks to the West, seeking to remain true to the agrarian past. The problem, of course, is that Iowa is neither totally one nor the other. As Iowa historian Joseph Wall correctly pointed out, each state must develop its own culture, because it cannot survive for long on one that is imported. Even with many similarities to other midwestern states, Iowa has clearly etched out a distinctive place for itself with its particular prairie environment, its reformist social nature, its political moderation, and its agrarian stability. Iowa remains the middle land.

NOTES

1. Quoted in Lewis Atherton, *Main Street on the Middle Border* (reprinted New York, 1975); see 65–88 for a discussion of McGuffey's views.
2. Ibid., 112–17.
3. Curtis Harnack, *We Have All Gone Away* (Ames, Iowa, 1981), 129.

BIBLIOGRAPHY

A bibliographical survey on Iowa can be divided into three parts: general studies and reference guides, standard monographs published before 1970, and monographs published after 1970. Materials published in the state history journals *Iowa Journal of History* (discontinued in 1961), *Annals of Iowa*, and *Palimpsest* should also be acknowledged for their wealth of information on Iowa history, although articles from these journals are not included in this bibliography.

A number of general studies have been written on Iowa, including three multivolume series. The oldest is Benjamin Gue's four-volume *History of Iowa* (New York, 1903). In the early thirties Edgar Harlan published the five-volume *Narrative History of the People of Iowa* (Chicago, 1931), and in 1952 William Petersen wrote a four-volume study, *A History of Iowa* (New York, 1952). Two recent single-volume histories are Leland Sage, *A History of Iowa* (Ames, Iowa, 1974), basically a political history, and Joseph Wall, *Iowa: A History* (New York, 1978), an interpretive essay written as a part of the bicentennial state history series. Dorothy Schwieder's *Patterns and Perspectives in Iowa History* (Ames, 1973) is a collection of articles dealing mainly with social and economic history. Two useful reference guides are William J. Petersen, *Iowa History Reference Guide* (Iowa City, 1942), and *Guide to Manuscripts* (Iowa City, 1978), a listing of holdings of the State Historical Society in Iowa City.

Older but still highly useful monographs include Earle Ross, *Iowa Agriculture* (Iowa City, 1951); Allan G. Bogue, *From Prairie to Cornbelt: Farming on the Illinois and Iowa Prairies in the Nineteenth Century* (Chicago, 1963); Louise R. Noun, *Strong-Minded Women: The Emergence of the Woman-Suffrage Movement in Iowa* (Ames, 1969); Donald Jackson, ed., *Black Hawk: An Autobiography* (Urbana, Ill., 1969), and Lewis Atherton, *Main Street on the Middle Border* (Bloomington, Ind., 1954).

Since 1970 there has been a significant increase in the number of books published in Iowa history. In keeping with trends in national historiography, many of these books deal with topics related to the new social history. A sampling include Clarence Andrews, *A Literary History of Iowa* (Iowa City, 1972); Elmer and Dorothy Schwieder, *A Peculiar People: Iowa's Old Order Amish* (Ames, 1975); James Larew, *A Party Reborn: The Democrats of Iowa, 1950–1974* (Iowa City, 1980); Hubert H. Wubben, *Civil War Iowa and the Copperhead Movement* (Ames, 1980); Glenda Riley, *Frontierswomen: The Iowa Experience* (Ames, 1981); Dorothy Schwieder, *Black Diamonds: Life and Work in Iowa's Coal Mining Communities, 1895–1925* (Ames, 1983); Diane L. Barthel, *Amana: From Pietist Sect to American Community* (Lincoln, Nebr., 1984); Curtis Harnack, *We Have All Gone Away*, the story of farm life in northwest Iowa in the 1940s (Garden City, N.Y., 1973); Curtis Harnack, *Gentlemen on the Prairie*, an account of English settlement in northwest Iowa in the 1870s (Ames, 1985); and Deborah Fink, *Open Country, Iowa: Rural Women, Tradition, and Change* (Albany, N.Y., 1986).

Recently initiated is the Henry A. Wallace Series on Agricultural History and Rural Studies with Richard Kirkendall serving as general editor. Two recent books in this series are Harold Lee, *Roswell Garst: A Biography* (Ames, 1984), and Alan I Marcus, *Agricultural Science and the Quest for Legitimacy: Farmers, Agricultural Colleges, and Experiment Stations, 1870–1890* (Ames, 1985).

Contributors

ANNETTE ATKINS has been on the Saint John's University (College-ville, Minnesota) faculty since 1980. Educated at Southwest State University (Marshall, Minnesota) and Indiana University, she is the author of *Harvest of Grief* (1984) and is currently studying adult brothers and sisters in nineteenth-century United States and Canada.

MARTHA MITCHELL BIGELOW is the Director of the Bureau of History, Michigan Department of State, and State Historic Preservation Officer for Michigan. She received her Ph.D. from the University of Chicago and taught at Memphis State University and the University of Mississippi. Before coming to Michigan she was Chairman of the Department of History and Political Science of Mississippi College, Clinton, Mississippi. She has written widely in the field of state and local history and is a past president of the American Association of State and Local History.

JOHN D. BUENKER is Professor of History at the University of Wisconsin–Parkside. He has written extensively on the Progressive Era, especially at the state level, and on immigration and ethnicity. He is the author of *Urban Liberalism and Progressive Reform* (1973, 1977), *Progressivism* (1977), and *The Income Tax and the Progressive Era* (1985). He is editing the *Historical Dictionary of the Progressive Era* and writing *Wisconsin: The Progressive Era, 1893–1915*.

LAWRENCE O. CHRISTENSEN received the Ph.D. degree from the University of Missouri–Columbia. Since 1969 he has taught at the University of Missouri–Rolla, where he is Professor and Chairman of the Department of History and Political Science. He coauthored *Missouri: The Heart of the Nation* (1980) and *UM–Rolla: A History of MSM/UMR* (1983). He serves on the board of editors of the *Missouri Historical Review* and is the recipient of the Author's Award from the State Historical Society of Missouri.

DAVID B. DANBOM is Professor of History at North Dakota State University, where he has taught since 1974. His major publications include *The Resisted Revolution: Urban America and the Industrialization of Agriculture, 1900–1930* (1979) and *"The World of Hope": Progressives and the Struggle for an Ethical Public Life* (1987).

CULLOM DAVIS is Professor of History at Sangamon State University, where he also directs a major oral history center. A native Illinoisan, he has degrees from Princeton and the University of Illinois. His writings have centered on modern United States political history, oral history methodology, and Illinois history.

PETER T. HARSTAD who was educated at Bethany Lutheran College in Minnesota and the University of Wisconsin, taught at Idaho State University from 1963 to 1972. He then spent a decade as director of the State Historical Society of Iowa and three years as development officer at Bethany. In 1984 he became executive officer of the Indiana Historical Society. He publishes in the area of regional history.

HERBERT T. HOOVER of the University of South Dakota specializes in American frontier history, particularly the history of Indian-white relations in Sioux Country. His interest in cross-cultural affairs at the grass roots is reflected in *To Be an Indian* (1971), *The Chitimacha People* (1975), and *Bibliography of the Sioux* (1980).

R. DOUGLAS HURT is Associate Director of the State Historical Society of Missouri. Before moving to Missouri he served as a curator and editor at the Ohio Historical Society. He holds a Ph.D. degree from Kansas State University, and he is the author of *The Dust Bowl: An Agricultural and Social History* (1981), *American Farm Tools: From Hand Power to Steam Power* (1982), and *Indian Agriculture in America: From Prehistory to the Present* (1987).

FREDERICK C. LUEBKE is Professor of History and Director of the Center for Great Plains Studies at the University of Nebraska–Lincoln. A specialist in both state history and European immigration to the United States, he is the author or editor of eight books and a score of articles. His most recent book is *Germans in Brazil: A Comparative History of Cultural Conflict during World War I* (1987). He has been a Fulbright senior research fellow in Germany and a scholar-in-residence at the Rockefeller Foundation Study Center in Bellagio, Italy.

JAMES H. MADISON is Editor of the *Indiana Magazine of History* and Associate Professor of History at Indiana University, Bloomington. He has written on state and regional history and rural history and is working on a biography of Eli Lilly (1885–1977). His most recent book is *The Indiana Way: A State History* (1986).

LEO E. OLIVA, Visiting Professor of History at Fort Hays State University, is former chairman of the History Department there and has taught Kansas history for twenty years. Author of seven books and numerous articles about Kansas, Oliva is a frequent lecturer for community organizations.

DOROTHY SCHWIEDER received her Ph.D. degree from the University of Iowa and is presently an Associate Professor of History at Iowa State University. She has coauthored, with Elmer Schwieder, *A Peculiar People: Iowa's Old Order Amish* and is author of *Black Diamonds: Life and Work in Iowa's Coal Mining Communities*. Her most recent work is *Buxton: Work and Racial Equality in a Coal Mining Community*, authored with Joseph Hraba and Elmer Schwieder.

Index